The Writer
and the Worlds
of Words

The Writer
and the Worlds
of Words

edited by
ROBERT BAIN and **DENNIS G. DONOVAN**
University of North Carolina, Chapel Hill

PRENTICE-HALL, INC., ENGLEWOOD CLIFFS, N.J.

Library of Congress Cataloging in Publication Data

BAIN, ROBERT A   comp.
  The writer and the worlds of words.

  Includes index.
    1. College readers. 2. English language—Rhetoric.
I. Donovan, Dennis G., joint comp. II. Title.
PE1417.B27   808'.04275   74-23662
ISBN 0-13-969980-5

10 9 8 7 6 5 4 3 2 1

Printed in the United States of America

PRENTICE-HALL INTERNATIONAL, INC., *London*
PRENTICE-HALL OF AUSTRALIA, PTY. LTD., *Sydney*
PRENTICE-HALL OF CANADA, LTD., *Toronto*
PRENTICE-HALL OF INDIA PRIVATE LIMITED, *New Delhi*
PRENTICE-HALL OF JAPAN, INC., *Tokyo*

CONTENTS

3 The Writer as Word-Maker and World-Maker

4 The Writer as Workman: Occupational Hazards

5 The Writer's Words: Social and Human Implications

Introduction   227

6 Writers Making Words Work

PREFACE

This book is about the practical problems of making words work in writing. The authors represented in this collection are all word-workers: journalists, poets, advertising writers, cartoon strip authors, essayists, humorists, news commentators, fiction writers, linguists. They share a fascination for one of our most human activities—making signs, sounds, and symbols to tell others how we feel and think about ourselves and the world. These writers do not all agree that man "simply does not know what his life means until he says it," but they are concerned with the way that language shapes meaning and attitudes, conveys our profundities and perversities, reveals or conceals our feelings and ideas. They acknowledge a connection between the way we see and the way we say. The problems of seeing and saying are the subjects of this book.

To reflect these concerns, we have gathered readings about people as users of language, not as specialists in linguistics. These readings demonstrate effective use of language in a variety of forms and genres, show strategies and choices available to us when we write, dramatize problems facing us as word-workers, and raise questions about language and its users. To avoid riding a hobby horse, we have tried to present many views of language and to ask readers to formulate their own beliefs.

We have arranged the readings in six sections. "The Worlds of Words" looks at language, the medium of speaking and writing, to see how naming things affects the way we see the world and how the way we see the world influences the words we use to describe it. Words, however, are not the only ways people talk with each other. Space and gesture are powerful ways of speaking, and so is the language of pictures. Because people see in pictures and gestures, we have included readings on these subjects.

The next two sections have to do with seeing and saying. Section 2, "The Writer as See-er and Thinker," focuses upon the difference between looking at experience and seeing it, between simply reporting an event and understanding its implications. These readings examine the lenses through which we see, and ask us to think about the way we think. Just as the limits of language are acknowledged in Section 1, the limits of logic and vision are noted in Section 2. In the third section, "The Writer as Word-Maker and World-Maker," the focus is upon the writer as a shaper of words, ideas, and feelings; these readings pose questions about audience, attitudes toward subject, and awareness of style.

Section 4, "The Writer as Workman: Occupational Hazards," defines language traps that conceal meaning—frequently from the writer himself and usually from his audience. These readings show how jargon, clichés, and gobbledygook not only fog meaning for the reader but also dim the writer's eyesight.

Section 5, "The Writer's Words: Social and Human Implications," looks briefly at what happens to our words once we let them go. No matter how carefully we choose our options, no matter how hard we strive for clarity, we always run the risk of being misunderstood. Along with sticks and stones, words sometimes lead to bone-breaking. One man's wit may be another's poison; one man's art may be another's pornography; one man's liberty may be another's license. The readings in this section explore some social and human implications of our words.

The last section, "Writers Making Words Work," is simply a *tour de force* celebrating man's capacity to convey forcefully his feelings and ideas. Chosen from a variety of genres, these readings show what writers have accomplished when they were in control of their feelings, their ideas, and their language.

Study questions aimed at developing reading and writing skills and at increasing awareness of language accompany the readings in the first five sections. Each set begins with questions about "Words and Sentences," asking students to define words and to study and to imitate sentence patterns that can strengthen their prose. Questions about "Ideas and Implications" follow; these ask students to test the writer's thesis and to see any complications that might arise from his views. The "Strategies" questions explore problems of organization and development, of the way the writer has chosen to present his ideas. These questions sometimes ask students to propose alternate strategies. Finally, each set of questions concludes with "Suggestions for Writing."

As students work through the readings and the study questions, they should be assembling a glossary of rhetorical terms and composing their own rhetorics. Though we have assumed that most teachers will use this book with a rhetoric or handbook, such complementary texts are not necessary. Desk dictionaries give succinct and useful definitions of most of the rhetorical terms we have used in the study questions.

To make it easy to locate specific problems raised in the study questions, we have numbered paragraphs in the readings. In selections where paragraphs are short, we have numbered every fifth paragraph.

We believe that organizing the book around the perspectives described above is a valid approach to the problems of language and writing. But it is not the only approach. For those who prefer to teach "à la mode," we have included an alternate table of contents at the back, listing the readings by the principal rhetorical modes employed in each. The index also refers to rhetorical problems treated in the study questions.

As anthologizers, we are first of all indebted to the many authors whose work appears here. We would also like to thank those who have made suggestions along the way: Neal L. Goldstien, Meredith Lynn Bratcher Murphy, Jay Dowd, Pattie McIntyre, Carol Bombay, Doris Betts, Connie C. Eble, William A. McQueen, Richard D. Rust, Fred H. MacIntosh, and especially, Shirley Donovan and Bonnie Bain.

1 The Worlds of Words

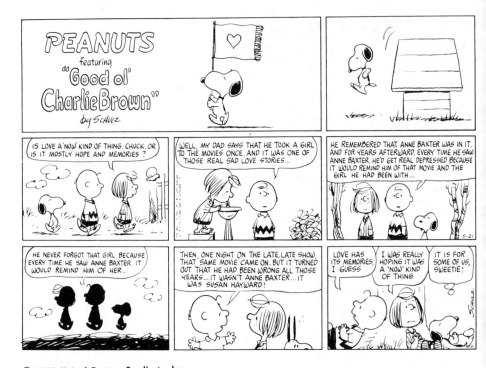

INTRODUCTION

Charles Schulz's "Peanuts" dramatizes the difficulty of making sense to ourselves about the world and our experience. Peppermint Patti and Good Ole Charlie Brown wrestle with a definition important to them. Neither is sure: "Love has its memories I guess," says Charlie Brown; "I was really hoping it was a 'now' kind of thing," says Peppermint Patti doubtfully. Only Snoopy seems certain. In six panels, Schulz has his little people confront one of the most troublesome words in the language. Their solutions amuse because they are not really solutions at all, but the world demands that most of us come to terms with troublesome words like, *love, courage,* and *friendship*. Like Peppermint Patti and Charlie Brown, we all search for meanings. By examining the meanings of words and the things they stand for, we attempt to understand the meanings of our world—and our lives.

Schulz's characters use words to mirror the sense they have gathered from their experience. Though their word-worlds touch at points, each sees the meaning of *love* through a different lens and chooses different words to mirror meaning. The connection between the worlds of words and the things and ideas words stand for is the subject of the readings in this section.

In Lewis Carroll's *Through the Looking Glass,* Humpty Dumpty solves the problem of connecting words with things and ideas by making words mean what he wants them to. After Humpty Dumpty defines *impenetrability* for Alice, she tells him, "That's a great deal to make one word mean." He answers, "When I make a word do a lot of work, I always pay it extra." The world Alice visits when she steps through the looking glass confuses her because its landscape and people are alien, but mainly because characters like Humpty Dumpty define their experience without regard for the world outside themselves.

Julius Fast and Paul R. Wendt look at forms of non-verbal communication. Fast believes that our bodies talk more than we think they do, and that the way we share space with others reveals something about us and our relationships with them. Fast calls his study *Body Language*. In "The Language of Pictures," Wendt compares the grammar, syntax, and style of photographs and film with the grammar, syntax, and style of the word-world, and argues that picture language is more complicated than we sometimes think.

The next two readings by Emily Dickinson and William Shakespeare discuss connecting words with things and ideas. Miss Dickinson tells what makes words live for her in "A Word Is Dead," and Shakespeare's Falstaff turns the word *honour* about in his head to see if it is worth dying for.

The language Falstaff uses to explain *honour* tells us something about him and how he sees the world. An old playground rhyme says:

> Twinkle, twinkle, little star,
> What you say, is what you are.

Several readings plumb this connection between what we say and what we are. S. I. Hayakawa shows "How Words Change Our Lives" because the "meaning of words (or other symbols) is not in the words, but in our own semantic reactions." He defines *semantics* as the "comparative study of the kinds of responses people make to symbols and signs around them." Hayakawa believes that once we understand the "difference between words and what they stand for," we are ready to see the world with clearer eyes and to act in it with better sense.

In "We Cover up Our Faults with Words," Sydney J. Harris looks at the numerous synonyms for words like *drunkenness, lying,* and *stealing,* and concludes that language is often a "means of barricading ourselves against the impact of reality." Marsteller Inc., an advertising agency, sees "The Wonderful World of Words" as a way "to make corporations personable, to make useful products desirable, to clarify ideas, and to create friendships in the mass for our employers." Instead of using language to "barricade," Marsteller believes that language has the power to create good will and to clarify.

Irving J. Lee argues that there is "a world of words which must be sharply distinguished from a world of not-words" before men and women can begin to understand themselves, the world, and each other. "The Useful Use of Words," says Lee, depends upon our fitting together the world of fact and idea with the word-world. To illustrate his point, Lee calls words *maps* and what the words represent *territories.* Whether we are talking about *love* or *apples,* we must make the *map* and *territory* fit before words can be useful.

Sydney J. Harris performs "Antics with Semantics" to show how we sometimes distort maps and territories to celebrate ourselves and to put others down. Among his examples are:

I am "cautious."	My candidate is "silver-tongued."
You are "timid."	Yours is "leather-lunged."
He is "cowardly."	His is a "a windbag."

Harris's antics ironically suggest that such celebration often leads to self-deception.

In "Expressive Language," Imamu Amiri Baraka (LeRoi Jones) reflects on the multiplicities of meaning as he explores how different cultures and groups within cultures express themselves with words, especially the spoken word. Baraka compares the sentence "God don't never change!" with "God does not ever change!" to dramatize how each statement tells about the speaker's culture. The same statement—"God don't never change!"—in the mouth of a rich man and in the mouth of a "blind hopeless black American" means something very different. Baraka believes the difference is in "the final human reference, in the form of passage through the world" of the person speaking.

In "The Limitations of Language," Melvin Maddocks talks about word pollution; he calls it semantic aphasia, "that numbness of ear, mind and heart —that tone deafness to the very meaning of language—which results from the habitual and prolonged abuse of words." Maddocks's culprits are the over-simplifiers who speak in slogans and grunts, and the overcomplicators who use specialized and high-falutin language to "inflate the trivial." There are no simple remedies for word pollution, but Maddocks believes man's "Adam urge" to know by naming is a sign of hope.

Maddocks and the other authors of this section explore the raw materials —words and experience—that writers use to explain what is in their hearts and in their heads. Any worker needs to know his tools. Carpenters must know about levels and plumbs, about cross-cut and rip saws, and writers need to know their tools—how their language works and how they can use it to free ideas and feelings so that others may share them.

As writers, we create word-worlds for our readers. That word-world may change as our audience changes. What we do with the raw materials—words and experience—makes a considerable difference, for writers must choose what details to emphasize and what words to convey their ideas and feelings. The choices we make are crucial because they shape the word-worlds we try to communicate to others; these choices also separate us from other people by showing how our world-view is different from theirs.

Three versions of "Little Red Riding Hood" demonstrate how choices of detail and language create three different word-worlds. The first is the story as it was told by Charles Perrault in 1697 in *Contes de ma mère l'Oye* and translated into English by Robert Samber in 1729 as *Mother Goose's Tales*.

LITTLE RED RIDING-HOOD

Once upon a time, there lived in a certain village, a little country girl, the prettiest creature was ever seen.—Her mother was excessively fond of her; and her grandmother doated on her much more. This good woman got made for her a little red Riding-Hood; which became the girl so extremely well, that every body called her Little Red Riding-Hood.

One day, her mother, having made some custards, said to her, "Go, my dear, and see how thy grand-mamma does, for I hear she has been very ill, carry her a custard, and this little pot of butter." Little Red Riding-Hood sets out immediately to go to her grand-mother, who lived in another village. As she was going thro' the wood, she met with Gaffer Wolf, who had a very great mind to eat her up, but he durst not, because of some faggot makers hard by in the forest.

He asked her, whither she was going: The poor child, who did not know that it was dangerous to stay and hear a Wolf talk, said to him, "I am going to see my grand-mamma, and carry her a custard, and a little pot of butter, from my mamma." "Does she live far off?" said the Wolf. "Oh! ay," answered Little Red

Riding-Hood, "it is beyond that mill you see there, at the first house in the village." "Well," said the Wolf, "and I'll go and see her too: I'll go this way, and you go that, and we shall see who will be there soonest."

The Wolf began to run as fast as he could, taking the nearest way; and the little girl went by that farthest about, diverting herself in gathering nuts, running after butterflies, and making nosegays of such little flowers as she met with. The Wolf was not long before he got to the old woman's house: he knocked at the door, tap, tap. "Who's there?" "Your grand-child, Little Red Riding-Hood" (replied the Wolf, counterfeiting her voice) "who has brought you a custard, and a little pot of butter, sent you by mamma."

The good grand-mother, who was in bed, because she found herself somewhat ill, cry'd out, "Pull the bobbin, and the latch will go up." The Wolf pull'd the bobbin, and the door opened, and then presently he fell upon the good woman, and eat her up in a moment; for it was above three days that he had not touched a bit. He then shut the door, and went into the grand-mother's bed, expecting Little Red Riding-Hood, who came some time afterwards, and knock'd at the door, tap, tap. "Who's there?" Little Red Riding-Hood, hearing the big voice of the Wolf, was at first afraid; but believing her grand-mother had got a cold, and was hoarse, answered, " 'Tis your grand-child, Little Red Riding-Hood, who has brought you a custard, and a little pot of butter, mamma sends you." The Wolf cried out to her, softening his voice as much as he could, "Pull the bobbin, and the latch will go up." Little Red Riding-Hood pulled the bobbin, and the door opened.

The Wolf seeing her come in, said to her, hiding himself under the bedclothes; "Put the custard, and the little pot of butter upon the stool, and come and lye down with me." Little Red Riding-Hood undressed herself, and went into bed; where, being greatly amazed to see how her grand-mother looked in her night-cloaths, said to her, "Grand-mamma, what great arms you have got!" "That is the better to hug thee, my dear." "Grand-mamma, what great legs you have got!" "That is to run the better, my child." "Grand-mamma, what great ears you have got!" "That is to hear the better, my child." "Grand-mamma, what great eyes you have got!" "It is to see the better, my child." "Grand-mamma, what great teeth you have got!" "That is to eat thee up." And, saying these words, this wicked Wolf fell upon poor Little Red Riding-Hood, and eat her all up.

THE MORAL

From this short story easy we discern
What conduct all young people ought to learn.
But above all, young, growing misses fair,
Whose orient rosy blooms begin t'appear:
Who, beauties in the fragrant spring of age,
With pretty airs young hearts are apt t'engage.
Ill do they listen to all sorts of tongues,
Since some inchant and lure like Syrens *songs.*
No wonder therefore tis, if over-power'd,
So many of them has the Wolf devour'd.
The Wolf, I say, for Wolves too sure there are
Of every sort, and every character.
Some of them mild and gentle-humour'd be,
Of noise and gall, and rancour wholly free
Who tame, familiar, full of complaisance

Ogle and leer, languish, cajole and glance;
With luring tongues, and language wond'rous sweet,
Follow young ladies as they walk the street,
Ev'n to their very houses, nay, beside,
And, artful, tho' their true designs they hide:
Yet ah! these simpering Wolves who does not see
Most dang'rous of all Wolves in fact to be?

The second version is from a modern children's book distributed by Child Guidance Products. This telling, or one much like it, is probably more familiar to modern readers than is the Perrault tale.

LITTLE RED RIDING HOOD*

Once upon a time, there lived a little girl whose grandmother made her a beautiful bright red cape with a hood. She wore it so often that everyone called her Red Riding Hood. One morning, Red Riding Hood's mother said, "Grandma is sick, dear. I have packed a basket full of custard and cookies for you to take her. But be careful. Don't stop along the way until you get to grandmother's house on the far side of the forest."

Red Riding Hood skipped through the woods. She stopped only to pick some wildflowers. But before very long, she met a wolf. Red Riding Hood had never seen a wolf before, and she was pleased to have some company. "Where are you going?" the wolf asked sweetly, sniffing at her basket. "I am bringing custard and cookies to my grandmother who is sick," Red Riding Hood said. The Wolf loved custard and cookies as well as little children. He decided he would like all three for dinner.

"Where does your grandma live, my sweet?" the wolf asked. As soon as Red Riding Hood told him, he bounded off into the woods. The wolf raced to the grandmother's house and knocked gently at the door. "Lift the latch, my dear, and come in," the grandmother said weakly, thinking it was Red Riding Hood. When she saw the wolf, she became very frightened! She jumped out of bed and ran into the closet. With one great leap the wolf slammed the door and locked her inside.

Then he put on the grandmother's night cap and climbed into bed. Soon Red Riding Hood knocked on the door. "Lift the latch, my dear, and come in," the wolf said weakly. Red Riding Hood came in and walked toward the bed. "Why, Grandma, what big eyes you have!" she said. "The better to see you with, my dear," the wolf said softly. "And what big ears, Grandma!" "The better to hear you with, my dear," the wolf said more loudly. "And what big teeth, Grandma!" Then the wolf leaped from the bed, shouting, "The better to eat you with, my dear!"

Red Riding Hood screamed with all her might. A woodsman, who was chopping trees nearby, heard her. He came running ready to swing his enormous axe at the wolf. The wolf ran out the back door and into the forest. The woodsman and Red Riding Hood unlocked the closet door and freed Red Riding Hood's grandmother. Then Red Riding Hood unpacked the basket, while her grandmother made a pot of steaming hot tea. They all had a wonderful party.

* Originally published by Platt & Munk Publishers. Reprinted by permission of Questor Education Products Company.

James Thurber is the author of the third version, entitled "The Little Girl and the Wolf" and published in *Fables for Our Time*.

THE LITTLE GIRL AND THE WOLF*

One afternoon a big wolf waited in a dark forest for a little girl to come along carrying a basket of food to her grandmother. Finally a little girl did come along and she was carrying a basket of food. "Are you carrying that basket to your grandmother?" asked the wolf. The little girl said yes, she was. So the wolf asked her where her grandmother lived and the little girl told him and he disappeared into the wood.

When the little girl opened the door of her grandmother's house she saw that there was somebody in bed with a nightcap and nightgown on. She had approached no nearer than twenty-five feet from the bed when she saw that it was not her grandmother but the wolf, for even in a nightcap a wolf does not look any more like your grandmother than the Metro-Goldwyn lion looks like Calvin Coolidge. So the little girl took an automatic out of her basket and shot the wolf dead.

Moral: It is not so easy to fool little girls nowadays as it used to be.

All three versions tell of a little girl, a grandmother, and a wolf. Perrault gives the woodsmen minor roles; Thurber omits this detail; the children's story makes the woodsman a major character. Obviously, the plots of the tales are different, but more important are the differences in the selection and arrangement of the words in each, for the language of each story carries explicit assumptions about little girls, grandmothers, wolves—and the world. Though the outlines of the stories are the same, each word-world projects a different view of reality.

What makes these word-worlds so different from each other? What assumptions do Perrault, Thurber, and the anonymous author of the child's story make about wolves? The Child Guidance story ends with, "And they all had a party." Do stories about little girls, wolves, and grandmothers always end in parties? Perrault makes very different assumptions. Do his assumptions have to do with the purpose of his story? How is his purpose different from that of Thurber or Child Guidance? Danger is present in all three versions, but how does each writer treat this danger? Thurber inverts the roles of the little girl and the wolf. What are the implications of this reversal? Whose view of the world most approximates your own—Perrault's, Thurber's, or Child Guidance Products'?

From the worlds of words men and women use to describe what they see and feel, each of the writers about Little Red Riding has chosen language and details to create different word-worlds about little girls, grandmothers, and wolves. Their word-worlds are different because they see differently, because their audiences are different, and because their purposes are different. Each has made conscious choices of language and detail to construct the three tales.

As writers, speakers, and human beings, we constantly choose language and details to project our views of reality. Sometimes our choices are highly conscious, sometimes not. Understanding how words work may make us see our choices more clearly, may make us better builders of our word-worlds.

Lewis Carroll

from **Through the Looking Glass**

[1] "What a beautiful belt you've got on!" Alice suddenly remarked. (They had had quite enough of the subject of age, she thought; and if they really were to take turns in choosing subjects, it was her turn now.) "At least," she corrected herself on second thoughts, "a beautiful cravat, I should have said—no, a belt, I mean—I beg your pardon!" she added in dismay, for Humpty Dumpty looked thoroughly offended, and she began to wish she hadn't chosen that subject. "If only I knew," she thought to herself, "which was neck and which was waist!"

Evidently Humpty Dumpty was very angry, though he said nothing for a minute or two. When he *did* speak again, it was in a deep growl.

"It is a—*most—provoking—*thing," he said at last, "when a person doesn't know a cravat from a belt!"

"I know it's very ignorant of me," Alice said, in so humble a tone that Humpty Dumpty relented.

[5] "It's a cravat, child, and a beautiful one, as you say. It's a present from the White King and Queen. There now!"

"Is it really?" said Alice, quite pleased to find that she *had* chosen a good subject, after all.

"They gave it to me," Humpty Dumpty continued thoughtfully, as he crossed one knee over the other and clasped his hands around it, "they gave it me—for an un-birthday present."

"I beg your pardon?" Alice said with a puzzled air.

"I'm not offended," said Humpty Dumpty.

[10] "I mean, what *is* an un-birthday present?"

"A present given when it isn't your birthday, of course."

Alice considered a little. "I like birthday presents best," she said at last.

"You don't know what you're talking about!" cried Humpty Dumpty. "How many days are there in a year?"

"Three hundred and sixty-five," said Alice.

[15]   "And how many birthdays have you?"

"One."

"And if you take one from three hundred and sixty-five, what remains?"

"Three hundred and sixty-four, of course."

Humpty Dumpty looked doubtful. "I'd rather see that done on paper," he said.

[20]   Alice couldn't help smiling as she took out her memorandum book, and worked the sum for him:

$$\begin{array}{r} 365 \\ 1 \\ \hline 364 \end{array}$$

Humpty Dumpty took the book, and looked at it carefully. "That seems to be done right—" he began.

"You're holding it upside down!" Alice interrupted.

"To be sure I was!" Humpty Dumpty said gayly, as she turned it round for him. "I thought it looked a little queer. As I was saying, that *seems* to be done right—though I haven't time to look it over thoroughly just now—and that shows that there are three hundred and sixty-four days when you might get un-birthday presents—"

"Certainly," said Alice.

[25]   "And only *one* for birthday presents, you know. There's glory for you!"

"I don't know what you mean by 'glory,'" Alice said.

Humpty Dumpty smiled contemptuously. "Of course you don't—till I tell you. I meant 'there's a nice knock-down argument for you!'"

"But 'glory' doesn't mean 'a nice knock-down argument,'" Alice objected.

"When *I* use a word," Humpty Dumpty said in rather a scornful tone, "it means just what I choose it to mean—neither more nor less."

[30]   "The question is," said Alice, "whether you *can* make words mean so many different things."

"The question is," said Humpty Dumpty, "which is to be master—that's all."

Alice was too much puzzled to say anything, so after a minute Humpty Dumpty began again. "They've a temper, some of them—particularly verbs, they're the proudest—adjectives you can do anything with, but not verbs—however, I can manage the whole lot of them! Impenetrability! That's what I say!"

"Would you tell me, please," said Alice, "what that means?"

"Now you talk like a reasonable child," said Humpty Dumpty, looking very much pleased. "I meant by 'impenetrability' that we've had enough of that subject, and it would be just as well if you'd mention what you mean to do next, as I suppose you don't mean to stop here all the rest of your life."

[35] "That's a great deal to make one word mean," Alice said, in a thoughtful tone.

"When I make a word do a lot of work like that," said Humpty Dumpty, " I always pay it extra."

"Oh!" said Alice. She was too much puzzled to make any other remark.

"Ah, you should see 'em come round me of a Saturday night," Humpty Dumpty went on, wagging his head gravely from side to side: "for to get their wages, you know."

(Alice didn't venture to ask what he paid them with; and so you see I can't tell *you*.)

[40] "You seem very clever at explaining words, sir," said Alice. "Would you kindly tell me the meaning of the poem called 'Jabberwocky?'"

"Let's hear it," said Humpty Dumpty. "I can explain all the poems that ever were invented—and a good many that haven't been invented just yet."

This sounded very hopeful, so Alice repeated the first verse:

" 'Twas brillig, and the slithy toves
   Did gyre and gimble in the wabe:
All mimsy were the borogroves,
   And the mome raths outgrabe."

"That's enough to begin with," Humpty Dumpty interrupted: "there are plenty of hard words there. *'Brillig'* means four o'clock in the afternoon—the time when you begin *broiling* things for dinner."

"That'll do very well," said Alice: "and *'slithy?'*"

[45] "Well, *'slithy'* means lithe and slimy. 'Lithe' is the same as 'active.' You see it's like a portmanteau—there are two meanings packed up into one word."

"I see it now," Alice remarked thoughtfully: "and what are *'toves?'*"

"Well, *'toves'* are something like badgers—they're something like lizards—and they're something like corkscrews."

"They must be very curious-looking creatures."

"They are that," said Humpty Dumpty, "also they make their nest under sundials—also they live on cheese."

[50] "And what's to *'gyre'* and to *'gimble'?*"

"To *'gyre'* is to go round and round like a gyroscope. To *'gimble'* is to make holes like a gimlet."

"And *'the wabe'* is the grass-plot round a sundial, I suppose?" said Alice, surprised at her own ingenuity.

"Of course it is. It's called *'wabe,'* you know, because it goes a long way before it, and a long way behind it—"

"And a long way beyond it on each side," Alice added.

[55] "Exactly so. Well then, *'mimsy'* is 'flimsy and miserable'—there's another portmanteau for you. And a *'borogove'* is a thin shabby-looking bird with its feathers sticking out all round—something like a live mop."

"And then *'mome raths?'*" said Alice. "I'm afraid I'm giving you a great deal of trouble."

"Well, a *'rath'* is a sort of green pig: but *'mome'* I'm not certain about. I think it's short for 'from home'—meaning that they'd lost their way, you know."

"And what does *'outgrabe'* mean?"

"Well, *'outgribing'* is something between bellowing and whistling, with a kind of sneeze in the middle: however, you'll hear it done, maybe —down in the wood yonder—and when you've once heard it you'll be *quite* content. Who's been repeating all that hard stuff to you?"

[60]   "I read it in a book," said Alice. "But I had some poetry repeated to me, much easier than that, by—Tweedledee, I think it was."

"As to poetry, you know," said Humpty Dumpty, stretching out one of his great hands, "*I* can repeat poetry as well as other folk, if it comes to that—"

words and sentences

1. Vocabulary: *cravat* (¶ 1); *provoking* (3); *relented* (4); *contemptuously* (27); *impenetrability* (32); *portmanteau* (45) ; *gyroscope, gimlet* (51).
2. Check a dictionary for the meaning of the word *context*. Words have contexts, and so do people. Write a paragraph describing your context at this moment.
3. Check the dictionary definition of *reasonable*. In its context, what does the word *reasonable* mean in ¶ 34? Do the same for *glory* (¶ 25).
4. Make up a half dozen portmanteau words and write your definitions for them. Then use these words in sentences. Exchange papers with classmates to see if they can understand your words.
5. Check the words *coin* and *coinage* in a dictionary. Try to coin two or three words of your own and write definitions for them. Then write sentences using your words. Again, share these sentences with classmates to see if they understand your coined words.
6. Change the word order of the sentences in ¶s 6 and 7. Does changing the word order alter the meaning? Does it alter the effectiveness of these sentences in their context?

ideas and implications

1. Underline or list the words Carroll uses to describe the moods and attitudes of Alice and Humpty Dumpty. How does Humpty Dumpty see Alice and how does he see himself? Do the same for Alice.
2. Humpty Dumpty and Alice (see ¶s 25-38 especially) have different notions about language and meaning. Describe their notions about language and meaning. Which one is closer to your ideas about language?
3. How do the two characters' ideas about language affect the way they see the world?
4. In ¶ 32, Humpty Dumpty says that you can do anything with adjectives, but that verbs are proud and have a temper. Why?

5. Could Carroll be using Humpty Dumpty to represent the adult world and its attitudes? Why and how?
6. Carroll's "Jabberwocky" poem has been described as "nonsense verse." Can nonsense sometimes make sense? Under what circumstances?
7. Alice tells Humpty Dumpty that he is holding the paper upside down (¶ 22). What might Carroll be suggesting with this detail?

strategies

1. In ¶s 1 and 6, Alice is concerned with "choosing a subject." Does the problem of choosing a subject help Carroll give sequence and order to his scene?
2. What are the subjects of the conversation between Humpty Dumpty and Alice? Can you list them? How does the conversation shift from one subject to another? Would you describe the progression of the conversation as a logical progression or as a progression by association?

suggestions for writing

1. Write a short dialogue in which two characters try to discover the meaning of a word that is important to them. Carroll's scene and the "Peanuts" cartoon might give you some suggestions.
2. Drawing from your childhood, write a paper about an event that some adult or older person tried to explain to you.
3. Write a paper proposing a different reading of the "Jabberwocky" poem.
4. Write a short nonsense poem and then write an explanation of your poem.
5. Write a paper using several nonsense words. Do not try to conceal the meaning of your nonsense words; try to make the context in which these words appear clarify their meaning.

Julius Fast

from **Body Language**

A Science Called Kinesics

[1]   Within the last few years a new and exciting science has been uncovered and explored. It is called body language. Both its written form and the scientific study of it have been labeled kinesics. Body language

From Julius Fast, *Body Language.* © 1970 by Julius Fast. Reprinted by permission of the publisher, M. Evans and Company, New York.

and kinesics are based on the behavioral patterns of nonverbal communication, but kinesics is still so new as a science that its authorities can be counted on the fingers of one hand.

[2]   Clinical studies have revealed the extent to which body language can actually contradict verbal communications. A classic example is the young woman who told her psychiatrist that she loved her boyfriend very much while nodding her head from side to side in subconscious denial.

[3]   Body language has also shed new light on the dynamics of inter-family relationships. A family sitting together, for example, can give a revealing picture of itself simply by the way its members move their arms and legs. If the mother crosses her legs first and the rest of the family then follows suit, she has set the lead for the family action, though she, as well as the rest of the family, may not be aware she is doing it. In fact her words may deny her leadership as she asks her husband or children for advice. But the unspoken, follow-the-leader clue in her action gives the family setup away to someone knowledgeable in kinesics.

A New Signal from the Unconscious

[4]   Dr. Edward H. Hess told a recent convention of the American College of Medical Hypnotists of a newly discovered kinesic signal. This is the unconscious widening of the pupil when the eye sees something pleasant. On a useful plane, this can be of help in a poker game if the player is in the "know." When his opponent's pupils widen, he can be sure that his opponent is holding a good hand. The player may not even be conscious of his ability to read this sign, any more than the other person is conscious of telegraphing his own luck.

[5]   Dr. Hess has found that the pupil of a normal man's eye becomes twice as large when he sees a picture of a nude woman.

[6]   On a commercial level, Dr. Hess cites the use of this new kinesic principle to detect the effect of an advertising commercial on television. While the commercial is being shown to a select audience, the eyes of the audience are photographed. The film is then later carefully studied to detect just when there is any widening of the eye; in other words, when there is any unconscious, pleasant response to the commercial.

[7]   Body language can include any non-reflexive or reflexive movement of a part, or all of the body, used by a person to communicate an emotional message to the outside world.

[8]   To understand this unspoken body language, kinesics experts often have to take into consideration cultural differences and environmental differences. The average man, unschooled in cultural nuances of body language, often misinterprets what he sees. . . .

A Space to Call Your Own

[9]   Among Quakers, the story is told of an urban Friend who visited a Meeting House in a small country town. Though fallen into disuse, it

was architecturally a lovely building, and the city Quaker decided to visit
it for Sunday meeting athough he was told that only one or two Quakers
still attended meetings there.

[10]   That Sunday he entered the building to find the meeting hall completely empty, the morning sun shafting through the old, twelve-paned
windows, the rows of benches silent and unoccupied.

[11]   He slipped into a seat and sat there, letting the peaceful silence fill
him. Suddenly he heard a slight cough and, looking up, saw a bearded
Quaker standing near his bench, an old man who might well have
stepped out of the pages of history.

[12]   He smiled, but the old Quaker frowned and coughed again, then
said, "Forgive me if I offend, but thee art sitting in my place."

[13]   The old man's quaint insistence on his own space, in spite of the
empty meeting house, is amusing, but very true to life. Invariably, after
you attend any church for any period of time, you stake out your own
spot.

[14]   In his home Dad has his own particular chair, and while he may
tolerate a visitor sitting there, it is often with poor grace. Mom has her
own kitchen, and she doesn't like it one bit when her mother comes to
visit and takes over "her" kitchen.

[15]   Men have their favorite seats in the train, their favorite benches in
the park, their favorite chairs at conferences, and so on. It is all a need
for territory, for a place to call one's own. Perhaps it is an inborn and
universal need, though it is shaped by society and culture into a variety
of forms. An office may be adequate for a working man or it may be too
small, not according to the actual size of the room but according to place-
ment of desk and chair. If the worker can lean back without touching a
wall or a bookcase, it will usually seem big enough. But in a larger room,
if his desk is placed so that he touches a wall when he leans back, the
office may seem to be cramped from his viewpoint.

A Science Called Proxemics

[16]   Dr. Edward T. Hall, professor of anthropology at Northwestern
University, has long been fascinated by man's reaction to the space about
him, by how he utilizes that space and how his spatial use communicates
certain facts and signals to other men. As Dr. Hall studied man's personal
space, he coined the word *proxemics* to describe his theories and observations about zones of territory and how we use them.

[17]   Man's use of space, Dr. Hall believes, has a bearing on his ability
to relate to other people, to sense them as being close or far away. Every
man, he says, has his own territorial needs. Dr. Hall has broken these
needs down in an attempt to standardize the science of proxemics and
he has come up with four distinct zones in which most men operate. He
lists these zones as 1) intimate distance, 2) personal distance, 3) social distance and 4) public distance.

[18]   As we might guess, the zones simply represent different areas we
move in, areas that increase as intimacy decreases. Intimate distance can

either be *close,* that is, actual contact, or *far,* from six to eighteen inches. The close phase of intimate distance is used for making love, for very close friendships and for children clinging to a parent or to each other. [19] When you are at *close intimate* distance you are overwhelmingly aware of your partner. For this reason, if such contact takes place between two men, it can lead to awkwardness or uneasiness. It is most natural between a man and a woman on intimate terms. When a man and a woman are not on intimate terms the close intimate situation can be embarrassing.

[20] Between two women in our culture, a close intimate state is acceptable, while in an Arab culture such a state is acceptable between two men. Men will frequently walk hand in hand in Arab and in many Mediterranean lands.

[21] The far phase of intimate distance is still close enough to clasp hands, but it is not considered an acceptable distance for two adult male Americans. When a subway or an elevator brings them into such crowded circumstances, they will automatically observe certain rigid rules of behavior, and by doing so communicate with their neighbors.

[22] They will hold themselves as stiff as possible trying not to touch any part of their neighbors. If they do touch them, they either draw away or tense their muscles in the touching area. This action says, "I beg your pardon for intruding on your space, but the situation forces it and I will, of course, respect your privacy and let nothing intimate come of this."

[23] If, on the other hand, they were to relax in such a situation and let their bodies move easily against their neighbors' bodies and actually enjoy the contact and the body heat, they would be committing the worst possible social blunder.

[24] I have often seen a woman in a crowded subway car turn on an apparently innocent man and snarl, "Don't do that!" simply because the man had forgotten the rules and had relaxed against her. The snarls are worse when a man relaxes against another man.

[25] Nor must we, in the crowded car or elevator, stare. There is a stated time interval during which we can look, and then we must quickly look away. The unwary male who goes beyond the stated time interval risks all sorts of unpleasant consequences.

[26] I rode an elevator down in a large office building recently with another man. A pretty young girl got on at the fourteenth floor, and my friend looked at her absently but thoroughly. She grew redder and redder, and when the elevator stopped at the lobby, turned and snapped, "Haven't you ever seen a girl before, you—you dirty old man!"

[27] My friend, still in his thirties, turned to me bewilderedly as she stormed out of the car and asked, "What did I do? Tell me, what the hell did I do?"

[28] What he had done was to break a cardinal rule of nonverbal communication. "Look, and let your eyes slide away when you are in far intimate contact with a stranger."

[29]   The second zone of territory charted by Dr. Hall is called the *personal* distance zone. Here, too, he differentiates two areas, a *close personal* distance and a *far personal* distance. The close area is one and a half to two and a half feet. You can still hold or grasp your partner's hand at this distance.

[30]   As to its significance, he notes that a wife can stay within the close personal distance zone of her husband, but if another woman moves into this zone she presumably has designs on him. And yet this is obviously the comfortable distance at cocktail parties. It allows a certain intimacy and perhaps describes an intimate zone more than a personal zone. But since these are simply attempts by Dr. Hall to standardize a baby science, there may be a dozen clarifications before proxemics gets off the ground.

[31]   The far phase of personal distance, Dr. Hall puts at two and one half to four feet and calls this the limit of physical domination. You cannot comfortably touch your partner at this distance, and so it lends a certain privacy to any encounter. Yet the distance is close enough so that some degree of personal discussion can be held. When two people meet in the street, they usually stop at this distance from each other to chat. At a party they may tend to close in to the close phase of personal distance.

[32]   A variety of messages are transmitted by this distance and they range from, "I am keeping you at arm's length," to "I have singled you out to be a little closer than the other guests." To move too far in when you are on a *far personal* relationship with an acquaintance is considered pushy, or, depending on the sexual arrangement, a sign of personal favor. You make a statement with your distance, but the statement, to mean anything, must be followed up.

Social and Public Space

[33]   *Social* distance too has a close phase and a far phase. The *close* phase is four to seven feet and is generally the distance at which we transact impersonal business. It is the distance we assume when, in business, we meet the client from out of town, the new art director or the office manager. It is the distance the housewife keeps from the repairman, the shop clerk or the delivery boy. You assume this distance at a casual social gathering, but it can also be a manipulative distance.

[34]   A boss utilizes just this distance to dominate a seated employee—a secretary or a receptionist. To the employee, he tends to loom above and gain height and strength. He is, in fact, reinforcing the "you work for me" situation without ever having to say it.

[35]   The *far* phase of social distance, seven to twelve feet, is for more formal social or business relationships. The "big boss" will have a desk large enough to put him this distance from his employees. He can also remain seated at this distance and look up at an employee without a loss of status. The entire man is presented for his view.

[36]   To get back to the eyes, at this distance it is not proper to look briefly and look away. The only contact you have is visual, and so tradition dictates that you hold the person's eyes during conversation. Failing to hold his eyes is the same as excluding him from the conversation, according to Dr. Hall.

[37]   On the positive side, this distance allows a certain protection. You can keep working at this distance and not be rude, or you can stop working and talk. In offices it is necessary to preserve this far social distance between the receptionist and the visitor so that she may continue working without having to chat with him. A closer distance would make such an action rude.

[38]   The husband and wife at home in the evening assume this far social distance to relax. They can talk to each other if they wish or simply read instead of talking. The impersonal air of this type of social distance makes it an almost mandatory thing when a large family lives together, but often the family is arranged for this polite separation and must be pulled more closely together for a more intimate evening.

[39]   Finally, Dr. Hall cites *public* distance as the farthest extension of our territorial bondage. Again there is a close phase and a far phase, a distinction which may make us wonder why there aren't eight distances instead of four. But actually, the distances are arrived at according to human interaction, not to measurement.

[40]   The *close* phase of public distance is twelve to twenty-five feet, and this is suited for more informal gatherings, such as a teacher's address in a roomful of students, or a boss at a conference of workers. The *far* phase of public distance, twenty-five feet or more, is generally reserved for politicians where the distance is also a safety or a security factor, as it is with animals. Certain animal species will let you come only within this distance before moving away.

[41]   While on the subject of animal species and distance, there is always the danger of misinterpreting the true meaning of distance and territorial zones. A typical example is the lion and the lion tamer. A lion will retreat from a human when the human comes too close and enters his "danger" zone. But when he can retreat no longer and the human still advances, the lion will turn and approach the human.

[42]   A lion tamer takes advantage of this and moves toward the lion in his cage. The animal retreats, as is its nature, to the back of the cage as the lion tamer advances. When the lion can go no farther, he turns and, again in accordance with his nature, advances on the trainer with a snarl. He invariably advances in a perfectly straight line. The trainer, taking advantage of this, puts the lion's platform between himself and the lion. The lion, approaching in a straight line, climbs on the platform to get at the trainer. At this point the trainer quickly moves back out of the lion's danger zone, and the lion stops advancing.

[43]   The audience watching this interprets the gun that the trainer holds, the whip and the chair in terms of its own inner needs and fantasies. It feels that he is holding a dangerous beast at bay. This is the nonverbal communication of the entire situation. This, in body lan-

guage, is what the trainer is trying to tell us. But here body language lies.
[44] In actuality, the dialogue between lion and tamer goes like this—
Lion: "Get out of my sphere or I'll attack you." Trainer: "I am out of
your sphere." Lion: "All right. I'll stop right here."
[45] It doesn't matter where *here* is. The trainer has manipulated things
so that *here* is the top of the lion's platform.
[46] In the same way the far public sphere of the politician or the actor
on a stage contains a number of body language statements which are
used to impress the audience, not necessarily to tell the truth.
[47] It is at this far public distance that it is difficult to speak the truth
or, to turn it around, at this far public distance it is most easy to lie
with the motions of the body. Actors are well aware of this, and for centuries they have utilized the distance of the stage from the audience to
create a number of illusions.
[48] At this distance the actor's gestures must be stylized, affected and
far more symbolic than they are at closer public, social or intimate distances.
[49] On the television screen, as in the motion picture, the combination
of long shots and close-ups calls for still another type of body language.
A movement of the eyelid or the eyebrow or a quiver of the lip in a
close-up can convey as much of a message as the gross movement of arm
or an entire body in a long shot.
[50] In the close-up the gross movements are usually lost. This may be
one of the reasons television and motion picture actors have so much
trouble adapting to the stage.
[51] The stage often calls for a rigid, mannered approach to acting because of the distance between actors and audience. Today, in revolt
against this entire technique, there are elements of the theatre that try
to do away with the public distance between actor and stage.
[52] They either move down into the audience, or invite the audience
up to share the stage with them. Drama, under these conditions, must
be a lot less structured. You can have no assurance that the audience will
respond in the way you wish. The play therefore becomes more formless,
usually without a plot and with only a central idea.
[53] Body language, under these circumstances, becomes a difficult vehicle for the actor. He must on the one hand drop many of the symbolic
gestures he has used, because they just won't work over these short distances. He cannot rely on natural body language for the emotions he
wishes to project no matter how much he "lives" his part. So he must
develop a new set of symbols and stylized body motions that will also lie
to the audience.
[54] Whether this "close-up" lying will be any more effective than the
far-off lying of the proscenium stage remains to be seen. The gestures of
the proscenium or traditional stage have been refined by years of practice. There is also a cultural attachment involved with the gestures of
the stage. The Japanese kabuki theater, for example, contains its own
refined symbolic gestures that are so culture-oriented that more than half
of them may be lost on a Western audience.

words and sentences

1. Vocabulary: *subconscious* (¶ 2); *dynamics* (3); *unconscious* (4); *reflexive* (7); *nuances* (8); *anthropology* (16); *cardinal* (28); *manipulative* (33); *mandatory* (38); *stylized* (48); *mannered* (51).
2. In international relations, what does the phrase "violation of space" mean? Does Fast give examples of violation of personal space?
3. Rewrite the first sentence of ¶ 1, changing the voice of the verbs. Have you saved any words and improved the sentence in your rewriting?
4. Could Fast have placed all the sentences of ¶s 9-13 in a single paragraph? Why? What reasons might Fast have for arranging the paragraphs and sentences as he has?
5. Check the word *conciseness* in a dictionary. Rewrite the sentences of ¶s 9-13, placing them in a single paragraph. These paragraphs contain 193 words; try to reduce the number of words and sentences without changing the meaning.

ideas and implications

1. What evidence does Fast offer to prove that kinesics is a science?
2. What warning does Fast give to readers about their ability to interpret body language? Why? What must one know to read this special language?
3. Why does Fast say that much of the body's language is unconscious? Are people sometimes unaware of the effects of the words they use? Under what circumstances might this be true?
4. Not all of our body language is unconscious. Think of some gesture or body language that is not unconscious. What do these gestures say?
5. In ¶ 20, Fast comments on acceptable spatial contact between men and men and women and women in Arab and American cultures. What has his example to do with contexts? Explain.
6. In ¶ 15, Fast writes, "It is all a need for territory, for a place to call one's own. Perhaps it is an inborn universal need, though it is shaped by society and culture into a variety of forms." Does he make further distinctions about what is inborn and what is cultural?

strategies

1. Fast develops many of his ideas with examples and incidents. Cite four of these examples and comment on the purpose of each in its context.
2. ¶s 9-54 treat the topic of space in personal relationships. How does Fast introduce his topic and how does he conclude his discussion?
3. How has Fast ordered his ideas about one's need for space in ¶s 9-54? How important are ¶s 16 and 17 in determining the order in which Fast presents his ideas?
4. Transitional words and phrases not only connect sentences and paragraphs, but also show logical relationships between ideas. Examine some of Fast's transitions to see what kinds of relationships they establish in the presentation of his ideas.

suggestions for writing

1. Sit in a restaurant or coffee shop so that you can observe those around you. Select the people seated at one table and observe their spatial relationships to each other and their gestures. Sit far enough away that you cannot overhear their conversation. You might even want to take some notes. Then write a paper describing the people, their spatial relationships, and their gestures.
2. Rewrite the paper above, adding conversation that you imagine took place.
3. From your experience, write a paper describing a situation in which you think spatial relationships were important.
4. Elsewhere in his book, Fast writes of going to lunch with a "psychiatrist friend" who after eating lit a cigarette and placed the package three-quarters of the way across the table in Fast's direction. As the two talked, the psychiatrist moved the cigarettes and the tableware further in Fast's direction. Fast records that he felt uncomfortable and troubled. The psychiatrist explained that he had been performing a "demonstration of a very basic step in body language." By pushing the cigarettes and tableware to Fast's half of the table, the psychiatrist had aggressively threatened and challenged Fast. Try a similar experiment with an acquaintance and then write a paper describing the incident.

Paul R. Wendt

The Language of Pictures

[1]   Man has been communicating by pictures longer than he has been using words. With the development of photography in this century we are using pictures as a means of communication to such an extent that in some areas they overshadow verbal language. The science of semantics has studied the conveyance of meaning by language in considerable detail. Yet very little is known as to how pictures convey meaning and what their place is in the life of man.

[2]   Perhaps this neglect may be due to the poor repute pictures have in our society as a means of communication. For example, in the field of education, pictures, as a part of the group of audio-visual materials available to teachers, are still considered supplementary rather than complementary to other teaching materials such as textbooks or other purely

Reprinted from *ETC.*, Vol. XIII, No. 4, by permission of the International Society for General Semantics.

verbal materials. The term audio-visual "aids" persists, although a number of educators have tried for a decade to persuade their colleagues to discontinue its use on the basis of its connotation of (1) something used by poor teachers who cannot teach without gadgets, (2) a luxury to be trimmed off the budget in hard times, and (3) a mental crutch for backward pupils.

[3] Pictures are of course surrogates for experience. As such they may be said to be closer to extensional meaning than to intensional meaning. At least their position lies in between these two. They are not always close to the actual experience even though the school of "you press the button and we do the rest" implies that merely pointing the camera at Aunt Minnie results in a good likeness to cherish when she is not around. Neither are pictures symbols as words are symbols, since even Aunt Minnie's nephew, age four, can recognize her snapshot though he cannot read.

[4] Pictures are a language in themselves. They are not merely limited representations of reality operating within narrow limits of expression. On the contrary photography is a very flexible medium with a wide range whose limits have not yet been sighted. The range extends from absorbing realism to a fairly high level of abstraction. Let us consider the realistic end of the scale.

[5] The tendency today is to say that the heydey of the movies is over. Television is gnawing at the vitals of Hollywood. But the powerfully realistic effect of the film remains. The other day the writer showed to one of his classes a film, *The Cinematographer,* which purports to show the work of the director of photography in a large studio. Excerpts from several dramatic films were shown to illustrate the different types of scenes a cinematographer encounters. None of these excerpts was longer than one minute. After the film ended some members of the class complained that the excerpts were so realistic and exciting that they "lost" themselves in the content of the episodes and completely forgot that the purpose of the film showing was to study cinematography. Each episode in turn caught these students up in a rich representation of reality. The excerpts were very dissimilar in content so that it was a wrench to change from one scene to another. Nevertheless the students were deeply involved in each excerpt in turn, and only when the lights came on in the classroom did they remember where they were.

[6] Motion pictures are a powerful medium of persuasion. Hitler's films of the bombing of Warsaw were such terribly realistic records that they could be used as a tool of conquest. At times a motion picture may seem even more realistic than the real experience.

[7] At the other end of the scale from realism to abstraction, pictures have many qualities of language. Like words every picture has a content of meaning partly intensional, partly extensional. Whether this meaning is more or less extensionally clear or abstractly difficult to understand depends of course on many factors inherent in the viewer, such as his past experience. But it also is dependent on factors in the picture itself which we might call the grammar of photography.

[8]   Composition is all important. In chirographic, or hand-made, pictures composition is achieved sometimes by selection of the point of view but more often by manipulation of space relationships of objects perceived or imagined. The still photographer, unless he is using techniques which are essentially chirographic, such as retouching, montage, or collage, is bound by the objects of reality as the eye of his camera sees them. He achieves composition by painstaking selection of the camera angle, by using a variety of lenses, by choice of filters and emulsions, and by controlling lighting on the subject or scene. Choosing a camera angle may take a professional photographer days of continuous effort, even though television camera operators may be forced to do it in seconds. The angle and the lens used for the shot determine the basic composition. The lighting, however, gives the photographer an enormous range of control over the representation of reality. High key photography in which all the values are crowded toward the whites and light grays, gives the impressions of light, of lightness, or happiness, or innocent pleasures. Low key photography with many shadows and low values is appropriate for mystery, danger, depression. Every textbook in photography contains the series of portraits of a model taken with different lighting effects, showing how one face can be made to look like many strange people. Pictures have affective connotations.

[9]   These constitute the grammar of photographs. The analogy holds even down to details such as synizesis. Two crucial objects in a picture, like two syllables, can be blended and not discriminated from each other, thereby changing the meaning entirely. Even though the photographer uses lighting and other techniques to separate the two objects, the viewer may still misread the picture because of lack of experience or poor viewing conditions. Always it is important to remember that pictures, like words, are merely surrogates for reality, not reality itself.

[10]   In motion pictures we find the syntax of photography. Motion pictures present a flowing discourse in picture surrogates. Like a paragraph, a motion picture sequence is a highly structured time-space analysis and synthesis of reality. Using individual "shots" like words, the sequence inflects the static frame of film by motion. One scene with motion by actors or by the camera resembles a sentence. Short dynamic scenes have the same effect as blunt statements. Longer scenes with complicated changes in composition created by camera movement have somewhat the effect of compound sentences.

[11]   Pictures, like words, must make a logical continuity, according to accepted rules. For example, a motion picture showing two people conversing must first show them more or less side-to, to establish their relative positions. Then as each speaks he is shown over the other's shoulder. This is the familiar "reverse-angle" shot. That this is a culturally based convention of film syntax is shown by the experience of representatives of the U. S. Office of Information who have found that natives of foreign countries who have not seen motion pictures cannot "understand" the reverse-angle shot. They cannot adjust to our stereotyped representations of reality. They don't understand our language of pictures. Similarly,

most of the action in a motion picture must be "matched." That is, if
an actor is shown walking up to a door in a distant shot, the following
close-up should show him approximately in the same position as he was
in the last frame of the long shot. "Matching the action" is a convention
in cinematography, part of the film language. It is not always used.
When the tempo of the film is fast it is common practice for the editor
to elide some of the action, as an author does when he wants the same
effect. And of course films *can* compress time dramatically.

[12]   Paragraphing is accomplished by the traditional fade-out and
fade-in, or by the dissolve or optical effect as soft or hard "wipes." The
pace of the narrative is determined more by the film editor than by the
script. The editor of words clarifies the presentation of content by eliminating words, sentences, paragraphs, and even chapters. The film editor
clips out frames, scenes, sequences, and even large parts of a film (resulting sometimes in "the face on the cutting room floor"). The book editor
may achieve lucidity by rearranging the author's text, moving paragraphs
and chapters. The film editor boldly changes the order of film sequences.
Both the book editor and the film editor can have a decisive influence
on the style of the finished work. Both can call for rewriting or new
photography. Both can affect the pace of the manuscript or the "rough
cut." Both are experts in grammar, syntax, and style.

[13]   More important than the mechanical analogy to words are the semantic dimensions of pictures. Every photograph is an abstraction of an
object or an event. Even the amateur, ignorant of the plasticity of the
medium, makes an abstraction of Aunt Minnie when he presses the button. Only a few of Aunt Minnie's characteristics are recorded on the film.

[14]   The professional photographer in control of his medium knows he
is abstracting. If he is competent he abstracts to a purpose. Knowing he
cannot possibly record the whole event, he sees to it that the abstracting
preserves those features he wants to present to the picture-reader. By
manipulation of the variables at his command, he lets us "see" the event
as he thinks it should be "seen." If he is a news photographer he probably
wants to present a "realistic" event, full of details, although often he is
working under such handicaps of haste that the picture as we see it in
the newspaper has become simplified and perhaps indistinct. Then it
lacks background or environment, it lacks the richness and crispness
which a realistic picture must have. Some news pictures are so simplified
that they look like symbolization. They fit the definition of a symbol as
"that which suggests something else by convention."

[15]   The fashion photographer, however, preparing for an advertisement in *The New Yorker,* controls the photographic medium to produce
a simple, stylized figure, often against a blank background. This picture
is realistic only to a limited extent and approaches the characteristics
of a symbol. Carried even further a photograph can be almost purely
symbolic, devoid of the very characteristics that are usually associated
with photography. Take as an example the famous combat photo of the
planting of the American flag by Marines on the summit of Mount Suri-
bachi. There is nothing in the frame but the men struggling to raise the

flag and a few rocks of the mountain top. This picture has been accepted as a symbol. It has even been reproduced in bronze in Washington, D.C., as a memorial to the Marines. We accept a statue as a symbol. But here is a case where the statue was copied directly *with little change* from a press shot.

[16]   At this point we may consider a paradox. *Life* magazine a few years ago ran a series of photographs called "What's in a Picture." One showed a tired interne in a hospital having a quick cup of coffee while still in his surgical gown. Another showed a boy and his dog walking the railroad track. In a third Cardinal Mindszenty was on trial in Hungary. A fourth showed the exhaustion in the face of a combat Marine. There is no doubt that these pictures rate among the most graphic that have ever been taken. In fact, this is why *Life* ran them as a separate series, to show that some of the best pictures need no explanation. This, however, is a characteristic of symbols, and these pictures achieve their greatness because they present symbols—the American doctor, a typical boy, the horror of brain-washing behind the Iron Curtain, and the life of a front-line soldier. It is a paradox that these most graphic pictures are symbolic. They are *at the same time* very real and very symbolic.

[17]   A picture is a map, since there is not a one-to-one correspondence between elements of the picture and elements of the event. We might say, as J. J. Gibson says about the retinal image, that a picture is a good correlate *but not a copy* of the scene photographed. A picture definitely has structure. It is a configuration of symbols which make it possible for

THE MAP IS NOT THE TERRITORY

us to interpret the picture, provided that we have enough experience with these symbols to read the picture.

[18]   Pictures can be manipulated like words so as to seem to change their referents. The motion picture editor can lengthen and shorten individual scenes and place them in such a juxtaposition in a carefully planned tempo as to create an impression foreign to the events photographed. It would be possible to assemble a number of pictures of active American businessmen and cut them together to give the impression of frantic competition for money when this did not exist in the actual situations.

[19]   Once we have established the fact that photographs of events are

not the events, that they show by intent or accident only a few characteristics of events, we have the perspective to question some reactions
of people to pictures. In spite of decades of visual education there still
are teachers who will not use teaching films when they are easily available. This refusal has been dismissed as conservatism, laziness, and poor
teaching. Could it be that some of these teachers, projecting films in
undarkened rooms on a wall (for want of a proper screen) and with a
screen image not large enough to give a realistic effect, have unconsciously concluded that motion pictures are not enough different from
words to bother with? Obviously the great asset of films is realism, which
gives the pupils a chance to identify with characters on the screen and
"lose" themselves in the picture. When this realism is wiped out by
poor reproduction or poor projection, the faint images on the wall lose
details, become more outlined and stylized, and have little advantage,
if any, over words. Like words they are so vague that they can be interpreted individually by each viewer. Pictures, unlike words, depend very
much indeed on the quality of their reproduction for the kind and
amount of meaning the picture-reader gets from them.

[20]   Because of the plasticity of the photographic medium it is well that
there are few pictures that do not have captions. In a sense these are
indices like Interne$_1$, Interne$_2$. We feel the need of captions on pictures
as we do not feel the need for indices on words. Yet we usually feel that
pictures are much more likely to be completely self-explanatory than
words.

[21]   General semanticists know it is hard to make the average person
realize that he brings meaning to the word, that the word does *not* contain any meaning. A word is just a series of hentracks which we are told
authoritatively stands for a certain concept.

[22]   It is still harder to convince anyone that we also bring meaning to
a picture. If the picture is well within our previous experience it means
something. What it means depends on the kind of our experience. The
picture of any political figure is interpreted in radically different manners by opposing parties. City children react differently to a picture of a
cow than do farm children. Thus pictures can reinforce stereotypes because the characteristics of people or events which the photographer
presents through the medium are not strong enough to overcome the
"embedded canalizations" in the reader.

[23]   When the picture is not within the range of our experience we
react to it almost as little as to an unknown word. Scenes of mass calis-
thenics performed by ten thousand Russians mean to us little more than
"mass conformity," whereas they may originally have been meant to express "ideals." Strange animals are to us just configurations of light and
shade on paper. If they move on the screen we can apply more of our
experience to understanding what we see. Professional photographers,
like teachers, have their readers carefully estimated. Like teachers, they
see to it that their pictures contain plenty of the familiar (to their particular reader) and some of the unusual. We are able to reach out a
short distance into the unknown from the solid base of our own ex-

perience. The difference here between words and pictures is that the distinction between the known and the unknown is sharpened by pictures. If we read that an emu is like an ostrich, only larger, we have a vague idea about it. If we see a picture of an emu we remember more clearly the features similar to an ostrich and perhaps notice how the emu is different and new.

[24] Pictures are multiordinal. They are interpreted on different levels of abstraction. We have seen this happen in the *Life* series mentioned above. Our Aunt Minnie is just another aunt to strangers; they think she looks like the Genus Aunt. The fact that pictures are interpreted on different levels is the basis for some items in some common intelligence scales. The lowest level is that in which the child merely enumerates objects and people: "I see a woman and a girl and a stove," etc. This is analogous to the descriptive level of words. A higher level of reaction would be description and interpretation such as, "The woman is probably the girl's mother and she is cooking her supper."

[25] A picture causing a semantic disturbance is familiar to everyone. "Oh, that doesn't look like me at all. What a terrible picture!" Or the vacationers who have rented a lake cottage on the basis of glamorous pictures in an advertising folder get a shock when they find that the lake is much smaller than they thought, that the trees are scrubby, and that the cottage is in disrepair. Visitors to California complain that the "blue Pacific" is not always blue, as the postcards invariably show it. Or they say, "Is *that* Velma Blank, the great movie star?" It is in situations like these that we can best realize that pictures, although somewhat better than words, are only maps of the territory they represent.

[26] Pictures can be self-reflexive. A photograph of a photograph is a standard method of reproduction, for example, in the making of filmstrips. It is by such reproduction that it is possible to present to congressional committees photographs which seem to show members of the cabinet or senators in conversation with persons with whom they never exchanged more than a word.

[27] Pictures, then, have many of the characteristics of language, not in the figurative sense of "the language of flowers" but in the very real characteristics of structure (syntax, grammar, style) and of semantics. The most crucial characteristic is that pictures are abstractions of reality. A picture can present only a few of the aspects of the event. It may, under the strict control of the photographer, become as abstract as a symbol.

[28] It is most urgent that there should be more awareness of the abstracting power of photography, that pictures *do lie*. Instead we find great naïveté. People believe what they see in pictures. "One picture is worth a thousand words" not only because it is more graphic but because it is believed to be the gospel truth, an incontrovertible fact. A teacher may present her pupils in a big city with a side view of a cow. They should then know what a cow is! Little do they dream that to a farm boy a cow is a complex of associations which even four hours of movies could not present. We find pictures used as "illustrations." They are inserted in textbooks as a last resort to relieve the copy. One picture of

Iowa in the geography text must suffice for Iowa. The author says, "This is Iowa." The general semanticists would recognize this as the error of "allness," ascribing to a word all the characteristics of the thing abstracted from. The danger of "allness" is so much more lively in the case of pictures than in the case of words because everyone assumes pictures *are* reality.

[29] Of course pictures provide us with more cues from reality itself (cues for eliciting the meaning we bring to the picture) than the arbitrary hen tracks we call "words." But the basic error is to fail to realize that the meanings of pictures are not in the pictures, but rather in what we bring to them.

words and sentences

1. Vocabulary: *semantics, conveyance* (¶ 1) ; *connotation* (2); *surrogates* (3); *purports, excerpts* (5); *inherent* (7); *chirographic, montage, collage* (8); *analogy, synizesis* (9); *syntax, synthesis, inflects* (10); *stereotyped, elide* (11); *lucidity* (12); *plasticity* (13); *paradox* (16); *juxtaposition* (18); *eliciting* (29).
2. Change the word order and rewrite the opening sentences of ¶s 8, 9, 10, and 11. Does changing the word order alter the meaning of these sentences? Is Wendt's choice of word order more or less effective than your rewriting?

ideas and implications

1. Wendt argues three or four principal points in his essay. List these points, and then write a single paragraph summarizing his major points.
2. What distinction does Wendt make between *symbol (abstraction)* and *realism?* In ¶ 16, he speaks of a paradox that complicates his distinction. Define that paradox in your own words.
3. Does the line drawing (¶ 17) help to illustrate Wendt's point that "Pictures . . . are only maps of the territory they represent" (¶ 25)? What does this suggest about the relationship between pictures and words?
4. What faulty reasoning about photographs does Wendt describe in ¶ 28?
5. In ¶ 29, Wendt notes, "But the basic error is to fail to realize that meanings of pictures are not in the pictures, but rather in what we bring to them." According to this statement, where does meaning lie? Does Wendt ever qualify this statement?

strategies

1. What is a topic sentence? Check a dictionary or a handbook if you are uncertain. Find several topic sentences in Wendt's essay. Do these topic sentences determine the way Wendt discusses the subject of a particular paragraph? Are many of Wendt's topic sentences simple sentences? Why?
2. What is the purpose of the first three paragraphs of Wendt's essay?
3. Beginning with ¶ 4, Wendt employs a specific method to develop his ideas about pictures. Describe that method. How many paragraphs does

Wendt employ in this explanation? Where does this section of his presentation end?

4. What sentence pattern is Wendt using in the last four sentences of ¶ 12? Why does he use this pattern?

5. Does the first sentence of ¶ 13 signal to the reader the introduction of a new topic? How does Wendt connect ¶ 13 with his previous observations?

suggestions for writing

1. Find examples in magazines or newspapers of photographs that Wendt would label symbolic and realistic. Select one of each kind and write a paper explaining why these two photographs are realistic and symbolic. Attach to your paper copies of the photographs you discuss.

2. From magazine and newspaper photographs create your own picture, collage, or montage. Then write a paper describing your intentions in this work. Attach your collage, etc., to your paper.

3. Find a photograph or a painting that interests you. Then write a paper defining the point of view of the photographer or painter. Attach a copy of the photo or painting to your paper.

4. Describe a photograph in which you appear or which you took yourself. Perhaps an old yearbook photo or a snapshot from your wallet would suffice. Make your description as specific as you can—so that your classmates might draw a fairly accurate representation of the photo from your description. Then reconstruct from memory the context of the actual events surrounding the taking of the photo. Try to determine how much the photo "lies" (¶ 28) or tells the truth.

5. Take a photograph of yourself (a driver's licence picture, etc.) that causes you "semantic disturbance." Compare it with a photo which you believe is truer of you. Write a paper about the differences between the two.

6. Choose a photograph or a painting that a classmate or an acquaintance finds appealing. Then write a character sketch of that person based on his liking for the work. In short, try to determine what that person brings to the work (see ¶ 29).

Emily Dickinson

"A Word Is Dead"

1212

A word is dead
When it is said,
Some say.
I say it just
Begins to live
That day.

From *The Complete Poems of Emily Dickinson,* ed. Thomas H. Johnson (Little, Brown and Co., 1960).

William Shakespeare

Falstaff's Speech on Honour
from *Henry IV, Part 1**

FALSTAFF. 'Tis not due yet; I would be loath to pay him before his day. What need I be so forward with him that calls not on me? Well, 'tis no matter; honour pricks me on. Yea, but how if honour prick me off when I come on? how then? Can honour set to a leg? no: or an arm? no: or take away the grief of a wound? no. Honour hath no skill in surgery, then? no. What is honour? a word. What is in that word honour? what is that honour? air. A trim reckoning! Who hath it? he that died o' Wednesday. Doth he feel it? no. Doth he hear it? no. 'Tis insensible, then? Yea, to the dead. But will it not live with the living? no. Why? detraction will not suffer it. Therefore I'll none of it. Honour is a mere scutcheon: and so ends my catechism.

* In the speech just before Falstaff's soliloquy, Prince Hal has said to Falstaff: "Why, thou owest God a death." Prince Hal and Falstaff are getting ready for battle against the enemies of Henry IV, Prince Hal's father.

words and sentences

1. How many words of more than one syllable appear in Emily Dickinson's poem? What kind of language does she use to present her idea?
2. Vocabulary from Falstaff's speech: *loath, pricks, trim, reckoning, detraction, catechism.*
3. Does the word *insensible* in Falstaff's speech have more than a single meaning in its context? Why?

ideas and implications

1. Miss Dickinson plays with the words *dead* and *live.* For her, what gives words life? Is an audience necessary for that life to occur?
2. Where does meaning lie for Falstaff? Is he about to die for a word? Why or why not? Is Falstaff's attitude toward language similar to other authors in this section?

strategies

1. Miss Dickinson's poem employs two sentences. Rewrite these sentences placing the words in "normal" English word order (subject, verb, object). Note, too, that each sentence omits one word—the understood relative pronoun *that.* Why might Miss Dickinson have changed the word order from the usual subject, verb, object sequence?
2. Does Falstaff's soliloquy resemble the form of a catechism? How? Or is there another way to describe the way Shakespeare orders this speech?

suggestions for writing

1. Abstract words like *honor, courage, love, truth,* etc., have always posed problems for people. Write a paper about one of your attempts to learn the meaning of an abstract word.
2. Write a paper comparing and contrasting Miss Dickinson's and Falstaff's attitudes towards words.
3. Write a paper about a situation in which you gave life to words by saying them to another person or another person gave life to words by saying them to you. What was the importance of the situation, the words, and the feelings associated with this event?

S. I. Hayakawa

How Words Change Our Lives

[1]   The end product of education, yours and mine and everybody's, is the total pattern of reactions and possible reactions we have inside ourselves. If you did not have within you at this moment the pattern of reactions that we call "the ability to read English," you would see here only meaningless black marks on paper. Because of the trained patterns of response, you are (or are not) stirred to patriotism by martial music, your feelings of reverence are aroused by the symbols of your religion, you listen more respectfully to the health advice of someone who has "M.D." after his name than to that of someone who hasn't. What I call here a "pattern of reactions," then, is the sum total of the ways we act in response to events, to words, and to symbols.

[2]   Our reaction patterns—our semantic habits, as we may call them— are the internal and most important residue of whatever years of education or miseducation we may have received from our parents' conduct toward us in childhood as well as their teachings, from the formal education we may have had, from all the sermons and lectures we have listened to, from the radio programs and the movies and television shows we have experienced, from all the books and newspapers and comic strips we have read, from the conversations we have had with friends and associates, and from all our experiences. If, as the result of all these influences that make us what we are, our semantic habits are reasonably similar to those of most people around us, we are regarded as "well-adjusted," or "normal," and perhaps "dull." If our semantic habits are noticeably different from those of others, we are regarded as "individualistic" or "original," or, if the differences are disapproved of or viewed with alarm, as "screwballs" or "crazy."

[3]   Semantics is sometimes defined in dictionaries as "the science of the meaning of words"—which would not be a bad definition if people didn't assume that the search for the meanings of words begins and ends with looking them up in a dictionary.

[4]   If one stops to think for a moment, it is clear that to define a word, as a dictionary does, is simply to explain the word with more words. To be thorough about defining, we should next have to define the words used in the definition, then define the words used in defining the words used in the definition . . . and so on. Defining words with more words, in short, gets us at once into what mathematicians call an "infinite regress." Alternatively, it can get us into the kind of run-around we sometimes encounter when we look up "impertinence" and find it defined as "impudence," so we look up "impudence" and find it defined as "impertinence." Yet—and here we come to another common reaction pattern

—people often act as if words can be explained fully with more words. To a person who asked for a definition of jazz, Louis Armstrong is said to have replied, "Man, when you got to ask what it is, you'll never get to know," proving himself to be an intuitive semanticist as well as a great trumpet player.

[5]   Semantics, then, does not deal with the "meaning of words" as that expression is commonly understood. P. W. Bridgman, the Nobel Prize winner and physicist, once wrote, "The true meaning of a term is to be found by observing what a man does with it, not by what he says about it." He made an enormous contribution to science by showing that the meaning of a scientific term lies in the operations, the things done, that establish its validity, rather than in verbal definitions.

[6]   Here is a simple, everyday kind of example of "operational" definition. If you say, "This table measures six feet in length," you could prove it by taking a foot rule, performing the operation of laying it end to end while counting, "One . . . two . . . three . . . four. . . ." But if you say—and revolutionists have started uprisings with just this statement—"Man is born free, but everywhere he is in chains!"—what operations could you perform to demonstrate its accuracy or inaccuracy?

[7]   But let us carry this suggestion of "operationalism" outside the physical sciences where Bridgman applied it, and observe what "operations" people perform as the result of both the language they use and the language other people use in communicating to them. Here is a personnel manager studying an application blank. He comes to the words "Education: Harvard University," and drops the application blank in the wastebasket (that's the "operation") because, as he would say if you asked him, "I don't like Harvard men." This is an instance of "meaning" at work—but it is not a meaning that can be found in dictionaries.

[8]   If I seem to be taking a long time to explain what semantics is about, it is because I am trying, in the course of explanation, to introduce the reader to a certain way of looking at human behavior. Semantics—especially the general semantics of Alfred Korzybski (1879-1950), Polish-American scientist and educator—pays particular attention not to words in themselves, but to semantic reactions—that is, human responses to symbols, signs, and symbol-systems, including language.

[9]   I say *human* responses because, so far as we know, human beings are the only creatures that have, over and above that biological equipment which we have in common with other creatures, the additional capacity for manufacturing symbols and systems of symbols. When we react to a flag, we are not reacting simply to a piece of cloth, but to the meaning with which it has been symbolically endowed. When we react to a word, we are not reacting to a set of sounds, but to the meaning with which that set of sounds has been symbolically endowed.

[10]   A basic idea in general semantics, therefore, is that the meaning of words (or other symbols) is not in the words, but in our own semantic reactions. If I were to tell a shockingly obscene story in Arabic or Hindustani or Swahili before an audience that understood only English, no one would blush or be angry; the story would be neither shocking

nor obscene—indeed, it would not even be a story. Likewise, the value of a dollar bill is not in the bill, but in our social agreement to accept it as a symbol of value. If that agreement were to break down through the collapse of our government, the dollar bill would become only a scrap of paper. We do not understand a dollar bill by staring at it long and hard. We understand it by observing how people act with respect to it. We understand it by understanding the social mechanisms and the loyalties that keep it meaningful. Semantics is therefore a social study, basic to all other social studies.

[11] It is often remarked that words are tricky—and that we are all prone to be deceived by "fast talkers," such as high-pressure salesmen, skillful propagandists, politicians, or lawyers. Since few of us are aware of the degree to which we use words to deceive ourselves, the sin of "using words in a tricky way" is one that is always attributed to the other fellow. When the Russians use the word "democracy" to mean something quite different from what we mean by it, we at once accuse them of "propaganda," of "corrupting the meanings of words." But when we use the word "democracy" in the United States to mean something quite different from what the Russians mean by it, they are equally quick to accuse us of "hypocrisy." We all tend to believe that the way we use words is the correct way, and that people who use the same words in other ways are either ignorant or dishonest.

[12] Leaving aside for a moment such abstract and difficult terms as "democracy," let us examine a common, everyday word like "frog." Surely there is no problem about what "frog" means! Here are some sample sentences:

> "If we're going fishing, we'll have to catch some frogs first." (This is easy.)
> "I have a frog in my throat." (You can hear it croaking.)
> "She wore a loose silk jacket fastened with braided frogs."
> "The blacksmith pared down the frog and the hoof before shoeing the horse."
> "In Hamilton, Ohio, there is a firm by the name of American Frog and Switch Company."

In addition to these "frogs," there is the frog in which a sword is carried, the frog at the bottom of a bowl or vase that is used in flower arrangement, and the frog that is part of a violin bow. The reader can no doubt think of other "frogs."

[13] Or take another common word such as "order." There is the *order* that the salesman tries to get, which is quite different from the *order* that a captain gives to his crew. Some people enter holy *orders*. There is the *order* in the house when mother has finished tidying up; there is the batting *order* of the home team; there is an *order* of ham and eggs. It is surprising that with so many meanings to the word, people don't misunderstand one another oftener than they do.

[14] The foregoing are only striking examples of a principle to which we are all so well accustomed that we rarely think of it; namely, that

most words have more meanings than dictionaries can keep track of. And when we consider further that each of us has different experiences, different memories, different likes and dislikes, it is clear that all words evoke different responses in all of us. We may agree as to what the term "Mississippi River" stands for, but you and I recall different parts of the river; you and I have had different experiences with it; one of us has read more about it than the other; one of us may have happy memories of it, while the other may recall chiefly tragic events connected with it. Hence your "Mississippi River" can never be identical with my "Mississippi River." The fact that we can communicate with each other about the "Mississippi River" often conceals the fact that we are talking about two different sets of memories and experiences.

[15] Words being as varied in their meanings as they are, no one can tell us what the correct interpretation of a word should be in advance of our next encounter with that word. The reader may have been taught always to revere the word "mother." But what is he going to do the next time he encounters this word, when it occurs in the sentence "Mother began to form in the bottle"? If it is impossible to determine what a single word will mean on next encounter, is it possible to say in advance what is the correct evaluation of such events as these: (1) next summer, an individual who calls himself a socialist will announce his candidacy for the office of register of deeds in your city; (2) next autumn, there will be a strike at one of your local department stores; (3) next week, your wife will announce that she is going to change her style of hairdo; (4) tomorrow, your little boy will come home with a bleeding nose?

[16] A reasonably sane individual will react to each of these events in his own way, according to time, place, and the entire surrounding set of circumstances; and included among those circumstances will be his own stock of experiences, wishes, hopes, and fears. But there are people whose pattern of reactions is such that some of them can be completely predicted in advance. Mr. A will never vote for anyone called "socialist," no matter how incompetent or crooked the alternative candidates may be. Mr. B_1 always disapproves of strikes and strikers, without bothering to inquire whether or not this strike has its justifications; Mr. B_2 always sympathizes with the strikers because he hates all bosses. Mr. C belongs to the "stay sweet as you are" school of thought, so that his wife hasn't been able to change her hairdo since she left high school. Mr. D always faints at the sight of blood.

[17] Such fixed and unalterable patterns of reaction—in their more obvious forms we call them prejudices—are almost inevitably organized around words. Mr. E distrusts and fears all people to whom the term "Catholic" is applicable, while Mr. F, who is Catholic, distrusts and fears all non-Catholics. Mr. G is so rabid a Republican that he reacts with equal dislike to all Democrats, all Democratic proposals, all opposite proposals if they are also made by Democrats. Back in the days when Franklin D. Roosevelt was President, Mr. G disliked not only the Democratic President but also his wife, children, and dog. His office was on Roosevelt Road in Chicago (it had been named after Theodore Roose-

velt), but he had his address changed to his back door on 11th Street, so that he would not have to print the hated name on his stationery. Mr. H, on the other hand, is an equally rabid Democrat, who gave up golf during the Eisenhower adminstration (he resumed it after Kennedy took up the game). People suffering from such prejudice seem to have in their brains an uninsulated spot which, when touched by such words as "capitalist," "boss," "striker," "scab," "Democrat," "Republican," "socialized medicine," and other such loaded terms, results in an immediate short circuit, often with a blowing of fuses.

[18]   Korzybski called such short-circuited responses "identification reactions." He used the word "identification" in a special sense; he meant that persons given to such fixed patterns of response identify (that is, treat as identical) all occurrences of a given word or symbol; they identify all the different cases that fall under the same name. Thus, if one has hostile identification reactions to "women drivers," then all women who drive cars are "identical" in their incompetence.

[19]   Korzybski believed that the term "identification reaction" could be generally used to describe the majority of cases of semantic malfunctioning. Identification is something that goes on in the human nervous system. "Out there" there are no absolute identities. No two Harvard men, no two Ford cars, no two mothers-in-law, no two politicians, no two leaves from the same tree are identical with each other in all respects. If, however, we treat all cases that fall under the same class label as one at times when the differences are important, then there is something wrong with our semantic habits.

[20]   We are now ready, then, for another definition of general semantics. It is a comparative study of the kind of responses people make to the symbols and signs around them; we may compare the semantic habits common among the prejudiced, the foolish, and the mentally ill with those found among people who are able to solve their problems successfully, so that, if we care to, we may revise our own semantic habits for the better. In other words, general semantics is the study of how not to be a damn fool.

[21]   Identification reactions run all the way through nature. The capacity for seeing similarities is necessary to the survival of all animals. The pickerel, I suppose, identifies all shiny, fluttery things going through the water as minnows, and goes after them all in pretty much the same way. Under natural conditions, life is made possible for the pickerel by this capacity. Once in a while, however, the shiny, fluttery thing in the water may happen to be not a minnow but an artificial lure on the end of a line. In such a case, one would say that the identification response, so useful for survival, under somewhat more complex conditions that require differentiation between two sorts of shiny and fluttery objects, proves to be fatal.

[22]   To go back to our discussion of human behavior, we see at once that the problem of adequate differentiation is immeasurably more complex for men than it is for the pickerel. The signs we respond to, and

the symbols we create and train ourselves to respond to, are infinitely greater in number and immeasurably more abstract than the signs in a pickerel's environment. Lower animals have to deal only with certain brute facts in their physical environment. But think, only for a moment, of what constitutes a human environment. Think of the items that call for adequate responses that no animal ever has to think about: our days are named and numbered, so that we have birthdays, anniversaries, holidays, centennials, and so on, all calling for specifically human responses; we have history, which no animal has to worry about; we have verbally codified patterns of behavior which we call law, religion, and ethics. We have to respond not only to events in our immediate environment, but to reported events in Washington, Paris, Tokyo, Moscow, Beirut. We have literature, comic strips, confession magazines, market quotations, detective stories, journals of abnormal psychology, bookkeeping systems to interpret. We have money, credit, banking, stocks, bonds, checks, bills. We have the complex symbolisms of moving pictures, paintings, drama, music, architecture, and dress. In short, we live in a vast human dimension of which the lower animals have no inkling, and we have to have a capacity for differentiation adequate to the complexity of our extra environment.

[23]   The next question, then, is why human beings do not always have an adequate capacity for differentiation. Why are we not constantly on the lookout for differences as well as similarities instead of feeling, as so many do, that the Chinese (or Mexicans, or ballplayers, or women drivers) are "all alike"? Why do some people react to words as if they were the things they stand for? Why do certain patterns of reaction, both in individuals and in larger groups such as nations, persist long after the usefulness has expired?

[24]   Part of our identification reactions are simply protective mechanisms inherited from the necessities of survival under earlier and more primitive conditions of life. I was once beaten up and robbed by two men on a dark street. Months later, I was again on a dark street with two men, good friends of mine, but involuntarily I found myself in a panic and insisted on our hurrying to a well-lighted drugstore to have a soda so that I would stop being jittery. In other words, my whole body responded with an identification reaction of fear of these two men, in spite of the fact that I "knew" that I was in no danger. Fortunately, with the passage of time, this reaction has died away. But the hurtful experiences of early childhood do not fade so readily. There is no doubt that many identification reactions are traceable to childhood traumas, as psychiatrists have shown.

[25]   Further identification reactions are caused by communal patterns of behavior which were necessary or thought necessary at one stage or another in the development of a tribe or nation. General directives such as "Kill all snakes," "Never kill cows, which are sacred animals," "Shoot all strangers on sight," "Fall down flat on your face before all members of the aristocracy," or, to come to more modern instances, "Never vote

for a Republican," "Oppose all government regulation of business," "Never associate with Negroes on terms of equality," are an enormous factor in the creation of identification reactions.

[26] Some human beings—possibly in their private feelings a majority—can accept these directives in a *human* way: that is, it will not be impossible for them under a sufficiently changed set of circumstances to kill a cow, or not to bow down before an aristocrat, to vote for a Republican, or to accept a Negro as a classmate. Others, however, get these directives so deeply ground into their nervous systems that they become incapable of changing their responses no matter how greatly the circumstances may have changed. Still others, although capable of changing their responses, dare not do so for fear of public opinion. Social progress usually requires the breaking up of these absolute identifications, which often make necessary changes impossible. Society must obviously have patterns of behavior; human beings must obviously have habits. But when those patterns become inflexible, so that a tribe has only one way to meet a famine, namely, to throw more infants as sacrifices to the crocodiles, or a nation has only one way to meet a threat to its security, namely, to increase its armaments, then such a tribe or such a nation is headed for trouble. There is insufficient capacity for differentiated behavior.

[27] Furthermore—and here one must touch upon the role of newspapers, radio, and television—if agencies of mass communication hammer away incessantly at the production of, let us say, a hostile set of reactions at such words as "Communists," "bureaucrats," "Wall Street," "international bankers," "labor leaders," and so on, no matter how useful an immediate job they may perform in correcting a given abuse at a given time and place, they can in the long run produce in thousands of readers and listeners identification reactions to the words—reactions that will make intelligent public discussion impossible. Modern means of mass communication and propaganda certainly have an important part to play in the creation of identification reactions.

[28] In addition to the foregoing, there is still another source of identification reactions; namely, the language we use in our daily thought and speech. Unlike the languages of the sciences, which are carefully constructed, tailor-made, special-purpose languages, the language of everyday life is one directly inherited and haphazardly developed from those of our prescientific ancestors: primitive Indo-Europeans, primitive Germanic tribes, Anglo-Saxons. With their scant knowledge of the world, they formulated descriptions of the world before them in statements such as "The sun rises." We do not today believe that the sun "rises." Nevertheless, we still continue to use the expression, without believing what we say.

[29] But there are other expressions, quite as primitive as the idea of "sunrise," which we use uncritically, fully believing in the implications of our terms. Having observed (or heard) that *some* Negroes are lazy, an individual may say, making a huge jump beyond the known facts, "Negroes are lazy." Without arguing for the moment the truth or falsity of this statement, let us examine the implications of the statement as it is

ordinarily constructed: "Negroes are lazy." The statement implies, as common sense or any textbook on traditional logic will tell us, that "laziness" is a "quality" that is "inherent" in Negroes.

[30] What are the facts? Under conditions of slavery, under which Negroes were not paid for working, there wasn't any point in being an industrious and responsible worker. The distinguished French abstract artist Jean Hélion once told the story of his life as a prisoner of war in a German camp, where, during World War II, he was compelled to do forced labor. He told how he loafed on the job, how he thought of device after device for avoiding work and producing as little as possible—and, since his prison camp was a farm, how he stole chickens at every opportunity. He also described how he put on an expression of good-natured imbecility whenever approached by his Nazi overseers. Without intending to do so, in describing his actions, he gave an almost perfect picture of the literary type of the Southern Negro of slavery days. Jean Hélion, confronted with the fact of forced labor, reacted as intelligently as Southern Negro slaves, and the slaves reacted as intelligently as Jean Hélion. "Laziness," then, is not an "inherent quality" of Negroes or of any other group of people. It is a *response* to a work situation in which there are no rewards for working, and in which one hates his taskmasters.

[31] Statements implying inherent qualities, such as "Negroes are lazy" or "There's something terribly wrong with young people today," are therefore the crudest kind of unscientific observation, based on an out-of-date way of saying things, like "The sun rises." The tragedy is not simply the fact that people make such statements; the graver fact is that they believe themselves.

[32] Some individuals are admired for their "realism" because, as the saying goes, they "call a spade a spade." Suppose we were to raise the question "Why should anyone call it a spade?" The reply would obviously be, "Because that's what it is!" This reply appeals so strongly to the common sense of most people that they feel that at this point discussion can be closed. I should like to ask the reader, however, to consider a point which may appear at first to him a mere quibble.

[33] Here, let us say, is an implement for digging made of steel, with a wooden handle. Here, on the other hand, is a succession of sounds made with the tongue, lips, and vocal cords: "spade." If you want a digging implement of the kind we are talking about, you would ask for it by making the succession of sounds "spade" if you are addressing an English-speaking person. But suppose you were addressing a speaker of Dutch, French, Hungarian, Chinese, Tagolog? Would you not have to make completely different sounds? It is apparent, then, that the common-sense opinion of most people, "We call a spade a spade because that's what it is," is completely and utterly wrong. We call it a "spade" because we are English-speaking people conforming, in this instance, to majority usage in naming this particular object. The steel-and-iron digging implement is simply an object standing there against the garage door; "spade" is what we *call* it—"spade" is a *name*.

[34] And here we come to another source of identification reactions—

an unconscious assumption about language epitomized in the expression "a spade is a spade," or even more elegantly in the famous remark "Pigs are called pigs because they are such dirty animals." The assumption is that everything has a "right name" and that the "right name" names the "essence" of that which is named.

[35]   If this assumption is at work in our reaction patterns, we are likely to be given to premature and often extremely inappropriate responses. We are likely to react to names as if they gave complete insight into the persons, things, or situations named. In spite of the fact that my entire education has been in Canada and the United States and I am unable to read and write Japanese, I am sometimes credited with, or accused of, having an "Oriental mind." Now, since Buddha, Confucius, General Tojo, Mao Tse-tung, Syngman Rhee, Pandit Nehru, and the proprietor of the Golden Pheasant Chop Suey House all have "Oriental minds," it is hard to imagine what is meant. The "Oriental mind," like the attribute of "Jewishness," is purely and simply a fiction. Nevertheless, I used to note with alarm that newspaper columnists got paid for articles that purported to account for Stalin's behavior by pointing out that since he came from Georgia, which is next to Turkey and Azerbaijan and therefore "more a part of Asia than of Europe," he too had an "Oriental mind."

[36]   To realize fully the difference between words and what they stand for is to be ready for differences as well as similarities in the world. This readiness is mandatory to scientific thinking, as well as to sane thinking. Korzybski's simple but powerful suggestion is to add "index numbers" to all terms according to the formula: A_1 is not A_2; it can be translated as follows: Cow_1 is not cow_2; cow_2 is not cow_3; $politician_1$ is not $politician_2$; ham and eggs (Plaza Hotel) are not ham and eggs (Smitty's Café); socialism (Russia) is not socialism (England); private enterprise (Joe's Shoe Repair Shop) is not private enterprise (A.T.&T.).

[37]   This device of "indexing" will not automatically make us wiser and better, but it's a start. When we talk or write, the habit of indexing our general terms will reduce our tendency to wild and woolly generalization. It will compel us to think before we speak—think in terms of concrete objects and events and situations, rather than in terms of verbal associations. When we read or listen, the habit of indexing will help us visualize more concretely, and therefore understand better, what is being said. And if nothing is being said except deceptive windbaggery, the habit of indexing may—at least part of the time—save us from snapping, like the pickerel, at phony minnows. Another way of summing up is to remember, as Wendell Johnson said, that "To a mouse, cheese is cheese—that's why mousetraps work."

words and sentences

1. Vocabulary: *martial* (¶ 1); *residue* (2); *regress, impertinence, impudence, intuitive* (4); *hypocrisy* (10); *codified, ethics* (22); *persist* (23); *traumas* (24); *haphazardly, scant* (28); *epitomized* (34).

2. How and why does Hayakawa define the following: *patterns of reaction* (1); *operationalism* (7); *identification reactions* (17); *index numbers* (36)?
3. How does Hayakawa define *prejudice?* Compare his definition with a dictionary definition. Which definition is clearer?
4. What pattern does Hayakawa use to insure clarity in the first sentence of ¶ 2?
5. How many times does Hayakawa define *semantics?* Why?
6. Check a dictionary for the following: *loose sentence* and *periodic sentence.* Is the last sentence in ¶ 20 a loose or a periodic sentence? What emotional impact does a writer gain with the periodic sentence?
7. Describe the pattern of the first sentence in ¶ 36, and write a sentence imitating that pattern.

ideas and implications

1. What is Hayakawa's attitude towards dictionaries? Why?
2. Why does Hayakawa call the study of semantics "a certain way of looking at human behavior" (¶ 8)?
3. How does Hayakawa see the relationship between words and the things they stand for? Does he regard language as fixed or fluid?
4. According to Hayakawa, how does our association of meaning with words affect our conduct? How are beliefs and language related? Does he believe that by changing language habits we can change our attitudes? How interested is he in changing his readers' attitudes towards language?
5. What is Hayakawa's attitude towards generalization? Why does he stress the necessity for concreteness in thinking, speaking, and writing?

strategies

1. How does Hayakawa's use of the first person pronoun ("I") affect the tone of his essay?
2. What methods of development does Hayakawa use in ¶s 2, 4, and 5? Is his strategy in ¶5 different from that of ¶s 2 and 4? Why? How does a writer's purpose affect his choices of methods of development?
3. What idea is Hayakawa developing in ¶s 21 and 22? How does dramatizing the idea affect the choice of method of development of these paragraphs?
4. ¶s 29-31 comprise a unit within the larger plan of Hayakawa's essay. Do these paragraphs have topic sentences? And do these sentences determine the way Hayakawa talks about the main idea of each paragraph?

suggestions for writing

1. Select a person you know fairly well and write a paper showing how that person's use of language affects his way of looking at the world.
2. Select a public figure whom you know only through his public utterances. Write a paper examining his attitudes by examining his use of language.

3. From your experience, try to recall and recount a situation in which your attitude was changed by a new understanding of words and a new association with those words.
4. Make a list of slogans you have heard. Then write a paper examining the meaning and implications of those slogans.

Sydney J. Harris

We Cover up Our Faults with Words

[1]   A workman in Finland recently won a competition, based on knowledge of the Finnish vocabulary, when he sent in 747 synonyms for "drunkenness."

The competition, reported by the London *Times,* was sponsored by the Finnish Broadcasting Company, in co-operation with the Foundation for Research into the Finnish Language.

Other winning categories included 203 synonyms for "lying," and 170 words that mean "stealing."

I am sure that a contest would disclose the same volume and variety in English. A man rarely speaks of being "drunk"—he is plastered, boiled, stewed, crocked, loaded, tipsy, and scores of other kind euphemisms.

[5]   Likewise, we never "lie." We prevaricate, fib, stretch, exaggerate, color, and so forth. Children don't "steal"—they filch, snitch, borrow, find, and walk off with.

Yet, for the antonyms of these words, we have few or no substitutes. For "sober," or "truth," or "honest," we use the same word. Now, the student of languages may find this interesting in a verbal way; but I think that the psychologist and the moralist can make more significance out of it.

One of the most ingrained and dangerous of human habits is the refusal to face our badness. The alcoholic calls himself a "social drinker" —and, indeed, not until he is ready to change his verbal habit and admit he is an alcoholic can he be helped to change his drinking habit.

Criminals rarely think of themselves as "thieves." A man who makes a living illegally will tell you he is "in the rackets"—which puts a kind of tough-guy glamour into his occupation. And a liar, of course, lies to himself more than to anyone else.

We think of language as a means of communication; but just as

From Sydney J. Harris, *Majority of One.* © 1957 by Sydney J. Harris. Reprinted by permission of the publisher, Houghton Mifflin Company.

often it is a means of barricading ourselves against the impact of reality. For every person who uses words to express what he really thinks and feels, a hundred persons use words to escape from the necessity of confronting their true selves.

[10] Everyone will admit, in the abstract, that he has faults. Asked to enumerate them, however, most people pick their slightest and most harmless flaws, while placidly ignoring their deeper defects. A friend of mine once asked his mother, "What do you think is your biggest fault?"

She thought for a moment, and then replied, with complete sincerity, "I think that my biggest fault is being too good to people!"

words and sentences

1. Vocabulary: *euphemisms* (¶ 1); *prevaricate* (5); *antonyms* (6); *enumerate, placidly* (10).
2. In ¶ 9, Harris chooses the word *barricading* to describe the way we cover our faults with words. Does this choice seem appropriate?
3. Is the first sentence in ¶ 7 a loose or a periodic sentence? Does the sound and form of the last word in the sentence seem appropriate for the idea that Harris is trying to emphasize?
4. Find examples of transitional words or phrases. Comment on the function of the transitional words and phrases Harris uses.

ideas and implications

1. In eleven short paragraphs, Harris makes a rather telling observation about language and one of its functions. Why does he say that "the psychologist and the moralist can make more significance" of his observation than the student of language?
2. Check a dictionary of slang and a desk dictionary for synonyms of one of the following: *lie, drunk, thief,* or *steal.* How many synonyms did you find? Do the same for *sober, honesty,* and *truth.* Does Harris appear correct in his observation that we use language frequently to escape from the truth?

strategies

1. Does Harris put his thesis into a single sentence? If so, what is that sentence and where does it appear in his essay?
2. Harris develops his thesis largely through examples and incidents. Could he have made his lists of examples longer? Why doesn't he?
3. Harris devotes his last two paragraphs to a single example. Comment on the appropriateness of his choice of example for the conclusion.

suggestions for writing

1. Write a paper showing or explaining how you or one of your friends used language to hide or to escape from the truth.
2. In a newspaper, magazine, or television program, find an example of what you believe to be the use of language to escape the truth. Write

a paper describing the occasion and pointing out how you think words were used to avoid what Harris calls "the impact of reality."

3. A public service announcement on radio and television suggests that "If you need a drink to be social, you are not a social drinker." Examine in detail the implications of this statement.

Marsteller, Inc.

The Wonderful World of Words

[1]   *Human beings come in all sizes, a variety of colors, in different ages, and with unique, complex and changing personalities. So do words.*

There are tall, skinny words and short, fat ones, and strong ones and weak ones, and boy words and girl words.

For instance, title, lattice, latitude, lily, tattle, Illinois and intellect are all lean and lanky. While these words get their height partly out of "t's" and "l's" and "i's," other words are tall and skinny without a lot of ascenders and descenders. Take, for example, Abraham, peninsula and ellipsis, all tall.

Here are some nice short-fat words: hog, yogurt, bomb, pot, bon-bon, acne, plump, sop and slobber.

[5]   Sometimes a word gets its size from what it means but sometimes it's just how the word sounds. Acne is a short-fat word even though pimple, with which it is associated, is a puny word.

Puny words are not the same as feminine words. Feminine words are such as tissue, slipper, cute, squeamish, peek, flutter, gauze and cumulus. Masculine words are like bourbon, rupture, oak, cartel, steak and socks. Words can mean the same thing and be of the opposite sex. Naked is masculine, but nude is feminine.

Sex isn't always a clear-cut, yes-or-no thing and there are words like that, too. On a fencing team, for instance, a man may compete with a sabre and that is definitely a masculine word. Because it is a sword of sorts, an épée is also a boy word, but you know how it is with épées.

Just as feminine words are not necessarily puny words, masculine words are not necessarily muscular. Muscular words are thrust, earth, girder, ingot, cask, Leo, ale, bulldozer, sledge and thug. Fullback is very muscular; quarterback is masculine but not especially muscular.

Words have colors, too.

[10]   Red: fire, passion, rape, explode, smash, murder, lightning, attack.

From *Time* (July 18, 1969). Reprinted by permission of Marsteller Inc., Advertising Agency.

Green: moss, brook, cool, comfort, meander, solitude, hammock.

Black: glower, agitate, funeral, dictator, anarchy, thunder, tomb, somber, cloak.

Beige: unctuous, abstruse, surrender, clerk, conform, observe, float.

San Francisco is a red city, Cleveland is beige, Asheville is green and Buffalo is black.

[15] Shout is red, persuade is green, rave is black and listen is beige.

One of the more useful characteristics of words is their age.

There's youth in go, pancake, hamburger, bat, ball, frog, air, surprise, morning and tickle. Middle age brings moderate, agree, shade, stroll and uncertain. Fragile, lavender, astringent, fern, velvet, lace, worn and Packard are old. There never was a young Packard, not even the touring car.

Mostly, religion is old. Prayer, vespers, choir, Joshua, Judges, Ruth and cathedral are all old. Once, temple was older than cathedral and still is in some parts of the world, but in the United States temple is now fairly young.

Saturday, the seventh day of the week, is young, while Sunday, the first day of the week, is old. Night is old, and so, although more old people die in the hours of the morning just before dawn, we call that part of the morning, incorrectly, night.

[20] Some words are worried and some radiate disgusting self-confidence. Pill, ulcer, twitch, itch, stomach and peek are all worried words. Confident, smug words are like proud, major, divine, stare, dare, ignore, demand. Joe is confident; Horace is worried.

Now about shapes.

For round products, round companies or round ideas use dot, bob, melon, loquacious, hock, bubble and bald. Square words are, for instance, box, cramp, sunk, block and even ankle. Ohio is round but Iowa, a similar word, is square but not as square as Nebraska. The roundest city is, of course, Oslo.

Some words are clearly oblong. Obscure is oblong (it is also beige) and so are platter and meditation (which is also middle-aged). The most oblong lake is Ontario, even more than Michigan, which is also surprisingly muscular for an oblong, though not nearly as strong as Huron, which is more stocky. Lake Pontchartrain is almost a straight line. Lake Como is round and very short and fat. Lake Erie is worried.

Some words are shaped like Rorschach ink blots. Like drool, plot, mediocre, involvement, liquid, amoeba and phlegm.

[25] At first blush (which is young), fast words seem to come from a common stem (which is puny). For example, dash, flash, bash and brash are all fast words. However, ash, hash and gash are all slow. Flush is changing. It used to be slow, somewhat like sluice, but it is getting faster. Both are wet words, as is Flushing, which is really quite dry compared to New Canaan, which sounds drier but is much wetter. Wilkinsburg, as you would expect, is dry, square, old and light gray. But back to motion.

Raid, rocket, piccolo, hound, bee and rob are fast words. Guard, drizzle, lard, cow, sloth, muck and damp are slow words. Fast words are often young and slow words old, but not always. Hamburger is young and slow, especially when uncooked. Astringent is old but fast. Black is old, and yellow—almost opposite on the spectrum—is young, but orange and brown are nearly next to each other and orange is just as young as yellow while brown is only middle-aged. Further, purple, though darker than lavender, is not as old; however, it is much slower than violet, which is extremely fast.

Lavender is actually a rather hard word. Not as hard as rock, edge, point, corner, jaw, trooper, frigid or trumpet, but hard nevertheless. Lamb, lip, thud, sofa, fuzz, stuff, froth and madam are soft. Although they are the same thing, timpani are harder than kettle drums, partly because drum is a soft word (it is also fat and slow), and as pots and pans go, kettle is one of the softer.

There is a point to all this.

Ours is a business of imagination. We are employed to make corporations personable, to make useful products desirable, to clarify ideas, to create friendships in the mass for our employers.

[30] We have great power to do these things. We have power through art and photography and graphics and typography and all the visual elements that are part of the finished advertisement.

And these are great powers. Often it is true that one picture is worth ten thousand words.

But not necessarily worth one word.

If it's the *right* word.

words and sentences

1. Vocabulary: *épée* (¶ 7), *unctuous* (13); *loquacious* (22); *Rorschach* (24); *astringent* (26).
2. According to the author, what is "wonderful" about the world of words?
3. In its context, the word *right* has a specific meaning. What is that meaning and what are the implications of that meaning?
4. The advertisement includes verbal play. In ¶ 19, how is the word *morning* treated?
5. Does the writer of the advertisement use many sentence fragments? What is the purpose of these fragments?

ideas and implications

1. What is the purpose of the Marsteller essay? Point to specific sentences which define that purpose explicitly. Are there also implicit statements of this purpose?
2. In what way is Marsteller's business one "of imagination" (¶ 29)?
3. How might Marsteller's attitude towards language be described? Does this attitude allow for much flexibility of meaning? How does Marsteller's attitude towards language compare with Falstaff's? What are

the implications of this statement, "We are employed . . . to create friendships in the mass for our employers"?

strategies

1. Classification is the principal strategy used in presenting Marsteller's view of language. How many classes of words does the advertisement describe? List them. Do some words belong to more than one class? Cite examples. Might another strategy of organization have been chosen?
2. The advertisement begins with an analogy. State that analogy in a single sentence. Does the analogy seem appropriate to the message Marsteller addresses to its readers?
3. Describe the character or personality of the voice projected in the advertisement. That voice is important for a number of reasons. Why? Is that voice arguing a specific point?

suggestions for writing

1. Write an original advertisement for a product you admire. Use pictures as well as words if you wish. Pay attention to the voice you project to your reader.
2. Examine an advertisement or television commercial that has appealed to you. Write a paper in which you discuss the reasons for this appeal.
3. Choose a group of words (perhaps color words) and classify them according to Marsteller's system. Does such a classification reveal anything to you about colors, about Marsteller's purpose, about yourself, about an acquaintance to whom you show your list?
4. Take the words from your list or classification and organize them in an essay to make three or four points about their qualities.

Irving J. Lee

The Useful Use of Words

The Work of Words

[1] Though widely differing in statement, much agreement may be found about what it is that words are supposed to do for us. Some typical definitions:

From Irving J. Lee, *Language Habits in Human Affairs.* Copyright 1941 by Harper & Row, Publishers, Inc.; renewed 1959 by Laura Louise Lee. Reprinted by permission of the publisher.

A sign or expression may concern or designate or describe something, or, rather, he who uses the expression may intend to refer to something by it, e.g., to an object, or a property, or a state of affairs.

Words are vocal sounds or letter combinations which symbolize or signify something. They . . . have no other function except to direct attention. The words now being read by the reader for instance are directing his attention to something; to the fact that words are attention directors. . . . Thus the word gold directs attention to a yellow, incorrodible, dense metal of atomic weight 197, and the word vertebrate to a class of animals having a spinal column.

Words may be thought of as signs which *name* that for which they are signs: "*table* is the name of an object, *red* of a quality, *run* of an activity, *over* of a relation."

[2]   Thus, words may be considered as *pointers, indicators, forms of representation,* which are intended to correspond to anything whatsoever that may exist, that may be experienced, or that anyone might want to talk about. Or put another way, words may be used for the almost *endless naming* of the inexhaustible electronic events, objects, persons, situations, relations, etc., observed in the world outside-our-skins, along with the sensations, feelings, beliefs, opinions, values, tensions, affective states, etc., experienced inside-our-skins.

Note the Two Media

[3]   Such an analysis of the work of words makes one point inevitable: the phenomenon of language is different from the non-verbal phenomena which we represent by it. We live in two worlds which must not be confused, a world of words, and a world of not-words. If a word is not what it represents, then whatever you might say about anything will not be *it*. If in doubt, you might try eating the word *steak* when hungry, or wearing the word *coat* when cold. In short, the universe of discourse *is not* the universe of our direct experience.

[4]   If a word *were* what it used to stand for, that is, a "complete reproduction," it would then be no word, but one more non-verbal fact. For words have aspects and functions quite different from the non-verbal

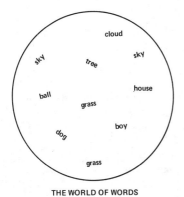

THE WORLD OF WORDS

THE WORLD OF NOT-WORDS

facts which they may represent. William James once remarked that words should be taken as "summaries of things to look for," and not, it should be added, as the actual existent "things." A book on astronomy is not the heavenly bodies, distances, and movements which make up the stellar universe, and the calculations and hypotheses which result from studying the stars clearly are not the phenomena in space. And the names and addresses on envelopes are not the human beings who receive them.

[5] There exists, then, a world of words which must be sharply distinguished from a world of not-words about which talk occurs, even though frequently we tend to identify them.

Fitting the Two

[6] Language will have maximum usefulness when it properly corresponds to what it is supposed to represent. We need to know what constitutes adequate representation. This may be illustrated in reverse. Suppose that a thermomenter registered at freezing point when the liquid in which it was placed boiled furiously; a speedometer recorded only a thousand miles when the auto had been driven from New York to Denver; a road-marker showed the arrow pointing to the left, while the actual road turned to the right. One can say that each of these symbolic recording devices was "wrong," "inaccurate," "erroneous," "misleading," etc. Such evaluations, however, though understandable, do not in themselves account for the wrongness. We get that in the suggestion that the recording did not *fit* the facts.

[7] But what of words? When are they "adequate" and "useful"? Korzybski has said, "If we reflect upon our languages, we find that at best they must be considered *only as maps.*" And further, "A language, to be useful, should be similar in its structure to the structure of the events which it is supposed to represent."

[8] An example may help. Suppose you receive a book entitled *Guide to Beautiful Bali,* which you read carefully. Never having been there, how can you know that such a place exists, and that what is said is correct to fact? A friend who has been there asserts that the book can be read with confidence. He argues further that if passage be taken to Bali, the directions followed, and the places visited, the book will be found to correspond to what is seen. If the trip is taken, and if the book is verified —that is, if the descriptions of Bali parallel the experienced Bali—then we can say that the language of the book was an accurate representation of the non-verbal facts. In the normal run of affairs we cannot personally corroborate what we read. But whenever we do, this notion of correspondence of words with facts will become clear.

[9] Korzybski's famous analogy makes the point even more graphically, so that the notion of "usefulness" becomes readily apparent.

> Let us take some actual territory in which cities appear in the following order: San Francisco, Chicago, New York, when taken from the West to the East. If we were to build a *map* of this territory and place San Francisco *between* Chicago and New York thus:

Actual territory

	*		*		*
	San Francisco	Chicago		New York

Map

	*		*		*
	Chicago	San Francisco		New York

we should say that the map was wrong, or that it was an incorrect map, or that the map has a *different structure* from the territory. If, speaking roughly, we should try, in our travels, to orient ourselves by such a map, we should find it misleading. It would lead us astray, and we might waste a great deal of unnecessary effort. In some cases, even, a map of wrong structure would bring actual suffering and disaster, as, for instance, in a war, or in the case of an urgent call for a physician.

With Words Alone

[10]   Even though language can be made to fit life facts, it is essential that another point be clearly understood, that words can be manipulated independently without corresponding to any non-verbal facts.

[11]   Just as it is easy to make a map without bothering to survey the terrain, or address letters to imaginary people, so one can indulge in verbalism, using words at random. No inner necessity governs the use of words in their relationship to things, feelings, and circumstances. Stories of people may be manufactured, nonexistent places may be talked about, situations may be verbally distorted beyond recognition, and denials and affirmations may be made regardless of what happens. Nothing *in the nature of language* could have prevented Bismarck from altering the Ems telegram, could have stopped the writing of the letter which helped convict Alfred Dreyfus, or hindered Mencken's hoax about the first American bathtub.

[12]   If in 1938 Adolf Hitler could say that he "wants no more land in Europe," even as his armies mobilized for invasion; and if astrologers can assert that those born under Libra should have musical talent, while a researcher finds that the birth dates of 1498 musicians show that almost "fewer are born under Libra than under any sign except Scorpio"—if these things can be said, it should begin to be clear that words *may be used according to the whim of the user*. Without checking and testing with life it is impossible by merely looking at statements to know whether or not they represent some existing territory in the world of happenings. Without an "inner check" one may turn out a false war communiqué, forge the "Protocols of the Elders of Zion," concoct nonverifiable racist dogmas, maintain the prophetic virtues of crystal-gazing, tell a yarn in contest for the "Liar's Championship," and on occasion provide pleasant diversion:

> Two of Joe Cook's favorite "gags" in *Why I Will Not Imitate Four Hawaiians* are a note reading "See frontispiece" and another "See page 226," the frontispiece being totally irrelevant to the matter in question, and the book having only 64 pages. Josh Billings had a similar gag. At the bottom of the card advertising his lecture on milk—in which, moreover, the subject of milk was never mentioned—he printed the word *over* in large type, and the other side was blank.

[13] John Locke argued that "in inquiries after philosophical knowledge . . . names must be conformable to things." More recently Bridgman agreed that language "owes whatever success it attains to its ability to set up and maintain certain correspondences with experience." However, one who uses words does not have to be governed by such demands. By itself language cannot force a user to seek that correspondence with actual facts. Indeed, there is a certain convenience in avoiding it. As Vilfredo Pareto says,

> It is much easier to talk about antipodes than to go out and see if they are really there. To discuss the implication of a "principle of fire" or "damp" is much more expeditious than to prosecute all the field studies that have made up the science of geology. To ruminate on "natural law" is a much more comfortable profession than to dig out the legal codes of the various countries in various periods of history. To prattle about "value" and ask when and under what circumstances it is said that "a thing has value" is much less difficult than to discover and comprehend the laws of economic equilibrium.

[14] Relevant here is a story of the small Austrian village under attack from hostile forces. To preserve the priceless possession of the community, a bell in the tower of the *Rathaus,* three of the elders rowed with it to the center of a nearby lake. To remember the place where it was dropped overboard, a deep mark was cut on the side of the boat.
[15] Just as that boat mark can be moved, unrelated to its object, so, too, can words be handled and bandied about without regard to what they are supposed to represent.

On Adjustment

[16] Mr. George had never given a speech to youngsters. But the Principal assured him that they would listen quietly and eagerly and that it was as easy to talk to them as to adults. Mr. George was satisfied and looked forward to the occasion. For the first three minutes the children paid careful attention. Then a few up in front began to wiggle. Then the group burst into laughter at something he thought not at all funny. When a door at the other end of the corridor slammed, they all turned in that direction. And after that they began to whisper. . . . In the next five minutes the confusion increased, and Mr. George, much distraught, mumbled a "Thank you" and sat down.
[17] That the speaker lost control is not too surprising. He was led to expect simplicity and found complexity. His adjustment was affected when the circumstances ran counter to what he expected. The verbal assurances given him had low predictability value.
[18] This suggests a general principle: Our adjustment (and ultimately, survival) is correlated with our expectations, that is, our ability to predict happenings accurately. This is a way of saying that the correctness of our expectations depends upon the similarity of structure of the language used and the happenings represented. If the statements by means of which

we are oriented are not adequate representations, it will be difficult to prepare for what is to be met in the world of direct experience.

[19]   But a nice problem thus emerges. If it becomes necessary to check everything anyone says with our own personal experience of the life facts, we should have time for little else. In this highly technical and minutely specialized civilization much must be taken on "faith," on the say-so of those who are supposed to know and expected to be responsible. One of the great sources of confusion in our time, however, lies in the fact that many find it profitable and expedient to betray this faith by making "maps" which do not fit the facts. This may be readily documented by reference to the findings of the Better Business Bureaus, the Food and Drug Administration, the Department of Weights and Measures, the Underwriters' Laboratory, the Bureau of Investigation of the American Medical Association, the Federal Trade Commission, Consumers Union, Federal Bureau of Investigation, Senate Investigating Committees, etc. In one form or another these organizations serve as reminders that *complete* faith in what is said, and expectations based on that faith, too often end in disappointment and disaster.

[20]   Awareness, then, of the different characteristics of words (map) and what they stand for (territory) should lead to the understanding that all utterance is to be neither blindly rejected nor blindly accepted. To know that language can be false to fact should make for more searching consideration of the nature of language. Those who argue that *all* public statements must be discounted suffer in their cynicism from delusions no less harmful than those who insist that if important men and official statements say so, then it must be so. What is urged here is something quite different: that men and women should be conscious of the *possibility* of structural dissimilarity between words and "things," and further, that a large step is taken toward proper evaluation, predictability, and adjustment, when they begin to ask whether or not the map fits the territory.

In Short

[21]   A map is not the territory. To be most useful, statements must fit, must be similar in structure to the life facts being represented. Words can

be manipulated independently of what they represent, and so made false to fact both consciously and unconsciously. In either case their reliability and our predictability are impaired.

[22]   The basic question: not, What did he say? but, Did what he said fit the life facts?

words and sentences

1. Vocabulary: *phenomena, discourse* (¶ 3); *corroborate* (8); *concoct* (12); *antipodes, expeditious, ruminate* (13); *correlated* (18); *cynicism* (20).
2. Does Lee's definition of *useful* add anything to your understanding of this word? If so, how?
3. Explain *symbolic recording devices* (6). List some devices not mentioned by Lee.
4. Describe the pattern of the first sentence in ¶ 12, and write a sentence imitating this pattern.
5. Find a topic sentence in the essay. If a topic sentence does its job, it promises the reader something. What promise does Lee make in the topic sentence you have chosen? Does Lee keep his promise?

ideas and implications

1. What distinction does Lee make between the world of words and the world of not-words? How important is this distinction to seeing experience and the world?
2. What confusion can arise when the relationship between words and experience does not fit? You might look back at Humpty Dumpty's remarks on words at the beginning of this section.
3. Lee uses a metaphor—"A map is not the territory"—to describe the relationship between words and the things they stand for. Why do people use maps? Can maps sometimes "lie" or be out of date? What happens to a traveller when a map is faulty? Or what happens when a prankster turns a roadsign the wrong way? Can you think of occasions when a traveller might prefer not to have a map? Does Lee's metaphor open more possibilities than he explores?
4. In ¶ 18, Lee says that our survival depends upon our ability to adjust expectations and happenings. How does he see the role of language in making such adjustments?
5. Can the language of poetry and prose fiction be "useful"? How? Would Lee exclude such language as being useful? Why or why not?

strategies

1. Compare and contrast Lee's opening and closing strategies. Why does he turn to authorities for his opening strategy? Why doesn't he return to those authorities for his closing?
2. How important are the illustrations (¶ 4) to clarifying Lee's distinction between the world of words and the world of not-words? Does the right-hand picture tell a story? What is missing from the left-hand picture that keeps it from telling a story?
3. How much does Lee rely on example, anecdote, and metaphor to develop his ideas? Point to specific examples, anecdotes, or metaphors and comment on their function in the development of his ideas.
4. How does Lee develop his idea in ¶ 8? Can you suggest another strategy for clarifying the idea presented in ¶ 7?

suggestions for writing

1. Write a paper about a personal experience in which the map and the territory did not resemble each other.
2. Write a paper describing a situation in which your survival depended upon adjusting your expectations. What part did words play in this adjustment?
3. Write a paper giving a classmate directions to your house in your hometown. Or to your college residence. Your classmate might want to test your language map to see if it fits experience by trying to look you up. Where would you have to begin your language map if you wished the classmate to find you?
4. Television dramas draw maps for viewers. Write a paper about a television drama which provides you with (a) an accurate map of experience, or (b) a faulty map of experience.

Sydney J. Harris

Antics with Semantics

Antics with Semantics: 4

[1]   A politician I approve of has "friends"; a politician I am doubtful of has "cronies"; a politician I dislike has "confederates" or "camp followers."

Likewise, my political party needs a stronger "organization," but your political party has too strong a "machine."

My candidate is "silver-tongued"; yours is "leather-lunged"; his is "a windbag."

My statesman is "firm"; yours is "authoritarian"; his "runs roughshod over all opposition."

[5]   What the government gives me is a "subsidy"; what it gives you is a "handout."

Our participation in Vietnam is "advisory intervention"; but the other side's participation in Vietnam is "Red domination."

I am for "individualism" in the market place, but when I run across someone who wants to express his individualism by wearing a beard, I suspect him of being "un-American."

In the political sphere, I have "principles"; you have "ideology"; he has "dogmas."

Our military makes "surprise sorties"; their military makes "terrorist raids."

[10] We "indoctrinate" with "information"; they "brainwash" with "propaganda."

The candidate I voted for won "because of the good common sense of the people"; the candidate I voted for lost "because not enough people have good common sense."

I am for "leadership" when the mayor I supported is in office, but I am against "bossism" when the mayor I opposed is in office.

My relative is in "public service"; yours is in "politics"; his is "a payroller."

As an officeholder, I accepted a "gift"; you took a "rake-off"; he was guilty of soliciting a "kickback."

[15] My alderman did me a "favor," but your alderman "put in the fix."

When I run for office, it is because I am "civic-minded"; when you run, it is because you "have a taste for power"; when he runs, it is because he "is out to get everything he can."

A "sincere" politician is one who sincerely wants you to believe what he says; a "hypocritical" politician is the same.

Antics with Semantics: 5

My senator is making a "probe"; your senator is on a "fishing expedition"; his senator is starting a "witch-hunt."

I am "cautious"; you are "timid"; he is "cowardly."

[20] I believe something to be a fact because "I saw it in black and white"; but you mustn't believe something to be a fact "just because you happened to see it in print somewhere."

Our country is engaged in "security measures"; your country is engaged in an "arms race"; his country is engaged in "stockpiling weapons."

My church denomination lives by a "creed," but yours subscribes to a "dogma."

The ceremony I approve of had "dignity and grandeur"; the ceremony I disapprove of had "pomp and ostentation."

I believe in "authority"; you believe in "force"; he believes in "violence."

[25] I am a "man of few words"; you are "taciturn"; he is "unresponsive."

My outburst was "indignation"; yours was "anger"; his was "petulance."

My crude friend is "a diamond in the rough"; yours is "a touch on the common side"; his is "a loudmouthed boor."

If she picks up men in bars, she is a "floozie"; if she picks up men at a Hollywood shindig, she is a "swinger"; if she picks up men at a fashionable garden party, she is a "femme fatale."

I am a great champion of "tolerance"—as long as you let me define the precise point at which it becomes intolerable.

[30] My cutting remark is an "epigram"; yours is a "wisecrack"; his is
a "cheap jeer."

I am a "realist" when I am doing to you that which, if you were
doing it to me, I would call "ruthless."

If it was your fault, we had a "collision," but if it was my fault,
we just "banged the bumpers up a little."

There are really no "juvenile gang leaders" because, according to
the parents, each of the boys "just happened to get in with the wrong
crowd."

I am opposed to your newfangled ideas because I believe in "the
value of tradition," but you are opposed to my sensible reforms because
you are "blindly clinging to the past."

[35] Why is the female of the species called a "songstress," when the male
isn't called a "songster"?

words and sentences

1. Vocabulary: *ideology, dogmas* (¶ 8); *sorties* (9); *soliciting* (14); *witch-hunt*
   (18); *taciturn* (25); *petulance* (26); *epigram* (30).
2. Describe one of the sentence patterns that Harris repeats. Then write
   a sentence of your own using the same pattern.
3. What is the principal punctuation mark Harris uses? Why? Note where
   this mark goes when it appears with a quotation mark.
4. Describe the sentence pattern used in ¶ 28. Then write a sentence of
   your own using this pattern.

ideas and implications

1. The thesis of Harris's essays is implicit, not explicit. Write a sentence
   which states explicitly Harris's thesis, and then compare your sentence
   with those of your classmates.
2. What point does Harris demonstrate about maps and territories with
   his examples?
3. What profession provides Harris with his examples in "Antics with
   Semantics: 4"? Why is the language of this profession particularly rich
   in such examples? Are the examples in "Antics with Semantics: 5" from
   the same source?

strategies

1. Harris's principal strategy is listing examples. Does he vary the patterns
   for presenting items in his list? How? Would the same technique work
   effectively in the Marstellar advertisement?
2. One pattern Harris uses resembles the conjugation of verbs. How effective is this pattern for his purpose?
3. In listing his examples, does Harris call attention to the point of view
   of a speaker? How?

suggestions for writing

1. Write a paper examining a political or social issue that interests you. Pay attention to your own antics with semantics.
2. In a magazine or newspaper, find an editorial essay dealing with a controversial issue. Examine the language of the essay for any antics with semantics.

Imamu Amiri Baraka (LeRoi Jones)

Expressive Language

[1]   Speech is the effective form of a culture. Any shape or cluster of human history still apparent in the conscious and unconscious habit of groups of people is what I mean by culture. All culture is necessarily profound. The very fact of its longevity, of its being what it is, *culture,* the epic memory of practical tradition, means that it is profound. But the inherent profoundity of culture does not necessarily mean that its *uses* (and they are as various as the human condition) will be profound. German culture is profound. Generically. Its uses, however, are specific, as are all uses . . . of ideas, inventions, products of nature. And specificity, as a right and passion of human life, breeds what it breeds as a result of its context.

[2]   Context, in this instance, is most dramatically social. And the social, though it must be rooted, as are all evidences of existence, in culture, depends for its impetus for the most part on a multiplicity of influences. Other cultures, for instance. Perhaps, and this is a common occurrence, the reaction or interreaction of one culture on another can produce a social context that will extend or influence any culture in many strange directions.

[3]   *Social* also means *economic,* as any reader of nineteenth-century European philosophy will understand. The economic is part of the social—and in our time much more so than what we have known as the spiritual or metaphysical, because the most valuable canons of power have either been reduced or traduced into stricter economic terms. That is, there has been a shift in the actual meaning of the world since Dante lived. As if Brooks Adams were right. Money does not mean the same thing to me it must mean to a rich man. I cannot, right now, think of

From *Home: Social Essays* by LeRoi Jones. © 1963 by LeRoi Jones. Reprinted by permission of William Morrow and Company, Inc.

one meaning to name. This is not so simple to understand. Even as a simple term of the English language, *money* does not possess the same meanings for the rich man as it does for me, a lower-middle-class American, albeit of laughably "aristocratic" pretensions. What possibly can "money" mean to a poor man? And I am not talking now about those courageous products of our permissive society who walk knowledgeably into "poverty" as they would into a public toilet. I mean, The Poor.

[4]   I look in my pocket; I have seventy cents. Possibly I can buy a beer. A quart of ale, specifically. Then I will have twenty cents with which to annoy and seduce my fingers when they wearily search for gainful employment. I have no idea at this moment what that seventy cents will mean to my neighbor around the corner, a poor Puerto Rican man I have seen hopefully watching my plastic garbage can. But I am certain it cannot mean the same thing. Say to David Rockefeller, "I have money," and he will think you mean something entirely different. That is, if you also dress the part. He would not for a moment think, "Seventy cents." But then neither would many New York painters.

[5]   Speech, the way one describes the natural proposition of being alive, is much more crucial than even most artists realize. Semantic philosophers are certainly correct in their emphasis on the final dictation of words over their users. But they often neglect to point out that, after all, it is the actual importance, *power,* of the words that remains so finally crucial. Words have users, but as well, users have words. And it is the users that establish the world's realities. Realities being those fantasies that control your immediate span of life. Usually they are not your own fantasies, *i.e.,* they belong to governments, traditions, etc., which, it must be clear by now, can make for conflict with the singular human life all ways. The fantasy of America might hurt you, but it is what should be meant when one talks of "reality." Not only the things you can touch or see, but the things that make such touching or seeing "normal." Then words, like their users, have a hegemony. Socially— which is final, right now. If you are some kind of artist, you naturally might think this is not so. There is the future. But *immortality* is a kind of drug, I think—one that leads to happiness at the thought of death. Myself, I would rather live forever . . . just to make sure.

[6]   The social hegemony, one's position in society, enforces more specifically one's terms (even the vulgar have "pull"). Even to the mode of speech. But also it makes these terms an available explanation of any social hierarchy, so that the words themselves become, even informally, laws. And of course they are usually very quickly stitched together to make formal statutes only fools or the faithfully intrepid would dare to question beyond immediate neccessity.

[7]   The culture of the powerful is very infectious for the sophisticated, and strongly addictive. To be any kind of "success" one must be fluent in this culture. Know the words of the users, the semantic rituals of power. This is a way into wherever it is you are not now, but wish, very desperately, to get into.

[8]   Even speech then signals a fluency in this culture. A knowledge at

least. "He's an educated man," is the barest acknowledgment of such fluency . . . in any time. "He's hip," my friends might say. They connote a similar entrance.

[9]   And it is certainly the meanings of words that are most important, even if they are no longer consciously acknowledged, but merely, by their use, trip a familiar lever of social accord. To recreate instantly the understood hierarchy of social, and by doing that, cultural, importance. And cultures are thought by most people in the world to do their business merely by being hierarchies. Certainly this is true in the West, in as simple a manifestation as Xenophobia, the naïve bridegroom of anti-human feeling, or in economic terms, Colonialism. For instance, when the first Africans were brought into the New World, it was thought that it was all right for them to be slaves because "they were heathens." It is a perfectly logical assumption.

[10]   And it follows, of course, that slavery would have been an even stranger phenomenon had the Africans spoken English when they first got here. It would have complicated things. Very soon after the first generations of Afro-Americans mastered this language, they invented white people called Abolitionists.

[11]   Words' meanings, but also the rhythm and syntax that frame and propel their concatenation, seek their culture as the final reference for what they are describing of the world. An A flat played twice on the same saxophone by two different men does not have to sound the same. If these men have different ideas of what they want this note to do, the note will not sound the same. Culture is the form, the overall structure of organized thought (as well as emotion and spiritual pretension). There are many cultures. Many ways of organizing thought, or having thought organized. That is, the form of thought's passage through the world will take on as many diverse shapes as there are diverse groups of travelers. Environment is one organizer of *groups,* at any level of its meaning. People who live in Newark, New Jersey, are organized, for whatever purpose, as Newarkers. It begins that simply. Another manifestation, at a slightly more complex level, can be the fact that blues singers from the Midwest sing through their noses. There is an explanation past the geographical, but that's the idea in tabloid. And singing through the nose does propose that the definition of singing be altered . . . even if ever so slightly. (At this point where someone's definitions must be changed, we are flitting around at the outskirts of the old city of Aesthetics. A solemn ghost town. Though some of the bones of reason can still be gathered there.)

[12]   But we still need definitions, even if there already are many. The dullest men are always satisfied that a dictionary lists everything in the world. They don't care that you may find out something *extra,* which one day might even be valuable to them. Of course, by that time it might even be in the dictionary, or at least they'd hope so, if you asked them directly.

[13]   But for every item in the world, there are a multiplicity of definitions that fit. And every word we use *could* mean something else. And at

the same time. The culture fixes the use, and usage. And in "pluralistic" America, one should always listen very closely when he is being talked to. The speaker might mean something completely different from what we think we're hearing. "Where is your pot?"

[14] I heard an old Negro street singer last week, Reverend Pearly Brown, singing, "God don't never change!" This is a precise thing he is singing. He does not mean "God does not ever change!" He means "God don't never change!" The difference, and I said it was crucial, is in the final human reference . . . the form of passage through the world. A man who is rich and famous who sings, "God don't never change," is confirming his hegemony and good fortune . . . or merely calling the bank. A blind hopeless black American is saying something very different. He is telling you about the extraordinary order of the world. But he is not telling you about his "fate." Fate is a luxury available only to those fortunate citizens with alternatives. The view from the top of the hill is not the same as that from the bottom of the hill. Nor are most viewers at either end of the hill, even certain that, in fact, there is any other place from which to look. Looking down usually eliminates the possibility of understanding what it must be like to look up. Or try to imagine yourself as not existing. It is difficult, but poets and politicians try every other day.

[15] Being told to "speak proper," meaning that you become fluent with the jargon of power, is also a part of not "speaking proper." That is, the culture which desperately understands that it does not "speak proper," or is not fluent with the terms of social strength, also understands somewhere that its desire to gain such fluency is done at a terrifying risk. The bourgeois Negro accepts such risk as profit. But does *close-ter* (in the context of "jes a close-ter, walk wi-thee") mean the same thing as *closer?* Close-ter, in the term of its user is, believe me, exact. It means a quality of existence, of actual physical disposition perhaps . . in its manifestation as a *tone* and *rhythm* by which people live, most often in response to common modes of thought best enforced by some factor of environmental emotion that is exact and specific. Even the picture it summons is different, and certainly the "Thee" that is used to connect the implied "Me" with, is different. The God of the damned cannot know the God of the damner, that is, cannot know he is God. As no Blues person can really believe emotionally in Pascal's God, or Wittgenstein's question, "Can the concept of God exist in a perfectly logical language?" Answer: "God don't never change."

[16] Communication is only important because it is the broadest root of education. And all cultures communicate exactly what they have, a powerful motley of experience.

words and sentences

1. Vocabulary: *profound, longevity, generically* (¶ 1); *impetus* (2); *metaphysical, canons, traduced* (3); *hegemony* (5); *hierarchy* (6); *Xenophobia*

(9); *concatenation, Aesthetics* (11); *pluralistic* (13); *bourgeois* (15); *motley* (16).

2. Besides being a prose writer, Baraka is a poet. Are there any examples of the telescoped or telegraphic language of poetry in the essay?

3. How does Baraka define *culture?* What metaphor is central in his definition? What does the metaphor say about Baraka's attitude towards culture?

4. How many different meanings can you list for the sentence, "Where is your pot?"

5. In ¶ 15, Baraka speaks of *tone* and *rhythm.* Say aloud with as many different intonations and inflections as you can: "God don't never change." Does meaning change as intonation and inflection change? Can this kind of tone and rhythm be conveyed in the written sentence as well as the spoken?

ideas and implications

1. For Baraka, what is the relationship between *words* and *power?* Why is he concerned with words and their power? How do "words themselves become, even informally, laws" (¶ 6)?

2. According to Baraka, who makes meaning?

3. What is Baraka's attitude towards the dictionary? Does he share this attitude with other authors represented in this section?

4. Baraka says that language and meaning have changed since Dante's time. Why?

5. How important is context for Baraka? Does he define *context* in the same way that Hayakawa defines it?

6. In ¶ 5, Baraka discusses realities and fantasies. Comment on his distinction between the two.

strategies

1. Does Baraka state his thesis explicitly or implicitly? Where in the essay does he present his main idea? Why?

2. In ¶s 2, 3, and 4, Baraka talks of contexts. In what direction do these three paragraphs move?—from the inside to the outside or vice versa? Why has Baraka used the strategy he has employed in these three paragraphs?

3. In ¶ 14, Baraka uses the analogy of looking from the top and from the bottom of a hill to illustrate his point. Does this analogy also argue the point for Baraka?

suggestions for writing

1. Collect three or four sentences like "Where is your pot?" or "God don't never change." Then write a paper showing how context, tone, and rhythm can alter the meaning of one or more of these sentences.

2. Write a paper about an incident in which you heard a person use "expressive language." Baraka's example of the Negro street singer (¶ 14) might provide you with some suggestions.

3. Frequently, we hear friends make statements which appear to have one meaning, but when we begin to think about the statement and its context, that meaning may change for us. Write a paper about such an incident in your experience.

Melvin Maddocks

The Limitations of Language

[1]   In J.M.G. Le Clézio's novel *The Flood,* the anti-hero is a young man suffering from a unique malady. Words—the deluge of daily words —have overloaded his circuits. Even when he is strolling down the street, minding his own business, his poor brain jerks under the impact of instructions (WALK—DON'T WALK), threats (TRESPASSERS WILL BE PROSE-CUTED), and newsstand alarms (PLANE CRASH AT TEL AVIV). Finally, Le Clézio's Everyman goes numb—nature's last defense. Spoken words be-come mere sounds, a meaningless buzz in the ears. The most urgent printed words—a poem by Baudelaire, a proclamation of war—have no more profound effect than the advice he reads (without really reading) on a book of matches: PLEASE CLOSE COVER BEFORE STRIKING.

[2]   If one must give a name to Le Clézio's disease, perhaps semantic aphasia will do. Semantic aphasia is that numbness of ear, mind and heart—that tone deafness to the very meaning of language—which results from the habitual and prolonged abuse of words. As an isolated phe-nomenon, it can be amusing if not downright irritating. But when it becomes epidemic, it signals a disastrous decline in the skills of com-munication, to that mumbling low point where language does almost the opposite of what it was created for. With frightening perversity— the evidence mounts daily—words now seem to cut off and isolate, to cause more misunderstandings than they prevent.

[3]   Semantic aphasia is the monstrous insensitivity that allows generals to call war "pacification," union leaders to describe strikes or slowdowns as "job actions," and politicians to applaud even moderately progressive programs as "revolutions." Semantic aphasia is also the near-pathological blitheness that permits three different advertisers in the same women's magazine to call a wig and two dress lines "liberated."

[4]   So far, so familiar. Whenever the ravishing of the English language comes up for perfunctory headshaking, politicians, journalists, and ad writers almost invariably get cast as Three Horsemen of the Apocalypse.

The perennially identified culprits are guilty as charged, God knows. At their worst—and how often they are!—they seem to address the world through a bad PA system. Does it matter what they actually say? They capture your attention, right? They are word manipulators—the carnival barkers of life who misuse language to pitch and con and make the quick kill.

[5]   So let's hear all the old boos, all the dirty sneers. Paste a sticker proclaiming STAMP OUT AGNEWSPEAK on every bumper. Take the ribbons out of the typewriters of all reporters and rewritemen. Force six packs a day on the guy who wrote "Winston tastes good *like . . . .*" Would that the cure for semantic aphasia were that simple.

[6]   What about, for example, the aphasics of the counterculture? The ad writer may dingdong catch phrases like Pavlov's bells in order to produce saliva. The Movement propagandist rings his chimes ("Fascist!" "Pig!" "Honky!" "Male chauvinist!") to produce spit. More stammer than grammar, as Dwight Macdonald put it, the counterculture makes inarticulateness an ideal, debasing words into clenched fists ("Right on!") and exclamation points ("Oh, wow!"). Semantic aphasia on the right, semantic aphasia on the left. Between the excesses of square and hip rhetoric the language is in the way of being torn apart.

[7]   The semantic aphasia examined so far might be diagnosed as a hysterical compulsion to simplify. Whether pushing fluoride toothpaste or Women's Lib, the rhetoric tends to begin, rather than end, at an extreme. But there is a second, quite different variety of the disease: overcomplication. It damages the language less spectacularly but no less fatally than oversimplification. Its practitioners are commonly known as specialists. Instead of unjustified clarity they offer unjustified obscurity. Whether his discipline is biophysics or medieval Latin, the specialist jealously guards trade secrets by writing and speaking a private jargon that bears only marginal resemblances to English. Cult words encrust his sentences like barnacles, slowing progress, affecting the steering. And the awful truth is that everybody is a specialist at something.

[8]   If the oversimplifier fakes being a poet, the oversimplicator fakes being a scientist. Perhaps it is unfair to pick on economists rather than anybody else—except that they are, after all, talking about money. And as often as not it turns out to be our money. Here is a master clarifier-by-smokescreen discussing the recruiting possibilities of a volunteer army if wages, military (W_m) are nudged seductively in the direction of wages, civilian (W_c): "However, when one considers that a military aversion factor must be added to W_c or subtracted from W_m, assuming average aversion is positive, and that only a portion of military wages are perceived, the wage ratio is certainly less than unity and our observations could easily lie on the increasing elasticity segment of the supply curve." All clear, everyone?

[9]   The ultimate criticism of the overcomplicator is not that he fuzzes but that he fudges. If the cardinal sin of the oversimplifier is to inflate the trivial, the cardinal sin of the overcomplicator is to flatten the magnificent—or just pretend that it is not there. In the vocabulary of the

'70s, there is an adequate language for fanaticism, but none for ordinary, quiet conviction. And there are almost no words left to express the concerns of honor, duty or piety.

[10] For the noble idea leveled with a thud, see your nearest modern Bible. "Vanity of vanities, saith the Preacher . . ." In one new version his words become, "A vapor of vapors! Thinnest of vapors! All is vapor!" —turning the most passionate cry in the literature of nihilism into a spiritual weather report. The new rendition may be a more literal expression of the Hebrew original, but at what a cost in grace and power.

[11] Who will protect the language from all those oversimplifiers and overcomplicators who kill meaning with shouts or smother it with cautious mumbles? In theory, certain professions should serve as a sort of palace guard sworn to defend the mother tongue with their lives. Alas, the enemy is within the gates. Educators talk gobbledygook about "non-abrasive systems intervention" and "low structure-low consideration teaching style." Another profession guilty of non-defense is lexicography. With proud humility today's dictionary editor abdicates even as arbiter, refusing to recognize any standards but usage. If enough people misuse disinterested as a synonym for uninterested, Webster's will honor it as a synonym. If enough people say infer when they mean imply, then that becomes its meaning in the eyes of a dictionary editor.

[12] Con Edison can be fined for contaminating the Hudson. Legislation can force Detroit to clean up automobile exhausts. What can one do to punish the semantic aphasics for polluting their native language? None of man's specialties of self-destruction—despoliation of the environment, overpopulation, even war—appear more ingrained than his gift for fouling his mother tongue. Yet nobody dies of semantic aphasia, and by and large it gets complained about with a low-priority tut-tut.

[13] The reason we rate semantic aphasia so low—somewhere between athlete's foot and the common cold on the scale of national perils—is that we don't understand the deeper implications of the disease. In his classic essay, *Politics and the English Language,* George Orwell pointed out what should be obvious—that sloppy language makes for sloppy thought. Emerson went so far as to suggest that bad rhetoric meant bad men. Semantic aphasia, both men recognized, kills after all. "And the Lord said: 'Go to, let us go down, and there confound their language, that they may not understand one another's speech.'" Is there a more ominous curse in the Bible? It breathes hard upon us at this time of frantic change, when old purposes slip out from under the words that used to cover them, leaving the words like tombstones over empty graves.

[14] How, then, does one rescue language? How are words repaired, put back in shape, restored to accuracy and eloquence, made faithful again to the commands of the mind and the heart? There is, sadly enough, no easy answer. Sincerity is of little help to clichés, even in a suicide note, as Aldous Huxley once remarked. Read, if you can, the Latinized techno-pieties of most ecologists. Good intentions are not likely to produce another Shakespeare or a Bible translation equivalent to that produced by King James' bench of learned men. They wrote when English was

young, vital and untutored. English in 1971 is an old, overworked language, freshened sporadically only by foreign borrowings or the flickering, vulgar piquancy of slang. All of us—from the admen with their jingles to the tin-eared scholars with their jargon—are victims as well as victimizers of the language we have inherited.

[15] Concerning aphasia, the sole source of optimism is the logic of necessity. No matter how carelessly or how viciously man abuses the language he has inherited, he simply cannot live without it. Even Woodstock Nation cannot survive on an oral diet of grunts and expletives. Mankind craves definiton as he craves lost innocence. He simply does not know what his life means until he says it. Until the day he dies he will grapple with mystery by trying to find the word for it. "The limits of my language," Ludwig Wittgenstein observed, "are the limits of my world." Man's purifying motive is that he cannot let go of the Adam urge to name things—and finally, out of his unbearable solitude, to pronounce to others his own identity.

words and sentences

1. Vocabulary: *malady* (¶ 1); *aphasia, perversity* (2); *ravishing, perfunctory, Apocalypse, perennially* (4); *jargon* (7); *nihilism* (10); *lexicography, abdicates, arbiter* (11); *ominous* (13); *techno-pieties, piquancy* (14); *expletives* (15).
2. Maddocks employs the dash in his sentences frequently. Examine his sentences using the dash to determine why he relies on this punctuation mark. What do most grammars and handbooks say about the use of the dash?
3. How does Maddocks define *semantic aphasia*? Compare his definition with that of a dictionary.
4. Describe the structure of the second sentence in ¶ 2, and then write a sentence of your own using the same pattern.
5. Do the same for the following sentences: sentence four in ¶ 6, sentence eight in ¶ 7, sentence one in ¶ 9.
6. Maddocks employs a figure of speech in "proud humility" in sentence six of ¶ 11. What is the figure he is using? Write a sentence in which you use a similar figure of speech. Can you write such a sentence without naming the figure? Why or why not?

ideas and implications

1. According to Maddocks, who is generally blamed for word pollution? Why? Who else must share this blame?
2. Examine the metaphors of the first paragraph. What are the sources of these comparisons? And the implications?
3. What are the "deeper implications" of semantic aphasia? Does it ever kill? How?
4. Is Maddocks exaggerating when he writes that in the 1970's "there is an adequate language for fanaticism, but none for ordinary, quiet conviction" (¶ 9)?

5. Examine the metaphor of the last sentence in ¶ 13. What meaning does this metaphor convey?
6. Read further passages from the Book of Ecclesiastes in a modern translation of the Bible and in the King James Version. Compare the language of the two.
7. Does Maddocks support his statement that sloppy language makes for sloppy thought?
8. In ¶ 15, Maddocks writes, "He [man] simply does not know what his life means until he says it." What assumption does he make here about the way men know and understand?
9. Does Maddocks hope for a cure for semantic aphasia?

strategies

1. How does Maddocks begin and end his essay?
2. Describe the voice that Maddocks projects in his essay? Does the voice seem hysterical, reasonable, knowledgeable, or what? Support your judgment with specific details.
3. Maddocks uses many examples to illustrate his point. List those examples. Do the items on your list parallel the order that Maddocks has chosen for presenting his ideas?
4. Maddocks forwards his argument by metaphor as well as example. List a half dozen of his metaphors and explore the implications of each. Is there a way to describe generally the metaphors he uses?
5. Why does Maddox rely on authorities and sources for examples in his argument? How valuable is that strategy in his argument?

suggestions for writing

1. If you compared a King James Version and a modern biblical translation of the Book of Ecclesiastes, write a paper about differences in the language and meaning and feeling of a passage from the two versions.
2. Write a paper about an incident in which word pollution affected you.
3. Write a paper about a situation in which you called another person a "name." What were your reasons for using that name? Or you might write about a situation in which you were called a name.
4. Pay attention to the signs you see every day and write a paper about the meaning of some of those signs.

2 The Writer as See-er and Thinker

(A)

(B)

(C)

Three woodcuts by M. C. Escher. Escher Foundation. The Hague Museum.

INTRODUCTION

William Faulkner observed that "every time any character gets into a book, . . . he's actually telling his biography—that's all anyone ever does, he tells his own biography, talking about himself, in a thousand different terms, but himself." If we define *biography* in its broadest sense (as Faulkner does here), we might include not just characters in books, but all speakers and writers. When we tell others what we have seen, felt, and thought, we communicate a partial story of our lives and of our attitudes towards it. Our words are biographical—more precisely, autobiographical—because they describe what we have seen, felt, and thought at a specific time. No single utterance is likely to capture the whole of our biography; each utterance is one of "a thousand different terms" we use to describe ourselves and how we see. As we grow and change, so may our ability to see, to think, and to feel. But the means of telling others what we know will remain the worlds of words, though our ability to use words may increase as we learn more about them.

Before we can tell others about our ideas, attitudes, and feelings, we must *discover* what those ideas, attitudes, and feelings are. To discover what we know, we must *see* our experience, not merely *look* at it. At its simplest, the difference between looking and seeing is the difference between describing a plant as a "tree" when "loblolly pine" or "Douglas fir" is more precise and exact. But when we talk about "honor," "truth," or "courage," the problem of seeing gets complicated. Seeing abstractions like "truth" demands that we be able to connect ideas and to discriminate among them —in other words, to think clearly and honestly about our experience. Most of us spend our lives learning to see, discovering what it is that we know. And in our "Adam urge" to know by naming, we report our discoveries to our family and to our friends; if we are writers, we report them to the world.

Once we have begun to see, we are ready to say what we have discovered. Seeing, saying, and thinking are the subjects of the readings in this section.

If there were easy formulas for learning to see, someone would have invented them long ago. One way of discovering what we know is to ask ourselves questions about our experience—about our sense impressions, and our thoughts and feelings about these impressions. No list of questions can unlock the secrets that surround us, but answers to the questions *who, what, when, where, why,* and *how* provide a beginning. Any one of these questions is likely to lead us to other questions that may help us discover our attitudes and feelings and to communicate them to others. For example, much of our writing is about people or actors. Answers to questions about *who* might produce the following sequence: Who performed the action? What was his name? What does he look like? Are there any distinguishing physical characteristics about him? What are they? What color are his eyes and hair? Where is he from? Does he have brothers and sisters? Is he married? To whom? How does he talk? What does his voice sound like? Are there any peculiarities in his speech? Why? What kinds of stories does he tell? Do his stories tell anything about him? What? What was the particular action he performed? How did he perform it? What seems to have motivated this action? The list could go on and on. Asking such questions does not guarantee our seeing more clearly, but unless we ask questions which will lead us to understanding, what we say about our experience is likely to be fuzzy and general. Good writing depends upon specificity and concreteness; it depends upon our seeing clearly and conveying our perceptions with equal clarity of language.

"In the Laboratory with Agassiz" is Samuel H. Scudder's account of learning to see. As a freshman at Harvard University, Scudder enrolled in a science course taught by Louis Agassiz, who on the first day handed his student a *Haemulon* with these instructions: "Take this fish and look at it." Each time Scudder described his findings to Agassiz, his teacher told him to look at his fish again. Scudder looked until the fish began "to look loathsome"; then he began to observe the intricacies of his specimen. Scudder's essay is a tribute to Agassiz as a teacher, but it is also about his joyful discovery of learning to see.

Ezra Pound's "Tests and Composition Exercises" ask us to see others' prose with an editor's pencil and then to use that pencil to write descriptions of objects. His exercises are sprinkled with sound and witty observations about reading and writing.

The next five readings deal with keeping a diary, journal, or notebook as a way of seeing ourselves and our world more clearly—and sometimes as a practice field for learning to write. Virginia Woolf tells herself that she has improved her prose by writing during her "casual half hours after tea." The main thing, she says, "is not to play the part of censor, but to write as the mood comes or of anything whatever." Ralph Waldo Emerson uses his *Journal* "for a tablet to save the wear and tear of weak Memory," but he also confesses his hopes and fears. In *A Diary from Dixie,* Mary Boykin Chesnut records her impressions of life in the South during the Civil War; she stores in her diary conversations with friends, her feelings about the events between 1861 and 1865, and portraits of the many people she met during these years. Entries from Henry David Thoreau's *Journal* show a young man wondering about the kind of writer he would like to become. He asks, "But what does all this scribbling amount to?" As he matures, however, he begins to be more certain about his scribbling and about himself as a writer. Joan Didion keeps a notebook for several reasons. She wants to remember "*how it felt to me,*" and like the other diarists finds her notebook a way "to keep in touch" with herself and the world.

Robert Frost's couplet "The Secret Sits" wryly points to the difficulty of finding answers to the riddles in our lives. John Keats's "Upon First Looking into Chapman's Homer" celebrates George Chapman's skill as a translator. Chapman's voice, speaking "out loud and bold," brings to life for Keats the word-world of Homer; through Chapman's eyes and language, Keats sees anew and freshly the "wide expanse" of "deep-brow'd Homer" and is filled with awe, "like some watcher of the skies."

In "Denotation and Connotation," Richard D. Altick distinguishes between a word's dictionary definition and its emotional associations to show how word choices affect our seeing and saying. He warns about writing which conceals because the author is careless or because he is a propagandist. Language, says Altick, can both conceal and reveal; honest writing reveals. Ross Campbell's "Poetic Eclipse of the Moon" juxtaposes two views of the moon by recording the conversation of fictional astronauts—one much like our American space travellers and the other named Commander Shelley. The way his astronauts say tells us how they see.

Marchette Chute's "Getting at the Truth" discusses the problems of discovering what happened and what is. A biographer, Miss Chute recounts the problems she faced in finding out why Sir Philip Sidney failed to wear his leg armour to battle, a fact that led to his death. Like a lawyer, she examines evidence and questions the motives of witnesses to find what she believes is the truth. By focusing upon this single episode, Chute explores the larger problems of getting at the truth.

"Cool was I and logical," begins Max Shulman's comic tale, "Love Is a Fallacy." The narrator of the story is a young man who thinks he thinks logically, but finds that a woman's feelings (and his own) cannot always be measured by reason's ruler.

The three woodcuts by Maurits C. Escher at the opening of this section provide a place to test your ability to see, to look at your own fish. Do any of these woodcuts tell a story? What impressions or ideas is Escher trying to convey through the language of line and shadow? After you have looked carefully at the woodcuts, try to put titles on each. (The titles that Escher gave these woodcuts are printed upside down at the bottom of this page.) You may want to write a paper about the meaning of one or all three of the woodcuts, or you may want to write explaining the reasons for your titles. Whatever you write, you will be trying to tell readers what you see and feel and think about Escher's work.

(A) *Puddle*, (B) *Night and Day*, (C) *Predestination*.

Samuel H. Scudder

In the Laboratory with Agassiz

[1]   It was more than fifteen years ago that I entered the laboratory of Professor Agassiz, and told him I had enrolled my name in the scientific school as a student of natural history. He asked me a few questions about my object in coming, my antecedents generally, the mode in which I afterwards proposed to use the knowledge I might acquire, and finally, whether I wished to study any special branch. To the latter I replied that while I wished to be well grounded in all departments of zoölogy, I purposed to devote myself specially to insects.

"When do you wish to begin?" he asked.

"Now," I replied.

This seemed to please him, and with an energetic "Very well," he reached from a shelf a huge jar of specimens in yellow alcohol.

[5]   "Take this *fish*," said he, "and look at it; we call it a Hæmulon; by and by I will ask what you have seen."

With that he left me, but in a moment returned with explicit instructions as to the care of the object entrusted to me.

"No man is fit to be a naturalist," said he, "who does not know how to take care of specimens."

I was to keep the fish before me in a tin tray, and occasionally moisten the surface with alcohol from the jar, always taking care to replace the stopper tightly. Those were not the days of ground glass stoppers, and elegantly shaped exhibition jars; all the old students will recall the huge, neckless glass bottles with their leaky, wax-besmeared corks, half eaten by insects and begrimed with cellar dust. Entomology was a cleaner science than ichthyology, but the example of the professor, who had unhesitatingly plunged to the bottom of the jar to produce the fish, was infectious; and though this alcohol had "a very ancient and fish-like smell," I really dared not show any aversion within these sacred precincts, and treated the alcohol as though it were pure water. Still I was conscious of a passing feeling of disappointment, for gazing at a fish did not commend itself to an ardent entomologist. My friends at home, too, were annoyed, when they discovered that no amount of eau de cologne would drown the perfume which haunted me like a shadow.

In ten minutes I had seen all that could be seen in that fish, and started in search of the professor, who had however left the museum; and when I returned, after lingering over some of the odd animals stored in the upper apartment, my specimen was dry all over. I dashed the fluid over the fish as if to resuscitate the beast from a fainting-fit, and looked with anxiety for a return of the normal, sloppy appearance. This little excitement over, nothing was to be done but return to a steadfast gaze at my mute companion. Half an hour passed,—an hour,—another hour; the fish began to look loathsome. I turned it over and around; looked it in the face,—ghastly; from behind, beneath, above, sideways, at a three quarters' view,—just as ghastly. I was in despair; at an early hour I concluded that lunch was necessary; so, with infinite relief, the fish was carefully replaced in the jar, and for an hour I was free.

[10]   On my return, I learned that Professor Agassiz had been at the museum, but had gone and would not return for several hours. My fellow-students were too busy to be disturbed by continued conversation. Slowly I drew forth that hideous fish, and with a feeling of desperation again looked at it. I might not use a magnifying glass; instruments of all kinds were interdicted. My two hands, my two eyes, and the fish; it seemed a most limited field. I pushed my finger down its throat to feel how sharp the teeth were. I began to count the scales in the different rows until I was convinced that that was nonsense. At last a happy thought struck me—I would draw the fish; and now with surprise I began to discover new features in the creature. Just then the professor returned.

"That is right," said he; "a pencil is one of the best of eyes. I am glad to notice, too, that you keep your specimen wet and your bottle corked."

With these encouraging words, he added,—

"Well, what is it like?"

He listened attentively to my brief rehearsal of the structure of parts whose names were still unknown to me: the fringed gill-arches and movable operculum; the pores of the head, fleshy lips, and lidless eyes; the lateral line, the spinous fins, and forked tail; the compressed and arched body. When I had finished, he waited as if expecting more, and then, with an air of disappointment,—

[15]   "You have not looked very carefully; why," he continued, more earnestly, "you haven't even seen one of the most conspicuous features of the animal, which is as plainly before your eyes as the fish itself; look again, look again!" and he left me to my misery.

I was piqued; I was mortified. Still more of that wretched fish! But now I set myself to my task with a will, and discovered one new thing after another, until I saw how just the professor's criticism had been. The afternoon passed quickly, and when, toward its close, the professor inquired,—

"Do you see it yet?"

"No," I replied, "I am certain I do not, but I see how little I saw before."

"That is next best," said he, earnestly, "but I won't hear you now; put away your fish and go home; perhaps you will be ready with a better answer in the morning. I will examine you before you look at the fish."

[20]   This was disconcerting; not only must I think of my fish all night, studying, without the object before me, what this unknown but most visible feature might be; but also, without reviewing my new discoveries, I must give an exact account of them the next day. I had a bad memory; so I walked home by Charles River in a distracted state, with my two perplexities.

The cordial greeting from the professor the next morning was reassuring; here was a man who seemed to be quite as anxious as I, that I should see for myself what he saw.

"Do you perhaps mean," I asked, "that the fish has symmetrical sides with paired organs?"

His thoroughly pleased, "Of course, of course!" repaid the wakeful hours of the previous night. After he had discoursed most happily and enthusiastically—as he always did—upon the importance of this point, I ventured to ask what I should do next.

"Oh, look at your fish!" he said, and left me again to my own devices. In a little more than an hour he returned and heard my new catalogue.

[25] "That is good, that is good!" he repeated; "but that is not all; go on"; and so for three long days he placed that fish before my eyes, forbidding me to look at anything else, or to use any artificial aid. "Look, look, look," was his repeated injunction.

This was the best entomological lesson I ever had,—a lesson, whose influence has extended to the details of every subsequent study; a legacy the professor has left to me, as he has left it to many others, of inestimable value, which we could not buy, with which we cannot part.

A year afterward, some of us were amusing ourselves with chalking outlandish beasts upon the museum blackboard. We drew prancing star-fishes; frogs in mortal combat; hydra-headed worms; stately craw-fishes, standing on their tails, bearing aloft umbrellas; and grotesque fishes with gaping mouths and staring eyes. The professor came in shortly after, and was as amused as any, at our experiments. He looked at the fishes.

"Hæmulons, every one of them," he said; "Mr._____ drew them."

True; and to this day, if I attempt a fish, I can draw nothing but Hæmulons.

[30] The fourth day, a second fish of the same group was placed beside the first, and I was bidden to point out the resemblances and differences between the two; another and another followed, until the entire family lay before me, and a whole legion of jars covered the table and surrounding shelves; the odor had become a pleasant perfume; and even now, the sight of an old, six-inch, worm-eaten cork brings fragrant memories!

The whole group of Hæmulons was thus brought in review; and, whether engaged upon the dissection of the internal organs, the preparation and examination of the bony frame-work, or the description of the various parts, Agassiz' training in the method of observing facts and their orderly arrangement was ever accompanied by the urgent exhortation not to be content with them.

"Facts are stupid things," he would say, "until brought into connection with some general law."

At the end of eight months, it was almost with reluctance that I left these friends and turned to insects; but what I had gained by this outside experience has been of greater value than years of later investigation in my favorite groups.

words and sentences

1. Vocabulary: *antecedents* (¶ 1); *ichthyology, infectious, aversion* (8); *resuscitate, loathsome* (9); *interdicted* (10); *piqued* (16); *disconcerting* (20); *injunction* (25); *legacy, inestimable* (26); *grotesque* (27); *exhortation* (31).
2. In ¶s 8 and 30, Scudder speaks of "perfume." How does the meaning of this word change between ¶ 8 and ¶ 30? What causes this change of meaning?
3. Describe the structure of the second sentence in ¶ 8. Then write a sentence of your own imitating this pattern.
4. Does Scudder use the semicolon in many of his sentences? Why? Does his use of this punctuation mark tell something about the structure of his sentences?
5. Describe the structure of the first sentence in ¶ 14; then write a sentence of your own imitating this pattern.
6. Rewrite the sentence that comprises ¶ 15. Make more than one sentence if you wish. What other options might Scudder have selected for this sentence pattern?

ideas and implications

1. Louis Agassiz was a naturalist and professor at Harvard University. Scudder's essay is a portrait of Agassiz as a teacher. What is Scudder's attitude towards Agassiz? What picture of Agassiz emerges from Scudder's portrait?
2. Scudder's essay is also a story about his own experience. What picture of Scudder is presented? How long ago did the events described occur? Do you think Scudder's portrait of himself and Agassiz would have been the same if he had written the essay immediately following his experience with Agassiz? Why or why not?
3. Why does Agassiz refuse his students the use of artificial aids for examining their specimens?
4. Scudder says in ¶ 10 that the fish, his eyes, and his hands "seemed a most limited field." What does Scudder discover about the limitations of this "field"?
5. Agassiz says, "a pencil is one of the best of eyes." Explore the implications of this statement. Is the statement a metaphor?
6. Why does Agassiz assert that "Facts are stupid things"? Does Agassiz have much respect for facts? Why or why not?
7. Both Scudder and Agassiz make distinctions between looking and seeing. What are those distinctions? How does one learn to see? Make a list of the stages of Scudder's learning to see the Haemulons.
8. How important is the act of finding relationships to the act of seeing?

strategies

1. What is the person of the pronoun Scudder uses for telling of his experience? What would be the effect of third person pronouns in the essay?
2. How does Scudder focus his attention on his first year with Agassiz? Does he talk about the whole year? Why or why not?
3. How much dialogue is there in Scudder's essay? Is the use of dialogue an effective strategy in explaining and describing?
4. What is the function of the first paragraph of Scudder's essay?
5. Scudder begins looking at his fish by thinking the task is a simple one. He discovers, however, that what he viewed as a simple task turns out to be more complicated than he had imagined. How does he convey this idea to his readers? How many views of the fish does he present? Is there increasing complexity in his vision of the fish? Demonstrate your observations with specific examples.
6. Try to present the thesis idea of Scudder's essay in a single sentence.
7. Why does Scudder include the three paragraphs (27-29) about the chalkboard drawings? What point is he making about himself and Agassiz with this episode?
8. In ¶ 30, Scudder says that after he had seen clearly the Haemulon, a second fish "of the same group was placed beside the first." What point is he making about seeing by introducing this detail near the end of his essay?

suggestions for writing

1. Take a commonplace object that you use daily (a pencil, a cup, a bookbag, etc.) and draw it with a pencil. Then write a paper describing this object in detail—without using the name of the object itself.
2. Select from your experience an incident that has special meaning for you and write a paper telling what that meaning was.
3. Select an incident from one of your recent days and use that incident as the central event to characterize the meaning of that day.
4. Look carefully at your hands. Write a paper describing what you see. Then try an experiment for an entire day. Tape or tie your thumbs to your index fingers before you begin your day's work. Then write a second paper about your hands when you have completed the experiment.
5. Try another experiment. Blindfold yourself for a couple of hours and try to pursue your normal activities. Be sure that some friend can be with you during this time. Then write a paper about what happened to you during the time you were blindfolded.

Ezra Pound

Tests and Composition Exercises

I

[1] 1. Let the pupils exchange composition papers and see how many and what useless words have been used—how many words that convey nothing new.

2. How many words that obscure the meaning.

3. How many words out of their usual place, and whether this alteration makes the statement in any way more interesting or more energetic.

4. Whether a sentence is ambiguous; whether it really means more than one thing or more than the writer intended; whether it can be so read as to mean something different.

[5] 5. Whether there is something clear on paper, but ambiguous if spoken aloud.

II

It is said that Flaubert taught De Maupassant to write. When De Maupassant returned from a walk Flaubert would ask him to describe someone, say a concierge whom they would both pass in their next walk, and to describe the person so that Flaubert would recognize, say, the concierge and not mistake her for some other concierge and not the one De Maupassant had described.

SECOND SET

1. Let the pupil write the description of a tree.

2. Of a tree without mentioning the name of the tree (larch, pine, etc.) so that the reader will not mistake it for the description of some other kind of tree.

3. Try some object in the class-room.

[10] 4. Describe the light and shadow on the school-room clock or some other object.

5. If it can be done without breach of the peace, the pupil could write descriptions of some other pupil. The author suggests that the pupil should not describe the instructor, otherwise the description might

become a vehicle of emotion, and subject to more complicated rules of composition than the class is yet ready to cope with.

In all these descriptions the test would be accuracy and vividness, the pupil receiving the other's paper would be the gauge. He would recognize or not recognize the object or person described.

Rodolfo Agricola in an edition dating from fifteen hundred and something says one writes: *ut doceat, ut moveat ut delectet,* to teach, to move or to delight.

A great deal of bad criticism is due to men not seeing which of these three motives underlies a given composition.

[15] The converse processes, not considered by the pious teachers of antiquity, would be to obscure, to bamboozle or mislead, and to bore.

The reader or auditor is at liberty to remain passive and submit to these operations if he so choose.

words and sentences

1. Vocabulary: *ambiguous* (¶ 4); *bamboozle* (15).
2. Does ¶ 6 have a topic sentence? Describe the structure of the second sentence in this paragraph; then write a sentence of your own imitating Pound's sentence.
3. How does Pound use the word *seeing* in ¶ 14?

ideas and implications

1. How aware of audience is Pound in his exercises? Point to specific sentences to support your observations.
2. What is the cause of "a great deal of bad criticism"?
3. Could a composition have more than one purpose? Could it have as its purpose to teach and delight? to teach and move? Comment on the possible arrangements of these three purposes of writing.

strategies

1. Try to write the first five paragraphs in a single sentence. Can it be done? What reasons can you give for Pound's choice to list in these paragraphs?
2. What is the function of ¶ 6 in these exercises?
3. Does Pound develop a thesis in the first set of exercises (¶s 1 through 6)? Does he in the second set? State these theses in a sentence for each set.
4. What is the function of ¶ 15? What purpose does Pound seem to have in mind here?
5. Do Pound's exercises possess both form and strategy?

suggestions for writing

1. Pound's are excellent.
2. Write for your classmates an exercise directed towards a specific problem in composition. Without naming the problem itself, write your questions in such a way that your classmates will be able to identify the specific problem you are discussing.

Virginia Woolf

from A Writer's Diary

Easter Sunday, April 20th (1919)

In the idleness which succeeds any long article, and Defoe is the second leader this month, I got out this diary and read, as one always does read one's own writing, with a kind of guilty intensity. I confess that the rough and random style of it, often so ungrammatical, and crying for a word altered, afflicted me somewhat. I am trying to tell whichever self it is that reads this hereafter that I can write very much better; and take no time over this; and forbid her to let the eye of man behold it. And now I may add my little compliment to the effect that it has a slapdash and vigour and sometimes hits an unexpected bulls eye. But what is more to the point is my belief that the habit of writing thus for my own eye only is good practice. It loosens the ligaments. Never mind the misses and the stumbles. Going at such a pace as I do I must make the most direct and instant shots at my object, and thus have to lay hands on words, choose them and shoot them with no more pause than is needed to put my pen in the ink. I believe that during the past year I can trace some increase of ease in my professional writing which I attribute to my casual half hours after tea. Moreover there looms ahead of me the shadow of some kind of form which a diary might attain to. I might in the course of time learn what it is that one can make of this loose, drifting material of life; finding another use for it than the use I put it to, so much more consciously and scrupulously, in fiction. What sort of diary should I like mine to be? Something loose knit and yet not slovenly, so elastic that it will embrace any thing, solemn, slight or beautiful that comes into my mind. I should like it to resemble some deep old desk, or capacious hold-all, in which one flings a mass of odds and ends without looking them through. I should like to come back, after a year or two, and find that the collection had sorted itself and refined itself and coalesced, as such deposits so mysteriously do, into a mould, transparent enough to reflect the light of our life, and yet steady, tranquil compounds with the aloofness of a work of art. The main requisite, I think on re-reading my old volumes, is not to play the part of censor, but to write as the mood comes or of anything whatever; since I was curious to find how I went for things put in haphazard, and found the significance to lie where I never saw it at the time. But looseness quickly becomes slovenly. A little effort is needed to face a character or an incident which needs to be recorded. Nor can one let the pen write without guidance; for fear of becoming slack and untidy like Vernon Lee. Her ligaments are too loose for my taste.

words and sentences

1. Vocabulary: *capacious, coalesced.*
2. What does Virginia Woolf mean by "guilty intensity"? By the "loose, drifting material of life"?
3. Describe the pattern of the sentence beginning "Going at such a pace. . . ." Then write a sentence imitating this pattern.

ideas and implications

1. What does Virginia Woolf's conversation with herself tell readers about her? Point to specific details to support your findings.
2. Why does Virginia Woolf tell herself "not to play the part of censor"?
3. As she re-reads her diary, she notes that she sometimes "found the significance to lie where I never saw it at the time." Discuss the implications of this observation.

strategies

1. How important is the phrase "loosens the ligaments" in the organization of Virginia Woolf's diary entry?
2. Do metaphors and comparisons give a "loose" form to her diary entry?

suggestions for writing

1. Begin keeping a diary or journal of your own by answering the question Virginia Woolf asks; "What sort of diary should I like mine to be?"
2. Begin keeping a journal by writing about an event or feeling that occurred to you today. Make "direct and instant shots" at your subject without regard to form.

Ralph Waldo Emerson

from The Journals

[1]   Mixing with the thousand pursuits and passions and objects of the world as personified by Imagination, is profitable and entertaining. These pages are intended at their commencement to contain a record of new thoughts (when they occur); for a receptacle of all the old ideas that partial but peculiar peepings at antiquity can furnish or furbish; for tablet to save the wear and tear of weak Memory, and, in short, for all the various purposes and utility, real or imaginary, which are usually comprehended under that comprehensive title *Common Place book.* . . .

October 25, 1820

[2]   I find myself often idle, vagrant, stupid and hollow. This is somewhat appalling and, if I do not discipline myself with diligent care, I shall suffer severely from remorse and the sense of inferiority hereafter. All around me are industrious and will be great, I am indolent and shall be insignificant. Avert it, heaven! avert it, virtue! I need excitement.

March 9, 1822

[3]   The origin of Fiction is buried in the darkness of the remotest ages. If it were a question of any importance, perhaps its secret springs are not yet beyond the reach of the inquirer. To paint what is not should naturally seem less agreeable to the mind than to describe what is. "Nothing" (said the author of the Essay on the Human Understanding) "is so beautiful to the eye, as truth to the mind." But if we look again, I apprehend we shall find that the source of fable, is *human misery;* that to relieve one hour of life, by exciting the sympathies to a tale even of imaginary joy, was accounted a praiseworthy accomplishment; and honour and gold were due to him, whose rare talent took away, for the moment, the memory of care and grief. Fancy, which is ever a kind of contradiction to life and truth, set off in a path remote as possible from all human scenes and circumstances; and hence the first legends dealt altogether in monstrous scenes, and peopled the old mythology, and the nursery lore, with magicians, griffins, and metamorphoses which offend the ear of taste, and could only win away the credulity of a savage race, and the simplicity of a child. Reason, however, soon taught the bard that the deception was infinitely improved by being reduced within the compass of probability; and the second fictions introduced imaginary persons into the manners and dwellings of real life.

May 13, 1822

[4]   In twelve days I shall be nineteen years old; which I count a mis-

erable thing. Has any other educated person lived so many years and lost so many days? I do not say acquired so little, for by an ease of thought and certain looseness of mind I have perhaps been the subject of as many ideas as many of mine age. But mine approaching maturity is attended with a goading sense of emptiness and wasted capacity; with the conviction that vanity has been content to admire the little circle of natural accomplishments, and has travelled again and again the narrow round, instead of adding sedulously the gems of knowledge to their number. Too tired and too indolent to travel up the mountain path which leads to good learning, to wisdom and to fame, I must be satisfied with beholding with an envious eye the labourious journey and final success of my fellows, remaining stationary myself, until my inferiors and juniors have reached and outgone me. And how long is this to last? How long shall I hold the little acclivity which four or six years ago I flattered myself was enviable, but which has become contemptible now? It is a child's place, and if I hold it longer, I may quite as well resume the bauble and rattle, grow old with a baby's red jockey on my grey head and a picture-book in my hand, instead of Plato and Newton. Well, and I am he who nourished brilliant visions of future grandeur which may well appear presumptuous and foolish now. My infant imagination was idolatrous of glory, and thought itself no mean pretender to the honours of those who stood highest in the community, and dared even to contend for fame with those who are hallowed by time and the approbation of ages. It was a little merit to conceive such animating hopes, and afforded some poor prospect of the possibility of their fulfilment. This hope was fed and fanned by the occasional lofty communications which were vouchsafed to me with the Muses' Heaven, and which have at intervals made me the organ of remarkable sentiments and feelings which were far above my ordinary train. And with this lingering earnest of better hope (I refer to this fine exhilaration which now and then quickens my clay) shall I resign every aspiration to belong to that family of giant minds which live on earth many ages and rule the world when their bones are slumbering, no matter whether under a pyramid or a primrose? No, I will yet a little while entertain the angel.

December 10, 1824

[5]   I confess I am a little cynical on some topics, and when a whole nation is roaring Patriotism at the top of its voice, I am fain to explore the cleanness of its hands and purity of its heart. I have generally found the gravest and most useful citizens are not the easiest provoked to swell the noise, though they may be punctual at the polls. And I have sometimes thought the election an individual makes between right and wrong more important than his choice between rival statesmen, and that the loss of a novel train of thought was ill paid by a considerable pecuniary gain. It is pleasant to know what is doing in the world, and why should a world go on if it does no good? The man whom your vote supports is to govern some millions—and it would be laughable not to know the

issue of the naval battle. In ten years this great competition will be very stale, and a few words will inform you the result which cost you so many columns of the newsprints, so many anxious conjectures. Your soul will last longer than the ship; and will value its just and philosophical associations long after the memory has spurned all obtrusive and burdensome contents. . . .

words and sentences

1. Vocabulary: *furbish* (¶ 1); *indolent* (2); *sedulously, acclivity* (4); *obtrusive* (5).
2. Describe the sentence patterns in ¶ 2; then write a paragraph imitating these patterns. How much variety is there in the sentences?

ideas and implications

1. Compare and contrast Emerson's purpose in keeping a journal with that of Virginia Woolf. Are they different?
2. For Emerson, what are the sources of fiction? Who makes up the audience for fiction?
3. Describe Emerson's state of mind as he approaches his nineteenth birthday. How does he see himself? What are his fears and hopes?

strategies

1. In ¶ 3, Emerson attempts to define the term "fiction." How does he try to make the meaning of this word clear to himself?

suggestions for writing

1. In your journal, write your definition of "fiction." How is your view of the word different from Emerson's?
2. In your journal, write an entry about your reasons for attending college. Do not act as censor.

Mary Boykin Chesnut

from A Diary from Dixie

August 27th, 1861

[1]   Toady Barker and James Lowndes came today. A man told James Lowndes: "All that I wish on earth is to be at peace, and on my own plantation." Mr. Lowndes said quietly: "I wish I had a plantation to be

on, but just now I can't see how anyone would feel justified in leaving the army." The gentleman who had been answered so completely by James Lowndes answered spitefully: "Those women who are so frantic for their husbands to join the army would no doubt like them killed!" Things were growing rather uncomfortable, but an interruption came in the shape of a card. An old classmate of Mr. Chesnut's, Captain Archer, just now fresh from California, followed his card so quickly that Mr. Chesnut had hardly time to tell us that in Princeton College they called him Sally Archer, he was so pretty. He is good looking still, but the service and consequent rough life have destroyed all softness and girlishness. He will never be so pretty again.

[2]   Today I saw a letter from a girl crossed in love. Her parents object to the social position of her fiancé; in point of fact, they forbid the banns. She writes: "I am misserable." Her sister she calls a "mean retch." For such a speller, a man of any social status would do. They ought not to expect so much for her. If she wrote her "pah" a note I am sure that "stern parient" would give in.

[3]   I am miserable too today, but with one "s." The North is consolidated. They move as one man, with no states but with the army organized by the central power.

[4]   We see people here everywhere; I wonder why they let them stay. They are not true to us. Mr. Chesnut says I am like the man in the French convention who howled by the hour for the arrest of everyone. But Governor Letcher says: "Through the treachery of the guides, General Lee's plan for surprising Rosencrantz miscarried." I said: "I hope they hanged the guides!" "You hard-hearted, blood thirsty woman!" Custis Lee was present. He said simply: "I have heard nothing from my father."

[5]   I do not know when I have seen a woman without knitting in her hand. "Socks for the soldiers" is the cry. One poor man said he had dozens of socks and but one shirt. He preferred more shirts and fewer stockings. It gives a quaint look, the twinkling of needles, and the everlasting sock dangling. A Jury of Matrons, so to speak, sat at Mrs. Greenhow's. They say Mrs. Greenhow furnished Beauregard with the latest news of the Federal movements, and so made the Manassas victory a possibility. She sent us the enemy's plans. Everything she said proved true, numbers, route and all.

[6]   It is a despotism over there now, with Seward the despot; but our men say it enhances our chances three to one. David Power they outraged to the point of driving him in to us. They have arrested Wm. B. Reed and Miss Winder, she boldly proclaiming herself a secessionist. Why should she seek a martyr's crown? Writing people love notoriety. It is so delightful to be of enough consequence to be arrested. I have often wondered if such incense was ever offered as Napoleon's so-called persecution and alleged jealousy of Madame de Staël.

[7]   Today our assemblage of women, Confederate, talked pretty freely. Let us record some samples. "You people who have been stationed all over the United States and have been to Europe and all that; tell us

home-biding ones. Are our men worse than the others? Does Mrs. Stowe
know? You know what I mean?" "No, our men are no worse. Lady Mary
Montagu found we were all only men and women, everywhere. But Mrs.
Stowe's exceptional cases may be true. You can pick out horrors from
any criminal court record or newspaper in any country." "You see, irre-
sponsible men do pretty much as they please."

[8]   Russell now, to whom London and Paris and India were everyday
sights—and every night too, streets and all: for him to go on in indignation because there were women in Negro plantations who were not vestal
virgins! Negro women are married, and after marriage behave as well as
other people. Marrying is the amusement of their life. They take life
easily. So do their class everywhere. Bad men are hated here as elsewhere.

[9]   I hate slavery. You say there are no more fallen women on a plantation than in London, in proportion to numbers; but what do you say
to this? A magnate who runs a hideous black harem with its consequences under the same roof with his lovely white wife, and his beautiful
and accomplished daughters? He holds his head as high and poses as the
model of all human virtues to these poor women whom God and the laws
have given him. From the height of his awful majesty, he scolds and
thunders at them, as if he never did wrong in his life. Fancy such a man
finding his daughter reading "Don Juan." "You with that immoral
book!" And he orders her out of his sight. You see, Mrs. Stowe did not
hit the sorest spot. She makes Legree a bachelor.

[10]   Someone said: "Oh, I know half a Legree, a man said to be as cruel
as Legree. But the other half of him did not correspond. He was a man
of polished manners, and the best husband and father and church-
member in the world." "Can that be so?" "Yes, I know it. And I knew
the dissolute half of Legree. He was high and mighty, but the kindest
creature to his slaves; and the unfortunate results of his bad ways were
not sold. They had not to jump over ice blocks. They were kept in full
view, and were provided for, handsomely, in his will. His wife and
daughters, in their purity and innocence, are supposed never to dream
of what is as plain before their eyes as the sunlight. And they play their
parts of unsuspecting angels to the letter. They profess to adore their
father as the model of all earthly goodness."

[11]   "Well, yes. If he is rich, he is the fountain from whence all blessings
flow."

[12]   "The one I have in my eye, my half of Legree, the dissolute half,
was so furious in his temper, and so thundered his wrath at the poor
women that they were glad to let him do as he pleased if they could only
escape his everlasting fault-finding and noisy bluster."

[13]   "Now, now, do you know any woman of this generation who would
stand that sort of thing?"

[14]   "No, never, not for one moment. The make-believe angels were of
the last century. We know, and we won't have it. These are Old World
stories. Women were brought up not to judge their fathers or their husbands. They took them as the Lord provided, and were thankful."

[15]   "How about the wives of drunkards? I heard a woman say once, to

a friend, of her husband, as a cruel matter of fact without bitterness and without comment: 'Oh, you have not seen him. He is changed. He has not gone to bed sober in thirty years.' She has had her purgatory, if not what Mrs. _____ calls 'the other thing,' here in this world. We all know what a drunken man is. To think that for no crime a person may be condemned to live with one thirty years."

[16] "You wander from the question I asked. Are Southern men worse because of the slave system, and the facile black women?"

[17] "Not a bit! They see too much of them. The barroom people don't drink, the confectionary people loathe candy. Our men are sick of the black sight of them!"

[18] "You think a nice man from the South is the nicest thing in the world?" "I know it. Put him by any other man and see!" "And you say there are no saints and martyrs now; those good women who stand by bad husbands? Eh?" "No use to mince matters. Everybody knows the life of a woman whose husband drinks."

[19] "Some men have a hard time, too. I know women who are—well, the very devil and all his imps." "Ah, but men are dreadful animals." "Seems to me those of you who are hardest on men here are soft enough with them when they are present. Now everybody knows I am 'the friend of man' and I defend them behind their backs as I take pleasure in their society, well, before their faces."

[20] Our tongues went on. We heard that Mr. Mason* is going to be sent to England. My wildest imagination will not picture Mr. Mason as a diplomat. He will say 'chaw' for 'chew,' and he will call himself 'Jeems,' and he will wear a dress coat to breakfast. Over here, whatever a Mason does is right in his own eyes. He is above law. Somebody asked him how he pronounced his wife's maiden name. She was a Miss Chew from Philadelphia.

[21] "The finest and best of women! I don't care how he pronounces the nasty thing, but he will do it; I mean, chew tobacco. In England a man must expectorate like a gentleman, if he expectorates at all." "They say the English will like Mr. Mason; he is so manly, so straightforward, so truthful and bold. A fine old English gentleman—so said Russell—but for tobacco."

[22] And so on for hours.

words and sentences

1. Vocabulary: *purgatory* (¶ 15); *facile* (16); *expectorate* (21).

---

* James Mason, former United States Senator from Virginia, set out with John Slidell on a mission to England. They travelled on the British steamer Trent, and when she was stopped and searched by a Union vessel, Mason and Slidell were taken to Boston and imprisoned. The resulting diplomatic interchange brought England and the United States close to a severing of relations before the United States yielded.

ideas and implications

1. In this diary entry, does Mrs. Chesnut seem more or less introspective than Virginia Woolf or Emerson? Where does she find her material for composition? In the world inside herself or the world outside herself? Or both?
2. What is Mrs. Chesnut's attitude towards the young woman who cannot spell? What association does she make between social class and the ability to spell correctly?
3. Describe Mrs. Chesnut's attitude towards the North. How does she dramatize the intensity of her feeling?
4. What seems to be Mrs. Chesnut's attitude towards slavery? Why?
5. How do the Confederate ladies regard the role of women in society?

strategies

1. Paragraphs 7-19 record the conversation of the Confederate ladies. Does Mrs. Chesnut capture the random and wandering nature of most informal conversations? If so, how?
2. Paragraph 9 begins with, "I hate slavery." How does Mrs. Chesnut support this idea?

suggestions for writing

1. Begin a journal entry with, "I hate _____." Then develop that idea.
2. Write a journal entry in which you try to record a conversation you have taken part in.
3. Mrs. Chesnut draws a brief portrait of Captain Archer in her first paragraph; in your journal write a brief portrait of a person you have met in the last week or so.

Henry David Thoreau

from **The Journal**

March 5, 1838

[1] But what does all this scribbling amount to? What is now scribbled in the heat of the moment one can contemplate with somewhat of satisfaction, but alas! to-morrow—aye, to-night—it is stale, flat, and unprofitable,—in fine, is not, only its shell remains, like some red parboiled lobster-shell which, kicked aside never so often, still stares at you in the path.

[2]   What may a man do and not be ashamed of it? He may not do nothing surely, for straightway he is dubbed Dolittle—aye! christens himself first—and reasonably, for he was first to duck. But let him do something, is he the less a Dolittle? Is it actually something done, or not rather something undone; or, if done, is it not badly done, or at most well done comparatively?

[3]   Such is man,—toiling, heaving, struggling ant-like to shoulder some stray unappropriated crumb and deposit it in his granary; then runs out, complacent, gazes heavenward, earthward (for even pismires can look down, heaven and earth meanwhile looking downward, upward; there seen of men, world-seen, deed-delivered, vanishes into all-grasping night. And is he doomed ever to run the same course? Can he not, wriggling, screwing, self-exhorting, self-constraining, wriggle or screw out something that shall live,—respected, intact, intangible, not to be sneezed at?

January 5, 1842

[4]   I find that whatever hindrances may occur I write just about the same amount of truth in my Journal; for the record is more concentrated, and usually it is some very real and earnest life, after all, that interrupts. All flourishes are omitted. If I saw wood from morning to night, though I grieve that I could not observe the train of my thoughts during that time, yet, in the evening, the few scrannel lines which describe my day's occupations will make the creaking of the saw more musical than my freest fancies could have been. I find incessant labor with the hands, which engrosses the attention also, the best method to remove palaver out of one's style. One will not dance at his work who has wood to cut and cord before the night falls in the short days of winter; but every stroke will be husbanded, and ring soberly through the wood; and so will his lines ring and tell on the ear, when at evening he settles the accounts of the day. I have often been astonished at the force and precision of style to which busy laboring men, unpracticed in writing, easily attain when they are required to make the effort. It seems as if their sincerity and plainness were the main thing to be taught in schools,—and yet not in the schools, but in the fields, in actual service, I should say. The scholar not unfrequently envies the propriety and emphasis with which the farmer calls to his team, and confesses that if that lingo were written it would surpass his labored sentences.

[5]   Who is not tired of the weak and flowing periods of the politician and scholar, and resorts not even to the Farmer's Almanac, to read the simple account of the month's labor, to restore his tone again? I want to see a sentence run clear through to the end, as deep and fertile as a well-drawn furrow which shows that the plow was pressed down to the beam. If our scholars would lead more earnest lives, we should not witness those lame conclusions to their ill-sown discourses, but their sentences would pass over the ground like loaded rollers, and not mere hollow and wooden ones, to press in the seed and make it germinate.

[6]   A well-built sentence, in the rapidity and force with which it works, may be compared to a modern corn-planter, which furrows out, drops the seed, and covers it up at one movement.

[7]   The scholar requires hard labor as an impetus to his pen. He will learn to grasp it as firmly and wield it as gracefully and effectually as an axe or a sword. When I consider the labored periods of some gentleman scholar, who perchance in feet and inches comes up to the standard of his race, and is nowise deficient in girth, I am amazed at the immense sacrifice of thews and sinews. What! these proportions and these bones, and this their work! How these hands hewed this fragile matter, mere filagree or embroidery fit for ladies' fingers! Can this be a stalwart man's work, who has marrow in his backbone and a tendon Achilles in his heel? They who set up Stonehenge did somewhat,—much in comparison, —if it were only their strength was once fairly laid out, and they stretched themselves.

1845-1847

[8]   Exaggeration! was ever any virtue attributed to a man without exaggeration? was ever any vice, without infinite exaggeration? Do we not exaggerate ourselves to ourselves, or do we often recognize ourselves for the actual men we are? The lightning is an exaggeration of light. We live by exaggeration. Exaggerated history is poetry, and is truth referred to a new standard. To a small man every greater one is an exaggeration. No truth was ever expressed but with this sort of emphasis, so that for the time there was no other truth. The value of what is really valuable can never be exaggerated. You must speak loud to those who are hard of hearing; so you acquire a habit of speaking loud to those who are not. In order to appreciate any, even the humblest, man, you must not only understand, but you must first love him; and there never was such an exaggerator as love. Who are we? Are we not all of us great men? And yet what are we actually? Nothing, certainly, to speak of. By an immense exaggeration we appreciate our Greek poetry and philosophy, Egyptian ruins, our Shakespeares and Miltons, our liberty and Christianity. We give importance to this hour over all other hours. We do not live by justice, but by grace.

words and sentences

1. Vocabulary: *intangible* (¶ 3); *incessant, palaver* (4); *germinate* (5).
2. Describe the pattern of the second sentence in ¶ 5; then write a sentence imitating this pattern. Note the comparison Thoreau uses.
3. Describe the pattern of the single sentence in ¶ 6; then write a sentence imitating the pattern. Again, note Thoreau's use of analogy.

ideas and implications

1. Thoreau was twenty years old when he wrote the March 5, 1838, entry.

Describe his state of mind in this entry and compare that state of mind with his attitude in the January 5, 1842 entry.
2. What association does Thoreau make between physical labor and writing? Why?
3. What does Thoreau mean by "earnest lives" (¶ 5)?
4. Why does Thoreau say, "We live by exaggeration" (¶ 8)? What are the implications of this statement?

strategies

1. One strategy Thoreau uses in the January 5, 1842, entry is to compare and contrast. Point to some details which help Thoreau develop his notions on style.

suggestions for writing

1. Write a journal entry defining a word like "exaggeration." Again, do not act as censor; let your thoughts go.
2. In your journal, write a half dozen sentences in which you use a metaphor, simile, or comparison, to convey your idea.

Joan Didion

from On Keeping a Notebook

[1]   *How it felt to me:* that is getting closer to the truth about a notebook. I sometimes delude myself about why I keep a notebook, imagine that some thrifty virtue derives from preserving everything observed. See enough and write it down, I tell myself, and then some morning when the world seems drained of wonder, some day when I am only going through the motions of doing what I am supposed to do, which is write—on that bankrupt morning I will simply open my notebook and there it will all be, a forgotten account with accumulated interest, paid passage back to the world out there: dialogue overhead in hotels and elevators and at the hat-check counter in Pavillon (one middle-aged man shows his hat check to another and says, "That's my old football number"); impressions of Bettina Aptheker and Benjamin Sonnenberg and Teddy ("Mr. Acapulco") Stauffer; careful *aperçus* about tennis bums and failed fashion models and Greek shipping heiresses, one of whom taught me a significant lesson (a lesson I could have learned from F. Scott Fitzgerald, but perhaps we all must meet the very rich for ourselves) by

asking, when I arrived to interview her in her orchid-filled sitting room on the second day of a paralyzing New York blizzard, whether it was snowing outside.

[2]   I imagine, in other words, that the notebook is about other people. But of course it is not. I have no real business with what one stranger said to another at the hat-check counter in Pavillon; in fact I suspect that the line "That's my old football number" touched not my own imagination at all, but merely some memory of something once read, probably "The Eighty-Yard Run." Nor is my concern with a woman in a dirty crepe-de-Chine wrapper in a Wilmington bar. My stake is always, of course, in the unmentioned girl in the plaid silk dress. *Remember what it was to be me:* that is always the point. . . .

[3]   It is a good idea, then, to keep in touch, and I suppose that keeping in touch is what notebooks are all about. And we are all on our own when it comes to keeping those lines open to ourselves: your notebook will never help me, nor mine you. *"So what's new in the whiskey business?"* What could that possibly mean to you? To me it means a blonde in a Pucci bathing suit sitting with a couple of fat men by the pool at the Beverly Hills Hotel. Another man approaches, and they all regard one another in silence for a while. "So what's new in the whiskey business?" one of the fat men finally says by way of welcome, and the blonde stands up, arches one foot and dips it in the pool, looking all the while at the cabaña where Baby Pignatari is talking on the telephone. That is all there is to that, except that several years later I saw the blonde coming out of Saks Fifth Avenue in New York with her California complexion and a voluminous mink coat. In the harsh wind that day she looked old and irrevocably tired to me, and even the skins in the mink coat were not worked the way they were doing them that year, not the way she would have wanted them done, and there is the point of the story. For a while after that I did not like to look in the mirror, and my eyes would skim the newspapers and pick out only the deaths, the cancer victims, the premature coronaries, the suicides, and I stopped riding the Lexington Avenue IRT because I noticed for the first time that all the strangers I had seen for years—the man with the seeing-eye dog, the spinster who read the classified pages every day, the fat girl who always got off with me at Grand Central—looked older than they once had.

[4]   It all comes back. Even that recipe for sauerkraut: even that brings it back. I was on Fire Island when I first made that sauerkraut, and it was raining, and we drank a lot of bourbon and ate the sauerkraut and went to bed at ten, and I listened to the rain and the Atlantic and felt safe. I made the sauerkraut again last night and it did not make me feel any safer, but that is, as they say, another story.

words and sentences

1. Vocabulary: *voluminous, irrevocably* (¶ 3).
2. How does Joan Didion carry the reader from the first to the second paragraph? What kind of transition does she use?

92 THE WRITER AS SEE-ER AND THINKER

ideas and implications

1. Compare and contrast Joan Didion's attitude towards her notebook with those of Virginia Woolf, Emerson, Thoreau, and Mrs. Chesnut.
2. If a notebook is not about other people, why does Joan Didion observe and comment on people in her notebook?
3. With whom is Joan Didion really trying to keep in touch?
4. Does the last sentence in ¶ 4 in any way contradict Joan Didion's first two sentences in ¶ 1? Or does the final sentence suggest another function of notebook keeping?

strategies

1. What rhetorical strategy does Joan Didion use when she opens her last paragraph with, "It all comes back"?

suggestions for writing

1. Write in your journal an entry in which a half-remembered phrase or half-understood remark serves as a key to a person's character.
2. Find an advertisement which pictures several characters and write in your journal your observations—at random—about these characters. Then take your journal entries and from them shape a paper about the people pictured in the advertisement.

Robert Frost

The Secret Sits

We dance round in a ring and suppose,
But the Secret sits in the middle and knows.

From *The Poetry of Robert Frost,* ed. Edward Connery Lathem. Copyright 1942 by Robert Frost. © 1969 by Holt, Rinehart and Winston, Inc. © 1970 by Lesley Frost Ballatine. Reprinted by permission of the publisher.

John Keats

On First Looking into Chapman's Homer

Much have I travell'd in the realms of gold,
  And many goodly states and kingdoms seen;
  Round many western islands have I been
Which bards in fealty to Apollo hold.
Oft of one wide expanse had I been told   5
  That deep-brow'd Homer ruled as his demesne:
  Yet did I never breathe its pure serene
Till I heard Chapman speak out loud and bold:
Then felt I like some watcher of the skies
  When a new planet swims into his ken;   10
Or like stout Cortez when with eagle eyes
  He star'd at the Pacific—and all his men
Look'd at each other with a wild surmise—
  Silent, upon a peak in Darien.

words and sentences

1. Vocabulary in Keats: *fealty* (line 4); *ken* (l. 10); *surmise* (l. 13).
2. Describe the structure of the verse sentence in Frost's poem; then write a verse sentence imitating Frost's pattern.
3. How many verse sentences are there in Keats's poem? Write the first sentence of Keats's poem in its normal English word order (subject, verb, object). Does changing the order of the words of this verse sentence affect the meaning of these lines? How?

ideas and implications

1. Can you draw a pencil sketch of Frost's poem? Why or why not?
2. In Frost's poem, why does the *secret* "sit" and the *we* "dance"? What idea is Frost exploring here? Is the theme of Frost's poem in any way related to Scudder's experience with the fish?
3. In what way is Keats's poem about discovery? Cite specific examples to support your observation. What is the theme of Keats's poem?

strategies

1. What is the form of Frost's poem? Of Keats's?
2. Do these forms in any way confine the writers "to a most limited field"? In what way or ways, if any?
3. Frost's strategy depends, to some extent, upon a contrast. What word signals this contrast?
4. Why does Keats begin his poem with a statement about "travelling"?
5. Beginning with "Then felt I," Keats employs similes to explain his

response to Chapman's translation of Homer. Are these figures consistent with the figures he introduces at the beginning of the poem? Does the strategy of the last six lines seem to be appropriate to the theme Keats is conveying?

suggestions for writing

1. Write a paper describing a situation in which you felt you were *supposing* instead of *knowing*. Explain why you felt as you did.
2. Write a paper explaining a discovery you yourself made and the feeling you had upon making this discovery.
3. Take a photograph or a painting that you have seen many times and examine it carefully to see if you can discover something in it that went unnoticed before. Then write a paper about your discovery. Attach a copy of the photo or painting to your paper.

Richard D. Altick

Denotation and Connotation

[1]   Incidents like this are happening every day. A teacher in a college English course has returned a student's theme on the subject of a poem. One sentence in the theme reads, "Like all of Keats's best work, the 'Ode to Autumnn' has a sensual quality that makes it especially appealing to me." The instructor's red pencil has underscored the word *sensual*, and in the margin he has written "Accurate?" or whatever his customary comment is in such cases. The student has checked the dictionary and comes back puzzled. "I don't see what you mean," he says. "The dictionary says *sensual* means 'of or pertaining to the senses or physical sensation.' And that's what I wanted to say. Keats's poem is filled with words and images that suggest physical sensation."

[2]   "Yes," replies the instructor, "that's what the word *means*—according to the dictionary." And then he takes his copy of the *American College Dictionary,* which contains the definition the student quoted, and turns to the word *sensual.* "Look here," he says, pointing to a passage in small type just after the various definitions of the word:

> SENSUAL, SENSUOUS, VOLUPTUOUS refer to experience through the senses. SENSUAL refers, usually unfavorably, to the enjoyments derived from the senses, generally implying grossness or lewdness: *a sensual delight in eat-*

ing, sensual excesses. Sensuous refers, favorably or literally, to what is experienced through the senses: *sensuous impressions, sensuous poetry.* Voluptuous implies the luxurious gratification of sensuous or sensual desires: *voluptuous joys, voluptuous beauty.*[1]

[3]   The student reads the passage carefully and begins to see light. The word *sensual* carries with it a shade of meaning, an unfavorable implication, which he did not intend; the word he wanted was *sensuous.* He has had a useful lesson in the dangers of taking dictionary definitions uncritically, as well as in the vital difference between denotation and connotation.

[4]   The difference between the two is succinctly phrased in another of those small-type paragraphs of explanation, taken this time from *Webster's New Collegiate Dictionary:*

> *Denote* implies all that strictly belongs to the definition of the word, *connote* all of the ideas that are suggested by the term; thus, "home" *denotes* the place where one lives with one's family, but it usually *conntoes* comfort, intimacy, and privacy. The same implications distinguish *denotation* and *connotation.*[2]

The denotation of a word is its dictionary definition, which is what the word "stands for." According to the dictionary, *sensuous* and *sensual* have the same general denotation: they agree in meaning "experience through the senses." Yet they *suggest* different things. And that difference in suggestion constitutes a difference in connotation.

[5]   For another elementary example, take the word *tabloid,* the denotation of which refers to small size. For that reason, newspapers with pages that are half as large as regular ones and which specialize in very brief news articles are regularly called tabloids. But because the average tabloid newspaper emphasizes the racy and the bizarre in its attempt to appeal to a certain class of readers, the word's connotation introduces the idea of sensationalism, of "yellow journalism." Thus *tabloid,* not surprisingly, is applied to newspapers in a negative, or pejorative, sense. In such a fashion many words acquire additional meanings which are derived from common experience and usage. (Similarly, the term *prima donna* refers, strictly speaking, to the leading woman in an opera company. By what process has it come to be applied to a certain kind of man or woman, with no reference to opera?)

[6]   Nothing is more essential to intelligent, profitable reading than sensitivity to connotation. Only when we possess such sensitivity can we understand both what the author *means,* which may be quite plain, and what he wants to *suggest,* which may actually be far more important than the superficial meaning. The difference between reading a book, a story, an essay, or a poem for surface meaning and reading it for implication is the difference between listening to the New York Philharmonic Symphony Orchestra on a battered old transistor radio and listening to it on

1 *The American College Dictionary* (New York: Random House, Inc., 1947).
2 *Webster's New Collegiate Dictionary* (Springfield, Mass.: G. & C. Merriam Co., 1953).

a high-fidelity stereophonic record player. Only the latter brings out the nuances that are often more significant than the obvious, and therefore easily comprehended, meaning.

[7]   An unfailing awareness of the connotative power of words is just as vital, of course, to the writer. His ceaseless task is to select the word which will convey exactly what he wants to say. The practiced writer, like the practiced reader, derives his skill from his awareness that though many words may have substantially the same denotation, few are exactly synonymous in connotation. The inexperienced writer, forgetting this, often has recourse to a book like Roget's *Thesaurus,* where he finds, conveniently assembled, whole regiments of synonyms; not knowing which to choose, he either closes his eyes and picks a word at random or else chooses the one that "sounds" best. In either case he is neglecting the delicate shading in implication and applicability which differentiate each word in a category from its neighbors. Wishing to refer to the familiar terse expressions of wisdom in the Bible, for example, he has a number of roughly synonymous words at his disposal: *maxim, aphorism, apothegm, dictum, adage, proverb, epigram, saw, byword, motto,* among others. But if he chooses *saw* or *epigram* he chooses wrongly; for neither of these words is suitable to designate biblical quotations. (Why?) The way to avoid the all too frequent mistake of picking the wrong word from a list is to refer to those invaluable paragraphs in the dictionary which discriminate among the various words in a closely related group. (If the definition of the word in question is not followed by such a paragraph, there usually is a cross reference to the place where the differentiation is made.) For further help, consult the fuller discussions, illustrated by examples quoted from good writers, in *Webster's Dictionary of Synonyms.* But cheap pocket and desk dictionaries should always be avoided in any work involving word choice. They are frequently misleading because they oversimplify entries which are already reduced to a minimum in the larger, more authoritative dictionaries.

[8]   What has been said so far does not mean that the conscientious reader or writer is required to take up every single word and examine it for implications and subsurface meanings. Many words—articles, conjunctions, prepositions, and some adverbs—have no connotative powers, because they do not represent ideas but are used to connect ideas or to show some other relationship between them. Still other words, such as (usually) polysyllabled scientific or technical terms, have few if any connotations; that is, they call forth no vivid pictures, no emotional responses. *Psychomotor* and *cardiovascular* are neutral words in this sense; so are *acetylsalicylic acid* (aspirin) and *crustacean* (shellfish). The single word *eschatology* is colorless compared with the words for its chief concerns: *heaven, hell, death, judgment.* The fact remains, however, that most words which stand for ideas have some connotation, however limited, simply because ideas themselves have connotations. Some technical words, especially when they affect our daily lives, take on more and more connotation as they become familiar: *intravenous, angina pectoris, anxiety neurosis,* for example.

Connotations: Personal and General

[9]   There are two types of connotation: personal and general. Personal connotations result from our individual experience. The way we react to ideas and objects, and thus to the words that refer to them (this is why the ideas are often called "referents"), is determined by the precise nature of our earlier experience with these referents. Taken all together, the connotations that surround most of the words in our vocabulary are, though we may not recognize the fact, a complex and intimate record of our life. Our present reaction to a word may be the cumulative result of all our experiences with the word and its referent. In the case of another word, our reaction may have been determined once and for all by an early or a particularly memorable experience with it. A student's reaction to the word *teacher*, for instance, may be determined by all his experience with teachers, which has been subtly synthesized, in the course of time, into a single image or emotional response. In it are mingled memories of Miss Smith, the first-grade teacher who dried his tears when he lost a fight in the schoolyard at recess; of Miss Jones, the sixth-grade teacher who bored her pupils with thrice-told tales of her trip to Mexico ten years earlier; of Mr. Johnson, the high-school gym teacher who merely laughed when he saw the angry red brush burns a boy sustained when he inexpertly slid down a rope; of Mr. Miller, the college professor who somehow packed a tremendous amount of information into lectures that seemed too entertaining to be instructive. Or, on the other hand, when the student thinks of *teacher* he may think of a particular teacher who for one reason or another has made an especially deep impression upon him—such a person as the chemistry teacher in high school who encouraged him, by example and advice, to make chemistry his life work.

[10]   A moment's thought will show the relationship between personal and general connotations as well as the fact that there is no firm line of demarcation between the two types. Since "the mass mind" is the sum total of the individual minds that comprise it, general connotations result when the reaction of the great majority of people to a specific word is substantially the same. The reasons why one word should possess a certain connotation, while another word has a quite different connotation, are complex. We shall spend a little time on the subject later. Here it need only be said that differences in general connotation derive from at least two major sources. For one thing, the exact shade of meaning a word possesses in our language is often due to the use to which it was put by a writer who had especially great influence over the language because he was, and in some cases is, so widely read. The King James version of the Bible, for instance, is responsible for the crystallizing of many connotations. People came to know a given word from its occurrence in certain passages in the Bible, and thus the word came to connote to them on *all* occasions what it connoted in those familiar passages; it was permanently colored by particular associations. Such words include *trespass, money changers, manger, Samaritan* (originally the name of a person

living in a certain region of Asia Minor), *salvation, vanity, righteous, anoint,* and *charity.* The same is true of many words used in other books which, being widely read and studied, influenced the vocabularies of following generations—Shakespeare's plays, or *Paradise Lost,* or the essays of Addison and Steele.

[11]   But general connotation is not always a matter of literary development. It can result also from the experience that men as a social group have had with the ideas which words represent. Before 1938, the word *appease* had an inoffensive connotation. In the edition of *Webster's Collegiate Dictionary* current in that year it was defined simply as "to pacify, often by satisfying; quiet; calm; soothe; allay." But then the word became associated with the ill-fated attempts of Neville Chamberlain to stave off war with Hitler by giving in to his demands, and that association has now strongly colored its meaning. The latest edition of the same dictionary adds to the meaning quoted above this newer one: "to conciliate by political, economic, or other considerations;—now usually signifying a sacrifice of moral principle in order to avert aggression." Laden as the word is with its suggestions of the disaster of Munich, no British or American official ever uses it in referring to a conciliating move in foreign policy for which he wants to win public acceptance. On the other hand, opponents of that move use the word freely to arouse sentiment against it, even though the situation in question may have little or no resemblance to that of Munich. In other words, events have conditioned us to react in a particular way to the verb *appease* and the noun *appeasement.* If our support is desired for a policy of *give and take, live and let live, or peaceful coexistence* in international relations, its advocates will use the terms just italicized, as well as *negotiation* and *compromise,* which convey the idea of mutual concessions without sacrifice of principle; or *horse trading,* which has a homely American flavor, suggesting shrewd bargaining with the additional implication that a good profit can be made on the deal.

[12]   All general connotations thus have their origin in private connotations—in personal, individual, but generally shared reactions to words and the ideas for which they stand. But later, after general connotations have been established, the process works the other way: the individual, who may have had no personal experience with the idea represented by a given word, may acquire a personal attitude toward it by observing how society in general reacts to the word. In the future, men and women who were not yet born when Winston Churchill was delivering his famous Second World War speeches in Britain, or when Adolf Hitler was presiding over mass executions of the Jews, supposedly will continue to react admiringly or with revulsion to their names. In addition, some words pass into and then out of connotative "atmospheres." The word *quisling* probably inspires no feeling whatever in today's student, yet not too long ago it was synonymous with *traitor.* Yet the much older name of Benedict Arnold still serves the same purpose.

[13]   Every writer must cultivate his awareness of the distinction between general connotations and personal ones. It is the general ones—those he

can be reasonably sure his readers share with him—on which he must rely to convey the accurate spirit of his message. If he uses words for the sake of the additional connotations they have to him alone, he runs the risk of writing in a private shorthand to which he alone holds the key. Since there is no clear dividing line between general and personal connotations, it would, of course, be unrealistic to require that a writer absolutely confine himself to the former. Moreover, some of the subtle richness of poetry, and to some degree of imaginative prose, is derived (assuming that the reader discovers the secret) from the author's use of words in private senses. But in most forms of practical communication, the writer does well to confine himself to words whose connotations, he has reason to assume, are approximately the same to his readers as they are to him.

The Uses of Connotations

[14] What forms do our reactions to words take? As we have observed, by no means do all words evoke any distinguishable emotional response; *delusion* and *illusion,* for instance, probably do not do so for most people. Here the response is largely an intellectual one, a recognition that the two words are customarily used in different contexts, that they imply slightly different things.

[15] But for our purposes the most important words are those which appeal to the emotions, words which stir people to strong (but not always rational) judgment and may arouse them to action. Mention of *militarist* or *atheist* or *capitalist* or *communist* evokes deep-seated prejudice, for or against the ideas or ideologies behind the words, for or against the people who are called by those names. The adjectives *atomic* and *nuclear,* until 1945 purely technical terms in physics, have since acquired a variety of connotations—on the one hand, of unspeakable capacity for destruction (think how often the words are linked with and therefore colored by such nouns as *annihilation* and *holocaust*), and, on the other hand, of a certain measure of hope for human progress through medical applications and increased industrial efficiency.

[16] Many words lose much of their clear connotation, and in some instances much of their evocative power, through indiscriminate application. The word *bohemian* has been so overused that now it hazily covers nearly any form of untidy existence, as long as the "bohemians" in question are not genuinely poor and are living in unkempt quarters because they choose to do so. The term now has only vague connections, which once were much stronger, with the artist's life. For the same reason *streamlined* has lost its once-pleasant connotation; no advertising man would now consider using the word to describe the latest Pontiac model. *Streamlined* now suggests instead a slapdash glossing over or cutting corners (as in *streamlined* business operation or educational curriculum), because the word has so often been loosely applied in such contexts. A few years ago *space age,* which became current when the Russians orbited their first sputnik, contained the awe appropriate to a development which soon thereafter witnessed man himself voyaging into the cosmos. But

within a decade of its introduction *space age* was being applied to such mundane trivia as cosmetics, with the inevitable result that its initial power was entirely lost. It became merely another too-handy, threadbare word in the vocabulary of advertising and journalism.

[17]   Often the connotative power of a word is dependent on circumstances: who uses it, who is intended to read or hear it, and where. The connotations of the adjectives *hot* and *cool*, as slang terms, differ with the age of the user. *Debutante* means one thing to a New York society girl, who is actually going to have a costly debut, and another to the girl on an Iowa farm who buys *sub-deb* clothing from a mail order catalogue. *Nigger* connotes very different things to a diehard Mississippi segregationist and a member of the National Association for the Advancement of Colored People. *Draft, selective service,* and *conscription* mean the same thing, but one of these is never used in the United States, and of the remaining two, one has a more unpleasant connotation than the other. Both are widely used; who is likely to use which?

[18]   Intimately associated with emotional response, and often directly responsible for it, are the images that many words inspire in our minds. The commonest type of image is the visual: that is, a given word habitually calls forth a certain picture on the screen of our inner consciousness. Mention of places we have seen and people we have known produces a visual recollection of them. Of course the precise content of these pictures is determined by the sort of experience one has had with their originals. *Mary* may not recall the picture of one's childhood sweetheart, but it may evoke instead a picture of a pink hair ribbon which Mary must once have worn. *Boston* may recall only the picture of a street accident, which was the most vivid memory one carried away from that city. It is a fascinating game to examine in this fashion the mental images thus spontaneously conjured up by words. Equally rewarding is the effort to explain why many words evoke images which on first thought seem so completely irrelevant to their denotations.

[19]   It is not only words referring to concrete objects that have this power of evoking imaginative responses. Our picture-making faculty also enables us to visualize abstractions in concrete terms—and, as we shall see, it sometimes gets us into trouble on that account. Abstractions have little meaning unless we can concretize them in mental images; but we must take care not to allow abstractions, thus visualized, to become distorted by preconceptions or ingrained prejudices, which are inculcated emotionally rather than learned from our own experience. *Dictator* denotes a person who has absolute authority in any state; it does not necessarily mean that he is a tyrannical megalomaniac. But the most memorable dictators of history—Napoleon, Mussolini, Hitler—have also been ambitious egotists and demagogues. And so our understanding of the abstract word *dictator* is colored by a composite picture of the most flamboyant of the past's dictators: we perhaps envision a gesturing, ranting military figure, mesmerizing the crowd with four-hour-long appeals to national pride and hatred of enemies, watching with puffed-up chest an interminable military review complete with exaggerated parade step and fear-

some weapons of war flashing in the sun. The truth is that dictators from Caesar to Franco, in fact the great majority, have been far less colorful men than those mentioned. And in any case, personal flamboyance is not nearly as significant as a dictator's substantive actions. Our mental image of the dictator, then, is composed of what really amounts only to irrelevant window dressing. The word *dictator* serves to pull out many emotional stops in our minds; and emotion clouds any reasonable response we might be able to make to the idea. Therein lies the danger of connotation.

[20]   A further example: The picture that the word *artist* almost automatically calls forth in the imagination is of a pale, gaunt figure laboring fruitlessly in skylighted garret, scornful and defiant of a philistine society. His hands are long, sensitive looking (and bedaubed with paint), his eyes hollow, a little wild; his hair long and innocent of comb and brush. We envision him dying young through self-neglect, dissipation, and disappointment—the world has failed to recognize his genius. Such an image of "the artist" obviously is not fair; it may apply to a few individual specimens, but hardly to the profession of artists as a whole. It is a stereotype, a stock response cultivated in our minds by countless books, poems, and pictures: by the opera *La Bohéme*, by what is told of the "decadent" figures in the England of the 1890s and the Greenwich Villagers of our own century.

[21]   Out of similar materials, a fortuitous mixture of the truly typical with a great deal that is not typical but exceptional, are made the stereotypes which usually govern our idea of nationalities, races, parties, professions—in fact, of all kinds of groups—and our attitudes toward them.

[22]   In addition to visual responses in the imagination, words evoke responses associated with the other senses. Many have connotations that appeal most directly to our inward ear: *tick-tock, be-bop, slap, whir, squeak, splash, trumpet, dirge, shrill, thunder, shriek, croon, lisp, boom.* Others appeal to our sense of touch: *greasy, gritty, woolly, slick, silky, nettle, ice-cold, hairy, furry.* Another class invites palatal responses— *peppery, creamy, mellow, sugary, olive oil, menthol, salty, bitter.* Another brings olfactory responses, as in *burning rubber, incense, new-mown grass, pine forest, rancid, coffee roaster, ammonia, stench, diesel fumes, coal smoke.* Many words, of course, appeal to two or more senses at once; in addition to some of the above (which ones?) there are, for instance, *dry, effervescent, satin, lather, plastic, mossy, winy, slimy, wrinkle, sewage, frothy, sea breeze, misty, cigar.*

[23]   Because our sensory experience may be either pleasant or unpleasant, the words that evoke their imaginative equivalents have the power to sway us to accept or reject an idea. "So soft, yet manageable . . . so sweetly clean! Come-hither loveliness—that's what your hair has after a luxurious Prell shampoo! It's caressably soft, yet so *obedient!* Yes, angel-soft, smooth as satin, glowing with that 'Radiantly Alive' look *he'll* love!" Thus exclaims the advertising man who wants millions of women to buy a certain preparation for washing their hair. Or: "It's a

foul, evil-smelling mess!" says a minority-party congressman who is dissatisfied with something the administration has done.

[24] In some of the following pages, we shall concentrate upon this persuasive power of words, especially as found in advertising and political discussion. There is perhaps no simpler or better way of showing how connotation works. But this preliminary emphasis on the ways in which language may be manipulated for selfish purposes must not lead to the assumption that all, or even most, writers have wicked designs on their readers. On the contrary, the greater part of what people read has the sole purpose of informing or entertaining them—of giving them new knowledge, or fresh food for the imagination and the emotions. And here connotative language is used simply to heighten the effectiveness, the accuracy, and the vividness of the writer's communication.

[25] Take the best of today's journalism—not routine newspaper reporting, but, say, feature stories and magazine articles. Really good descriptive journalism requires a high degree of skill in the use of words; and the more skillfully and attentively we read what the author has set down, the greater will be our pleasure. Examine the sure sense of connotative values employed in this description of a Pennsylvania industrial town:

> Donora is twenty-eight miles south of Pittsburgh and covers the tip of a lumpy point formed by the most convulsive of the Monongahela's many horseshoe bends. Though accessible by road, rail, and river, it is an extraordinarily secluded place. The river and the bluffs that lift abruptly from the water's edge to a height of four hundred and fifty feet enclose it on the north and east and south, and just above it to the west is a range of rolling but even higher hills. On its outskirts are acres of sidings and rusting gondolas, abandoned mines, smoldering slag piles, and gulches filled with rubbish. Its limits are marked by sooty signs that read, "Donora. Next to Yours the Best Town in the U.S.A." It is a harsh, gritty town, founded in 1901 and old for its age, with a gaudy main street and a thousand identical gaunt gray houses. Some of its streets are paved with concrete and some are cobbled, but many are of dirt and crushed coal. At least half of them are as steep as roofs, and several have steps instead of sidewalks. It is treeless and all but grassless, and much of it is slowly sliding downhill. After a rain, it is a smear of mud. Its vacant lots and many of its yards are mortally gullied, and one of its three cemeteries is an eroded ruin of gravelly clay and toppled tombstones. Its population is 12,300.[3]

Here, in carefully chosen everyday words, the reporter has produced a graphic impression of a dismal community. He was clearly depressed by what he saw—a feeling he means us to have, too. And, were we to read on past the passage quoted, we would discover that even the seemingly casual reference to the population and the cemeteries is part of his plan; for the article as a whole is about the poison-laden smog that descended on Donora some years ago and killed at least a score of its inhabitants. The quoted passage, with its single-minded stress on language suggestive

3 Berton Roueché, "The Fog," *The New Yorker*, Sept. 30, 1950.

of griminess, ugliness, deterioration, prepares us for the disaster to come.
[26] In the same way, but on a less ephemeral plane of interest, with
more exalted purpose and greater intensity of feeling, poets too utilize
the connotative potentialities of language. They employ words lovingly,
unschemingly, wishing to delight and move the reader through an im-
parting of their own vivid experience:

> Here, where the reaper was at work of late—
>   In this high field's dark corner, where he leaves
>   His coat, his basket, and his earthen cruse,
>   And in the sun all morning binds the sheaves,
>   Then here, at noon, comes back his stores to use—
>   Here will I sit and wait,
>   While to my ear from uplands far away
>   The bleating of the folded flocks is borne,
>   With distant cries of reapers in the corn—
> All the live murmur of a summer's day.
>
> Screen'd is this nook o'er the high, half-reap'd field,
>   And here till sun-down, shepherd! will I be.
>   Through the thick corn the scarlet poppies peep
>   And round green roots and yellowing stalks I see
>   Pale blue convolvulus in tendrils creep;
>   And air-swept lindens yield
>   Their scent, and rustle down their perfumed showers
>   Of bloom on the bent grass where I am laid,
>   And bower me from the August sun with shade;
> And the eye travels down to Oxford's towers.

Or:

> It is a beauteous evening, calm and free,
> The holy time is quiet as a Nun
> Breathless with adoration; the broad sun
> Is sinking down in its tranquillity;
> The gentleness of heaven broods o'er the Sea:
> Listen! the mighty Being is awake,
> And doth with his eternal motion make
> A sound like thunder—everlastingly.

words and sentences

1. Check the definition of the word *context* again.
2. Vocabulary: *succinctly* (¶ 4); *pejorative* (5); *superficial* (6); *cumulative*
   (9); *evocative, mundane* (16); *conjured* (18); *preconceptions, inculcated, megalomaniac, demagogue, flamboyant, mesmerizing, substantive* (19); *philistine, dissipation* (20); *fortuitous* (21).

3. Describe the structure of the first sentence in ¶ 6; then rearrange the words in the sentence to see if you can improve on Altick's pattern. Is Altick's sentence a loose sentence or a periodic sentence?

4. Describe the pattern of the third sentence in ¶ 6; then write a sentence imitating that pattern. How effective is the analogy in this sentence?

5. If you have never examined Roget's *Thesaurus* (¶ 7), find a copy in the library and spend a few minutes examining this book.

6. Describe sentences four and six of ¶ 7. Then write sentences of your own imitating these patterns. Comment on the functions of the semicolon and the colon in these two sentences.

7. Describe the structure of the first sentence in ¶ 9. Is this sentence a topic sentence? Does the colon function in this sentence as it does in sentence six of ¶ 7? Does Altick use the colon frequently or infrequently in his essay?

8. Sentence one in ¶ 11 begins with a coordinating conjunction. Why? Is using a coordinating conjunction at the beginning of a sentence "incorrect"? What is the topic idea of ¶ 11? Is it expressed in a single sentence?

9. Describe the structure of the first sentence in ¶ 23. Is the sentence simple, compound, complex, compound-complex? Is it a periodic or a loose sentence? Is it a declarative, imperative, exclamatory, or interrogative sentence? Write a sentence of your own imitating Altick's pattern.

ideas and implications

1. Why does Altick say that sensitivity to connotation is important to intelligent reading and writing?

2. What words, according to Altick, have little or no connotative power? Can you think of any exceptions to Altick's observations?

3. What are the bases for Altick's distinction between general and personal connotations? List these distinctions and provide three of your own examples of the differences between the two.

4. What advice does Altick offer writers about the use of personal and general connotations?

5. What is Altick's attitude towards journalism and advertising? Why?

6. According to Altick, what accounts for our emotional responses to words? Cite specific sentences to support your answer.

7. How important is man's picture-making faculty in determining the connotative meaning of words? Does Altick believe that making abstractions as concrete as possible is valuable? Why or why not?

8. What role does Altick assign to the senses in determining connotative associations with words? Cite specific passages from the essay to support your answer.

9. What is Altick's attitude towards stereotypes? Cite specific sentences or paragraphs to support your answer. Then examine ¶ 17 again. Does Altick use any stereotypes in this paragraph?

10. What is Altick's attitude towards dictionaries and dictionaries of synonyms? Why does he hold this view?

strategies

1. Why does Altick divide his essay (really part of the first chapter of a book) into three sections? How much do his headings help a reader see his plan of organization? Does he allow his headings to substitute for thesis statements in each section, or does he state the thesis of each seciton clearly within the body of his text?
2. What is the function of ¶s 1-3? How would you describe Altick's opening strategy?
3. Point to the transition between ¶s 3 and 4. How does Altick link the material of ¶s 1-3 with that of ¶4 and the ensuing paragraphs of the first section?
4. In ¶ 4, does Altick define *connotation* and *denotation* more than one time?
5. What is the function of ¶ 8? How does this paragraph help forward Altick's ideas about connotation and denotation?
6. Is the first section (¶s 1-8) of Altick's essay devoted to definition? What strategies does Altick employ in his discussion of connotation and denotation? Only definition?
7. What is the thesis idea that Altick pursues in ¶s 9-13? Could you make a sentence outline of this section of the essay?
8. Make a list of the strategies Altick employs in ¶s 9-13. Does he give examples, define, compare and contrast, classify, illustrate process? Is more than one method of development present in each of his paragraphs?
9. What strategy does Altick use at the beginning of his third section (¶ 14)? What is he obligated to do in the ensuing paragraphs? Does he do what he promises in ¶ 14?
10. What is the function of ¶ 22? What is Altick's strategy here?
11. Look back through ¶s 14-26 to see what transitional devices Altick has used to link his paragraphs. Is there any variety in the transitional devices he uses?

suggestions for writing

1. In ¶ 25, Altick quotes at length Berton Roueché's observations about Donora, Pa. Rewrite this paragraph carefully, trying to alter the impression of the town. Keep as close as you can to the structure of Roueché's sentences, but change the language of the paragraph to produce another impression of the place.
2. In ¶ 18, Altick notes:

> *Boston* may recall only the picture of a street accident, which was the most vivid memory one carried away from that city. It is a fascinating game to examine in this fashion the mental images thus spontaneously conjured up by words. Equally rewarding is the effort to

explain why many words evoke images which on first thought seem so completely irrelevant to their denotations.

Select two or three names of places or people and jot down the images that come spontaneously to mind about them. Then write a paper in which you explain why these images are associated with a specific place or person.

3. Read the opening lines of Marc Antony's funeral oration in William Shakespeare's *Julius Caesar*, Act III, scene ii. Examine the language of the speech for connotative values of words to see how context changes meaning within the space of a few lines. Write a paper about what you discover.

Ross Campbell

Poetic Eclipse of the Moon

[1]   The moon journey of Apollo-10, while a great technical feat, was disappointing on its verbal side. The three brave officers who made the trip appeared to have a very limited command of language. Their inflight comments consisted of exclamations like: "Man, this is the greatest, Charlie!" "Babe, it's fantastic!" and "Boy, you wouldn't believe this thing!"

[2]   At critical moments they tended to lapse into a special space grammar. This occurred when the lunar module Snoopy was separated from the command module, Charlie Brown. The officer left in Charlie Brown said: "You'll never know how big this thing gets when there ain't nobody in here but one guy." From Snoopy came the cryptic report: "We is going! We is down among us, Charlie!"

[3]   It struck me as a pity that America's astronauts, provided at so much expense with an experience which nobody has had before, should be unable to describe it adequately. I therefore arranged for a representative to visit the U.S. National Aeronautics and Space Administration and ask whether it had paid any attention to this matter in its planning.

[4]   A spokesman for NASA replied: "We are by no means unaware of the problem. But we have had great difficulty in finding sensitive and articulate officers who also meet the exacting requirements for space personnel. We experimented for a time in training a man of literary tastes, Commander Shelley." He sighed. "Perhaps you would like to hear

From Ross Campbell, *She Can't Play My Bagpipes*. © 1970 by Shakespeare Head Press, Sydney, Australia. Reprinted by permission of the publisher.

some of the capsule communicator's tape for a simulated moon flight in which he took part."

[5]   My representative wrote down the recorded ground-space conversation, which went as follows:

CAPCOM: Houston to spacecraft. Are you guys OK?

SPACECRAFT: We are Diana's foresters, gentlemen of the shade, minions of the moon.

CAPCOM: Did not receive you. Repeat, over.

SPACECRAFT (Second voice): We is all systems go, Charlie babe.

[10]   CAPCOM: Roger. We copy.

SPACECRAFT:

> Ah, Moon of my delight that knowst no wane!
> The moon of heaven is rising once again.

CAPCOM: Houston to Commander Shelley. Check oxygen supply. You sound kinda dreamy.

SPACECRAFT (Singing):

> Oh, pray make no mistake,
> We are not shy,
> We're very wide awake,
> The moon and I!

Second voice: We done a real good exit burn, Charlie.

[15]   CAPCOM: Roger. Glad one of you guys is on the ball.

SPACECRAFT: The moon is advancing through a fairyland of silence —the Earth's Orphan.

CAPCOM: The Earth's often what?

SPACECRAFT: I was quoting Laforgue. He refers to *la terre et son Orpheline lunaire,* you remember.

CAPCOM: Houston to spacecraft. Warning, we show you close to gimbal lock. Are you gyrating?

[20]   SPACECRAFT: With the moon's beauty and the moon's soft pace.

Second voice: Son of a bitch, this module's gone crazy! I dunno how we'll reach the goddam moon.

First voice: Oh, swear not by the moon, the inconstant moon . . .

Second voice: Shuddup, will yer! Man, that was wild, Charlie babe.

CAPCOM: Are you stabilised, spacecraft?

[25]   SPACECRAFT (Second voice): Yeah. But we is going to abort the mission. Ain't no use carrying on with this nutcase aboard.

First voice: I feel like a Pierrot of space. The moon is my country. My collar of the moonshine's watery beams. (Singing) Shine on, shine on, harvest moon (*Thud*).

Second voice: I hit the guy with a spanner. Houston, stand by for re-entry burn.

CAPCOM: Roger. We copy . . .

The NASA spokesman switched off the tape.

[30] "We had to drop Commander Shelley from the program," he said. "As you could see, he had become moonstruck. It was a disappointment. Since then we have selected our space personnel from rugged, all-American guys." He added: "We would have had to dispense with Commander Shelley, anyway—his family life was not ideal enough for astronaut standards. His wife divorced him soon afterwards on multiple counts of adultery. More or less what you'd expect, I guess."

words and sentences

1. Vocabulary: *cryptic* (¶ 2), *simulated* (4); *minions* (7).
2. Look at the sentences spoken by the Second Voice in the dialogue between the spacecraft and CAPCOM. How would you describe the diction and grammar of these sentences? Has Campbell exaggerated the diction and grammar? If he has, why?
3. Rewrite the first sentence of ¶ 2 to see if you can reduce the number of words in the sentence without destroying its sense.

ideas and implications

1. What is Campbell's attitude towards Commander Shelley and the Second Voice in the spacecraft? What details tell of Campbell's attitude?
2. Why does Campbell name his unusual astronaut Commander Shelley?
3. Does the language of the two speakers from the spacecraft reflect the way they see? Is Campbell just having some fun with his speakers or is he suggesting that one view is better than the other? Or is he doing something else?
4. What stereotype is Campbell satirizing when the NASA spokesman discusses Commander Shelley in ¶ 30? Does the NASA spokesman also mention another stereotype in ¶ 30? Is the NASA spokesman a stereotype himself?
5. Does Campbell judge the value of the American space program in his essay? Point to specific words or phrases to support your view.

strategies

1. What is the thesis of Campbell's essay? Does he state it in any sentence in the essay? Or is his main idea implicitly presented?
2. What is the purpose of the first two paragraphs of Campbell's essay?
3. Is ¶ 3 in any way a transitional paragraph? Why or why not?
4. In the last part of Campbell's essay, there seem to be two units of organization: one encompassing ¶s 4-30, the other including ¶s 6-28. How would you describe the strategy Campbell has employed in presenting the material from ¶ 4 to the end of his essay?

suggestions for writing

1. Listen to some conversations of two or three people talking together. Try to record these conversations much as they occurred. Select one conversation and write a paper about it; try to show how the speakers'

language reflects the ways they say and see. Campbell's strategy might work for your paper, but do not limit yourself to his strategy if another seems more appropriate.

2. Write out the lyrics of a popular song and examine those lyrics for the relationships between saying and seeing. Or select a poem you admire and examine the language of the poem for the relationships between its words and the vision those words convey.

Marchette Chute

Getting at the Truth

[1]   This is a rather presumptuous title for a biographer to use, since truth is a very large word. In the sense that it means the reality about a human being it is probably impossible for a biographer to achieve. In the sense that it means a reasonable presentation of all the available facts it is more nearly possible, but even this limited goal is harder to reach than it appears to be. A biographer needs to be both humble and cautious when he remembers the nature of the material he is working with, for a historical fact is rather like the flamingo that Alice in Wonderland tried to use as a croquet mallet. As soon as she got its neck nicely straightened out and was ready to hit the ball, it would turn and look at her with a puzzled expression, and any biographer knows that what is called a "fact" has a way of doing the same.

[2]   Here is a small example. When I was writing my forthcoming biography, "Ben Jonson of Westminster," I wanted to give a paragraph or two to Sir Philip Sidney, who had a great influence on Jonson. No one thinks of Sidney without thinking of chivalry, and to underline the point I intended to use a story that Sir Fulke Greville told of him. Sidney died of gangrene, from a musket shot that shattered his thigh, and Greville says that Sidney failed to put on his leg armor while preparing for battle because the marshal of the camp was not wearing leg armor and Sidney was unwilling to do anything that would give him a special advantage.

[3]   The story is so characteristic both of Sidney himself and of the misplaced high-mindedness of late Renaissance chivalry that I wanted to use it, and since Sir Fulke Greville was one of Sidney's closest friends the information seemed to be reliable enough. But it is always well to check each piece of information as thoroughly as possible and so I con-

sulted another account of Sidney written by a contemporary, this time a doctor who knew the family fairly well. The doctor, Thomas Moffet, mentioned the episode but he said that Sidney left off his leg armor because he was in a hurry.

[4]   The information was beginning to twist in my hand and could no longer be trusted. So I consulted still another contemporary who had mentioned the episode, to see which of the two he agreed with. This was Sir John Smythe, a military expert who brought out his book a few years after Sidney's death. Sir John was an old-fashioned conservative who advocated the use of heavy armor even on horseback, and he deplored the current craze for leaving off leg protection, "the imitating of which . . . cost that noble and worthy gentleman Sir Philip Sidney his life."

[5]   So here I was with three entirely different reasons why Sidney left off his leg armor, all advanced by careful writers who were contemporaries of his. The flamingo had a legitimate reason for looking around with a puzzled expression.

[6]   The only thing to do in a case like this is to examine the point of view of the three men who are supplying the conflicting evidence. Sir Fulke Greville was trying to prove a thesis: that his beloved friend had an extremely chivalric nature. Sir John Smythe also was trying to prove a thesis: that the advocates of light arming followed a theory that could lead to disaster. Only the doctor, Thomas Moffet, was not trying to prove a thesis. He was not using his own explanation to reinforce some point he wanted to make. He did not want anything except to set down on paper what he believed to be the facts; and since we do not have Sidney's own explanation of why he did not put on leg armor, the chances are that Dr. Moffet is the safest man to trust.

[7]   For Moffet was without desire. Nothing can so quickly blur and distort the facts as desire—the wish to use the facts for some purpose of your own—and nothing can so surely destroy the truth. As soon as the witness wants to prove something he is no longer impartial and his evidence is no longer to be trusted.

[8]   The only safe way to study contemporary testimony is to bear constantly in mind this possibility of prejudice and to put almost as much attention on the writer himself as on what he has written. For instance, Sir Anthony Weldon's description of the Court of King James is lively enough and often used as source material; but a note from the publisher admits that the pamphlet was issued as a warning to anyone who wished to "side with this bloody house" of Stuart. The publisher, at any rate, did not consider Weldon an impartial witness. At about the same time Arthur Wilson published his history of Great Britain, which contained an irresistibly vivid account of the agonized death of the Countess of Somerset. Wilson sounds reasonably impartial; but his patron was the Earl of Essex, who had good reason to hate that particular countess, and there is evidence that he invented the whole scene to gratify his patron.

[9]   Sometimes a writer will contradict what he has already written, and in that case the only thing to do is to investigate what has changed his point of view. For instance, in 1608 Captain John Smith issued a description of his capture by Powhatan, and he made it clear that the Indian chief had treated him with unwavering courtesy and hospitality. In 1624 the story was repeated in Smith's "General History of Virginia," but the writer's circumstances had changed. Smith needed money, "having a prince's mind imprisoned in a poor man's purse," and he wanted the book to be profitable. Powhatan's daughter, the princess Pocahontas, had recently been in the news, for her visit to England had aroused a great deal of interest among the sort of people that Smith hoped would buy his book. So Smith supplied a new version of the story in which the once-hospitable Powhatan would have permitted the hero's brains to be dashed out if Pocahontas had not saved his life. It was the second story that achieved fame, and of course it may have been true. But it is impossible to trust it because the desire of the writer is so obviously involved; as Smith said in his prospectus, he needed money and hoped that the book would give "satisfaction."

[10]   It might seem that there was an easy way for a biographer to avoid the use of this kind of prejudiced testimony. All he has to do is to construct his biography from evidence that cannot be tampered with—from parish records, legal documents, bills, accounts, court records, and so on. Out of these solid gray blocks of impersonal evidence it should surely be possible to construct a road that will lead straight to the truth and that will never bend itself to the misleading curve of personal desire.

[11]   This might be so if the only problem involved were the reliability of the material. But there is another kind of desire that is much more subtle, much more pervasive, and much more dangerous than the occasional distortions of fact that contemporary writers may have permitted themselves to make; and this kind of desire can destroy the truth of a biography even if every individual fact in it is as solid and as uncompromising as rock. Even if the road is built of the best and most reliable materials it can still curve away from the truth because of this other desire that threatens it: the desire of the biographer himself.

[12]   A biographer is not a court record or a legal document. He is a human being, writing about another human being, and his own temperament, his own point of view, and his own frame of reference are unconsciously imposed upon the man he is writing about. Even if the biographer is free from Captain Smith's temptation—the need for making money—and wants to write nothing but the literal truth, he is still handicapped by the fact that there is no such thing as a completely objective human being.

[13]   An illustration of what can happen if the point of view is sufficiently strong is the curious conclusion that the nineteenth-century biographers reached about William Shakespeare. Shakespeare joined a company of London actors in 1594, was listed as an actor in 1598 and 1603, and was still listed as one of the "men actors" in the company in

1609. Shortly before he joined this company Shakespeare dedicated two narrative poems to the Earl of Southampton, and several years after Shakespeare died his collected plays were dedicated to the Earl of Pembroke. This was his only relationship with either of the two noblemen, and there is nothing to connect him with them during the fifteen years in which he belonged to the same acting company and during which he wrote nearly all his plays.

[14]   But here the desire of the biographers entered in. They had been reared in the strict code of nineteenth-century gentility and they accepted two ideas without question. One was that there are few things more important than an English lord; the other was that there are few things less important than a mere actor. They already knew the undeniable fact that Shakespeare was one of the greatest men who ever lived; and while they could not go quite so far as to claim him as an actual member of the nobility, it was clear to them that he must have been the treasured friend of both the Earl of Southampton and the Earl of Pembroke and that he must have written his plays either while basking in their exalted company or while he was roaming the green countryside by the waters of the river Avon. (It is another basic conviction of the English gentleman that there is nothing so inspiring as nature.) The notion that Shakespeare had spent all these years as the working member of a company of London actors was so abhorrent that it was never seriously considered. It could not be so; therefore it was not.

[15]   These biographers did their work well. When New South Wales built its beautiful memorial library to Shakespeare, it was the coat of arms of the Earl of Southampton that alternated with that of royalty in dignified splendor over the bookshelves. Shakespeare had been recreated in the image of desire, and desire will always ignore whatever is not relevant to its purpose. Because the English gentlemen did not like Shakespeare's background it was explained away as though it had never existed, and Shakespeare ceased to be an actor because so lowly a trade was not suited to so great a man.

[16]   All this is not to say that a biography should be lacking in a point of view. If it does not have a point of view it will be nothing more than a kind of expanded article for an encyclopedia—a string of facts arranged in chronological order with no claim to being a real biography at all. A biography must have a point of view and it must have a frame of reference. But it should be a point of view and a frame of reference implicit in the material itself and not imposed upon it.

[17]   It might seem that the ideal biographical system, if it could be achieved, would be to go through the years of research without feeling any kind of emotion. The biographer would be a kind of fact-finding machine and then suddenly, after his years of research, a kind of total vision would fall upon him and he would transcribe it in his best and most persuasive English for a waiting public. But research is fortunately not done by machinery, nor are visions likely to descend in that helpful manner. They are the product not only of many facts but also of much

thinking, and it is only when the biographer begins to get emotional in his thinking that he ought to beware.

[18] It is easy enough to make good resolutions in advance, but a biographer cannot altogether control his sense of excitement when the climax of his years of research draws near and he begins to see the pieces fall into place. Almost without his volition, A, B, and D fit together and start to form a pattern, and it is almost impossible for the biographer not to start searching for C. Something turns up that looks remarkably like C, and with a little trimming of the edges and the ignoring of one very slight discrepancy it will fill the place allotted for C magnificently.

[19] It is at this point that the biographer ought to take a deep breath and sit on his hands until he has had time to calm down. He has no real, fundamental reason to believe that his discovery is C, except for the fact that he wants it to be. He is like a man looking for a missing piece in a difficult jigsaw puzzle, who has found one so nearly the right shape that he cannot resist the desire to jam it in place.

[20] If the biographer had refused to be tempted by his supposed discovery of C and had gone on with his research, he might have found not only the connecting, illuminating fact he needed but much more besides. He is not going to look for it now. Desire has blocked the way. And by so much his biography will fall short of what might have been the truth.

[21] It would not be accurate to say that a biographer should be wholly lacking in desire. Curiosity is a form of desire. So is the final wish to get the material down on paper in a form that will be fair to the reader's interest and worthy of the subject. But a subconscious desire to push the facts around is one of the most dangerous things a biographer can encounter, and all the more dangerous because it is so difficult to know when he is encountering it.

[22] The reason Alice had so much trouble with her flamingo is that the average flamingo does not wish to be used as a croquet mallet. It has other purposes in view. The same thing is true of a fact, which can be just as self-willed as a flamingo and has its own kind of stubborn integrity. To try to force a series of facts into a previously desired arrangement is a form of misuse to which no self-respecting fact will willingly submit itself. The best and only way to treat it is to leave it alone and be willing to follow where it leads, rather than to press your own wishes upon it.

[23] To put the whole thing into a single sentence: you will never succeed in getting at the truth if you think you know, ahead of time, what the truth ought to be.

words and sentences

1. Vocabulary: *presumptuous* (¶ 1), *pervasive* (11); *abhorrent* (14); *volition* (18).
2. Describe the structure of the fourth sentence in ¶ 2. Is the sentence complicated in its structure? How does Miss Chute keep the references

clear in her sentence? Write a sentence imitating the pattern she has used.

3. Describe the structure of sentence two in ¶ 12. Then write a sentence imitating this pattern. Note that the sentence includes, among other things, some parallel constructions and ends with a preposition. What is a parallel construction? Is ending the sentence with a preposition "correct"?

4. Describe the structure of the first sentence in ¶ 18; then write a sentence imitating this pattern.

5. Describe the structure of the sentence in ¶ 23; then write a sentence imitating this pattern.

ideas and implications

1. If the truth is impossible to know, then why does Miss Chute write her essay? Comment also on the implications of the sentence in ¶ 23.

2. Why does Chute suggest that the only safe way to study contemporary testimony is "to put almost as much attention on the writer himself as on what he has written"?

3. What does Chute say about the objectivity of human beings? Why? What are some implications of this statement? about the language men use to describe their experience?

4. According to Chute, what happens to a writer when "desire" intrudes upon his attempt to find the truth? Why does she say curiosity is a form of desire? Does her statement about curiosity qualify some of her earlier observations?

5. What assumptions shaped nineteenth-century biographers' attitudes towards Shakespeare? Why?

6. What is Chute's attitude towards facts? Is her attitude different from that expressed by Agassiz?

7. Miss Chute has much to say about "point of view." How does one discover the point of view of a writer he reads? Is the biographer as a writer concerned with establishing a point of view? How?

8. How important are contexts in discovering the truth? What does Chute mean by contexts?

9. Though Chute focuses on the biographer's discovery of the truth, could her observations about the problems of the biographer be extended to other searches for truth? Are her statements about the difficulty of finding the truth applicable to any kind of research and thinking?

strategies

1. Miss Chute begins her essay by referring to Alice in Wonderland and the flamingo Alice tries to use as a croquet mallet. Does she allude to this analogy again? Where? What verbs in ¶s 5, 10, and 11 suggest an indirect allusion to this analogy? Does Chute's use of this analogy help her organize her observations? How?

2. ¶s 2-7 supply the reader with a "small example." What is the function of these paragraphs in the essay?

3. What strategy does Chute employ for supporting the statement in the first sentence of ¶ 8?
4. What analogy does Chute use in ¶s 10 and 11? For what purpose?
5. What is the function of ¶s 13-15? What strategy does Chute employ here? Does that strategy seem effective? What strategy does she use for moving from the subject of these paragraphs to the subject in the ensuing paragraphs?
6. What analogy does Chute use in ¶ 19 and what is its purpose?
7. What is the function of ¶ 22?
8. Miss Chute states her thesis idea in a single sentence at the end of the essay. Does she state her thesis elsewhere?

suggestions for writing

1. Clip an editorial or an article from a magazine; then examine the language and point of view of its author to determine his attitude towards his topic.
2. Write a brief biographical sketch of a friend. Try to be as objective as you can in your choice of language.
3. Select at random a biographical sketch from *The Dictionary of American Biography* or from a current magazine or newspaper. From the language and details used in the sketch, try to determine the author's point of view towards his subject.
4. Write a paper reporting on an event you have witnessed recently. Again, strive for objectivity in your paper.
5. Write a brief biographical sketch of yourself using the third person pronoun rather than the first. Again, work for objectivity. Then analyze carefully what you have written. Does it have a point of view? Can you explain what that point of view is? Does the appearance of a point of view affect your objectivity?

Max Shulman

Love Is a Fallacy

[1] Cool was I and logical. Keen, calculating, perspicacious, acute and astute—I was all of these. My brain was as powerful as a dynamo, as precise as a chemist's scales, as penetrating as a scalpel. And—think of it!—I was only eighteen.

It is not often that one so young has such a giant intellect. Take,

From Max Shulman, *The Many Loves of Dobie Gillis.* © 1951 by Max Shulman. Reprinted by permission of The Harold Matson Company, Inc.

for example, Petey Bellows, my roommate at the university. Same age, same background, but dumb as an ox. A nice enough fellow, you understand, but nothing upstairs. Emotional type. Unstable. Impressionable. Worst of all, a faddist. Fads, I submit, are the very negation of reason. To be swept up in every new craze that comes along, to surrender yourself to idiocy just because everybody else is doing it—this, to me, is the acme of mindlessness. Not, however, to Petey.

One afternoon I found Petey lying on his bed with an expression of such distress on his face that I immediately diagnosed appendicitis. "Don't move," I said. "Don't take a laxative. I'll get a doctor."

"Raccoon," he mumbled thickly.

[5]   "Raccoon?" I said, pausing in my flight.

"I want a raccoon coat," he wailed.

I perceived that his trouble was not physical, but mental. "Why do you want a raccoon coat?"

"I should have known it," he cried, pounding his temples. "I should have known they'd come back when the Charleston came back. Like a fool I spent all my money for textbooks, and now I can't get a raccoon coat."

"Can you mean," I said incredulously, "that people are actually wearing raccoon coats again?"

[10]   "All the Big Men on Campus are wearing them. Where've you been?"

"In the library," I said, naming a place not frequented by Big Men on Campus.

He leaped from the bed and paced the room. "I've got to have a raccoon coat," he said passionately. "I've got to!"

"Petey, why? Look at it rationally. Raccoon coats are unsanitary. They shed. They smell bad. They weigh too much. They're unsightly. They——"

"You don't understand," he interrupted impatiently. "It's the thing to do. Don't you want to be in the swim?"

[15]   "No," I said truthfully.

"Well, I do," he declared. "I'd give anything for a raccoon coat. Anything!"

My brain, that precision instrument, slipped into high gear. "Anything?" I asked, looking at him narrowly.

"Anything," he affirmed in ringing tones.

I stroked my chin thoughtfully. It so happened that I knew where to get my hands on a raccoon coat. My father had had one in his undergraduate days; it lay now in a trunk in the attic back home. It also happened that Petey had something I wanted. He didn't *have* it exactly, but at least he had first rights on it. I refer to his girl, Polly Espy.

[20]   I had long coveted Polly Espy. Let me emphasize that my desire for this young woman was not emotional in nature. She was, to be sure, a girl who excited the emotions, but I was not one to let my heart rule my head. I wanted Polly for a shrewdly calculated, entirely cerebral reason.

I was a freshman in law school. In a few years I would be out in practice. I was well aware of the importance of the right kind of wife in furthering a lawyer's career. The successful lawyers I had observed were, almost without exception, married to beautiful, gracious, intelligent women. With one omission, Polly fitted these specifications perfectly.

Beautiful she was. She was not yet of pin-up proportions, but I felt sure that time would supply the lack. She already had the makings.

Gracious she was. By gracious I mean full of graces. She had an erectness of carriage, an ease of bearing, a poise that clearly indicated the best of breeding. At table her manners were exquisite. I had seen her at the Kozy Kampus Korner eating the specialty of the house—a sandwich that contained scraps of pot roast, gravy, chopped nuts, and a dipper of sauerkraut—without even getting her fingers moist.

Intelligent she was not. In fact, she veered in the opposite direction. But I believed that under my guidance she would smarten up. At any rate, it was worth a try. It is, after all, easier to make a beautiful dumb girl smart than to make an ugly smart girl beautiful.

[25] "Petey," I said, "are you in love with Polly Espy?"

"I think she's a keen kid," he replied, "but I don't know if you'd call it love. Why?"

"Do you," I asked, "have any kind of formal arrangement with her? I mean are you going steady or anything like that?"

"No. We see each other quite a bit, but we both have other dates. Why?"

"Is there," I asked, "any other man for whom she has a particular fondness?"

[30] "Not that I know of. Why?"

I nodded with satisfaction. "In other words, if you were out of the picture, the field would be open. Is that right?"

"I guess so. What are you getting at?"

"Nothing, nothing," I said innocently, and took my suitcase out of the closet.

"Where you going?" asked Petey.

[35] "Home for the week end." I threw a few things into the bag.

"Listen," he said, clutching my arm eagerly, "while you're home, you couldn't get some money from your old man, could you, and lend it to me so I can buy a raccoon coat?"

"I may do better than that," I said with a mysterious wink and closed my bag and left.

"Look," I said to Petey when I got back Monday morning. I threw open the suitcase and revealed the huge, hairy, gamy object that my father had worn in his Stutz Bearcat in 1925.

"Holy Toledo!" said Petey reverently. He plunged his hands into the raccoon coat and then his face. "Holy Toledo!" he repeated fifteen or twenty times.

[40] "Would you like it?" I asked.

"Oh yes!" he cried, clutching the greasy pelt to him. Then a canny look came into his eyes. "What do you want for it?"

"Your girl," I said, mincing no words.

"Polly?" he said in a horrified whisper. "You want Polly?"

"That's right."

[45]   He flung the coat from him. "Never," he said stoutly.

I shrugged. "Okay. If you don't want to be in the swim, I guess it's your business."

I sat down in a chair and pretended to read a book, but out of the corner of my eye I kept watching Petey. He was a torn man. First he looked at the coat with the expression of a waif at a bakery window. Then he turned away and set his jaw resolutely. Then he looked back at the coat, with even more longing in his face. Then he turned away, but with not so much resolution this time. Back and forth his head swiveled, desire waxing, resolution waning. Finally he didn't turn away at all; he just stood and stared with mad lust at the coat.

"It isn't as though I was in love with Polly," he said thickly. "Or going steady or anything like that."

"That's right," I murmured.

[50]   "What's Polly to me, or me to Polly?"

"Not a thing," said I.

"It's just been a casual kick—just a few laughs, that's all."

"Try on the coat," said I.

He complied. The coat bunched high over his ears and dropped all the way down to his shoe tops. He looked like a mound of dead raccoons. "Fits fine," he said happily.

[55]   I rose from my chair. "Is it a deal?" I asked, extending my hand.

He swallowed. "It's a deal," he said and shook my hand.

I had my first date with Polly the following evening. This was in the nature of a survey; I wanted to find out just how much work I had to do to get her mind up to the standard I required. I took her first to dinner. "Gee, that was a delish dinner," she said as we left the restaurant. Then I took her to a movie. "Gee, that was a marvy movie," she said as we left the theater. And then I took her home. "Gee, I had a sensaysh time," she said as she bade me good night.

I went back to my room with a heavy heart. I had gravely underestimated the size of my task. This girl's lack of information was terrifying. Nor would it be enough merely to supply her with information. First she had to be taught to *think*. This loomed as a project of no small dimensions, and at first I was tempted to give her back to Petey. But then I got to thinking about her abundant physical charms and about the way she entered a room and the way she handled a knife and fork, and I decided to make an effort.

I went about it, as in all things, systematically. I gave her a course in logic. It happened that I, as a law student, was taking a course in logic myself, so I had all the facts at my finger tips. "Polly," I said to her when I picked her up on our next date, "tonight we are going over to the Knoll and talk."

[60]   "Oo, terrif," she replied. One thing I will say for this girl: you would go far to find another so agreeable.

We went to the Knoll, the campus trysting place, and we sat down under an old oak, and she looked at me expectantly. "What are we going to talk about?" she asked.

"Logic."

She thought this over for a minute and decided she liked it. "Magnif," she said.

"Logic," I said, clearing my throat, "is the science of thinking. Before we can think correctly, we must first learn to recognize the common fallacies of logic. These we will take up tonight."

[65] "Wow-dow!" she cried, clapping her hands delightedly.

I winced, but went bravely on. "First let us examine the fallacy called Dicto Simpliciter."

"By all means," she urged, batting her lashes eagerly.

"Dicto Simpliciter means an argument based on an unqualified generalization. For example: Exercise is good. Therefore everybody should exercise."

"I agree," said Polly earnestly. "I mean exercise is wonderful. I mean it builds the body and everything."

[70] "Polly," I said gently, "the argument is a fallacy. *Exercise is good* is an unqualified generalization. For instance, if you have heart disease, exercise is bad, not good. Many people are ordered by their doctors *not* to exercise. You must *qualify* the generalization. You must say exercise is *usually* good, or exercise is good *for most people.* Otherwise you have committed a Dicto Simpliciter. Do you see?"

"No," she confessed. "But this is marvy. Do more! Do more!"

"It will be better if you stop tugging at my sleeve," I told her, and when she desisted, I continued. "Next we take up a fallacy called Hasty Generalization. Listen carefully: You can't speak French. I can't speak French. Petey Bellows can't speak French. I must therefore conclude that nobody at the University of Minnesota can speak French."

"Really?" said Polly, amazed. "*Nobody?*"

I hid my exasperation. "Polly, it's a fallacy. The generalization is reached too hastily. There are too few instances to support such a conclusion."

[75] "Know any more fallacies?" she asked breathlessly. "This is more fun than dancing even."

I fought off a wave of despair. I was getting nowhere with this girl, absolutely nowhere. Still, I am nothing if not persistent. I continued. "Next comes Post Hoc. Listen to this: Let's not take Bill on our picnic. Every time we take him out with us, it rains."

"I know somebody just like that," she exclaimed. "A girl back home—Eula Becker, her name is. It never fails. Every single time we take her on a picnic——"

"Polly," I said sharply, "it's a fallacy. Eula Becker doesn't cause the rain. She has no connection with the rain. You are guilty of Post Hoc if you blame Eula Becker."

"I'll never do it again," she promised contritely. "Are you mad at me?"

[80] I sighed. "No, Polly, I'm not mad."

"Then tell me some more fallacies."

"All right. Let's try Contradictory Premises."

"Yes, let's," she chirped, blinking her eyes happily.

I frowned, but plunged ahead. "Here's an example of Contradictory Premises: If God can do anything, can He make a stone so heavy that He won't be able to lift it?"

[85] "Of course," she replied promptly.

"But if He can do anything, He can lift the stone," I pointed out.

"Yeah," she said thoughtfully. "Well, then I guess He can't make the stone."

"But He can do anything," I reminded her.

She scratched her pretty, empty head. "I'm all confused," she admitted.

[90] "Of course you are. Because when the premises of an argument contradict each other, there can be no argument. If there is an irresistible force, there can be no immovable object. If there is an immovable object, there can be no irresistible force. Get it?"

"Tell me some more of this keen stuff," she said eagerly.

I consulted my watch. "I think we'd better call it a night. I'll take you home now, and you go over all the things you've learned. We'll have another session tomorrow night."

I deposited her at the girls' dormitory, where she assured me that she had had a perfectly terrif evening, and I went glumly home to my room. Petey lay snoring in his bed, the raccoon coat huddled like a great hairy beast at his feet. For a moment I considered waking him and telling him that he could have his girl back. It seemed clear that my project was doomed to failure. The girl simply had a logic-proof head.

But then I reconsidered. I had wasted one evening; I might as well waste another. Who knew? Maybe somewhere in the extinct crater of her mind a few embers still smoldered. Maybe somehow I could fan them into flame. Admittedly it was not a prospect fraught with hope, but I decided to give it one more try.

[95] Seated under the oak the next evening I said, "Our first fallacy tonight is called Ad Misericordiam."

She quivered with delight.

"Listen closely," I said. "A man applies for a job. When the boss asks him what his qualifications are, he replies that he has a wife and six children at home, the wife is a helpless cripple, the children have nothing to eat, no clothes to wear, no shoes on their feet, there are no beds in the house, no coal in the cellar, and winter is coming."

A tear rolled down each of Polly's pink cheeks. "Oh, this is awful, awful," she sobbed.

"Yes, it's awful," I agreed, "but it's no argument. The man never answered the boss's question about his qualifications. Instead he appealed to the boss's sympathy. He committed the fallacy of Ad Misericordiam. Do you understand?"

[100] "Have you got a handkerchief?" she blubbered.

I handed her a handkerchief and tried to keep from screaming while she wiped her eyes. "Next," I said in a carefully controlled tone, "we will discuss False Analogy. Here is an example: Students should be allowed to look at their textbooks during examinations. After all, surgeons have X rays to guide them during an operation, lawyers have briefs to guide them during a trial, carpenters have blueprints to guide them when they are building a house. Why, then, shouldn't students be allowed to look at their textbooks during an examination?"

"There now," she said enthusiastically, "is the most marvy idea I've heard in years."

"Polly," I said testily, "the argument is all wrong. Doctors, lawyers, and carpenters aren't taking a test to see how much they have learned, but students are. The situations are altogether different, and you can't make an analogy between them."

"I still think it's a good idea," said Polly.

[105] "Nuts," I muttered. Doggedly I pressed on. "Next we'll try Hypothesis Contrary to Fact."

"Sounds yummy," was Polly's reaction.

"Listen: If Madame Curie had not happened to leave a photographic plate in a drawer with a chunk of pitchblende, the world today would not know about radium."

"True, true," said Polly, nodding her head. "Did you see the movie? Oh, it just knocked me out. That Walter Pidgeon is so dreamy. I mean he fractures me."

"If you can forget Mr. Pidgeon for a moment," I said coldly, "I would like to point out that the statement is a fallacy. Maybe Madame Curie would have discovered radium at some later date. Maybe somebody else would have discovered it. Maybe any number of things would have happened. You can't start with a hypothesis that is not true and then draw any supportable conclusions from it."

[110] "They ought to put Walter Pidgeon in more pictures," said Polly. "I hardly ever see him any more."

One more chance, I decided. But just one more. There is a limit to what flesh and blood can bear. "The next fallacy is called Poisoning the Well."

"How cute!" she gurgled.

"Two men are having a debate. The first one gets up and says, 'My opponent is a notorious liar. You can't believe a word that he is going to say.' . . . Now, Polly, think. Think hard. What's wrong?"

I watched her closely as she knit her creamy brow in concentration. Suddenly a glimmer of intelligence—the first I had seen—came into her eyes. "It's not fair," she said with indignation. "It's not a bit fair. What chance has the second man got if the first man calls him a liar before he even begins talking?"

[115] "Right!" I cried exultantly. "One hundred per cent right. It's not fair. The first man has *poisoned the well* before anybody could drink

from it. He has hamstrung his opponent before he could even start. . . . Polly, I'm proud of you."

"Pshaw," she murmured, blushing with pleasure.

"You see, my dear, these things aren't so hard. All you have to do is concentrate. Think—examine—evaluate. Come now, let's review everything we have learned."

"Fire away," she said with an airy wave of her hand.

Heartened by the knowledge that Polly was not altogether a cretin, I began a long, patient review of all I had told her. Over and over and over again I cited instances, pointed out flaws, kept hammering away without letup. It was like digging a tunnel. At first everything was work, sweat, and darkness. I had no idea when I would reach the light, or even *if* I would. But I persisted. I pounded and clawed and scraped, and finally I was rewarded. I saw a chink of light. And then the chink got bigger and the sun came pouring in and all was bright.

[120] Five grueling nights this took, but it was worth it. I had made a logician out of Polly; I had taught her to think. My job was done. She was worthy of me at last. She was a fit wife for me, a proper hostess for my many mansions, a suitable mother for my well-heeled children.

It must not be thought that I was without love for this girl. Quite the contrary. Just as Pygmalion loved the perfect woman he had fashioned, so I loved mine. I decided to acquaint her with my feelings at our very next meeting. The time had come to change our relationship from academic to romantic.

"Polly," I said when next we sat beneath our oak, "tonight we will not discuss fallacies."

"Aw, gee," she said, disappointed.

"My dear," I said, favoring her with a smile, "we have now spent five evenings together. We have gotten along splendidly. It is clear that we are well matched."

[125] "Hasty Generalization," said Polly brightly.

"I beg your pardon," said I.

"Hasty Generalization," she repeated. "How can you say that we are well matched on the basis of only five dates?"

I chuckled with amusement. The dear child had learned her lessons well. "My dear," I said, patting her hand in a tolerant manner, "five dates is plenty. After all, you don't have to eat a whole cake to know that it's good."

"False Analogy," said Polly promptly. "I'm not a cake. I'm a girl."

[130] I chuckled with somewhat less amusement. The dear child had learned her lessons perhaps too well. I decided to change tactics. Obviously the best approach was a simple, strong, direct declaration of love. I paused for a moment while my massive brain chose the proper words. Then I began:

"Polly, I love you. You are the whole world to me, and the moon and the stars and the constellations of outer space. Please, my darling, say that you will go steady with me, for if you will not, life will be meaningless. I will languish. I will refuse my meals. I will wander the face of the earth, a shambing, hollow-eyed hulk."

There, I thought, folding my arms, that ought to do it.

"Ad Misericordiam," said Polly.

I gound my teeth. I was not Pygmalion; I was Frankenstein, and my monster had me by the throat. Frantically I fought back the tide of panic surging through me. At all costs I had to keep cool.

[135] "Well, Polly," I said, forcing a smile, "you certainly have learned your fallacies."

"You're darn right," she said with a vigorous nod.

"And who taught them to you, Polly?"

"You did."

"That's right. So you do owe me something, don't you, my dear? If I hadn't come along you never would have learned about fallacies."

[140] "Hypothesis Contrary to Fact," she said instantly.

I dashed perspiration from my brow. "Polly," I croaked, "you mustn't take all these things so literally. I mean this is just classroom stuff. You know that the things you learn in school don't have anything to do with life."

"Dicto Simpliciter," she said, wagging her finger at me playfully.

That did it. I leaped to my feet, bellowing like a bull. "Will you or will you not go steady with me?"

"I will not," she replied.

[145] "Why not?" I demand.

"Because this afternoon I promised Petey Bellows that I would go steady with him."

I reeled back, overcome with the infamy of it. After he promised, after he made a deal, after he shook my hand! "The rat!" I shrieked, kicking up great chunks of turf. "You can't go with him, Polly. He's a liar. He's a cheat. He's a rat."

"Poisoning the Well," said Polly, "and stop shouting. I think shouting must be a fallacy too."

With an immense effort of will, I modulated my voice. "All right," I said. "You're a logician. Let's look at this thing logically. How could you choose Petey Bellows over me? Look at me—a brilliant student, a tremendous intellectual, a man with an assured future. Look at Petey—a knothead, a jitterbug, a guy who'll never know where his next meal is coming from. Can you give me one logical reason why you should go steady with Petey Bellows?"

[150] "I certainly can," declared Polly. "He's got a raccoon coat."

words and sentences

1. Vocabulary: *perspicacious, astute* (¶ 1); *acme* (2); *incredulously* (9); *trysting* (61); *desisted* (72); *contritely* (79); *fraught* (94); *infamy* (147); *modulated* (149).

2. Are there any phrases, words, and allusions which help to date Shulman's story? If so, make a list of them.

3. How does Shulman use the word *cool* in ¶ 1? Describe the structure of the first sentence in ¶ 1.

4. Examine the structure and the rhythm of the sentences in ¶ 47. Are the structure and rhythm of these sentences related to the mood and idea Shulman is trying to communicate?

5. How much does Shulman depend upon italics for emphasis? Point to specific instances.

6. Describe the first sentences of ¶s 22, 23, and 24. What pattern has Shulman used in these sentences? What is the effect of this pattern?

ideas and implications

1. "Love Is a Fallacy" has been called a short story. Examine the form of Shulman's story, of Scudder's "In the Laboratory with Agassiz," and of Chute's "Getting at the Truth." How are these writings alike and different? List the likenesses and differences. Does your list tell you anything about the names of the forms? Or their definitions?

2. What is the theme of Shulman's tale? Can you state that theme in a single sentence?

3. Are the characters of Shulman's story stereotypes? Point to specific passages to support your conclusions.

strategies

1. Can you outline Shulman's story? Can it be divided into scenes which have purposes in illuminating both character and theme?

2. What is the function of ¶ 2 of the story? What strategy is he using in this paragraph? What strategy in ¶s 23 and 24?

3. Shulman's handling of point of view is important in the story. Why? What is the narrator's or speaker's attitude towards himself? What is Shulman's attitude towards the speaker? How does Shulman inform his reader of these attitudes? Point to specific sentences to support your observations.

4. How does the speaker characterize Polly Espy and Petey Bellows? How does Shulman characterize them? Are there differences in attitude towards these characters on the part of Shulman and the speaker in the story?

5. What provides the "conflict" of Shulman's story?

6. Check your dictionary for the distinction between *verbal irony* and *dramatic irony*. How much does Shulman's story depend upon these two types of irony? List some examples of both kinds of irony.

suggestions for writing

1. From your own experience, write a paper which shows how logic failed. Try to focus your paper upon a single episode.

2. From a movie or a book that you know, select a scene in which dramatic

irony was present. Describe the scene and then comment upon the importance of point of view in the presentation of the scene.

3. A recent book included the statement that being in love meant never having to say one was sorry. Examine that statement for its logic. Write a paper on the subject.

3 The Writer as Word-Maker and World-Maker

INTRODUCTION

To get the chuckle from his "Peanuts" cartoon, Charles Schulz has created two worlds of words—one within the other. In one, Snoopy tells about his hero and heroine; in the other, Schulz creates a word and picture world showing Snoopy in action. But the stances and the styles of the two authors are different.

Stance is where one has his feet and how he stands—his physical position and posture. It is also his emotional and intellectual attitudes towards his material. With Snoopy, stance is where he has his seat, before the typewriter spinning his yarn. When his hero says, "My love for you is higher than the highest mountain which is. . . ," Snoopy is serious about his characters and their language. He stands too close to his characters and the words they say to see the truth about them—until the eye-opening discovery of the last panel.

Schulz plants his seat before his drawing board, and by doing so, he is physically farther from Snoopy's typewriter, characters, and language than is the world-famous author. Not only is Schulz physically farther away, but his emotional and intellectual attitudes are quite different. What Snoopy takes seriously, Schulz sees comically. Snoopy's discovery in the last panel is what Schulz has known all along, that Snoopy's language, characters, and story are the hogwash of daytime television and maudlin movies. The distance between Snoopy's earnestness about his characters and language and Schulz's parody of that language and those characters makes us chuckle. It is the difference in stance and style.

Stance and style, the subjects of the readings in this section, are like a man and his shadow on a sunny day. There can be no shadow without the man, nor can the man stand in the sunlight without casting a shadow. Yet for convenience of discussion, writers sometimes talk about stance and style as if they were separate. But only for a while. Like the man and his shadow, stance and style are finally inseparable.

Several authors in this section discuss the problems of finding a place to stand physically, emotionally, and intellectually. While they express different attitudes, they all work within the contexts described by this diagram:

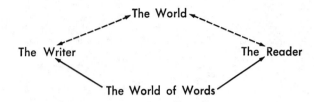

Readers and writers live in, look at, and respond to the world, and both have their own notions about its goings on. To tell others what he sees, feels, and thinks about himself and the world, the writer makes a world of words to inform readers about his discoveries "out there" and his inner responses to these discoveries. That world of words is a representation of his observations, feelings, and thoughts, *and it is through that world of words alone that readers understand what the writer knows.* It is also through the world of words that readers test the writer's perceptions against their own experience in the world. Thus, finding a place to stand becomes an important task for the writer as a maker of word-worlds.

"Whose Eye Is on the Sparrow?" by Doris Betts describes how finding a place to stand affects the way a writer tells what he knows. She believes that the writer's choice of point of view (first, third, omniscient) is "not simply a choice in method, but will result in a different story." Though Mrs. Betts discussses the problem of finding a place to stand as it concerns fiction writers, much of what she says applies to writers of exposition and argument as well. She notes that "how someone feels about an event begins to be story"; then she shows how changing stance affects the language and details a writer employs.

Wayne Booth argues that rhetorical stance "depends on discovering and maintaining in any writing situation a proper balance among the three elements at work in any communicative effort: the available arguments about the subject itself, the interests and peculiarities of the audience, and the voice, the implied character, of the speaker." He shows how writers sometimes reduce a stance to a slouch by losing their balance or by muting their voices. H. L. Mencken points out that President Warren G. Harding spoke eloquently on the "ideals of the Elks," but wrote nonsense about the poet Dante because he knew "no more about Dante than a Tennessee county judge knows about the Institutes of Justinian." Mencken believes that President Harding found a place to stand on the subject of Elks; on the subject of Dante, he slouched and was therefore ludicrous without knowing it.

Once a writer believes he has found a place to stand, he must put words in sentences and paragraphs to share his understanding with others. The way he chooses and arranges words is his style. In choosing and arranging words, he may change his mind about his subject because he discovers new feelings and thoughts by making these choices. Since writing is one way of discovering what we feel and know, those first choices and arrangements are usually tentative; at this stage of composition the writer is still testing his stance to see if it is sound. As he discovers his way, as he revises and changes, he may shift his stance to accommodate his subject or his audience—or both. Thus a change in style may result in a change in stance, just as a change in stance may be a change in style.

If finding a stance is frequently troublesome, finding a style is an even more shadowy matter.

One way to talk about style is to see it in action. Here is a passage from *The Sun Also Rises* by Ernest Hemingway, one of the great prose stylists of the twentieth century. The speaker in the passage is Jake Barnes, the teller of Hemingway's story. Jake has spent a week in Pamplona, Spain, celebrating the Festival of San Fermin by watching bullfights and drinking mightily. Jake is describing Pamplona the day after the Festival ends:

> In the morning it was all over. The fiesta was finished. I woke about nine o'clock, had a bath, dressed, and went down-stairs. The square was empty and there were no people on the streets. A few children were picking up rocket-sticks in the square. The cafés were just opening and the waiters were carrying out the comfortable white wicker chairs and arranging them around the marble-topped tables in the shade of the arcade. They were sweeping the streets and sprinkling them with a hose.
>
> I sat in one of the wicker chairs and leaned back comfortably. The waiter was in no hurry to come. The white-paper announcements of the unloading of the bulls and the big schedules of special trains were still up on the pillars of the arcade. A waiter wearing a blue apron came out with a bucket of water and a cloth, and commenced to tear down the notices, pulling the paper off in strips and washing and rubbing away the paper that stuck to the stone. The fiesta was over.[1]

Here is another sample of Hemingway's prose, a story about a sea voyage:

MY FIRST SEA VOUGE

I was born in a little white house on the island of Marthas Vineyard in the State of Massachuset. My mother died when I was four years old and my father, the captain of the three masted schooner "Elizabeth" took me and my little brother around the "Horn" with him to Australia.

Going we had fine weather and we would see the porpoises playing around the ship and the big white albatross winging its way across the ocean or following the brig for scraps of food; the sailors caught one on a huge hook baited with a biscuit but they let him go as soon as they had caught him for they are very superstitious about these big birds.

One time the sailors went out on a barrel fastened on the bow sprit and speared a porpoise (or sea pig as they call them) and hauled him up on deck and cut out the the liver and we had it fried for supper it tasted like pork only it was greesier.

[1] Excerpt from *The Sun Also Rises* by Ernest Hemingway is used by permission of Charles Scribner's Sons. Copyright 1926 by Charles Scribner's Sons; renewal copyright 1954 Ernest Hemingway.

> We arrived in Sydney Australia after a fine vouge and had just as good a vouge going back.[2]

Hemingway was about twenty-five years old when he wrote *The Sun Also Rises.* He wrote "My First Sea Vouge," complete with misspellings, when he was twelve years old and a sixth-grader. The prose of *The Sun Also Rises* is not stylistically the same as that of "My First Sea Vouge." But in the sixth-grader's story, we can hear some stylistic qualities that Hemingway cultivated and practiced as a mature writer: the specific and concrete details that give a sense of place and scene, the verbs and verbals that give his prose a sense of movement and action, the effective repetitions, and the linking of details and events with words like *and, but, then.*

What, then, is style? How does one get it? Can it be taught or learned? Is the style the man? These are some questions that authors in this section discuss. Most of their answers are tentative, and they talk about style in different ways.

Sydney Harris talks about developing an ear for words just as a musician learns to hear notes, and Benjamin Franklin describes how he learned to write by imitating the works of others.

Mencken believes that to write clearly one must be able to think clearly. He believes that no one can teach the art of thinking any more than he can teach the art of writing, and hence style "is not acquired, but congenital." George Jean Nathan disagrees with Mencken. Clear thinking, says Nathan, does not mean that writing will be clear. Nathan believes that personality is the outgrowth of style and that style is "less often the man than the concept of him he wishes his readers to have."

Clemens, Art Buchwald, and Dan Greenburg play with style by writing parodies. To write a parody of another's style, one must know well the ways his words fall into sentences and paragraphs. Clemens and Buchwald rewrite Shakespeare to show how alterations in language change the playwright's noble speeches into comic ones. Buchwald parodies modern translations of the Bible for similar reasons. Greenburg has sophisticated fun telling the story of Goldilocks and the Three Bears in the distinctive styles of J. D. Salinger, James Joyce, and Ernest Hemingway.

For Donald Hall, "Style is the manner of a sentence, not its matter." He argues that writers must be clear, honest, and sincere. Bad prose, says Hall, results from a writer's deception of himself as much as from his deception of others. "A writer of bad prose, to become a writer of good prose, must alter his character." He must close the gap between his real and his declared aims or purposes. Hall concludes that the only way to change one's style is to change one's character, to change oneself.

The readings in this section, then, deal with one of the most complex problems writers must solve—finding a place to stand and putting words together in ways that work.

---

[2] Excerpt from *Ernest Hemingway: A Life Story* by Carlos Baker is reprinted by permission of Charles Scribner's Sons. Copyright © 1969 Mary Hemingway.

Doris Betts

Whose Eye Is on the Sparrow?

[1]   When we observe a quarrel in real life, we take in all sensory impressions at once, and our brains arrange the details in a unity. Our ears hear words at the same time our eyes are watching angry people, and should a rose be blooming on their left, its fragrance will be simultaneously smelled. Even the green grass, the airplane overhead, will be perceived. Yet in life while we absorb a thousand details, our nervous system will still "rate" these in some order and allow us to focus on what is most important. How can we put things down one-at-a-time on paper, and still feel we are observing a single scene? How can we reproduce "focus" on the page?

[2]   Add to these problems the kinship of a writer to a witness at an automobile accident. Where was he standing when the two cars crashed? Did the passenger bus block his vision? Could he tell what color the stoplight was and which driver violated the law? What a shame the witness wasn't conveniently high in a sycamore tree when the wreck occurred, armed with a camera having long-range as well as close-up lenses!

[3]   In any fiction you read, these questions have plagued writers and been solved in a variety of ways. You should begin judging the method each writer chose for the purposes he wished to achieve.

[4]   Robie Macauley and George Lanning's *Technique in Fiction* offers one simple way to consider viewpoint as not merely a *way* to write, but a device which actually changes one story into another! [1]

[5]   Study first the following sketch:

From *English c34F, Creative Writing: The Short Story,* © 1969 by Doris Betts. Reprinted by permission of Doris Betts.

[1] The material about the Gamma family has been adapted from Macauley and Lanning, *Technique in Fiction,* pp. 100–104, by permission of Harper & Row, Publishers.

[6]   On the left, in a clearing in the woods, the Gamma family is having a picnic: Mr. and Mrs. Gamma, their young son, about eight, and their teenage daughter. They believe they are alone but nearby, hidden behind a bush, is Mr. Beta, one of their neighbors. He can overhear everything they say and, being a neighbor, knows something about each member of the family. Still a sixth person is present, a mysterious and powerful Mr. Alpha, more distant from the picnic scene. However, he is on a hillside and can see everything, and has brought his telescope with him. Perhaps he can even see Mr. Beta spying.

[7]   It hardly matters what happens at the picnic. Let us say only that a disagreement takes place between Mr. and Mrs. Gamma; the discussion mounts to a quarrel, and finally he slaps her in the face. That is the raw event. It is the story to be told, the scene to be shown. How?

[8]   A writer might first consider telling the story through a member of the Gamma family. They, after all, were closest. Two of them took part in the fight. The writer might pick any of the four Gammas and tell, or show, the event through that individual, calling him either "I" or "he" or "she." Since Mr. Gamma was provoked enough to strike, his emotion must be the most intense and the story-writer would probably consider him first.

[9]   An important thing to notice here is that any choice the writer makes will not simply be a choice in method, but will result in a different story. Obviously the one who struck the blow has a different view of events from the one on whose face it fell. "She asked for it," might be Mr. Gamma's underlying prejudice, and this would color everything he reported—even the way he described his wife's appearance. His wife's chief emotion might be. "He never understood me, just like Mama said." The facial expression Mr. Gamma meant to be righteous would appear to her eyes selfish and mean. Even in choosing between Mr. and Mrs. Gamma, with the emotional tones each would bring, the writer can select from four different stories, two "I's" and two he/she's. An "I" approach would usually be more intimate, more internal; it might even become stream-of-consciousness.

[10]   Now you begin to see why viewpoint is the first means by which, as Henry James said, "facts pass into fiction." Events are only raw material. How someone feels about an event begins to be story.

[11]   To many modern writers, the attractive viewpoint on the Gamma quarrel would be that of either child, because a choice here offers opportunities for subtle treatment. The innocent child, who sees what happens but will not understand its full implications as the reader may, is a refracting lens. The small boy cannot judge who is right and who is wrong; he may be loyal to the wrong side altogether and the reader's own judgment may differ from how the child feels and form a running counterpoint. The reader who thinks about a story, makes comments on it, and comes to decisions about it, grows deeply involved and will read to the end. He wants *his* view of reality to be the "right" one.

[12]   The adolescent girl, also, is an attractive viewpoint choice. At an

intense time in her life, entering her own womanhood, how will she feel when her father strikes her mother? To what might she compare it?

[13]   So a writer might choose any viewpoint from the Gamma family. He might never violate that choice throughout the story—that is, if he chose the child, he would use no language a child that age did not know, make no observations beyond the eight-year-old level. If he picked Mrs. Gamma, he would try to think in a feminine way. Mr. Gamma's hand would be apt to come down on her face like a swung broom, but not like a crowbar; because one description would be more natural for her than the other.

[14]   Suppose the writer rejects all these eight viewpoints (four first-person, four third-person) and decides to tell the story through Mr. Beta, called in some texts a narrator-agent, or a dramatized narrator-observer. Mr. Beta can judge and evaluate the quarrel in a broader, more objective way than any of the Gammas. He can compare them, speculate on what each feels. He may remember the husband and wife quarreled Saturday night on the patio as well. He may know the neighborhood is already gossiping about the likelihood of their divorce. He may know Mr. Gamma drinks too much and Mrs. Gamma flirts with the milkman. In short, he may know more than the quarrelers themselves! Through him the author may or may not comment and interpret. On the other hand, Mr. Beta may be an absolute scoundrel. He may be in love with Mrs. Gamma himself. He may be Mr. Gamma's employer. He need not be "objective," but a character whose own bias will color the story in a different way.

[15]   Many novels have been written through Beta narrators. In *The Great Gatsby,* Nick Carraway is one kind of Beta. He is not just another name for the writer, but a real character in his own right, present at someone else's love story. Conrad's Marlow is a Beta. In *Moby Dick,* Ishmael is a Beta, though he has a role in the story of his own, and although Melville did not allow Ishmael to tell the whole story and would not restrict himself to what Ishmael alone could see, know, experience. Faulkner's sharecroppers speak in a rhetoric sharecroppers seldom use; obviously Faulkner is present himself, but he so overpowers us with his language that we allow him to carry us away in suspended disbelief. Some writers complicate their narrators—in *Huckleberry Finn,* the narrator keeps telling us he is wicked, but the reader likes him and does not accept Huck's stated low opinion of himself. Some narrators can be trusted and some cannot. If you have read Henry James' "The Turn of the Screw," do you believe or disbelieve the governess' account of what actually occurred?

[16]   Don't forget that on the far hillside, Mr. Alpha is still waiting and would also be willing to tell the story of the Gammas' quarrel. Mr. Alpha is omniscient, like God. He sees everything, even inside the minds of the characters. He is the very one who would know that the man in the land of Uz was named Job, and might report on what happened in an empty room when nobody was there to see it. An old riddle about sound vi-

bration asks: "If a tree falls in the forest and there isn't an ear within ten miles, does the tree make any noise?" Mr. Alpha would hear the noise. He would also know the precise moment Eve took the first bite of the serpent's apple.

[17]   These supernatural skills explain why Mr. Alpha is so useful for long novels, where he can see all the way from France to China and be inside the crippled beggar as well as the sage priest. In some texts, he is called an author-narrator. ("I created this whole fictional universe, so naturally not a sparrow falls but I know it.")

[18]   Modern short story writers usually save Mr. Alpha for novels, too, where he has the sweep and space to do his best work. They are inclined to tell a short story, by definition an intense emotional experience, through a viewpoint closer to the action, where feelings are strongest and can be most easily held together through a single personality. A story needs a single effect, not a scattering of attention into this mind and that.

words and sentences

1. Vocabulary: *stream-of-consciousness* (¶ 9); *refracting* (11).
2. Describe the sentence patterns in ¶ 7. How many kinds of sentences appear in this paragraph (simple, complex, etc.)? Write a paragraph imitating these sentence patterns. What are the purposes of this paragraph in the context of the essay?
3. How important are adverbs to the shaping of meaning in ¶ 7? What is the purpose of each adverb in the paragraph? If they were deleted, what would happen to the meaning of ¶ 7?

ideas and implications

1. What distinction does Mrs. Betts make between fact and fiction?
2. How important is "feeling" in the transferring of fact to fiction? Why?
3. Why has the viewpoint of children been appealing to modern writers?
4. Why does Betts insist that a short story "needs a single effect"?
5. In ¶ 15, Betts says, "Some narrators can be trusted and some cannot." Why?
6. Which viewpoint does Betts advocate as the most appropriate for the short story? Which for the novel? Why?
7. Betts writes about point of view in prose fiction; can one apply her observations about viewpoint to exposition, description, or argument? How?

strategies

1. Mrs. Betts employs eighteen paragraphs in her discussion of point of view. The following paragraphs comprise units of her essay: ¶s 1-3, 4-7, 8-13, 14-15, 16-17, and 18. What is the purpose of each of these groups of paragraphs? Note that she has chosen to begin her discussion with the Gamma family and to work out from that center. Why?

2. How helpful is the diagram in dramatizing Mrs. Betts's observations about viewpoint?
3. What strategy does Betts use in ¶ 15 and why?

suggestions for writing

1. Select an event you witnessed or took part in during the last few days and write a paper from first-person point of view. Then rewrite the paper from another viewpoint. Are the papers really "different," as Mrs. Betts suggests (¶ 9)?
2. Find a brief account of a dramatic event in a newspaper and rewrite that story using a different viewpoint. Turn in the newspaper clipping with your paper.
3. Find a short editorial in a newspaper or magazine and write a paper which takes a viewpoint different from the editorial. Turn in a copy of the editorial with your paper.
4. Look back at the three versions of Little Red Riding Hood in the introduction to Section 1. Take a different point of view and re-tell that story. Or you might wish to retell another familiar story from a new point of view.

Wayne C. Booth

The Rhetorical Stance

[1]   Last fall I had an advanced graduate student, bright, energetic, well-informed, whose papers were almost unreadable. He managed to be pretentious, dull, and disorganized in his paper on *Emma,* and pretentions, dull, and disorganized on *Madame Bovary.* On *The Golden Bowl* he was all these and obscure as well. Then one day, toward the end of term, he cornered me after class and said, "You know, I think you were all wrong about Robbe-Grillet's *Jealousy* today." We didn't have time to discuss it, so I suggested that he write me a note about it. Five hours later I found in my faculty box a four-page polemic, unpretentious, stimulating, organized, convincing. Here was a man who had taught freshman composition for several years and who was incapable of committing any of the more obvious errors that we think of as characteristic of bad writing. Yet he could not write a decent sentence, paragraph, or

From *College Composition and Communication* (October, 1963). © 1963 by the National Council of Teachers of English. Reprinted by permission of the publisher and Wayne C. Booth.

paper until his rhetorical problem was solved—until, that is, he had found a definition of his audience, his argument, and his own proper tone of voice.

[2]   The word "rhetoric" is one of those catch-all terms that can easily raise trouble when our backs are turned. As it regains a popularity that it once seemed permanently to have lost, its meanings seem to range all the way from something like "the whole art of writing on any subject," as in Kenneth Burke's *The Rhetoric of Religion,* through "the special arts of persuasion," on down to fairly narrow notions about rhetorical figures and devices. And of course we still have with us the meaning of "empty bombast," as in the phrase "merely rhetorical."

[3]   I suppose that the question of the role of rhetoric in the English course is meaningless if we think of rhetoric in either its broadest or its narrowest meanings. No English course could avoid dealing with rhetoric in Burke's sense, under whatever name, and on the other hand nobody would ever advocate anything so questionable as teaching "mere rhetoric." But if we settle on the following, traditional, definition, some real questions are raised: "Rhetoric is the art of finding and employing the most effective means of persuasion on any subject, considered independently of intellectual mastery of that subject." As the students say, "Prof. X knows his stuff but he doesn't know how to put it across." If rhetoric is thought of as the art of "putting it across," considered as quite distinct from mastering an "it" in the first place, we are immediately landed in a bramble bush of controversy. Is there such an art? If so, what does it consist of? Does it have a content of its own? Can it be taught? Should it be taught? If it should, how do we go about it, head on or obliquely?

[4]   Obviously it would be foolish to try to deal with many of these issues in twenty minutes. But I wish that there were more signs of our taking all of them seriously. I wish that along with our new passion for structural linguistics, for example, we could point to the development of a rhetorical theory that would show just how knowledge of structural linguistics can be useful to anyone interested in the art of persuasion. I wish there were more freshman texts that related every principle and every rule to functional principles of rhetoric, or, where this proves impossible, I wish one found more systematic discussion of why it is impossible. But for today, I must content myself with a brief look at the charge that there is nothing distinctive and teachable about the art of rhetoric.

[5]   The case against the isolability and teachability of rhetoric may look at first like a good one. Nobody writes rhetoric, just as nobody ever writes writing. What we write and speak is always *this* discussion of the decline of railroading and *that* discussion of Pope's couplets and the other argument for abolishing the poll-tax or for getting rhetoric back into English studies.

[6]   We can also admit that like all the arts, the art of rhetoric is at best very chancy, only partly amenable to systematic teaching; as we are all painfully aware when our 1:00 section goes miserably and our 2:00 section of the same course is a delight, our own rhetoric is not entirely under control. Successful rhetoricians are to some extent like poets, born, not

made. They are also dependent on years of practice and experience. And we can finally admit that even the firmest of principles about writing cannot be taught in the same sense that elementary logic or arithmetic or French can be taught. In my first year of teaching, I had a student who started his first two essays with a swear word. When I suggested that perhaps the third paper ought to start with something else, he protested that his high school teacher had taught him always to catch the reader's attention. Now the teacher was right, but the application of even such a firm principle requires reserves of tact that were somewhat beyond my freshman.

[7] But with all of the reservations made, surely the charge that the art of persuasion cannot in any sense be taught is baseless. I cannot think that anyone who has ever read Aristotle's *Rhetoric* or, say, Whateley's *Elements of Rhetoric* could seriously make the charge. There is more than enough in these and the other traditional rhetorics to provide structure and content for a year-long course. I believe that such a course, when planned and carried through with intelligence and flexibility, can be one of the most important of all educational experiences. But it seems obvious that the arts of persuasion cannot be learned in one year, that a good teacher will continue to teach them regardless of his subject matter, and that we as English teachers have a special responsibility at all levels to get certain basic rhetorical principles into all of our writing assignments. When I think back over the experiences which have had any actual effect on my writing, I find the great good fortune of a splendid freshman course, taught by a man who believed in what he was doing, but I also find a collection of other experiences quite unconnected with a specific writing course. I remember the instructor in psychology who pencilled one word after a peculiarly pretentious paper of mine: *bull.* I remember the day when P. A. Christensen talked with me about my Chaucer paper, and made me understand that my failure to use effective transitions was not simply a technical fault but a fundamental block in my effort to get him to see my meaning. His off-the-cuff pronouncement that I should never let myself write a sentence that was not in some way explicitly attached to preceding and following sentences meant far more to me at that moment, when I had something I wanted to say, than it could have meant as part of a pattern of such rules offered in a writing course. Similarly, I can remember the devastating lessons about my bad writing that Ronald Crane could teach with a simple question mark on a graduate seminar paper, or a pencilled "Evidence for this?" or "Why this section here?" or "Everybody says so. Is it true?"

[8] Such experiences are not, I like to think, simply the result of my being a late bloomer. At least I find my colleagues saying such things as "I didn't learn to write until I became a newspaper reporter," or "The most important training in writing I had was doing a dissertation under old *Blank.*" Sometimes they go on to say that the freshman course was useless; sometimes they say that it was an indispensable preparation for the later experience. The diversity of such replies is so great as to suggest that before we try to reorganize the freshman course, with or without

explicit confrontations with rhetorical categories, we ought to look for whatever there is in common among our experiences, both of good writing and of good writing instruction. Whatever we discover in such an enterprise ought to be useful to us at any level of our teaching. It will not, presumably, decide once and for all what should be the content of the freshman course, if there should be such a course. But it might serve as a guideline for the development of widely different programs in the widely differing institutional circumstances in which we must work.

[9]   The common ingredient that I find in all of the writing I admire— excluding for now novels, plays and poems—is something that I shall reluctantly call the rhetorical stance, a stance which depends on discovering and maintaining in any writing situation a proper balance among the three elements that are at work in any communicative effort: the available arguments about the subject itself, the interests and peculiarities of the audience, and the voice, the implied character, of the speaker. I should like to suggest that it is this balance, this rhetorical stance, difficult as it is to describe, that is our main goal as teachers of rhetoric. Our ideal graduate will strike this balance automatically in any writing that he considers finished. Though he may never come to the point of finding the balance easily, he will know that it is what makes the difference between effective communication and mere wasted effort.

[10]   What I mean by the true rhetorician's stance can perhaps best be seen by contrasting it with two or three corruptions, unbalanced stances often assumed by people who think they are practicing the arts of persuasion.

[11]   The first I'll call the pedant's stance; it consists of ignoring or underplaying the personal relationship of speaker and audience and depending entirely on statements about a subject—that is, the notion of a job to be done for a particular audience is left out. It is a virtue, of course, to respect the bare truth of one's subject, and there may even be some subjects which in their very nature define an audience and a rhetorical purpose so that adequacy to the subject can be the whole art of presentation. For example, an article on "The relation of the ontological and teleological proofs," in a recent *Journal of Religion,* requires a minimum of adaptation of argument to audience. But most subjects do not in themselves imply in any necessary way a purpose and an audience and hence a speaker's tone. The writer who assumes that it is enough merely to write an exposition of what he happens to know on the subject will produce the kind of essay that soils our scholarly journals, written not for readers but for bibliographies.

[12]   In my first year of teaching I taught a whole unit on "exposition" without ever suggesting, so far as I can remember, that the students ask themselves what their expositions were *for.* So they wrote expositions like this one—I've saved it, to teach me toleration of my colleagues: the title is "Family relations in More's *Utopia.*" "In this theme I would like to discuss some of the relationships with the family which Thomas More elaborates and sets forth in his book, *Utopia.* The first thing that I would like to discuss about family relations is that overpopulation, according

to More, is a just cause of war." And so on. Can you hear that student sneering at me, in this opening? What he is saying is something like "you ask for a meaningless paper, I give you a meaningless paper." He knows that he has no audience except me. He knows that I don't want to read his summary of family relations in *Utopia*, and he knows that I know that he therefore has no rhetorical purpose. Because he has not been led to see a question which he considers worth answering, or an audience that could possibly care one way or the other, the paper is worse than no paper at all, even though it has no grammatical or spelling errors and is organized right down the line, one, two, three.

[13]   An extreme case, you may say. Most of us would never allow ourselves that kind of empty fencing? Perhaps. But if some carefree foundation is willing to finance a statistical study, I'm willing to wager a month's salary that we'd find at least half of the suggested topics in our freshman texts as pointless as mine was. And we'd find a good deal more than half of the discussions of grammar, punctuation, spelling, and style totally divorced from any notion that rhetorical purpose to some degree controls all such matters. We can offer objective descriptions of levels of usage from now until graduation, but unless the student discovers a desire to say something to somebody and learns to control his diction for a purpose, we've gained very little. I once gave an assignment asking students to describe the same classroom in three different statements, one for each level of usage. They were obedient, but the only ones who got anything from the assignment were those who intuitively imported the rhetorical instructions I had overlooked—such purposes as "Make fun of your scholarly surroundings by describing this classroom in extremely elevated style," or "Imagine a kid from the slums accidentally trapped in these surroundings and forced to write a description of this room." A little thought might have shown me how to give the whole assignment some human point, and therefore some educative value.

[14]   Just how confused we can allow ourselves to be about such matters is shown in a recent publication of the Educational Testing Service, called "Factors in Judgments of Writing Ability." In order to isolate those factors which affect differences in grading standards, ETS set six groups of readers—business men, writers and editors, lawyers, and teachers of English, social science and natural science—to reading the same batch of papers. Then ETS did a hundred-page "factor analysis" of the amount of agreement and disagreement, and of the elements which different kinds of graders emphasized. The authors of the report express a certain amount of shock at the discovery that the median correlation was only .31 and that 94% of the papers received either 7, 8, or 9 of the 9 possible grades.

[15]   But what *could* they have expected? In the first place, the students were given no purpose and no audience when the essays were assigned. And then all these editors and business men and academics were asked to judge the papers in a complete vacuum, using only whatever intuitive standards they cared to use. I'm surprise that there was any correlation at all. Lacking instructions, some of the students undoubtedly wrote

polemical essays, suitable for the popular press; others no doubt imagined an audience, say, of *Reader's Digest* readers, and others wrote with the English teachers as implied audience; an occasional student with real philosophical bent would no doubt do a careful analysis of the pros and cons of the case. This would be graded low, of course, by the magazine editors, even though they would have graded it high if asked to judge it as a speculative contribution to the analysis of the problem. Similarly, a creative student who has been getting A's for his personal essays will write an amusing colorful piece, failed by all the social scientists present, though they would have graded it high if asked to judge it for what it was. I find it shocking than tens of thousands of dollars and endless hours should have been spent by students, graders, and professional testers analyzing essays and grading results totally abstracted from any notion of purposeful human communication. Did nobody protest? One might as well assemble a group of citizens to judge students' capacity to throw balls, say, without telling the students or the graders whether altitude, speed, accuracy or form was to be judged. The judges would be drawn from football coaches, hai-lai experts, lawyers, and English teachers, and asked to apply whatever standard they intuitively apply to ball throwing. Then we could express astonishment that the judgments did not correlate very well, and we could do a factor analysis to discover, lo and behold, that some readers concentrated on altitude, some on speed, some on accuracy, some on form—and the English teachers were simply confused.

[16] One effective way to combat the pedantic stance is to arrange for weekly confrontations of groups of students over their own papers. We have done far too little experimenting with arrangements for providing a genuine audience in this way. Short of such developments, it remains true that a good teacher can convince his students that he is a true audience, if his comments on the papers show that some sort of dialogue is taking place. As Jacques Barzun says in *Teacher in America,* students should be made to feel that unless they have said something to someone, they have failed; to bore the teacher is a worse form of failure than to anger him. From this point of view we can see that the charts of grading symbols that mar even the best freshman texts are not the innocent time savers that we pretend. Plausible as it may seem to arrange for more corrections with less time, they inevitably reduce the student's sense of purpose in writing. When he sees innumerable W13's and P19's in the margin, he cannot possibly feel that the art of persuasion is as important to his instructor as when he reads personal comments, however few.

[17] This first perversion, then, springs from ignoring the audience or over-reliance on the pure subject. The second, which might be called the advertiser's stance, comes from *under*valuing the subject and overvaluing pure effect: how to win friends and influence people.

[18] Some of our best freshman texts—Sheridan Baker's *The Practical Stylist,* for example—allow themselves on occasion to suggest that to be controversial or argumentative, to stir up an audience is an end in itself. Sharpen the controversial edge, one of them says, and the clear

implication is that one should do so even if the truth of the subject is honed off in the process. This perversion is probably in the long run a more serious threat in our society than the danger of ignoring the audience. In the time of audience-reaction meters and pre-tested plays and novels, it is not easy to convince students of the old Platonic truth that good persuasion is honest persuasion, or even of the old Aristotelian truth that the good rhetorician must be master of his subject, no matter how dishonest he may decide ultimately to be. Having told them that good writers always to some degree accommodate their arguments to the audience, it is hard to explain the difference between justified accommodation—say changing *point one* to the final position—and the kind of accommodation that fills our popular magazines, in which the very substance of what is said is accommodated to some preconception of what will sell. "The publication of *Eros* [magazine] represents a major breakthrough in the battle for the liberation of the human spirit."

[19]   At a dinner about a month ago I sat between the wife of a famous civil rights lawyer and an advertising consultant. "I saw the article on your book yesterday in the Daily News," she said, "but I didn't even finish it. The title of your book scared me off. Why did you ever choose such a terrible title? Nobody would buy a book with a title like that." The man on my right, whom I'll call Mr. Kinches, overhearing my feeble reply, plunged into a conversation with her, over my torn and bleeding corpse. "Now with my *last* book," he said, "I listed 20 possible titles and then tested them out on 400 business men. The one I chose was voted for by 90 percent of the businessmen." "That's what I was just saying to Mr. Booth," she said. "A book title ought to grab you, and *rhetoric* is not going to grab anybody." "Right," he said. "My *last* book sold 50,000 copies already; I don't know how this one will do, but I polled 200 businessmen on the table of contents, and . . ."

[20]   At one point I did manage to ask him whether the title he chose really fit the book. "Not quite as well as one or two of the others," he admitted, "but that doesn't matter, you know. If the book is designed right, so that the first chapter pulls them in, and you *keep* 'em in, who's going to gripe about a little inaccuracy in the title?"

[21]   Well, rhetoric is the art of persuading, not the art seeming to persuade by giving everything away at the start. It presupposes that one has a purpose concerning a subject which itself cannot be fundamentally modified by the desire to persuade. If Edmund Burke had decided that he could win more votes in Parliament by choosing the other side—as he most certainly could have done—we would hardly hail this party-switch as a master stroke of rhetoric. If Churchill had offered the British "peace in our time," with some laughs thrown in, because opinion polls had shown that more Britishers were "grabbed" by these than by blood, sweat, and tears, we could hardly call his decision a sign of rhetorical skill.

[22]   One could easily discover other perversions of the rhetorician's balance—most obviously what might be called the entertainer's stance—the willingness to sacrifice substance to personality and charm. I admire

Walker Gibson's efforts to startle us out of dry pedantry, but I know from experience that his exhortations to find and develop the speaker's voice can lead to empty colorfulness. A student once said to me, complaining about a colleague, "I soon learned that all I had to do to get an A was imitate Thurber."

[23]   But perhaps this is more than enough about the perversions of the rhetorical stance. Balance itself is always harder to describe than the clumsy poses that result when it is destroyed. But we all experience the balance whenever we find an author who succeeds in changing our minds. He can do so only if he knows more about the subject than we do, and if he then engages us in the process of thinking—and feeling—it through. What makes the rhetoric of Milton and Burke and Churchill great is that each presents us with the spectacle of a man passionately involved in thinking an important question through, in the company of an audience. Though each of them did everything in his power to make his point persuasive, including a pervasive use of the many emotional appeals that have been falsely scorned by many a freshman composition text, none would have allowed himself the advertiser's stance; none would have polled the audience in advance to discover which position would get the votes. Nor is the highly individual personality that springs out at us from their speeches and essays present for the sake of selling itself. The rhetorical balance among speakers, audience, and argument is with all three men habitual, as we see if we look at their non-political writings. Burke's work on the Sublime and Beautiful is a relatively unimpassioned philosophical treatise, but one finds there again a delicate balance: though the implied author of this work is a far different person, far less obtrusive, far more objective, than the man who later cried *sursum corda* to the British Parliament, he permeates with his philosophical personality his philosophical work. And though the signs of his awareness of his audience are far more subdued, they are still here: every effort is made to involve the *proper* audience, the audience of philosophical minds, in a fundamentally interesting inquiry, and to lead them through to the end. In short, because he was a man engaged with men in the effort to solve a human problem, one could never call what he wrote dull, however difficult or abstruse.

[24]   Now obviously the habit of seeking this balance is not the only thing we have to teach under the heading of rhetoric. But I think that everything worth teaching under that heading finds its justification finally in that balance. Much of what is now considered irrelevant or dull can, in fact, be brought to life when teachers and students know what they are seeking. Churchill reports that the most valuable training he ever received in rhetoric was in the diagramming of sentences. Think of it! Yet the diagramming of a sentence, regardless of the grammatical system, can be a live subject as soon as one asks not simply "How is this sentence put together," but rather "Why is it put together in this way?" or "Could the rhetorical balance and hence the desired persuasion be better achieved by writing it differently?"

[25]   As a nation we are reputed to write very badly. As a nation, I would say, we are more inclined to the perversions of rhetoric than to the rhetorical balance. Regardless of what we do about this or that course in the curriculum, our mandate would seem to be, then, to lead more of our students than we now do to care about and practice the true arts of persuasion.

words and sentences

1. Vocabulary: *pretentious, polemic* (¶ 1); *rhetoric* (2); *isolability* (5); *amenable* (6); *ontological, teleological* (11); *exhortations* (22); *abstruse, permeates* (23).

2. Why does Booth use the word *perversion* to describe the absence of "rhetorical balance"? What other word choices were available to Booth? Might some other word choice be more appropriate? Why or why not?

3. Look up some definitions of the word *rhetoric* and compare them with the definition Booth presents. How are they alike and different?

4. Restate in your own words Booth's definition of "rhetorical stance." Limit yourself to one sentence.

5. What does Booth mean by "implied characters" (¶ 4) and "implied author" (¶ 23)?

6. Write a sentence of your own imitating the pattern of sentence six in ¶ 7. Describe the structure of this sentence.

7. Write a sentence of your own imitating the pattern of sentence six in ¶ 23. Then rewrite Booth's sentence, rearranging the patterns. Try to make your rewriting more effective than Booth's sentence.

8. Write a paragraph of your own imitating the patterns of ¶ 4. Note Booth's use of repetition. Comment on the effect of this repetition in Booth's paragraph and your own.

ideas and implications

1. What does Booth mean by "rhetorical balance"? How does one achieve it?

2. How much emphasis does Booth place on writing as an act of discovery? Why?

3. In ¶ 5, Booth says, "Nobody writes rhetoric, just as nobody ever writes writing." What are the implications of his statement?

4. Does Booth believe that writing can be taught? Does he believe that rhetoricians are born and not made? Support your answers with specific sentences from the essay.

5. How much emphasis does Booth place on audience? Why?

6. Does Booth tell his readers how he has learned to write? Point to specific sentences to support your answer.

7. What audience is Booth apparently addressing? How do you know?

8. Does Booth define good writing as "correctness"?

strategies

1. How does Booth open his essay? What strategy is he employing in the opening and how effective is that strategy?
2. What is the function of ¶ 15? Is the final sentence of this paragraph effective?
3. In what paragraph does Booth state the thesis of his essay? Could he have stated his thesis earlier in the essay? Why doesn't he?
4. Booth uses many anecdotes to illustrate his points. What are the sources of these anecdotes? Do these anecdotes tell us anything about the speaker in the essay?
5. What is the function of ¶ 17? What words in this paragraph signal its function?
6. In ¶s 10-22, Booth discusses "two or three" corruptions of rhetorical balance. How many paragraphs does he devote to each of these corruptions? On which one does he place the greatest emphasis? Could you outline ¶s 10-22? What is the function, then, of ¶ 23?

suggestions for writing

1. Write a paper for which you have clearly ascertained a specific audience. For example, you might write for the reader of *Scientific American, The Ladies' Home Journal, The Progressive Farmer,* etc. Be prepared to discuss how aiming at a specific audience influences your organization, your word choice, and your voice.
2. Write a paper about a situation in which a speaker or writer completely misjudged his audience. Be certain that you explain what went wrong.
3. Collect and comment upon some examples of writing in which the authors have assumed an "unbalanced rhetorical stance." You might profitably use the categories Booth cites.
4. Look back at the three versions of "Little Red Riding Hood" in the introduction to Section 1. Try to determine the audiences of these three versions. Then write a paper of your own directed at one of these audiences.
5. Find a story in the King James Bible—a story that you like. Then retell that story using the "pedantic" stance Booth discusses. Compare the King James version of the story and your retelling of it. What is the effect of the pedantic stance? What does this stance do to the story and the language used to tell it?

Sydney J. Harris

You Need an Ear for Words to Write

[1] While reading the entries, as one of the judges in a collegiate writing contest, I was reminded of Mark Twain's annoyed remark that "the difference between the right word and the *almost* right word is the difference between lightning and the lightning bug."

Most persons—and this includes aspiring writers—simply fail to recognize that there are very few true synonyms in the language, no matter what the dictionary may insist.

The dictionary, for instance, gives "devour" as a synonym for "eat." But no woman would care to have it said of her that she "devoured her dinner," which sounds more like an animal than a human. (Indeed, German has "essen" for human eating, and "fressen" for animal eating.)

Again, a woman's eyes may "glow" with affection, but they do not "glitter," although the two words are roughly synonymous. Eyes "glitter" with greed or contempt, but they "glow" with love or compassion.

[5] Distinguishing between two words that seem to mean the same, but have different colors and shapes and suggestions—that is essential to the art of writing, and also of speaking. The dictionary can tell you only what a word points to; it cannot tell you what it feels like.

An interesting example is the word "fat." The unabridged dictionary gives as synonyms: fleshy, plump, corpulent, obese, stocky, portly, tubby, and thick, among others.

Obviously, different people are fat in different ways—a woman may be "fleshy," but a man is "portly." "Obese" carries the connotation of a glandular sickness. "Stocky" involves size as well as shape. We speak of a "plump" or "tubby" baby, but nobody would call him "corpulent."

The same is true of hundreds of words which only superficially resemble one another. "Unspeakable" in the dictionary means the same as "unutterable"—but the former is always used to mean something base or vile, while the latter usually means some rapturous or divine thought or emotion.

The right word is as important to the writer as the right note to the composer or the right line to the painter. Hemingway's prose is so compelling (despite his defects of mind) precisely because he always knows the right word to capture the essence of a situation or the feel of a person. A writer needs an "ear" as much as a musician does.

[10] And without this ear, he is lost and groping in a forest of words, where all the trees look much alike.

From Sydney J. Harris, *Last Things First.* © 1961 by Sydney J. Harris. Reprinted by permission of the publisher, Houghton Mifflin Company.

words and sentences

1. Vocabulary: *superficially, rapturous* (¶ 8).
2. Write a sentence imitating the pattern of the sentence in ¶ 1. Is this sentence pattern loose or periodic? Describe the structure of the sentence you have written.
3. Write a sentence imitating the pattern of the sentence in ¶ 10. Is this a loose or a periodic sentence?
4. Write a sentence imitating the pattern of the first sentence in ¶ 5. Note Harris's use of the dash in this sentence. Describe the pattern of the sentence you have written.

ideas and implications

1. What is Harris's attitude towards the unabridged dictionary? And dictionaries generally?
2. What are the implications of Harris's statement that "there are very few true synonyms in the language"?
3. What does Harris mean when he says that the dictionary cannot tell us what a word "feels like"?

strategies

1. What strategy does Harris use for beginning his essay? Why?
2. What is the principal strategy that Harris employs for presenting his ideas? Give examples to support your observation.
3. Could ¶s 6 and 7 be joined in a single paragraph? Why might Harris choose to make two paragraphs here instead of one?
4. In ¶ 9, Harris uses a comparison to illustrate his point. How appropriate is that comparison? Does the comparison help the reader understand what a word "feels like"?
5. Does Harris state his thesis in the essay? If so, in what paragraph does that statement appear?

suggestions for writing

1. Collect and comment on some examples of writing in which the author's "ear for words" has failed him. In your paper, try to explain why this failure occurred.
2. Write a paper describing a situation in which your failure to have an "ear for words" proved embarrassing.
3. Check a word that interests you in an unabridged dictionary; look at the synonyms given. Then write a paper about the word and its synonyms. In your paper, try to show how the synonyms "feel" different from the word you have looked up.

Benjamin Franklin

from **The Autobiography**

[1]   From a child I was fond of reading, and all the little money that came into my hands was ever laid out in books. Pleased with the Pilgrim's Progress, my first collection was of John Bunyan's works in separate little volumes. I afterward sold them to enable me to buy R. Burton's Historical Collections; they were small champmen's books, and cheap, 40 or 50 in all. My father's little library consisted chiefly of books in polemic divinity, most of which I read, and have since often regretted that, at a time when I had such a thirst for knowledge, more proper books had not fallen in my way, since it was now resolved I should not be a clergyman. Plutarch's Lives there was in which I read abundantly, and I still think that time spent to great advantage. There was also a book of De Foe's, called an Essay on Projects, and another of Dr Mather's, called Essays to do Good, which perhaps gave me a turn of thinking that had an influence on some of the principal future events of my life.

[2]   This bookish inclination at length determined my father to make me a printer, though he had already one son (James) of that profession. In 1717 my brother James returned from England with a press and letters to set up his business in Boston. I liked it much better than that of my father, but still had a hankering for the sea. To prevent the apprehended effect of such an inclination, my father was impatient to have me bound to my brother. I stood out some time, but at last was persuaded, and signed the indentures when I was yet but twelve years old. I was to serve as an apprentice till I was twenty-one years of age, only I was to be allowed journeyman's wages during the last year. In a little time I made great proficiency in the business, and became a useful hand to my brother. I now had access to better books. An acquaintance with the apprentices of booksellers enabled me sometimes to borrow a small one, which I was careful to return soon and clean. Often I sat up in my room reading the greatest part of the night, when the book was borrowed in the evening and to be returned early in the morning, lest it should be missed or wanted.

[3]   And after some time an ingenious tradesman, Mr. Matthew Adams, who had a pretty collection of books, and who frequented our printing-house, took notice of me, invited me to his library, and very kindly lent me such books as I chose to read. I now took a fancy to poetry, and made some little pieces; my brother, thinking it might turn to account, encouraged me, and put me on composing occasional ballads. One was called *The Lighthouse Tragedy,* and contained an account of the drowning of Captain Worthilake, with his two daughters: the other was a sailor's song, on the taking of *Teach* (or Blackbeard) the pirate. They were wretched stuff, in the Grub-street-ballad style; and when they were printed he sent me about the town to sell them. The first sold wonder-

fully, the event being recent, having made a great noise. This flattered my vanity; but my father discouraged me by ridiculing my performances, and telling me verse-makers were generally beggars. So I escaped being a poet, most probably a very bad one; but as prose writing has been of great use to me in the course of my life, and was a principal means of my advancement, I shall tell you how, in such a situation, I acquired what little ability I have in that way.

[4]   There was another bookish lad in the town, John Collins by name, with whom I was intimately acquainted. We sometimes disputed, and very fond we were of argument, and very desirous of confuting one another, which disputatious turn, by the way, is apt to become a very bad habit, making people often extremely disagreeable in company by the contradiction that is necessary to bring it into practice; and thence, besides souring and spoiling the conversation, is productive of disgusts and, perhaps enmities where you may have occasion for friendship. I had caught it by reading my father's books of dispute about religion. Persons of good sense, I have since observed, seldom fall into it, except lawyers, university men, and men of all sorts that have been bred at Edinborough.

[5]   A question was once, somehow or other, started between Collins and me, of the propriety of educating the female sex in learning, and their abilities for study. He was of opinion that it was improper, and that they were naturally unequal to it. I took the contrary side, perhaps a little for dispute's sake. He was naturally more eloquent, had a ready plenty of words; and sometimes, as I thought, bore me down more by his fluency than by the strength of his reasons. As we parted without settling the point, and were not to see one another again for some time, I sat down to put my arguments in writing, which I copied fair and sent to him. He answered, and I replied. Three or four letters of a side had passed, when my father happened to find my papers and read them. Without entering into the discussion, he took occasion to talk to me about the manner of my writing; observed that, though I had the advantage of my antagonist in correct spelling and pointing (which I ow'd to the printing-house), I fell far short in elegance of expression, in method and in perspicuity, of which he convinced me by several instances. I saw the justice of his remarks, and thence grew more attentive to the manner in writing, and determined to endeavor at improvement.

[6]   About this time I met with an odd volume of the *Spectator*. It was the third. I had never before seen any of them. I bought it, read it over and over, and was much delighted with it. I thought the writing excellent, and wished, if possible, to imitate it. With this view I took some of the papers, and, making short hints of the sentiment in each sentence, laid them by a few days, and then, without looking at the book, try'd to compleat the papers again, by expressing each hinted sentiment at length, and as fully as it had been expressed before, in any suitable words that should come to hand. Then I compared my *Spectator* with the original, discovered some of my faults, and corrected them. But I found I wanted a stock of words, or a readiness in recollecting and using them,

which I thought I should have acquired before that time if I had gone on making verses; since the continual occasion for words of the same import, but of different length, to suit the measure, or of different sound for the rhyme, would have laid me under a constant necessity of searching for variety, and also have tended to fix that variety in my mind, and make me master of it. Therefore I took some of the tales and turned them into verse; and, after a time, when I had pretty well forgotten the prose, turned them back again. I also sometimes jumbled my collections of hints into confusion, and after some weeks endeavored to reduce them into the best order, before I began to form the full sentences and compleat the paper. This was to teach me method in the arrangement of thoughts. By comparing my work afterwards with the original, I discovered many faults and amended them; but I sometimes had the pleasure of fancying that, in certain particulars of small import, I had been lucky enough to improve the method or the language, and this encouraged me to think I might possibly in time come to be a tolerable English writer, of which I was extreamly ambitious. My time for these exercises and for reading was at night, after work or before it began in the morning, or on Sundays, when I contrived to be in the printing-house alone, evading as much as I could the common attendance on public worship which my father used to exact on me when I was under his care, and which indeed I still thought a duty, though I could not, as it seemed to me, afford time to practise it.

words and sentences

1. Vocabulary: *polemic* (¶ 1); *apprehended* (2); *disputatious, enmities* (4); *perspicuity* (5).
2. The pattern of sentence two in ¶ 4 is very complicated. Describe this pattern and then write a sentence of your own imitating Franklin's sentence.
3. Describe the patterns of the first six sentences in ¶ 6. Label these sentences simple, complex, compound, compound-complex. Does the structure of these sentences parallel in any way the ideas that Franklin communicates in each of these structures? In other words, do the structures of the sentences reflect the complexities of the ideas Franklin discusses in each?

ideas and implications

1. How important is reading in the development of Franklin's prose style? Why is reading significant?
2. Does Franklin speak humorously at points in his recounting of how he learned to write? If so, point to specific instances of his humor.
3. How important is imitation in Franklin's learning to write? Why?
4. For Franklin, what is the value of writing verses? Why?
5. How influential is Franklin's father in calling attention to writing problems? Point to specific passages to support your observation.

strategies

1. What is Franklin's "rhetorical stance" in these paragraphs? How aware
   is Franklin of his audience? Can you describe that audience?
2. Can you outline the major points of Franklin's observations?
3. What method of development does Franklin employ in ¶ 1? Does this
   paragraph have a topic sentence?
4. Is the first sentence in ¶ 3 a topic sentence? Why or why not? What
   method of development does Franklin use in this paragraph?

suggestions for writing

1. Choose an author whose style you admire and write a paper imitating
   that style. Xerox a page or two of the writer's prose and turn it in with
   your own paper.
2. Write a paragraph, then turn that paragraph into "verse." Then rewrite the paragraph in prose. Has your paragarph improved?
3. Rewrite one of Franklin's paragraphs to see if you can "improve" upon
   his style.
4. Write a paper in which you discuss how your own reading has influenced your writing. Be as specific as you can about these influences.
   Perhaps not all of these influences are written forms of prose.

H. L. Mencken

Literature and the Schoolma'm

[1]   With precious few exceptions, all the books on style in English are
by writers quite unable to write. The subject, indeed, seems to exercise a
special and dreadful fascination over schoolma'ms, bucolic college professors, and other such pseudo-literates. One never hears of treatises on
it by George Moore or James Branch Cabell, but the pedagogues, male
and female, are at it all the time. In a thousand texts they set forth
their depressing ideas about it, and millions of suffering high-school
pupils have to study what they say. Their central aim, of course, is to
reduce the whole thing to a series of simple rules—the overmastering
passion of their melancholy order, at all times and everywhere. They
aspire to teach it as bridge whist, the American Legion flag-drill and
double-entry bookkeeping are taught. They fail as ignominiously as

From H. L. Mencken, *Prejudices: Fifth Series.* © 1926 by Alfred A. Knopf, Inc. and
renewed 1954 by H. L. Mencken. Reprinted by permission of Alfred A. Knopf, Inc.

that Athenian of legend who essayed to train a regiment of grasshoppers in the goose-step.

[2]   For the essence of a sound style is that it cannot be reduced to rules—that it is a living and breathing thing, with something of the devilish in it—that it fits its proprietor tightly and yet ever so loosely, as his skin fits him. It is, in fact, quite as securely an integral part of him as that skin is. It hardens as his arteries harden. It has *Katzenjammer* on the days succeeding his indiscretions. It is gaudy when he is young and gathers decorum when he grows old. On the day after he makes a mash on a new girl it glows and glitters. If he has fed well, it is mellow. If he has gastritis it is bitter. In brief, a style is always the outward and visible symbol of a man, and it cannot be anything else. To attempt to teach it is as silly as to set up courses in making love. The man who makes love out of a book is not making love at all; he is simply imitating someone else making love. God help him if, in love or literary composition, his preceptor be a pedagogue!

[3]   The schoolma'm theory that the writing of English may be taught is based upon a faulty inference from a sound observation. The sound observation is that the great majority of American high-school pupils, when they attempt to put their thoughts upon paper, produce only a mass of confused and puerile nonsense—that they express themselves so clumsily that it is often quite impossible to understand them at all. The faulty inference is to the effect that what ails them is a defective technical equipment—that they can be trained to write clearly as a dog may be trained to walk on its hind legs. This is all wrong. What ails them is not a defective technical equipment but a defective natural equipment. They write badly simply because they cannot think clearly. They cannot think clearly because they lack the brains. Trying to teach them is as hopeless as trying to teach a dog with only one hind leg. Any human being who can speak English understandably has all the materials necessary to write English clearly, and even beautifully. There is nothing mysterious about the written language; it is precisely the same, in essence, as the spoken language. If a man can think in English at all, he can find words enough to express his ideas. The fact is proved abundantly by the excellent writing that often comes from so-called ignorant men. It is proved anew by the even better writing that is done on higher levels by persons of great simplicity, for example, Abraham Lincoln. Such writing commonly arouses little enthusiasm among pedagogues. Its transparency excites their professional disdain, and they are offended by its use of homely words and phrases. They prefer something more ornate and complex—something, as they would probably put it, demanding more thought. But the thought they yearn for is the kind, alas, that they secrete themselves—the muddled highfalutin, vapid thought that one finds in their own text-books.

[4]   I do not denounce them because they write so badly; I merely record the fact in a sad, scientific spirit. Even in such twilight regions of the intellect the style remains the man. What is in the head infallibly oozes out of the nub of the pen. If it is sparkling Burgundy the writing

is full of life and charm. If it is mush the writing is mush too. The late Dr. Harding, twenty-ninth President of the Federal Union, was a highly self-conscious stylist. He practiced prose composition assiduously, and was regarded by the pedagogues of Marion, Ohio, and vicinity as a very talented fellow. But when he sent a message to Congress it was so muddled in style that even the late Henry Cabot Lodge, a professional literary man, could not understand it. Why? Simply because Dr. Harding's thoughts, on the high and grave subjects he discussed, were so muddled that he couldn't understand them himself. But on matters within his range of customary meditation he was clear and even charming, as all of us are. I once heard him deliver a brief address upon the ideals of the Elks. It was a topic close to his heart, and he had thought about it at length and *con amore*. The result was an excellent speech— clear, logical, forceful, and with a touch of wild, romantic beauty. His sentences hung together. He employed simple words, and put them together with skill. But when, at a public meeting in Washington, he essayed to deliver an oration on the subject of the late Dante Alighieri, he quickly became so obscure and absurd that even the Diplomatic Corps began to snicker. The cause was plain: he knew no more about Dante than a Tennessee county judge knows about the Institutes of Justinian. Trying to formulate ideas upon the topic, he could get together only a few disjected fragments and ghosts of ideas—here an ear, there a section of tibia, beyond a puff of soul substance or other gas. The resultant speech was thus enigmatical, cacophonous and awful stuff. It sounded precisely like a lecture by a college professor on style.

[5]   A pedagogue, confronted by Dr. Harding in class, would have set him to the business of what is called improving his vocabulary—that is, to the business of making his writing even worse than it was. Dr. Harding, in point of fact, had all the vocabulary that he needed, and a great deal more. Any idea that he could formulate clearly he could convey clearly. Any idea that genuinely moved him he could invest with charm —which is to say, with what the pedagogues call style. I believe that this capacity is possessed by all literate persons above the age of fourteen. It is not acquired by studying text-books; it is acquired by learning how to think. Children even younger often show it. I have a niece, now eleven years old, who already has an excellent style. When she writes to me about things that interest her—in other words, about the things she is capable of thinking about—she puts her thoughts into clear, dignified and admirable English. Her vocabulary, so far, is unspoiled by schoolma'ms. She doesn't try to knock me out by bombarding me with hard words, and phrases filched from Addison. She is unaffected, and hence her writing is charming. But if she essayed to send me a communication on the subject, say, of Balkan politics or government ownership, her style would descend instantly to the level of that of Dr. Harding's state papers.

[6]   To sum up, style cannot go beyond the ideas which lie at the heart of it. If they are clear, it too will be clear. If they are held passionately, it will be eloquent. Trying to teach it to persons who cannot think,

especially when the business is attempted by persons who also cannot think, is a great waste of time, and an immoral imposition upon the taxpayers of the nation. It would be far more logical to devote all the energy to teaching, not writing, but logic—and probably just as useless. For I doubt that the art of thinking can be taught at all—at any rate, by school-teachers. It is not acquired, but congenital. Some persons are born with it. Their ideas flow in straight channels; they are capable of lucid reasoning; when they say anything it is instantly understandable; when they write anything it is clear and persuasive. They constitute, I should say, about one-eighth of one per cent of the human race. The rest of God's children are just as incapable of logical thought as they are incapable of jumping over the moon. Trying to teach them to think is as vain an enterprise as trying to teach a streptococcus the principles of Americanism. The only thing to do with them is to make Ph.D.'s of them, and set them to writing handbooks on style.

words and sentences

1. Vocabulary: *bucolic, pedagogues, ignominiously* (¶ 1); *puerile, vapid* (3); *assiduously, disjected, cacophonous* (4).
2. Are there any words or phrases which date Mencken's essay? List any that you find. Does such language detract from Mencken's argument?
3. Why does *precious* in the first sentence of ¶ 1 seem appropriate? What sense of the word is conveyed by its context?
4. Describe the structure of the last sentence in ¶ 3; then write a sentence of your own imitating that structure. Does the word *secrete* have specific connotative associations in the context of the sentence?
5. Examine carefully the comparison Mencken uses in the last three sentences of ¶ 2. What is the purpose of the comparison?

ideas and implications

1. What is Mencken's attitude towards rules for writing?
2. For Mencken, what is the relationship between spoken language and written language? Be specific.
3. According to Mencken, why do most people write badly?
4. Does Mencken believe that a person's style can change?
5. For Mencken, how important is improving vocabulary in learning to write? Why?
6. Does Mencken believe that "style" can be taught?
7. How much of the populace writes clearly and persuasively? Does this observation contradict any of the statements in ¶ 3?
8. For Mencken, what is the relationship between the writer's feelings about a subject and the language he uses to talk about these feelings?

strategies

1. What is the thesis of Mencken's essay? Is that thesis stated explicitly or implicitly?

2. Do Mencken's paragraphs have topic sentences? If so, label them; if not, frame a topic sentence for each paragraph.

3. Examine the first and the last sentences of Mencken's essay. What strategy has Mencken employed in the way he begins and ends his essay?

4. How much does Mencken rely on examples to forward his argument? Point to specific instances and comment on the purposes of the examples.

5. How much does Mencken rely on comparisons or analogies to forward his argument? List four or five of these comparisons and comment on the purpose of each.

6. Examine carefully the strategy Mencken uses in ¶ 4. Here Mencken uses examples and incidents. What other strategy besides example is Mencken using? Point also to the transitional devices Mencken employs in the paragraph.

suggestions for writing

1. Find and xerox what you regard as a "muddled, highfalutin, vapid" page of prose and then rewrite the passage in clear and persuasive language.

2. Find and xerox a page of clear and persuasive prose and rewrite the passage in "muddled, highfalutin, vapid" prose. Then comment on what you had to do to write unclearly and unpersuasively.

3. Write a paper on a topic close to your heart. (See ¶ 4 for Mencken's observation on this point.) As you write, keep in mind Mencken's observations on style. Then revise your paper completely, and turn in both versions.

George Jean Nathan

Clear Writing

[1]   One of the fallacies that hovers over the literary art is that the writer who thinks clearly will pretty generally write clearly, whereas the one whose thought is muddled will write in a muddled manner. Conan Doyle, when he enters the field of spooks and metaphysics, shows a mind as muddled as a tureen of potage Mongol, yet he writes simply, clearly and, so far as mere writing goes, effectively. The same is true of G. K. Chesterton when he goes in for religion, as it is true of Benedetto Croce when he tackles the higher metaphysics of criticism. On the other hand, a measure of the writing of the world's first and clearest philosophical

From *The World of George Jean Nathan*, ed. Charles Angoff. © 1952 by Alfred A. Knopf, Inc. Reprinted by permission of Mrs. George Jean Nathan.

thinkers is, from the viewpoint of mere writing as writing, ambiguous, defective, involved and clumsy. For one Nietzsche or Huxley who has written as clearly as he thought, you will find sufficient instances of clear thought transcribed groggily to paper—by way of example, some portions of Spinoza's *Ethics* and many more in the works of Kant.

[2] The fallacy of the short sentence as a symbol of clear and direct thought is equally persistent. The clearest and most important philosophical thought that has been contributed to man has often been expressed in sentences so long that it is difficult to remember the beginning of them by the time one has plowed one's way past the middle. The most planless and idiotic thought of the most idiotic writers has been visited upon us in the crisp, short and speciously effective sentences of political diatribes, newspaper editorials and dime novels.

George Jean Nathan

Style

[1] The common statement that a writer's style is a true reflection of the man, that his style is an outgrowth of his personality, is often absurd. The truth is that, in the case of many a writer, the personality is an outgrowth of the style. The writer creates a fictitious picture of himself as man in his style and then takes color from his style by way of living up to the popular conception of him. Shaw is an excellent example. His style is of telegraphic dynamite all compact: mentally aphrodisiac adjectives, meat-eating verbs, sequences that are tipsy with the wine of gaiety. The man himself is intrinsically exactly the opposite. Shaw, the man, is no more the blood-brother of the Shaw style than Cabell, the man, is the blood-brother of the Cabell style. Shaw's style is less a true reflection of Shaw as man than, let us say, of John Maynard Keynes as man. Shaw, however, wise showman that he is, has simply created himself in its own image. He has carefully evolved a completely alien and artificial style, set it up as a dummy, and then appropriated the dummy's trousers for himself.

[2] Dreiser's style is Dreiser; Lewis' style is Lewis; Harold Bell Wright's style is Wright. But Lardner's style is no more Lardner, *Homo sapiens* and Great Neck householder, than Dunsany's style is Dunsany, *Homo sapiens* and Gargantuan oyster eater. The ivory elephant that the estimable and realistic Lord wears on a black ribbon around his neck is a

From *The World of George Jean Nathan*, ed. Charles Angoff. © 1952 by Alfred A. Knopf, Inc. Reprinted by permission of Mrs. George Jean Nathan.

concession to his style, just as the open-collar shirt and tousled hair of Jack London were a concession to his. Style is less often the man than the concept of him he wishes his readers to have. The sentence structure, the sequences, the juxtapositions and the verbal trickeries and cadences of many men of letters are no more reflections of their inner beings than the rôles most actors play are reflections of theirs.

words and sentences

1. Vocabulary: "Clear Writing"—*metaphysics* (¶ 1); *diatribes* (2). "Style"—*aphrodisiac* (1); *estimable, juxtapositions* (2).
2. If you are unfamiliar with many of the names Nathan alludes to, check these in a biographical dictionary. How important are these names in Nathan's argument?
3. Is the first sentence of ¶ 2 in "Clear Writing" a loose or a periodic sentence? Is the sentence effective?
4. Is Nathan using a sentence structure that parallels his idea in the second sentence of ¶ 2 in "Clear Writing"?
5. Compare and contrast the structures of the last sentences in "Clear Writing" and "Style." How are these sentences alike and different? Then write sentences of your own imitating these patterns.

ideas and implications

1. Explore the implications of Nathan's statement: "Style is less often the man than the concept of him he wishes his readers to have."
2. What kind of proof does Nathan offer to support his statement that style is sometimes not the man? Is that evidence convincing? Why or why not?
3. How do Nathan's ideas about style differ from Mencken's?

strategies

1. State in a sentence the thesis ideas of each of Nathan's brief essays.
2. Do Nathan's paragraphs contain topic sentences? If so, locate them.
3. What kind of evidence does Nathan present to develop his main ideas of his paragraphs? Be specific.

suggestions for writing

1. Collect a half dozen lengthy, involved sentences which seem clear to you. Then write a paper explaining why these sentences are clear.
2. Write a paper in which you create the voice and style of a person that is not you.
3. Write a short paper (about two paragraphs) giving *your* definition of *style*.
4. Using papers you have written earlier in the term, examine in detail your own prose style. Is the style a reflection of your personality and character? Are there elements of "posing" in your style? Is your style borrowed? Is your style really you?

William Shakespeare

"To Be, or Not to Be"
from *Hamlet*

HAMLET: To be, or not to be: that is the question:
Whether 'tis nobler in the mind to suffer
The slings and arrows of outrageous fortune,
Or to take arms against a sea of troubles,
And by opposing end them? To die: to sleep;   5
No more; and by a sleep to say we end
The heart-ache and the thousand natural shocks
That flesh is heir to, 'tis a consummation
Devoutly to be wish'd. To die, to sleep;
To sleep: perchance to dream: ay, there's the rub;   10
For in that sleep of death what dreams may come
When we have shuffled off this mortal coil,
Must give us pause: there's the respect
That makes calamity of so long life;
For who would bear the whips and scorns of time,   15
The oppressor's wrong, the proud man's contumely,
The pangs of despised love, the law's delay,
The insolence of office and the spurns
That patient merit of the unworthy takes,
When he himself might his quietus make   20
With a bare bodkin? who would fardels bear,
To grunt and sweat under a weary life,
But that the dread of something after death,
The undiscover'd country from whose bourn
No traveler returns, puzzles the will   25
And makes us rather bear those ills we have
Than fly to others that we know not of?
Thus conscience does make cowards of us all;
And thus the native hue of resolution
Is sicklied o'er with the pale cast of thought,   30
And enterprises of great pitch and moment
With this regard their currents turn awry,
And lose the name of action.—Soft you now!
The fair Ophelia! Nymph, in thy orisons
Be all my sins remember'd.   35

Samuel L. Clemens

Shakespeare Revised
from *Adventures of Huckleberry Finn*

[1]   It was after sun-up now, but we went right on and didn't tie up. The king and the duke turned out by and by looking pretty rusty; but after they'd jumped overboard and took a swim it chippered them up a good deal. After breakfast the king he took a seat on the corner of the raft, and pulled off his boots and rolled up his britches, and let his legs dangle in the water, so as to be comfortable, and lit his pipe, and went to getting his "Romeo and Juliet" by heart. When he had got it pretty good him and the duke begun to practise it together. The duke had to learn him over and over again how to say every speech; and he made him sigh, and put his hand on his heart, and after a while he said he done it pretty well; "only," he says, "you mustn't bellow out *Romeo!* that way, like a bull—you must say it soft and sick and languishy, so— R-o-o-meo! that is the idea; for Juliet's a dear sweet mere child of a girl, you know, and she doesn't bray like a jackass."

[2]   Well, next they got out a couple of long swords that the duke made out of oak laths, and begun to practise the sword-fight—the duke called himself Richard III.; and the way they laid on and pranced around the raft was grand to see. But by and by the king tripped and fell overboard, and after that they took a rest, and had a talk about all kinds of adventures they'd had in other times along the river.

After dinner the duke says:

"Well, Capet, we'll want to make this a first-class show, you know, so I guess we'll add a little more to it. We want a little something to answer encores with, anyway."

[5]   "What's onkores, Bilgewater?"

The duke told him, and then says:

"I'll answer by doing the Highland fling or the sailor's hornpipe; and you—well, let me see—oh, I've got it—you can do Hamlet's soliloquy."

"Hamlet's which?"

"Hamlet's soliloquy, you know; the most celebrated thing in Shakespeare. Ah, it's sublime, sublime! Always fetches the house. I haven't got it in the book—I've only got one volume—but I reckon I can piece it out from memory. I'll just walk up and down a minute, and see if I can call it back from recollection's vaults."

[10]   So he went to marching up and down, thinking, and frowning horrible every now and then; then he would hoist up his eyebrows; next he would squeeze his hand on his forehead and stagger back and kind of moan; next he would sigh, and next he'd let on to drop a tear. It was beautiful to see him. By and by he got it. He told us to give attention. Then he strikes a most noble attitude, with one leg shoved forwards, and his arms stretched away up, and his head tilted back, looking up at the

sky; and then he begins to rip and rave and grit his teeth; and after that, all through his speech, he howled, and spread around, and swelled up his chest, and just knocked the spots out of any acting ever *I* see before. This is the speech—I learned it, easy enough, while he was learning it to the king:

> To be, or not to be; that is the bare bodkin
> That makes calamity of so long life;
> For who would fardels bear, till Birnam Wood do come to Dunsinane,
> But that the fear of something after death
> Murders the innocent sleep,
> Great nature's second course,
> And makes us rather sling the arrows of outrageous fortune
> Than fly to others that we know not of.
> There's the respect must give us pause:
> Wake Duncan with thy knocking! I would thou couldst;
> For who would bear the whips and scorns of time,
> The oppressor's wrong, the proud man's contumely,
> The law's delay, and the quietus which his pangs might take,
> In the dead waste and middle of the night, when churchyards yawn
> In customary suits of solemn black,
> But that the undiscovered country from whose bourne no traveler returns,
> Breathes forth contagion on the world,
> And thus the native hue of resolution, like the poor cat i' the adage,
> Is sicklied o'er with care,
> And all the clouds that lowered o'er our housetops,
> With this regard their currents turn awry,
> And lose the name of action.
> 'Tis a consummation devoutly to be wished. But soft you, the fair Ophelia:
> Ope not thy ponderous and marble jaws,
> But get thee to a nunnery—go!

[11] Well, the old man he liked that speech, and he mighty soon got it so he could do it first rate. It seemed like he was just born for it; and when he had his hand in and was excited, it was perfectly lovely the way he would rip and tear and rair up behind when he was getting it off.

Art Buchwald

First the Bible, Then Shakespeare

[1]   Now that the best minds in the Western world have "improved" the Bible in the most modern edition, which is called the New English

From Art Buchwald, *Getting High in Government.* © 1968, 1970, 1971 by Art Buchwald. Reprinted by permission of G. P. Putnam's Sons.

Bible (the new Twenty-third Psalm begins, "The Lord is my shepherd, I shall want nothing. He makes me lie down in green pastures and leads me beside the waters of peace; He renews life within me and for His name's sake guides me in the right path. . . ."), it has been decided to update Shakespeare and make him easier for people to understand.

With this goal in mind and using the New English Bible as our inspiration, a group of us has already managed to update some of Hamlet's soliloquy.

"To be or not to be" will soon read as follows:

Should I or shouldn't I? That is the question.
I don't know whether it would be better for me to
Take
A lot of guff and that sort of thing
Or to fight back against all this trouble I've been
Having.
Maybe I should drop dead, and sleep;
That's all. And by sleeping hope to end
All this emotional conflict
That everyone goes through; boy, wouldn't that be a
Solution?
If you could just cop out, close your eyes and
Sleep. And maybe have a few good dreams. But that's
The trouble.
If you're dead, who knows what kind of bad trips
You're going to have
Leaving the station? It sure gives you something to
Think about.
You have to show some respect; if you don't, you
Could be in for real trouble.

That's as far as we got with Hamlet. But we have also been working on *Romeo and Juliet.*

[5]   So far, it goes like this:

JULIET (*on balcony to herself*): O Romeo, Romeo. Why are you Romeo? Why don't you change your name? Or if you can't do it, I'll work it out some way so I won't be known as a Capulet.

ROMEO (*underneath balcony to himself*): I wonder if I should stick around and listen to what she's saying, or speak up and jawbone with her.

JULIET: The only thing I hold against you, Romeo, is your name. Personally I like you for yourself, and not because you're a Montague.

Like, what's a Montague? It isn't your hand or your foot or your face, or any other part of your body belonging to a man. Gosh, I wish you had another name.

But what's in a name? Suppose you saw this flower which was called something else beside a rose. It would still smell pretty good, wouldn't it?

And that's the way it is with Romeo. If his name, for example, were Irving, he still would be perfect in my book. Romeo, get rid of your name because it has nothing to do with you, and in exchange, I'll do anything you want me to.

ROMEO (*out loud*): OK, Juliet, it's a deal. Forget I'm Romeo and call me Loverboy instead.

JULIET: Who is that listening in on everything I've been saying?

ROMEO: I can't tell you who I am because I hate my name, and from what I can tell, you do, too.

JULIET: Unless I'm stone-deaf, you sound like Romeo Montague. Are you or aren't you?

ROMEO: It all depends if it shakes you up or not.

As you see, we still have a little work to do, but if it took twenty years to rewrite the Bible, I believe we've gotten off to a pretty good start.

words and sentences

1. Vocabulary from Clemens: *sublime* (¶ 9); *contumely, consummation* (10).
2. The speaker in the Clemens selection is, of course, Huckleberry Finn, who tells the story of his adventures on the Mississippi River. Clemens creates in the speech of Huck Finn what has been called a "vernacular" voice, a voice different from the more formal speech of characters in novels. Underline all the coordinating conjunctions in ¶s 1, 2, and 10. Are there many coordinating conjunctions? Why?
3. Check these words in your dictionary: *hypotaxis, parataxis, polysyndeton, asyndeton.*
4. Describe the patterns of the first five sentences in ¶ 10; then write your own paragraph imitating these sentence patterns. What effect does polysyndeton and parataxis have on the movement of the action in these sentences?
5. Rewrite the first sentence of the Buchwald essay. How is your rewriting different from Buchwald's sentence?

ideas and implications

1. What seems to be Huck Finn's attitude towards the duke and the king and their acting? What seems to be Samuel Clemens attitude towards them? Are there any differences in these attitudes? If so, why?
2. What is Buchwald's attitude towards the revisions of the King James Bible? How does he convey his attitude to his readers?
3. Reread Buchwald's revisions of Shakespeare. What does his "revision" say about his attitudes towards language? Is Buchwald commenting on Shakespeare or on the inclination to "modernize"? Or both?
4. Compare Hamlet's soliloquy with the duke of Bilgewater's version and with Buchwald's revision. What do Clemens and Buchwald do to their language and the contexts of the speeches to change both style and stance?

strategies

1. What details allow the reader to distinguish the duke of Bilgewater from the king? Through whose eyes do we see these details? How would you describe the "rhetorical stance" of this teller?
2. What effect is Clemens working for by presenting the duke's version of Hamlet's soliloquy? What does Clemens assume about his audience?

3. What assumptions does Buchwald make about his audience? Give examples to support your statement.
4. How much does Buchwald depend upon examples to make his point?
5. What effect do ¶s 4 and 6 have upon Buchwald's "stance" towards his proposed revisions?

suggestions for writing

1. Write a paper comparing and contrasting the Clemens and Buchwald versions of Hamlet's soliloquy with Shakespeare's.
2. Rewrite (that is, construct a new "word-world") a familiar piece of writing as Buchwald has done in his essay. Be sure that you make clear to your reader the purpose of your rewriting.
3. Select a passage from the King James Bible and rewrite it in modern language. What effect has your rewriting on the sense of the original language?
4. Write a paper in which you use a "vernacular" voice to tell about some incident. Try to keep that voice as consistently "vernacular" as possible.
5. From your own observation, write a character sketch about someone who is forever constructing word-worlds which are different from their originals.
6. You might for pleasure create a new word-world based on one of your favorite speeches in Shakespeare. You might want your language to come from such sources as the leather-jacketed world of the motorcycle rider or the world of Women's Liberation.
7. Sometimes an instructor will construct a new word-world in order to teach an unfamiliar concept or idea. From your own experience, write about a teacher who created such a word-world effectively.

Dan Greenburg

Three Bears in Search of an Author

CATCH HER IN THE OATMEAL

[1]   If you actually want to hear about it, what I'd better do is I'd better warn you right now that you aren't going to believe it. I mean it's a true *story* and all, but it still sounds sort of phony.

[2]   Anyway, my name is Goldie Lox. It's sort of a boring name, but my parents said that when I was born I had this very blonde hair and all. Actually, I was born bald. I mean how many babies get born with blonde

hair? None. I mean I've *seen* them and they're all wrinkled and red and slimy and everything. And bald. And then all the phonies have to come around and tell you he's as cute as a bug's ear. A bug's ear, boy, that really kills me. You ever *seen* a bug's ear? What's cute about a bug's *ear*, for Chrissake! Nothing, that's what.

[3]   So, like I was saying, I always seem to be getting into these very stupid situations. Like this time I was telling you about. Anyway, I was walking through the forest and all when I see this very interesting house. A *house*. You wouldn't think anybody would be living way the hell out in the goddam *forest*, but they were. No one was home or anything and the door was open, so I walked in. I figured what I'd do is I'd probably horse around until the guys that lived there came home and maybe asked me to stay for dinner or something. Some people think they *have* to ask you to stay for dinner even if they *hate* you. Also I didn't exactly feel like going home and getting asked a lot of lousy questions. I mean that's *all* I ever seem to do.

[4]   Anyway, while I was waiting I sort of sampled some of this stuff they had on the table that tasted like oatmeal. *Oatmeal*. It would have made you puke, I mean it. Then something very spooky started happening. I started getting dizzier than hell. I figured I'd feel better if I could just rest for a while. Sometimes if you eat something like lousy oatmeal you can feel better if you just rest for a while, so I sat down. That's when the goddam *chair* breaks in half. No kidding, you start feeling lousy and some stupid *chair* is going to break on you every time. I'm not kidding. Anyway I finally found the crummy bedroom and I lay down on this very tiny bed. I was really depressed.

[5]   I don't know how long I was asleep or anything, but all of a sudden I hear this very strange voice say, "Someone's been sleeping in *my* sack, for Chrissake, and there she is!" So I open my eyes and here at the foot of the bed are these three crummy *bears*. *Bears!* I swear to God. By that time I was *really* feeling depressed. There's nothing more depressing than waking up and finding three *bears* talking about you, I mean.

[6]   So I didn't stay around and shoot the breeze with them or anything. If you want to know the truth, I sort of ran out of there like a madman or something. I do that quite a little when I'm depressed like that.

[7]   On the way home, though, I got to figuring. What probably happened is these bears wandered in when they smelled this oatmeal and all. Probably bears *like* oatmeal, *I* don't know. And the voice I heard when I woke up was probably something I dreamt.

[8]   So that's the story.

[9]   I wrote it all up once as a theme in school, but my crummy teacher said it was too *whimsical*. Whimsical. That killed me. You got to meet her sometime, boy. She's a real queen.

PORTRAIT OF GOLDILOCKS AS A YOUNG GIRL

[10]   ". . . I love porridge I'd love to have the whole place swimming in porridge but I ate it all up and broke his chair I hate chairs I remember

the first chair I broke they were playing the blue danube god how I hate the blue danube and the rhododendron was in bloom and I broke their chair because it was too warm in the room yes and now I have broken his chair yes and he is angry with me yes and he is standing over me yes and saying someone has been sleeping in my bed yes and there she is yes and I open my eyes to look at him yes and he looks like a little brown bear cub in the afterglow yes and he asks me with his eyes if I have eaten all his porridge yes and I ask him with my eyes to ask me again yes and he asks again yes did you eat my porridge yes and first I put my arms around him yes and draw him down to me so he can feel my breasts all perfume yes and his heart is going like mad and yes I say yes I did Yes. . . ."

A FAREWELL TO PORRIDGE

[11]   In the late autumn of that year we lived in a house in the forest that looked across the river to the mountains, but we always thought we lived on the plain because we couldn't see the forest for the trees.

[12]   Sometimes people would come to the door and ask if we would like to subscribe to *The Saturday Evening Post* or buy Fuller brushes, but when we would answer the bell they would see we were only bears and go away.

[13]   Sometimes we would go for long walks along the river and you could almost forget for a little while that you were a bear and not people.

[14]   Once when we were out strolling for a very long time we came home and you could see that someone had broken in and the door was open.

[15]   *"La porte est ouverte,"* said Mama Bear. "The door should not be open." Mama Bear had French blood on her father's side.

"It is all right," I said. "We will close it."

"It should not have been left open," she said.

"It is all right," I said. "We will close it. Then it will be good like in the old days."

"Bien," she said. "It is well."

[20]   We walked in and closed the door. There were dishes and bowls and all manner of eating utensils on the table and you could tell that someone had been eating porridge. We did not say anything for a long while.

"It is lovely here," I said finally. "But someone has been eating my porridge."

"Mine as well," said Mama Bear.

"It is all right," I said. "It is nothing."

"Darling," said Mama Bear, "do you love me?"

[25]   "Yes. I love you."

"You really love me?"

"I really love you. I'm crazy in love with you."

"And the porridge? How about the porridge?"

"That too. I really love the porridge too."

[30] "It was supposed to be a surprise. I made it as a surprise for you. But someone has eaten it all up."

"You sweet. You made it as a surprise. Oh, you're lovely," I said.

"But it is gone."

"It is all right," I said. "It will be all right."

Then I looked at my chair and you could see someone had been sitting in it and Mama Bear looked at her chair and someone had been sitting in that too and Baby Bear's chair was broken.

[35] "We will go upstairs," I said and we went upstairs to the bedroom but you could see that someone had been sleeping in my bed and in Mama Bear's bed too although that was the same bed but you have to mention it that way because that is the story. Truly. And then we looked in Baby Bear's bed and there she was.

"I ate your porridge and sat in your chairs and I broke one of them," she said.

"It is all right," I said. "It will be all right."

"And now I am lying in Baby Bear's bed."

"Baby Bear can take care of himself."

[40] "I mean that I am sorry. I have behaved badly and I am sorry for all of this."

"*Ça ne fait rien,*" said Mama Bear. "It is nothing." Outside it had started to rain again.

"I will go now," she said. "I am sorry." She walked slowly down the stairs.

I tried to think of something to tell her, but it wasn't any good. "Good-by," she said.

Then she opened the door and went outside and walked all the way back to her hotel in the rain.

words and sentences

1. Vocabulary: *whimsical* (¶ 9).
2. Check these words in your dictionary: *parody, stream of consciousness.*
3. If you have read J. D. Salinger's *Catcher in the Rye,* James Joyce's *Portrait of the Artist as a Young Man,* Ernest Hemingway's *A Farewell to Arms,* or other prose by these writers, you will recognize that Dan Greenburg has parodied the styles of each of these authors in the three versions of the Goldilocks story. If you have not read any of these authors, spend some time reading in a work by one; then list the stylistic qualities that Greenburg has parodied.
4. ¶ 10 is a long sentence using stream of consciousness technique. Write a sentence in which you use seriously this technique to convey a feeling or idea.

ideas and implications

1. How well did Greenburg have to know the "styles" of Salinger, Joyce,

and Hemingway to parody them? What is the difference between imitating a writer and parodying him?

2. What seems to be Greenburg's attitude towards the "styles" of Salinger, Joyce, and Hemingway?

3. Are Greenburg's parodies focused on style or on content? or both?

4. Parody is sometimes compared with caricature or cartooning in art— especially political cartoons. What are the purposes of parody and caricature?

5. Comedians like David Fry entertain audiences by caricaturing famous people. Are there similarities between the performances of comedians like Fry and Greenburg's parodies? If so, what are they?

strategies

1. What assumptions has Greenburg made about his audience? List these assumptions. "Three Bears in Search of an Author" was first published in *Esquire Magazine*. Does the place of publication tell you anything about audience?

2. What are the points of view of the three versions of the Goldilocks story? How do these points of view affect the way Greenburg writes his stories?

3. What purposes might Greenburg have had in choosing the Goldilocks story as the vehicle for his parodies? Is this choice part of Greenburg's strategy?

suggestions for writing

1. Write your own version of the Goldilocks story, parodying a writer whose works you know well. You might want to try the "style" of the King James Bible or some other famous book.

2. Select a fairy tale other than the Goldilocks story and write a parody in the style of a writer you know well.

3. Write a paper about a caricature you have clipped from a newspaper or magazine. Examine the caricature carefully to determine the techniques and purposes of the cartoonist or artist.

4. Analyze the performance of a comedian who parodies famous people. Try to find the elements of his performance that create the parody.

Donald Hall

An Ethic of Clarity

[1]   Ezra Pound, George Orwell, James Thurber, and Ernest Hemingway don't have much in common: a great poet who became a follower of Mussolini, a disillusioned left-wing satirist, a comic essayist and cartoonist, and a great novelist. If anything, they could represent the diversity of modern literature. Yet one thing unites them. They share a common idea of good style, an idea of the virtues of clarity and simplicity. This attitude toward style was not unknown to earlier writers, but never before has it been so pervasive and so exclusive.

[2]   Style is the manner of a sentence, not its matter. But the distinction between manner and matter is a slippery one, for manner affects matter. When *Time* used to tell us that President Truman slouched into one room, while General Eisenhower strode into another, their manner was trying to prejudice our feelings. The hotel that invites me to enjoy my favorite beverage at the Crown Room is trying not to sound crass: "Have a drink at the bar." One linguist, in discussing this problem, took Caesar's "I came; I saw; I conquered," and revised it as, "I arrived on the scene of the battle; I observed the situation; I won the victory." Here, the matter is the same, but Caesar's tone of arrogant dignity disappears in the palid pedantry of the longer version. It is impossible to say that the matter is unaffected. But, let us say that this kind of difference, in the two versions of Caesar, is what we mean by style.

[3]   In the expression "good writing" or "good style," the word "good" has usually meant "beautiful" or "proficient"—like a good Rembrandt or a good kind of soap. In our time it has come to mean honest as opposed to fake. Bad writing happens when the writer lies to himself, to others, or to both. Probably, it is usually necessary to lie to oneself in order to lie to others; advertising men use the products they praise. Bad writing may be proficient; it may persuade us to buy a poor car or vote for an imbecile, but it is bad because it is tricky, false in its enthusiasm, and falsely motivated. It appeals to a part of us that wants to deceive itself. I am encouraged to tell myself that I am enjoying my favorite beverage when, really, I am only getting sloshed.

[4]   "If a man writes clearly enough any one can see if he fakes," says Hemingway. Orwell reverses the terms: "The great enemy of clear language is insincerity. . . . When there is a gap between one's real and one's declared aims, one turns as it were instinctively to long words and exhausted idioms, like a cuttlefish squirting out ink." Pound talks about the "gap between one's real and one's declared aims" as the distance between expression and meaning. In "The New Vocabularianism,"

From *The Modern Stylists: Writers on the Art of Writing* by Donald Hall. © 1968 by The Free Press, a division of The Macmillan Company. Reprinted with permission of the publisher.

Thurber speaks of the political use of clichés to hide a "menacing Alice in Wonderland meaninglessness."

[5]   As Robert Graves says, "The writing of good English is thus a moral matter." And the morality is a morality of truth-telling. Herbert Read declares that "the only thing that is indispensable for the possession of a good style is personal sincerity." We can agree, but we must add that personal sincerity is not always an easy matter, nor is it always available to the will. Real aims, we must understand, are not necessarily conscious ones. The worst liars in the world may consider themselves sincere. Analysis of one's own style, in fact, can be a test of one's own feelings. And certainly, many habits of bad style are bad habits of thinking as well as of feeling.

[6]   There are examples of the modern attitude toward style in older writers. Jonathan Swift, maybe the best prose writer of the language, sounds like George Orwell when he writes:

> . . . Our English tongue is too little cultivated in this kingdom, yet the faults are nine in ten owing to affectation, not to want of understanding. When a man's thoughts are clear, the properest words will generally offer themselves first, and his own judgment will direct him in what order to place them, so as they may be best understood.

Here Swift appears tautological; clear thoughts only *exist* when they are embodied in clear words. But he goes on: "When men err against this method, it is usually on purpose," purposes, we may add, that we often disguise from ourselves.

[7]   Aristotle in his *Rhetoric* makes a case for plainness and truth-telling. "The right thing in speaking really is that we should be satisfied not to annoy our hearers, without trying to delight them: we ought in fairness to fight our case with no help beyond the bare facts." And he anticipates the modern stylist's avoidance of unusual words: "Clearness is secured by using the words . . . that are current and ordinary." Cicero attacks the Sophists because they are "on the lookout for ideas that are neatly put rather than reasonable. . . ."

[8]   Yet, when we quote Cicero, the master rhetorician, on behalf of honest clarity, we must remember that the ancients did not really think of style as we do. Style until recent times has been a division of rhetoric. To learn style, one learned the types of figures of speech and the appropriateness of each to different levels of discourse—high, middle, and low. The study of style was complex, but it was technical rather than moral. For some writers, Latin was high and the vernacular low, but in the Renaissance the vernacular took in all levels. It is only in modern times that style divorces itself from rhetoric—rhetoric belongs to the enemy, to the advertisers and the propagandists—and becomes a matter of ethics and introspection.

[9]   Ezra Pound, like some French writers before him, makes the writer's function social. "Good writers are those who keep the language efficient. That is to say, keep it accurate, keep it clear." We must ask why this idea of the function of good style is so predominantly a modern phe-

nomenon. Pound elsewhere speaks of the "assault," by which he means the attack upon our ears and eyes of words used dishonestly to persuade us, to convince us to buy or to believe. Never before have men been exposed to so many words—written words, from newspapers and billboards and paperbacks and flashing signs and the sides of buses, and spoken words, from radio and television and loudspeakers. Everyone who wishes to keep his mind clear and his feelings his own must make an effort to brush away these words like cobwebs from the face. The assault of the phoney is a result of technology combined with a morality that excuses any technique which is useful for persuasion. The persuasion is for purposes of making money, as in advertising, or winning power, as in war propaganda and the slogans of politicians. Politicians have always had slogans, but they never before had the means to spread their words so widely. The cold war of rhetoric between communism and capitalism has killed no soldiers, but the air is full of the small corpses of words that were once alive: "democracy," "freedom," "liberation."

[10] It is because of this assault, primarily, that writers have become increasingly concerned with the honesty of their style to the exclusion of other qualities. Concentration on honesty is the only way to exclude the sounds of the bad style that assault us all. These writers are concerned finally *to be honest about what they see, feel, and know.* For some of them, like William Carlos Williams, we can only trust the evidence of our eyes and ears, our real knowledge of our immediate environment.

[11] Our reading of good writers and our attempt to write like them can help to guard us against the dulling onslaught. But we can only do this if we are able to look into ourselves with some honesty. An ethic of clarity demands intelligence and self-knowledge. Really, the ethic is not only a defense against the assault (nothing good is ever merely defensive), but is a development of the same inwardness that is reflected in psychoanalysis. One cannot, after all, examine one's motives and feelings carefully if one takes a naïve view that the appearance of a feeling is the reality of that feeling.

[12] Sometimes, the assault is merely pompous. Some people say "wealthy" instead of "rich" in order to seem proper, or "home" instead of "house" in order to seem genteel. George Orwell translates a portion of *Ecclesiastes* into academic-pompous, for example; Quiller-Couch does something similar with Hamlet's soliloquy. Years ago, James Russell Lowell ridiculed the newspapers that translated "A great crowd came to see . . ." into "A vast concourse was assembled to witness. . . ." None of these examples is so funny as a colonel's statement on television that one of our astronauts "has established visual contact" with a piece of his equipment. He meant that the astronaut had *seen* it.

[13] Comic as these pomposities are, they are signs that something has gone wrong somewhere. (My father normally spoke a perfectly good plain English, but, occasionally, when he was unhappy with himself, he would fall off dreadfully; I remember him once admonishing me at dinner, "It is necessary to masticate thoroughly.") The colonel must have been worried about the intellectual respectability of the space program when

he resorted to phrases like "visual contact." The lady who speaks of
"luncheon" instead of "lunch" is worried about her social status. She
gives herself away. Something has gone wrong, and it has gone wrong
inside her mind and her emotions.

[14]   The style is the man. Again and again, the modern stylists repeat
this idea. By a man's metaphors you shall know him. When a commencement orator advises students to enrich themselves culturally, chances
are that he is more interested in money than in poetry. When a university
president says that his institution turned out 1,432 B.A.s last year, he
tells us that he thinks he is running General Motors. The style is the
man. Remy de Gourmont used the analogy that the bird's song is conditioned by the shape of the beak. And Paul Valery said ". . . what
makes the style is not merely the mind applied to a particular action;
it is the whole of a living system extended, imprinted and recognizable
in expression." These statements are fine, but they sound too deterministic,
as if one expresses an unalterable self and can no more change the style
of that self than a bird can change the shape of its beak. Man is a kind of
bird that can change his beak.

[15]   A writer of bad prose, to become a writer of good prose, must
alter his character. He does not have to become good in terms of conventional morality, but he must become honest in the expression of
himself, which means that he must know himself. There must be no gap
between expression and meaning, between real and declared aims. For
some people, some of the time, this simply means *not* telling deliberate
lies. For most people, it means learning when they are lying and when
they are not. It means learning the real names of their feelings. It means
not saying or thinking, "I didn't *mean* to hurt your feelings," when
there really existed a desire to hurt. It mean not saying "luncheon" or
"home" for the purpose of appearing upper-class or well-educated. It
means not using the passive mood to attribute to no one in particular
opinions that one is unwilling to call one's own. It means not disguising
banal thinking by polysyllabic writing or the lack of feeling by clichés
that purport to display feeling.

[16]   The style is the man, and the man can change himself by changing
his style. Prose style is the way you think and the way you understand
what you feel. Frequently, we feel for one another a mixture of strong
love and strong hate; if we call it love and disguise the hate to ourselves
by sentimentalizing over love, we are thinking and feeling badly. Style
is ethics and psychology; clarity is a psychological sort of ethic, since it
involves not general moral laws, but truth to the individual self. The
scrutiny of style is a moral and psychological study. By trying to scru-
tinize our own style, perhaps with the help of people like Orwell and
Pound, Hemingway and Thurber, we try to understand ourselves. Edit-
ing our own writing, or going over in memory our own spoken words, or
even inwardly examining our thought, we can ask *why* we resorted to
the passive in this case or to clichés in that. When the smoke of bad
prose fills the air, something is always on fire somewhere. If the style is
really the man, the style becomes an instrument for discovering and

changing the man. Language is expression of self, but language is also the instrument by which to know that self.

words and sentences

1. Vocabulary: *pervasive* (¶ 1); *pallid, pedantry* (2); *tautological* (6); *Sophists* (7); *banal, polysyllabic* (15).
2. Describe the pattern of the fifth sentence in ¶ 3 ("Bad writing . . .); then write a sentence imitating this pattern.
3. Rewrite sentence three of ¶ 14. How does your revision compare with Hall's sentence? Which seems more effective in the context of the paragraph?
4. Describe the pattern of sentence seven in ¶ 9; then write a sentence imitating this pattern. Be sure your sentence concludes with a simile.
5. Rewrite sentence three of ¶ 16. Again, compare your rewriting with Hall's sentence. How do the effects of the two sentences differ?

ideas and implications

1. "Style is the manner of a sentence, not its matter," says Hall in ¶ 2. What distinction does Hall make between manner and matter?
2. According to Hall, what are the causes of bad writing? What distinction does he make between the real and declared aims of writers or speakers? Why does Hall regard the matters of style and language as matters of morality?
3. Why is personal sincerity "not always an easy matter"? What is the distinction between the appearance of a feeling and the reality of that feeling? What connections does Hall make between style and psychology or psychoanalysis? Why?
4. In ¶ 8, Hall says that "rhetoric belongs to the enemy." What are the implications of this statement in the context of the paragraph and of the whole essay? Is Hall's attitude towards "rhetoric" different from Booth's in "The Rhetorical Stance"? How?
5. Why is the "assault" on clarity and honesty in language a particularly modern phenomenon?
6. In ¶ 9, Hall talks about the "small corpses of words" resulting from the cold war of rhetoric between communism and capitalism. According to Hall, why have these words died?
7. What does "an ethic of clarity" demand of a writer who wishes to live by it? Is this ethic more than a defense? If so, how?
8. Does Hall distinguish between conventional morality and personal morality? If so, how?
9. In ¶ 14, Hall says, "By a man's metaphors you shall know him." Discuss the implications of this observation. Then examine the metaphors in Hall's essay. What do Hall's metaphors say about him?
10. Why does Hall object to the statements on style by Remy de Gourmont and Paul Valery?
11. What is Hall's attitude toward the "passive mood"? Why?

12. What must a writer do to change his style? Why? How important to Hall is the idea that a person may change? Why?

strategies

1. How does Hall introduce the thesis idea of his essay? Comment on the effectiveness of this strategy.
2. Does ¶ 2 have a topic sentence? If so, which one? What method of development does Hall use in this paragraph? What is his purpose in this paragraph?
3. How much does Hall depend upon authorities to present his views? Comment on the effectiveness of this strategy.
4. How many major divisions appear in Hall's essay? Cite the paragraphs devoted to each of these major sections and then state the main idea of each section. Finally, establish the relationships between each of these major sections to the thesis idea.
5. Does ¶ 12 have a topic sentence? If so, which one? What method of development does Hall use in this paragraph?
6. Examine carefully Hall's concluding paragraph. What is the purpose of the analogy in the third sentence of the paragraph? How effective is Hall's conclusion?

suggestions for writing

1. Write a paper describing a situation in which a speaker or writer seemed to sacrifice sincerity of expression for convenience or manners.
2. Using Hall's observation about men and their metaphors, examine several paragraphs by a writer and then compose a paper telling what these metaphors reveal about that writer.
3. Write a paper about an incident in which you deliberately sacrificed sincerity for the sake of appearances. Try to explain specifically why you did so.
4. The pompous colonel of the space program (¶ 12) is one of many examples Hall could have cited. Collect similar examples from another field and write a paper in which you try to generalize about the use of such "respectable" words and phrases.

4 The Writer as Workman: Occupational Hazards

INTRODUCTION

Welders at work on high-rise buildings choose their steps carefully; truck drivers nodding at the wheel pull to the roadside for rest. Being alert to the dangers of their work keeps them alive. Avoiding the hazards of his craft may not keep a writer alive, but his work will be livelier if he recognizes language traps and circumvents them. In the "Peanuts" cartoon, Charles Schulz knows that Snoopy's story begins with a fleabitten sentence, agrees with his beagle that "Good writing is hard work," and amuses his readers because Snoopy's sentence and observation collide.

Like Snoopy, nearly everyone has fussed over sentences. George Bernard Shaw described that fussing as ten per cent inspiration and ninety per cent perspiration. Jonathan Swift's advice was to

> Blot out, correct, insert, refine,
> Enlarge, diminish, interline;
> Be mindful when invention fails
> To scratch your head and bite your nails.

Because knowing where to blot and correct can save a writer needless sweat and fuss, the readings in this section describe the kinds of words and phrases that short-circuit communication. Among these are clichés, jargon, euphemisms, gobbledygook, and mixed metaphors.

In "An Inflation Activity in the Communication Area," Calvin S. Brown laments that many radio and television announcers use nouns as adjectives to modify empty or redundant nouns such as *area, process, operation,* or *activity.* Among football announcers, for example, the "fourth down" is dead, replaced by the inflated "fourth-down situation"; on television it no longer rains, but there is much "precipitation activity." Brown speculates about the reasons for this verbiage.

Frank Sullivan's "The Cliché Expert Testifies on Politics" satirizes campaign oratory by interviewing Mr. Arbuthnot, who points with pride and views with alarm until he explodes in a blast of verbal flatulence. Sydney J. Harris collects "A Pretty Kettle of Clichés" that he would banish from the language, and Ross Campbell, an Australian journalist, questions the "benevolent clichés of the travel posters" depicting koalas as cute and cuddly. He says they aren't.

These writers object to clichés because such ready-made words and phrases require no thought, energy, or originality. We use them when we hurry or get lazy, but all acknowledge the difficulty of escaping clichés completely.

Stefan Kanfer writes more about puns than about politicians in "Punning: The Candidate at Word and Play." Kanfer shows that punning can be hazardous to public officials, but he also believes that the pun, a linguistic exercise reconciling opposites, can "sometimes lead to fresh revelations."

Other authors examine ways that language may become inflated or pretentious, may confuse or obfuscate. Two weeks as an editorial consultant in Washington, D.C., supplied Spencer Klaw with his eight rules for "A Field Guide to Government Jargon." One of these rules warns: "Beware of stating proposals in simple, commonsense terms; readers may conclude that you haven't given sufficient thought to the problems at hand." Art Buchwald's "All-Purpose Press Release" parodies the language and thought of that form of communication by offering a fill-the-blanks model. Both Klaw and Buchwald spoof this pompous and evasive language.

In "Dirty Words," Russell Lynes objects to words that "are substitutes for thought" and that "exude a mist which rises between a speaker and a listener so that all that can be perceived through it is a kind of fuzz." On Lynes's list of dirty words are creative, meaningful, and sensitive. He suggests that a sensitive man and woman who have a meaningful relationship probably deserve each other.

"Up Tight About Hang-Ups" (from Newsweek) chronicles words and phrases that have entered the language recently and speculates about their survival. A few are approved, but the Newsweek writer would need an army of pall-bearers to bury the "jargon and pretentious usages" he lists.

John Lardner collects his "Thoughts on Radio-Televese" to dramatize how talk-show personalities and sports announcers fracture the language. Lardner cites some examples: "Don't fail to miss tomorrow's doubleheader"; "The Yankees, as I told you later . . ."; and "Now, Jack, whaddya say we reminisce a little about tomorrow's fight?" This language, Lardner suggests wryly, is "proud and deliberate."

Stuart Chase's "Gobbledygook" is about removing the gobble from pretentious prose. Chase defines gobbledygook as "using two, or three, or ten words in place of one, or using a five-syllable word where a single syllable would suffice." He shows how foggy language affects the "common humanity" of people who deal with government agencies—sometimes with comic and sometimes with disastrous results. He believes that bureaucrats are not the only writers who gobble; lawyers and academicians often cloak simple ideas in mumbo-jumbo.

C. Hugh Holman defines "Metaphor and Mixed Figures" to show how effective metaphors can illuminate and how mixed figures can amuse. He cites William Shakespeare's Sonnets to illustrate metaphor working well; he quotes Lloyd George, a British statesman of the World War I era, to depict ways mixed figures can amuse. George is supposed to have observed, "I smell a rat. I see it floating in the air. I shall nip it in the bud." Another mixed figure that has amused is, "That is a virgin field, pregnant with opportunity."

No one avoids all the traps mentioned in this section; even the best writers get caught. But knowing what they are helps us to nip them in the bud, to expunge them from the face of the earth, eraserwise, that is, and to uproot this vast linguistic conspiracy that is a red-festering sore in the province of prose. Sometimes, that is.

Sydney J. Harris

Woe to the 'Hip' Language-Manglers

If I were king, I'd promptly rule it
Out of bounds to murmur, "Cool it."
I'd take a club and start out zapping
Folks who chat and call it rapping.
I'd even mutilate my queen   5
If she intoned, "Let's make the scene."
I'd fling in prison every flunky
Who'd even faintly whisper "Funky."
All courtiers would be put to flight
Who used clichés like "Out of sight."   10
The royal dungeon for the peon
Who dared exclaim, "It turns me on."
My mace I'd swing with all my might
At clowns who toss the term "uptight."
My greatest satisfaction is   15
Detecting where the action is,
And taking steps to end the days
Of all who perpetrate this phrase.
I'd disembowel without pity
Declaimers of the nitty-gritty.   20
I'd exile on the farthest frigate
Those who claim they really dig it.
Forty lashes on the hind
To him who utters, "blew my mind."
I'd trample down with elephants   25

From Syndicated Column, The *Chicago Daily News* (June 1, 1971). Reprinted by permission of Sydney J. Harris and Publishers-Hall Syndicate.

Demanders of more relevance;
And tear by tigers into shreds,
All who proudly wear their threads.
To coldest exile I would drive
Each ofay who pretends to jive.   30
And toss into the boiling vats
All who greet their friends as cats.
By fearful tax I'd put the bite on
All the squares who gargle "Right on!"

L'Envoi

Does it sound as though I'm ready to take   35
   my throne and heave it?
Cool friends and groovy subjects, you just
   better believe it!

words and sentences

1. What effect does Harris gain with the choice of the word *gargle* in line 34?
2. Describe the sentence pattern of lines 13 and 14. Does the structure of this sentence affect the rhyme? Rewrite the lines in normal English word order. Why might Harris have changed the word order in these lines? Examine the word order in other verse sentences for such effects.

ideas and implications

1. What is the significance of the words *woe* and *manglers* in the title?
2. Harris states his attitude towards "hip" language, but does he state why he has this attitude?
3. Does Harris seem to take seriously the violence in his verses?
4. How seriously does Harris seem to take his "poetic" effort? What details lead you to your conclusion?

strategies

1. What is the controlling metaphor of Harris's poem? How does this metaphor help him organize and develop his observations about "hip" language?
2. What is the principal method of development used in the poem?
3. What effect does Harris create with his word choices in the last line of the poem?

suggestions for writing

1. From your own experience, list several words and phrases which you used only a short while ago and which now seem less than satisfactory. Write a paper about the reasons for the fall from favor of these words and phrases.

2. Carl Sandburg is supposed to have said, "Slang is the language that takes off its coat, spits on its hands, and goes to work." Write a paper showing how slang might be effective in speech or writing.

Calvin S. Brown

An Inflation Activity in the Communication Area

[1]   Listening to the announcers of broadcast football games last year, I got the impression that something strange had happened to the game. The fourth down seemed to have disappeared. As the announcers told the story, there were plenty of fourth-down *situations,* but never an actual fourth down.

[2]   I soon realized, of course, that it was not the game that had changed, but the language. The announcers were merely falling in line with the latest big trend in English. This trend has already produced effects that are either amusing or annoying (depending on how gladly one suffers fools), and if it continues it may ultimately change the structure of our language. It can be accurately described in what may some day become a rule of English grammar: Use the noun that you really mean as an adjective, and let this adjective then modify some empty or redundant noun such as *area, process, operation,* or *activity.*

[3]   In the language of journalists, educationists, bureaucrats, and pompous speakers and writers generally, this rule is already in effect. Not only have town and country been entirely replaced by urban *areas* and rural *areas,* but the urban *areas* contain slum *areas* (or in the liberal euphemisms, blighted or disadvantaged *areas*), the rural *areas* contain wooded *areas,* and the parks in both have been replaced by recreational *areas.* Not only has democracy given way to the democratic *process,* but everyone who can afford a box of water-colors is studying the creative *process* in order to further his creative *activity.* The weatherman predicts thundershower *activity,* and not long ago I heard him reporting heavy rainfall *amounts* in (of course) local *areas.*

[4]   Such expressions as these have become so standard that they are hardly noticed, but they are insufficient for the more creative writers. A few recent examples will show what the real virtuoso can do. "Few two-year-olds are ready for the nursery school *experience.*" "An intermediate French textbook combining verbal *symbols* and visual *repre-*

From *The Georgia Review* (Winter, 1965, Vol. 19, No. 4). Reprinted by permission of *The Georgia Review.*

sentations"—which I take to be words and pictures. But the prize must go to the sportswriter who reported (libelously, I feel certain) that, "as the Tech coach says, improvement should set in with each new game-type *adventure."*

[5]   The redundant nouns mentioned above are somewhat different from the merely empty *areas* and *activities.* They have always existed, and they arise historically when a speaker uses a word that is not too familiar to him, and adds a familiar general word to help define it. Thus Americans, brought up in a prohibition-and-hard-liquor tradition without benefit of wines, often speak of sherry *wine,* whereas to the British sherry is simply sherry. In country newspapers (or should I say "in the news-*media* of the rural *areas*"?) one constantly sees references to edifices bearing names like Boggs Chapel *Church.* In such cases as these we have, in a way, the opposite of the *areas* and *activities,* for here the vague or fancy term is made into an adjective modifying a simple, everyday noun. Yet the redundant noun can be used much like the empty noun, and nowadays often is so used. The redundant *jaybird* is such an old formation that it has become a single word, but just the other day I saw an advertisement on an identical pattern for a "fly and mosquito *insect* killer." My finest specimen of a combination of emptiness and redundancy in the noun is a newspaper report that a man was resting comfortably after undergoing leg-amputation *surgery.*

[6]   Why should current English have developed these tricks? One can readily see why the radio and television announcers use them. These men have a simple task—to fill so many minutes with verbiage, whether they have anything to say or not—and obviously they are glad to have lots of linguistic padding at hand. The amusing thing is that they become so addicted to the readymade and roundabout expressions that even when, occasionally, they are actually pressed for time, they talk fast, but insist on talking as usual—that is, in padded language. It is as if a man packing something in a box *had* to use all the excelsior available, and made an issue of getting it all in. Most writers and speakers, however, do not have the announcer's excuse. They are simply pompous, and in their minds, the more and bigger the words, the more impressive the statement will be. The empty nouns spring from the same motive that makes some speakers always say *utilize* instead of *use,* and *donate* instead of *give*—and even, in advanced cases, *verbalize* instead of *talk.* Since such expressions are impressive (if at all) by being out of the ordinary, once they become ordinary their point is lost, and those who use them simply come to consider them as normal English, and the simpler words as somehow substandard. In the same way, I recently heard a weather broadcaster inadvertently say "rain," and then correct it to "precipitation *activity."* (Incidentally, the television weather girls are relatively free of this sort of jargon, doubtless because they count on quite different attributes to impress their audiences.) Since most people are usually out to impress, the only thing that could reverse the trend would be for the empty noun to become so standard and commonplace that the simple expression

would become, by contrast, impressive. Human nature being what it is, there is no reason to believe that this will ever happen.

[7]   If, then, the trend towards the use of empty nouns continues, where will it lead?

[8]   Many languages have words which grammarians call "classifiers"— words which *must* be used to put every specific noun into some general class. If, in English, we *had* to say "three *head* of cattle" instead of "three cows," and had to do the same thing for all quadrupeds, or domestic animals, or some other group, then *head* would be a classifier. Similarly, in classifying languages one might have to say so many *blade* of knives, axes, shovels, "church-keys," etc. Perhaps the function of classifiers is best illustrated by their use in pidgin English, where they have been carried over from various Oriental languages. Here the standard expressions (in fact, the only correct and intelligible expressions) are "four *fella* man" and "three *piece* shirt," *fella* and *piece* being the classifiers. Perhaps we are on the verge of such a development in English. It is not inconceivable that the time may come when *everything* mentioned will *have* to be classified as an *area,* a *process,* an *activity,* or something of the sort. We will need some more classifiers, especially for concrete objects, but what of that? I once asked an educationist why he insisted on saying "the education process," and he condescendingly explained that education *is* a process. By the same impeccable logic, since the pen I am writing with *is* an object, I suppose I really should call it a *pen object* instead of a pen. If we ever reach that point, the basic structure of English will have changed.

[9]   But there are other, even more fascinating possibilities. It would require at least several generations and an unconscious consensus to change the structure of the language, but in the meantime the individual speaker can explore new trails on his own. For example, if the adjective plus its empty noun becomes the standard formula, then it will be possible to make the whole thing into an adjective expression modifying a new and even emptier noun. In fact, this is already being done. From the beginning of the teaching of driving in the schools it had to have a more impressive name than its natural one, and consequently the schools have never taught driving, but only driver *education.* But recently I read the annunciation of a program for teaching driver education *skills.* Once you double the padding, the possibilities become literally infinite. If two empty nouns can be used, why not three, or five, or seventeen?

[10]   Or why any?

words and sentences

1. Vocabulary: *redundant* (¶ 2); *euphemisms, educationists* (3); *virtuoso* (4); *impeccable* (9).
2. Describe the pattern of the first sentence in ¶ 1, and write a sentence imitating that pattern. Then rewrite the sentence, changing the open-

    ing phrase to an adverbial clause. Which version of the sentence seems more effective?

3. Describe the pattern of the third sentence in ¶ 6; then write a sentence imitating that pattern.

4. What is "linguistic padding"? According to Brown, what does this padding do to writing and speech? Why? Can you think of any contexts in which *padding* has favorable connotative meanings?

5. Brown uses the word "church-keys" in ¶ 8. What is the meaning of that term? Is the term still used frequently?

ideas and implications

1. How does the title indicate Brown's attitudes? Explain.

2. In the first sentence of ¶ 3, Brown attributes an "inflation activity" in the language of several groups of writers and speakers. Why does he select these groups? Could others be added?

3. State in a sentence of your own the thesis of Brown's essay. Does Brown state his thesis explicitly? If so, where?

4. What distinction does Brown make between simplicity and pomposity? What seems to be his attitude towards reform in usage?

5. What comparison does Brown offer to clarify his notion about redundant and empty nouns? Does the comparison work? Why or why not?

strategies

1. Brown's first paragraph sets up his first sentence in ¶ 2. How effective is his opening strategy? Try to write a new opening paragraph for the essay, leaving the first sentence of the second paragraph intact (except for the word *game*).

2. Examine the transitional devices used in ¶s 2-6. How has Brown gotten from one idea to another?

3. ¶s 1-5 give many examples. In ¶ 6, Brown shifts his strategy. Is the direction from general to specific or from specific to general in the first six paragraphs? What, then, is the function of ¶ 6?

4. What is the function of ¶ 7? Why does Brown use a single sentence in this paragraph?

5. ¶s 8-10 comprise one unit of Brown's essay. What is the purpose of this section of the essay and how does Brown achieve this purpose?

6. Look at Brown's parenthetical remarks; there are a number of them in his essay. What do these parenthetical remarks do to his rhetorical stance?

suggestions for writing

1. Write a paragraph of "inflation activity" prose; then rewrite the paragraph in clear English.

2. Write a sketch of the language of a pompous speaker whom you know. Or you might try to write a parody of an imaginary pompous speaker. Select your subject with care.

3. If you have a country newspaper available, you might read two or three numbers and write a paper describing the language of the paper. You might want to talk about the paper's character, too.

4. Listen to the langauge of a sportscaster; then write a paper about the man and his language.

Frank Sullivan

The Cliché Expert Testifies on Politics

[1]   Q—Mr. Arbuthnot, I hear you've become a campaign orator.

A—Fellow American, you have heard correctly. I've been on the stump all fall.

Q—In that case you ought to be up on your campaign-oratory clichés.

A—Well, sir, it is not my wont to brag, but I believe I may say with all due modesty that I can point with pride and view with alarm as sententiously and bombastically as any senator who ever thrust one arm in his frock coat and with the other called upon high heaven to witness the perfidy of the Other Party.

[5]   Q—Describe your candidate, Mr. Arbuthnot.

A—My candidate is a man four-square, a true representative of the people, a leader worthy of the trust which has been placed in him, and a standard-bearer who will carry the banner of our ga-reat and ga-lorious party to victory.

Q—Is he a man of prophetic vision?

A—He is indeed. He is also a man of sterling character and a champion of the rights of the people.

Q—What kind of champion?

[10]   A—A stalwart champion.

Q—What is he close to?

A—The soil.

Q—Is his name Jones?

A—It is not. I have nothing against Mr. Jones personally, but I can't see where he's fitted to be President.

[15]   Q—Why not?

A—He may be a first-rate businessman, but what does he know about government?

From Frank Sullivan, *A Rock in Every Snowball.* © 1938, 1940, 1941, 1942, 1943, 1944, 1945, 1946 by Frank Sullivan. Reprinted by permission of Little, Brown and Co.

Q—Then your candidate's name is Brown.

A—Not at all. I'm a lifelong Democrat and I've always voted the straight Democratic ticket, but this year I'm taking a walk.

Q—Why?

[20] A—Because old party lines are disappearing. What this country needs is a *businessman* in the White House.

Q—Then your man is Jones, after all.

A—Jones is all right personally, but I don't like the crowd he's tied up with.

Q—What crowd?

A—Oh, the public utilities, the Old Guard, and so on. Besides, what does he know about foreign affairs?

[25] Q—Mr. Arbuthnot, I can't figure out *where* you stand. Let's get back to your campaign-oratory clichés. What kind of questions have you been discussing?

A—Burning questions. Great, underlying problems.

Q—What have you arrayed yourself against?

A—The forces of reaction. There must be no compromise with the forces of reaction.

Q—And now, Mr. Arbuthnot, may I ask you to characterize these times?

[30] A—These are troubled times, sir. We are met here today in an hour of grave national crisis.

Q—What do you, as a campaign orator, propose to do in this grave hour?

A—I shall demand, and denounce, and dedicate. I shall take stock. I shall challenge, pledge, stress, fulfill, indict, exercise, accuse, call upon, affirm, and reaffirm.

Q—Reaffirm what?

A—My undying faith in the principles laid down by the Founding Fathers. And I shall exercise eternal vigilance that our priceless heritage may be safeguarded.

[35] Q—Admirable, Mr. Arbuthnot. And that reminds me: What is it you campaign orators rise above?

A—Narrow partisanship. We must place the welfare of our country above all other considerations, including our desire to win.

Q—Mr. Arbuthnot, how do you campaign orators dedicate yourselves?

A—We dedicate ourselves anew to the task that lies before us.

Q—How does your party approach this task?

[40] A—With a solemn realization of the awful responsibility that rests upon us in this hour of unprecedented national stress.

Q—When our country is—

A—Sore beset by economic ills.

Q—How else do you approach the task?

A—With supreme confidence that our ga-reat party will prove worthy of its ga-lorious tradition.

[45]   Q—And if your party failed to approach the task in that spirit, Mr. Arbuthnot, would you say that—
A—It would indeed be recreant to its sacred trust.
Q—Ah. But you feel that it won't be recreant?
A—No, my fellow American, a tha-a-o-u-sand times no! The ga-reat party of Washington, and Jefferson, and Lincoln, and Wilson, and Roosevelt, and Cleveland, and Grant, Garfield, Hayes, and Arthur will not fail our country in this, her hour of need.
Q—Hurrah for Jones!
[50]   A—The candidate of Big Business?
Q—Then hurray for Brown!
A—He wants to be a dictator.
Q—Then three rousing cheers for Green!
A—If elected, he couldn't even control his own party.
[55]   Q—Then hurray for Smith!
A—Elect him and you'll *never* get rid of him.
Q—I'm afraid there's no pleasing you today, Mr. Arbuthnot. Would you mind telling me who's to blame for our country's hour of need?
A—The Other Party.
Q—What has the Other Party proved?
[60]   A—Its utter incapacity to govern. Its record is an unbroken record of failure, of forgotten campaign pledges, of callous disregard for the welfare of the country.
Q—What is the Other Party undermining?
A—The American way of life. It is spending vast sums of the tax-payers' money.
Q—For what?
A—To build up a huge political machine. It has aroused class hatred. Fellow American, in this solemn hour, when the sacred institutions of democracy are challenged on every side and the world is rent by strife, I charge the Other Party with having betrayed the pee-pul of these Yew-nited States.
[65]   Q—What must the pee-pul do?
A—They must rise in their wrath and elect my candidate.
Q—Mr. Arbuthnot, perhaps you'll tell us just what kind of leader the hour calls for?
A—A leader who will lead this country out of the wilderness, eliminate waste and extravagance in government, do away with red tape and bureaucratic inefficiency, solve the problem of unemployment, improve living conditions, develop purchasing power, raise the standard of living, provide better housing, and insure national defense by building a navy and air force second to none.
Q—What about the farmer?
[70]   A—The farmer must have relief.
Q—What kind of relief?
A—Farm relief. Labor must have the right to organize. Economy must be the watchword. Mounting deficits must cease; so must these

raids on the public treasury. I view with alarm the huge and unwarranted increase in our national debt. Generations yet unborn! Those who would undermine our sacred institutions! Bore from within! Freedom of speech! Monroe doctrine! I call upon every patriotic American—

Q—Regardless of race or creed?

A—Be quiet! . . . regardless of race or creed, from the snow-capped peaks of the Rockies—

[75]   Q—To the pine-clad shores of Maine?

A—Shut *up!* . . . to the pine-clad shores of Maine to have faith in the American way of life. Subversive doctrines! Undesirable aliens! Lincoln!

Q—What kind of Lincoln?

A—The Immortal Lincoln! The Immortal Washington! The Immortal Jefferson! The time for evasions has passed. We must face the facts, put our shoulders to the wheel, put our house in order, meet the challenge of the dictators, carry aloft the torch of liberty, fulfill our high destiny, face the future with confidence, and march forward to victory at the polls in November.

words and sentences

1. Vocabulary: *sententiously, perfidy* (¶ 4); *arrayed* (27); *recreant* (46).
2. Rewrite ¶ 6, trying to translate Mr. Arbuthnot's answer into clear English. Is that possible? Describe the sentence pattern Mr. Arbuthnot uses in ¶ 6. Is there any relationship between the pattern he uses and the words he chooses for his answer?
3. Does the connotation of the word "businessman" change between ¶ 16 and ¶ 20? If so, why?
4. Certain words in Sullivan's essay have favorable connotative meanings while others do not. List the favorable and unfavorable words and comment on the reasons for this distinction.
5. In ¶ 32, Sullivan has Mr. Arbuthnot answer with two sentences using parallel constructions. How are the intentions of Mr. Arbuthnot and Sullivan alike or different in these two sentences? Do the patterns of these sentences have any relationship to the intentions of Mr. Arbuthnot and Sullivan?
6. List about twenty of the clichés Mr. Arbuthnot uses. Examine these clichés for their meaning or absence of meaning.

ideas and implications

1. Sullivan's essay was first published more than twenty-five years ago. Are any of Mr. Arbuthnot's clichés still current in American political oratory? If they are, what are the implications of the continued use of such words and phrases? On the part of the speaker? On the part of the audience?
2. Write one sentence describing the quality of mind and thought of Mr. Arbuthnot. How does his language reflect his intelligence?

3. What is Sullivan's attitude towards Mr. Arbuthnot? Support your answer with specific details from the essay.

strategies

1. Sullivan presents his ideas in the form of an interview. List some advantages of this strategy. Are there any disadvantages?
2. For strategic purposes, does Sullivan use Mr. Arbuthnot as a "straw man" to be knocked down? If so, does this strategy affect the tone of Sullivan's essay?
3. Examine ¶ 78 and describe Sullivan's strategy for concluding his essay.

suggestions for writing

1. Using Sullivan's essay as a guide, write a dialogue on a subject other than political clichés.
2. If you can, interview a political figure in your home community or on your campus and write a paper about that interview.

Sydney J. Harris

A Pretty Kettle of Clichés

[1]   I should like to read or hear, just once, about tacks that aren't brass, questions that aren't moot, coasts that aren't clear, fates that aren't worse than death, and a mean that isn't golden.

[2]   And, just once, a null without a void, a might without a main, a far without a wide, a six of one without a half-dozen of the other, tooth without a nail, and ways without means.

[3]   And, just once, an unfit fiddle, a warm cucumber, a young hill, a stupid owl, a hard impeachment, a black elephant, a sage's paradise, feet of gold, the pepper of the earth, an unbloated plutocrat, and a sad Lothario.

[4]   And, just once, a social caterpillar, Father Nature, the orange of one's eye, an uncracked dawn, a picture of illness, ignorance after the event, a tower of weakness, an unsure slowness, a low dryness, and a lively earnestness.

[5]   And, just once, a fair without a square, a safe without a sound, a sackcloth without ashes, a wear without a tear, a fast without a loose, a rack without a ruin, a kill without a cure, a long without a short, and a storm without a port.

[6]   And, just once, a merciless errand, an ungrieved error, an un-

psychological moment, a light horse, a live certainty, an indecisive effect, an embarrassment of poverty, an eternal quadrangle, an emaciated calf, and someone who has been frightened into his wits.

[7]   And, just once, a nail that isn't hit on the head, a feather that can't knock you down, a gift that doesn't come from the gods, a bad Samaritan, a delicate exaggeration, and a pin that doesn't drop.

[8]   And, just once, an ungilded lily, good dirty fun, tepid congratulations, a wagon hitched to a meteorite, something that costs an ugly penny, someone who is gone and forgotten, and someone who would go through fire but not through water.

[9]   And, just once, a hue without a cry, a hem without a haw, a hit without a miss, a hither without a yon, a head without a shoulders, a spick without a span, a hammer without a tongs, fish on a string or a net or a pan but not in a kettle, a prophet with honor, and purely without simply.

[10]   And, just once, sweet grapes, soft facts, an unpicked bone, a tempest in a coffeepot, a ducksong or a goosesong but not a swansong, a bull that is taken by the tail, and a rhinestone in the rough.

words and sentences

  1. Vocabulary: *emaciated* (¶ 6), *tepid* (8).
  2. How many sentence patterns does Harris use in his essay? Does this number of sentence patterns affect Harris's prose adversely?

ideas and implications

  1. Do you recognize all of the clichés that Harris mentions? If not, does that fact say anything about the difficulty of discussing clichés?

strategies

  1. ¶s 2-10 begin with the phrase, "And, just once." What effect does Harris seem to be creating with that repetition?
  2. When Harris writes "a warm cucumber, a young hill, a stupid owl," what device is he using to discuss clichés? Does that strategy seem effective?

suggestions for writing

  1. The next time you watch the evening news, sit with a notepad and copy the clichés and stock phrases you hear. Then write a paper about the language of the evening news and the advertising that accompanies it.
  2. Listen to your own language the next time you discuss a controversial subject in a dormitory bull session or in a class. Make a list of some clichés or stock phrases that you use and then write a paper exploring the meaning of those phrases in the context of your discussion.

Ross Campbell

Cliché with Feet of Clay

[1] We in Australia suffer from a humiliating disability. The only other people with a comparable problem are those of East Africa. It is this: we are overshadowed by our fauna.

Tourists do not visit Kenya to make the acquaintance of its citizens, worthy as these may be. They go there to see, and in many cases to shoot, the local lions, antelopes, and elephants. Similarly, foreign visitors to this country are not interested in meeting, much less in shooting, a genuine Sydney estate agent or an Adelaide accountant. They want to see our kangaroos, hear our kookaburras laugh, and eat our oysters.

Noel Coward is a distinguished example of the attitude. His parting words after a stay here were: "I like Australia, and I love those wonderful oysters."

We, the human inhabitants, are regarded by the rest of the world simply as curators of wild life. Pre-eminent in interest for strangers are what they call our cute, cuddly koalas. As a result there has developed, I believe, a repressed resentment of the koala among people here. It is provoked whenever an actress goes through her koala-cuddling routine for photographers at the zoo.

[5] The thought must come to many: are koalas as lovable as they are made out to be? They are nocturnal animals, and when one sees them at the zoo are usually asleep. A koala's character, like a human being's, is hard to assess while it is sleeping. Only exceptional koalas with insomnia are available for daytime cuddling by visiting celebrities.

At last a man in a position to know has done some plain speaking about the species. He is Mr. Fred Pickersgill, who looks after a community of koalas at Phillip Island. The frank portrait he draws of them is very different from the benevolent cliché of the travel posters.

When they are annoyed, he says, they bite savagely and slash out with razor-sharp claws. The males fight over the females. They sometimes roll on the ground, as Mr. Pickersgill put it, "in a real good donnybrook."

Though male koalas are highly sexed, they treat the object of their love with no consideration. The female has a solitary existence while carrying young; her mate goes off with someone else. The male koala, as depicted by Mr. Pickersgill, is a marsupial Andy Capp.

The more one learns about the species, the more human its members appear. Mr. Pickersgill says koalas "spend the night prowling, eating and mating." The only significant difference between a koala sanctu-

From Ross Campbell, *She Can't Play My Bagpipes.* © 1970 by Shakespeare Head Press, Sydney, Australia. Reprinted by permission of the publisher.

ary and King's Cross is that koalas do not drink. (They get enough moisture from gumleaves.)

[10] By taking the creature down from its pedestal, this expert has made it more attractive to some people. An example is Les B———, a youth of 19 in our district. Previously Les had despised koalas. But when he read Mr. Pickersgill's disclosures of the animal's habits—its pugnacity, its promiscuity, and its nocturnal prowling—he was favorably impressed.

Last week Les was in trouble at home. He had gone off with a friend in a car, met a couple of girls, and stayed out till 4 a.m. When he showed up at breakfast, his father demanded to know what he had been doing.

The lad replied that he had been prowling, eating and mating, "like koalas do." Clearly he thought the example of the famous marsupial excused his conduct.

I do not suggest that everyone should imitate the koala's loose, brawling way of life. But there is need for a new note of realism in our thinking about them. It could be shown by fresh idioms: "fighting like koalas," "lustful as a koala," and so on. We should make visitors realise that koalas are morally no better than ourselves—if as good.

What matters is that Australians should creep out from behind the shadow of their fauna. For this purpose we should draw attention to our own good points, without being unduly boastful. True, we do not carry our young in pouches, but we invented the totalisator.

[15] The Federal Government has made a sound beginning by spicing its immigration propaganda with pictures of good-looking girls. We shall score an important point if we can convince the world that we have some cute, cuddly people.

words and sentences

1. Vocabulary: *donnybrook* (¶ 7); *marsupial* (8); *pugnacity, promiscuity* (10).
2. In ¶ 9, Campbell alludes to "King's Cross," a place in Sydney. Does the context of this allusion define the kind of place King's Cross is?
3. Campbell is using the word "cliché" in a more general sense than Harris. How does Campbell seem to define the word cliché?
4. List any clichés or stock phrases you find in Campbell's essay and suggest other word choices that might be appropriate.

ideas and implications

1. What are the implications of Campbell's comparison of koalas with people?
2. When Campbell says the koala is "a marsupial Andy Capp," what associations is he suggesting and why? What is the tone of Campbell's commentary on koalas?

strategies

1. Campbell seems to have organized his essay so that ¶s 1-4 comprise a

unit of discourse. What is the function of ¶s 1-4? And what is the function of ¶ 5?

2. What method of development does Campbell use in ¶s 5-9?
3. What is the relationship of ¶s 10-12 to the preceding unit of discourse?
4. What strategy does Campbell use for concluding his observations?
5. Describe Campbell's rhetorical stance.

suggestions for writing

1. Select a situation that you regard as a cliché and write a paper explaining why that situation is such.
2. From your viewing of television or the movies, select a scene that might qualify as a cliché. Describe the scene in detail and comment on your reasons for considering the scene a cliché.

Stefan Kanfer

Punning: The Candidate at Word and Play

[1]   In his scramble for the Democratic presidential nomination, Senator Edmund Muskie has uttered several statements so shocking to the sensibilities that his own aide has called them "a disease." Candidate Muskie obviously regards them as pretty amusing. Actually, both men are correct; Muskie has simply succumbed to paronophilia—the inordinate love of puns. Twice in New Hampshire he has assured audiences that the state cannot be taken for granite, and at the state capital he announced to a stunned reporter: "We just Concord the statehouse." At defenseless Coe College in Cedar Rapids, Iowa, he counted the house and cracked to his audience: "I can see that things are Coe-equal here."
[2]   Overseas, his punshots have gone wilder. While in Cairo before going on to Russia last year, he asked to visit the mosque containing Nasser's burial place. "After all," he said, "we're on our way to Mosque-Cow, aren't we?" At the tomb, when a member of his party removed his shoes according to Islamic custom and revealed a hole in his sock, Muskie shrugged: "We're in a holy place, aren't we?" When he learned that the Russians were being difficult and might not issue visas to his press entourage, he had one ready for that too: "Well, Soviet."
[3]   If Muskie is nominated, his aides will doubtless do their best to eliminate some of his worst puns from the national hustings. But once punning gets into the bloodstream, it seems to be as intoxicating as al-

From *Time Magazine*, Feb. 28, 1972. Reprinted by permission from TIME, The Weekly Newsmagazine; © Time Inc.

cohol. Even that master of precooked prose, Richard Nixon, could not resist a pun on the morning after he was elected to the presidency. Referring to a presidential seal that Julie had stitched and framed for him, Nixon described it as "the kindest thing that I had happen, even though it's crewel." That conjures up the frightening vision of a Nixon-Muskie race in which the two candidates pun for the presidency.

[4]   Puns are not newcomers to the primitive art of political mayhem. Adlai Stevenson, whose puns were superior to both Muskie's and Nixon's, once characterized Barry Goldwater as "a man who thinks everything will be better in the rear future"; he declared on another occasion: "He who slings mud generally loses ground." Franklin Roosevelt's foes insisted on calling his bright young advisers "the Drain Trust" and referring to some of his programs as ushering in a new "Age of Chiselry." In the 1800s the critics of British Prime Minister Benjamin Disraeli labeled him England's Jew d'Esprit.

[5]   Though puns may be used to political advantage—or disadvantage—punning has traditionally been more the farm of the artist than the playground of the politician. By punning, which probably derives from the Italian *puntiglio* (fine point), the writer grows ideas as well as wit. Aristophanes punned, with scatological exuberance, and so did Homer and Cicero. What was occasional in the classicists was fecund nature to Shakespeare. Because he had to play to the galleries, his plays were par for the coarse, brimming with such verbal pratfalls as "Discharge yourself of our company, Pistol." But Shakespeare could also buff the pun until it shone like art. Says the bleeding Mercutio: "Ask for me tomorrow and you shall find me a grave man." "You see how this world goes," Lear says to the blind Gloucester. "I see it feelingly," Gloucester replies.

[6]   Even with masters like Shakespeare, the pun is lagniappe, a trick to reconcile opposites, a method of giving a long sentence a parole. It was not until 1922 and *Ulysses* that James Joyce made it a literature unto itself. In *Finnegans Wake,* words become quintuple exposures; the reader has to search for a glimpse of something recognizable. In *A Skeleton Key to Finnegans Wake,* Joseph Campbell and Henry Morton Robinson explicate a typical and relatively easy example: "Into *boudoir* Joyce inserts the letter *l* and converts the word to *boudeloire,* thus adding a river association, 'Loire,' Clinging to the word also are the French associations, *bouder,* 'to pout' and *boue,* 'mud.'" Not to mention a reference to the poet Baudelaire. After you've grappled with *Finnegans Wake,* any pun seems accessible.

[7]   A simpler, journalistic style of punning was created by the Algonquin Round Table of the '20s and '30s. Dubbed the Vicious Circle, it became Prohibition's bottlefield, where columnists tailed their wags and reported puns the instant they were composed. When a Vassar girl eloped, Playwright George S. Kaufman announced that she had "put the heart before the course." Dorothy Parker confessed that in her own poetry she was always "chasing Rimbauds." Alexander Woollcott knew of "a cat hospital where they charged $4 a weak purr." Heywood Broun, drinking a bootleg liquor, sighed, "Any port in a storm." "The groans

that greet such puns," claims Milton Berle (who once joked that he had cut off his nose to spite his race), "are usually envious. The other person wishes he had said it."

[8]   Language, like the world it represents, can never be static. Even today the pun survives fitfully in tabloid headlines: JUDGES WEIGH FAN DANCER'S ACT, FIND IT WANTON. It survives in the humor of S. J. Perelman, the only post-Joycean writer capable of fluent bilingual flippancy: *"lox vobiscum,"* "the Saucier's Apprentice," and the neo-Joycean "Anna Trivia Pluralized." The pun makes its happiest regular appearance in the work of Novelist Peter De Vries, who writes stories about compulsive punners. "I can't stop," he claims. "I even *dream* verbal puns. Like the one in which a female deer was chasing a male deer. I woke up and realized it was a doe trying to make a fast buck."

[9]   Like the limerick, the pun may well be a folk-art form that defies condescension, scorn and contempt, and possesses the lust for survival of an amoeba. There will always be some, like that formidable adamant, Vladimir Nabokov, who believe that the pun is mightier than the word, that people who cannot play with words cannot properly work with them. "A man who could call a spade a spade," Oscar Wilde remarked, "should be compelled to use one."

[10]   With a little encouragement a man can bounce and juggle phrases all his life. That few do—and fewer still do well—may be the fault of formal education, which overstresses the discipline of sequential facts. Tired of such lock steps, the mind takes leaps—sometimes to fresh revelation. The pun is such a jump, but politicians, above all, should look before they leap. If puns are to be part of this year's political campaigns, it is to be hoped that the efforts will improve. Already Muskie's punning has begun to work up a backlash. His opponents are telling the apocryphal story of the Eskimo chairman of Senator George McGovern's Alaska campaign, who was giving a speech in favor of the Senator recently when a group of Muskie supporters began heckling him, drowning him out with boos and whistles. The Eskimo's comeback: "Hush, you Muskies!"

words and sentences

1. Vocabulary: *paronophilia* (¶ 1); *entourage* (2); *hustings, crewel* (3); *scatological, fecund, pratfalls* (5); *lagniappe, explicate* (6); *condescension, adamant* (9); *apocryphal* (10).
2. Describe the pattern of the first sentence in ¶ 5, and write a sentence imitating that pattern. Note Kanfer's use of the dashes.
3. Describe the pattern of the second sentence in ¶ 7, and write a sentence imitating that pattern.

ideas and implications

1. What is Kanfer's attitude towards punning? Does he pun in his essay? If so, list several of Kanfer's puns.

2. Is political punning the real subject of Kanfer's essay? Or does it simply supply him the occasion for writing an essay on puns?
3. Does Kanfer agree with Nabokov that "people who cannot play with words cannot properly work with them"? Cite evidence to support your answer.
4. According to Kanfer, why may formal education discourage punning? What must the mind do in order to pun?
5. How might puns lead to fresh revelations (¶ 10)? Can you think of any occasions when puns have led you to such revelations?

strategies

1. Kanfer divides his essay into three parts (¶s 1-4, 5-6, and 7-10). What is the subject of each of these sections of Kanfer's essay? How are these sections related to Kanfer's main idea?
2. Kanfer defines punning as the "farm of the artist" in ¶ 5. How does Kanfer develop his definition?
3. To understand a pun, one must understand the context in which it appears. How does Kanfer set the contexts for the puns he discusses? Point to two examples of his placing puns in context.

suggestions for writing

1. Write a paper in which you establish clearly the context which leads to a pun.
2. Write a dialogue in which one of your characters is a punster. Try to limit your topic to a single subject.
3. Write a paper describing a situation in which a pun led you to a fresh revelation.

Spencer Klaw

A Field Guide to Government Jargon

[1]   Not long ago, I had a chance to try my hand at a form of literary engineering for which there seems to be an unprecedented demand these days. For the better part of two weeks, I worked in Washington, D.C., as a consultant to a governmental advisory committee, one of those groups of prominent citizens that are now so frequently appointed to look into problems such as smog, or juvenile delinquency, or the plight of the humanities in an age of science. I will not identify the problem

handed to my particular committee to solve, although I may note that it is one which, in the words of a staff memorandum, "has a crucial bearing on both the short- and long-run performance capabilities of this nation and, indeed, of all free societies."

[2] At the time I was signed on as a consultant, the committee had been wrestling with this problem for almost a year, and my assignment was to assist as an editorial midwife at the birth of a preliminary draft of the committee's final report to the President and the nation. Writing committee prose is hard work—even harder, perhaps, than reading it. But I discovered that the job can be made somewhat easier if one keeps in mind certain fundamental rules, which I will list in summary form:

[3] ¶ In making recommendations, never state flatly that the people who will have to put them into effect have been doing a lousy job. Say, "While progress achieved over the past decade has been most gratifying, further improvement is not only possible but desirable."

[4] ¶ If the committee has no idea about how to effect such improvement, or if it is hopelessly divided over what concrete proposal should be made, it is customary to note that "The formulation of specific programs and procedures must, of course, await the availability of accurate information on which to base rational decisions."

[5] ¶ If it is necessary to make the foregoing point more than once—which I gathered it almost always is—beware of giving the reader the mistaken notion that the committee has been too lazy to collect the facts that are needed. One way to avoid this is to emphasize the need not so much for new facts as for new fact-finding machinery—by stating, for example, that "A system must be established and responsibility clearly pinpointed throughout the Executive branch, for ensuring an adequate flow of relevant and integrated information to decision-makers at all appropriate levels of government."

[6] ¶ Don't frighten people unnecessarily by evoking images of new bureaucratic controls. If the committee thinks, for instance, that there should be a tighter rein on government purchases of rocket fuel, say so as fuzzily as possible—e.g., "The evidence would seem to warrant the assignment within the departments concerned of responsibility for the establishment of appropriate policy guidelines governing the purchase of rocket fuel."

[7] ¶ Beware of stating proposals in simple, commonsense terms; readers may conclude that you haven't given sufficient thought to the problem at hand. It is poor tactics, for example, to point out that too many different agency chiefs are making decisions about the same thing, and to suggest that their heads should be knocked together. It is better to note that "Decision points are widely distributed throughout a complex and loosely articulated system," and then to say that "While gratifying progress has been made, further measures to facilitate improved co-ordination of this complex process within clearly defined parameters are nevertheless desirable." This formulation has the additional merit of suggesting, without the committee's coming right out and saying so, that more study is required.

[8]   ¶ Be sure to stress the extraordinary—indeed, the unique—complexity of the problem your committee has been asked to study. Make it clear at the outset that "The alternatives confronting decision-makers in this vital area of our national life have had to be weighed in the light of the subtle interplay of conflicting interests in a society that is itself changing with bewildering and unprecedented speed." A sentence like this helps to explain why, despite the $150,000 it has been given for research, the committee has been able only to scratch the surface of the problem.

[9]   ¶ In the interest of achieving a desirable textual density, it is a good idea to incorporate all the facts you can lay your hands on. Those that don't fit into your argument can be inserted at random, preceded in each instance by the phrase "It is interesting to note that . . ."

[10]   ¶ Finally, if it appears that the rocket-fuel situation is actually pretty well in hand and that there was probably no need in the first place for the appointment of a special advisory committee, the thing to do is to shift contexts. One may write, for example, that "Even though production and consumption of rocket fuel are for the moment in approximate balance, this committee would be derelict if it did not examine the supply-demand situation in the wider context of the complex interplay of shifting and conflicting forces that characterizes the nation's international environment." This lays the foundation for a ringing declaration to the effect that "In a true sense, indeed, this nation can never have too much rocket fuel."

[11]   ¶ While I would like to think that the foregoing list is fairly complete, I should point out that even after my two weeks in Washington I apparently still had much to learn. "The chairman is delighted," the committee's staff director wrote me a few days after I had returned to my home in New York. "He feels that commendable progress has been made toward drafting a report which adequately takes into account the many-faceted complexity of the problem. At the same time, he feels that certain improvements would be desirable. . . ."

words and sentences

1. Vocabulary: *jargon* (title); *parameters* (¶ 7); *derelict* (10).
2. What connotative associations does Klaw suggest with such phrases as "literary engineering" (¶ 1) and "editorial midwife" (¶ 2)?
3. Examine and describe the verbs in the sentences that Klaw quotes. In what voice are many of these verbs? Why?
4. Examine the modifiers of the nouns that Klaw quotes—for example, "performance capabilities" (¶ 1). What does this construction do to the prose of government jargon?
5. Rewrite the last sentence in ¶ 11. Translate this sentence into plain English.

ideas and implications

1. What does Klaw mean by "committee prose"? Why is writing com-

mittee prose hard work? Where might you find examples of committee prose?

2. According to Klaw, what is the purpose of most government reports?

strategies

1. Klaw's strategy is to list the rules for writing government jargon. Does he also use the journey or trip as a strategy for enclosing his list? In what way?
2. What effect does Klaw create by concluding his essay with the letter from the committee chairman? What are the implications of the chairman's remarks?

suggestions for writing

1. Take a sample of clear prose and rewrite it in government jargon. Include a copy of the prose with your rewritten version.
2. In a newspaper or magazine, find an example of prose that resembles government jargon. Then rewrite this prose in clear and concise language. Include with your rewritten version a xerox copy of the jargon.

Art Buchwald

All-Purpose Press Release

[1]   Things happen so fast these days that the State Department no longer has time to put out a statement for each crisis. To solve the problem a friend of mine has devised an all-purpose press release which is being sent out to newspapers, magazines and television stations throughout the country.

It goes like this:

DEPARTMENT OF STATE
ALL-PURPOSE PRESS STATEMENT
(Date)

For Release _____.

The United States government welcomes the progress, during the past 12 hours, toward freedom and increased stability in _____. While reluctant to condone any resort to violence, we regard the events in _____ as a significant step toward more orderly democracy and the strenthening of the _____ world. We pledge our firm support to Gen. _____ of the _____ party, and are encouraged by his promise to return _____ in due course to civilian rule.

His actions have spelled defeat for the tyrannical forces of (a) General (b) Colonel (c) President (d) Premier (e) Prince _____ of the badly split _____ party, and have given new hope for the free people of _____.

Our support for Gen. _____'s government represents no change in United States policy toward _____.

[5]   Nor does it change the United States posture vis-à-vis _____ or _____ or _____.

To help the people of _____ get back on their feet, the President has authorized a special fund of _____ dollars to pay for the salaries of the army and new government officials. The President has also promised _____ dollars in loans to _____ and has promised military aid and advisers to prevent another _____.

The _____ U.S. Fleet has been dispatched to _____ the capital of _____ to prevent further bloodshed and to protect American _____ there.

Secretary of State Dean Rusk denied that the Fleet was sent to _____ to influence in any way the internal affairs of the country. The Fleet had been requested by Gen. _____ and under the _____ agreement we had no choice but to provide American support to prevent a _____ take-over.

Mr. Rusk promised that as soon as things stabilized he would withdraw the _____ Fleet and the _____ Marine Brigade which was landed three days ago.

[10] The President and the National Security Council met today to discuss the _____ situation and the President is sending _____ as his personal representative to give him a firsthand report and to make future recommendations. This in no way shows his lack of confidence in Ambassador _____ _____, who has been called back to Washington for consultation.

Gen. _____ is considered a friend of the United States, having studied at the _____ War College, in Washington, and he has promised strong, forceful leadership for _____, something that has been lacking in the past under the weak regime of _____ and his so-called democratic government.

(a) General (b) Colonel (c) President (d) Premier (e) Prince _____ has sought political asylum in the _____ embassy and will probably be allowed to leave the country.

words and sentences

1. Vocabulary: *vis-à-vis* (¶ 5).
2. In ¶ 9, what is the effect of the final clause in that sentence? Write a sentence imitating Buchwald's pattern and effect.

3. List the words and phrases characterizing the former government in
   _____. What bias appears in these words?

ideas and implications

1. What attitude towards U.S. foreign policy appears in Buchwald's press release?
2. Examine several press releases in newspapers or magazines. Do they resemble Buchwald's? Can you generalize about the effectiveness of such communications?
3. Make a list of the implicit assumptions made in the press release. How many of these assumptions are related to power and the uses of power?

strategies

1. One of Buchwald's strategies is to include in his press release details which belie the truth of the report. Make a list of these details and comment on the effect of each.

suggestions for writing

1. Rewrite Buchwald's all-purpose press release from the point of view of the defeated faction in _____.
2. Write an all-purpose press release for another occasion. You might consider one of the following: the divorce or separation of a famous film couple, the resignation of some public official, the trading of a temperamental sports figure, or the publication of a new book by a famous writer.

Russell Lynes

Dirty Words

[1]   Possibly it is a reaction against the prevalence of four letter words in literature today, but there is a kind of dirty language that has become part of common parlance that seems to me far more pernicious than just plain - - - - ! Four-letter words, whatever one may think of their general use in fiction (where they mostly occur), at least have very specific meanings and convey images or ideas or situations that are at once graphic and

precise, and often emphatic. The dirty words to which I object are be-
fouling conversation and nonfiction and most especially the conversation
and prose of what is presumed to be the educated community. They are
substitutes for thought, most of them, or, to put it another way, they
exude a mist which rises between a speaker and his listener so that all
that can be perceived through it is a kind of fuzz. Some of the words to
which I refer unquestionably meant something once, but they are now
used to create an aura of sense, not sense itself.

[2]   But let me be meaningful.

[3]   If you know what I mean by *meaningful,* you know more than I do.
It is one of those words that sounds as though it were loaded and when
you fire it the noise is impressive but the blood it draws is none. A
"meaningful" conversation in my experience is one from which both
parties withdrew, each convinced that the other said nothing but that he
himself said something profound. A "meaningful" experience sometimes
seems to be one in which the emotions have been stirred but the precise
meaning of the situation escapes one. If the word serves any useful function at all it is as a cover-up for indecision. To some persons, for example,
looking at a sculpture of a goat by Picasso is a pleasure, to others it is a
joke or disgusting; to those who don't know what they think it is a
"meaningful experience." One never has to make up one's mind about
what is meaningful; the word does it for one.

[4]   Some of the dirty words come in pairs like *creative* and *constructive,*
both of which are examples of what happens to perfectly nice words when
they fall into bad company. "Creative people" are not what you would
think; they are not painters, sculptors, choreographers, poets, novelists,
or composers, all of whom are artists. Creative people do "constructive"
thinking in advertising agencies and in editorial offices and let somebody
else worry about the cost. "Creative" people, indeed, do "constructive"
thinking which, at its very best, is "meaningful."

[5]   One of the ways of promoting creative thinking in both business
and bureaucracy today is a method analogous to getting blood from a
stone known in the gutter slang of our time as *brainstorming.* It involves
another dirty word which I think it necessary to define at once because it
is impossible to talk the argot of today without using it. The word is
dialogue. Private individuals may still have conversations or they may
talk things over, but scholars, public servants, foundation executives,
radio and television commentators (if you'll excuse the expression), and
"generations" indulge in what is usually referred to in the singular as a
"dialogue." A dialogue rarely happens between two persons. A dialogue
is an attempt to relieve a situation defined by another cliché known as
lack of communication. But before we consider "communication," which
has a special darkness of its own, let us dispose of "brainstorming," which
is the miscellaneous use of untrained and undisciplined brains engaged
in a dialogue hoping to produce something that is meaningful. It assumes
that even the lamest brain under pressure—perhaps because it is a nerve
(or *nerve center,* a phrase now commonly used in the communications
business and other industries to indicate the office where the public-rela-

tions department keeps management from making a public fool of itself)
—can produce a *sensitive response.*

[6]   Recently there appeared in the *New York Times* a report of a young
lady who had got in trouble with the authorities at Barnard College because she was discovered to be living off-campus with a Columbia College
junior. She said she had gone to the office of Barnard's president, but
declared, "I just couldn't communicate with her. She seemed insensitive."

[7]   There in a single statement is the nub of the problem commonly
referred to as "the failure of communication between generations," which
is a newly devised verbal weapon used by the young when they do not
wish to admit that they know what their elders are talking about but
in fact know quite well, and used by the old to shield themselves from
having to bother. Almost the simplest definition of "communication" is
that it is something that doesn't happen between generations because of
the *generation gap.* (See below for a study of the importance of the "gap"
in modern society and politics.) Lack of communication between generations, however, is not communication's only kind of lack. It is the lack
of communication between those who are sensitive and those who are
insensitive which keeps the generations from being unified.

[8]   I can remember back to the time when *sensitive* was frequently used
to mean touchy, chip-on-shoulder, easily wounded, and when *insensitive*
meant thick-skinned, Philistine, boorish, and was frequently applied by
nonathletes to athletes and by English professors to scientists. Now a sensitive person is one who sees things as I do, and an insensitive person is
one who doesn't like the things I like and sees no reason to struggle to like
them. This is especially true in relation to the arts, but it also applies,
as in the case of the Barnard girl, to mores. There is, however, another
use of the word which cannot be overlooked by anyone who reads book
reviews. It is the equivalent of inertia, in the sense that the sensitive
novel is one in which almost nothing happens but in which the characters
(and most especially the one who represents the novelist him- or herself)
vibrates with reaction to a situation which is essentially static and which
nobody can do anything to change.

[9]   People who make a great many other people feel sensitive in the
current (and I contend bawdy) use of the word are, as I do not need to
remind you, *charismatic.* I sometimes wonder as I listen to my acquaintances, read the press, and hear wise men explain the world on television,
how we managed to communicate meaningfully at all until someone a
few years ago propelled the ancient word "charisma" into current slang.
Now if you haven't charisma you haven't spiritual or political *it,* which
was a simpler word in use in the 'twenties to mean much the same thing,
except that "it" had the added attraction of *sex appeal,* another phrase
that is all but extinct. It is as necessary for the political analyst to use
"charisma" today as it is for the political aspirant to incorporate it in his
(here's another) *ambience.** If you can project your charisma in the right

* The French spell it *ambiance.*

ambience you have achieved a position so invulnerable as to leave no room for dialogue, a situation for which we have invented another meaningful phrase, *credibility gap.*

[10]   I said we would come to the importance of "gap" to our society. Gap is a three-letter word, though it has the impertinence of a four-letter word. (Gap certainly sounds like - - - - , for example.) Used with the word credibility, it once may have had some meaning, but it has come to be an epithet and a slogan. Presumably it means the difference between the truth as "they" see it and the truth as "we" see it. There used to be a word "prevarication" which is no more cumbersome than "credibility gap" and suggests much the same thing. Prevarication, a minor kind of camouflage, has always been a part of daily life . . . a state of nature, you might say. Women lie about their age, men about their incomes, children about their marks in school, politicians about their intentions, and girls about their virginity. This is merely prevarication. I would call the distance between the knees and the hem of a miniskirt a genuine credibility gap.

[11]   Outside the ambience of political affairs, and the *ambivalence* (now *there's* one!) of political pundits, there are some phrases so benighted that I hesitate to mention them in this family magazine. Look upon the phrase "environmental management," for example, and blush for your native tongue. I am told that putting background music in an art gallery (or a dairy barn) is "e - - - - - - - - - - - m - - - - - - - - - ." There is no language so slovenly as that which is invented to make trades seem like professions. There is, indeed, a low expression for this process—to *upgrade.* "Upgrading" is frequently a matter of concealing a plain fact with a fancy phrase. I remember a tooth powder that used to carry on its container the legend, "also efficacious for cleansing artificial dentures."

[12]   Words like *empathize* and *ecumenism,* which we got along without perfectly well a few years ago, now fall like showers of commas into the most innocent conversations. I am not sure that to "empathize with" somebody is much worse than to "identify with" him, except for the sound reason that "to identify" is a respectable verb and "to empathize" is a noun that has lost its moorings. "Ecumenism," which used to have a certain theological standing, is rapidly becoming a synonym for "cool it, boys, let's get together." Even so, these two bits of intellectualistic slang are preferable to certain other clichés so commonly heard as to be allowed to befoul the language almost unnoticed. No study today is worth its salt unless it is *in depth;* no memorandum can be taken seriously unless it is a *position paper;* and everyone is at sea until he is *orientated.* No man takes a stand any more; he *assumes a posture* or a *stance,* soft words for soft convictions. I have even heard it said that no head of a family deserves the dignity of that position unless he *nest-eggs!*

[13]   I have left to the last the word of all words that seems to me the most offensive nine-letter word in common usage among the educated classes. The word is *dichotomy.*

[14]   As for dichotomy, I'm of two minds about it.

words and sentences

1. Vocabulary: *parlance, pernicious* (¶ 1); *Philistine* (8); *charismatic* (9); *epithet, prevarication* (10); *efficacious* (11); *dichotomy* (13).
2. Lynes redefines "dirty language." In a sentence, tell what Lynes means with this term.
3. Describe the sentence beginning "But before we consider . . ." in ¶ 5. Then write a sentence imitating this pattern. Is the sentence a loose or a periodic sentence? Can you predict the last word in that sentence before you read it? Now scan the sentence as you might scan a line of poetry. Can you comment on the rhythms in the sentence?
4. How is Lynes using the words "credibility gap" in the last sentence of ¶ 10?
5. Describe the pattern of the sentence in ¶ 14; then write a sentence imitating this pattern. How does the word *dichotomy* anticipate the main clause of this sentence?

ideas and implications

1. For Lynes, what is the relationship between dirty words and one's feelings?
2. Does Lynes object to dirty words because of the words themselves?
3. What would you guess Lynes's attitude to be towards four-letter words? Why?
4. In ¶ 8, Lynes mentions the relationship between "sensitivity" and mores. What does he suggest about the relationship between language and mores?

strategies

1. What method of development does Lynes use in ¶ 3? Does this paragraph have a topic sentence?
2. What is the function of ¶ 2?
3. In ¶ 4, Lynes introduces the words *creative* and *constructive*. Does he define these terms? How? What is the tone of his remarks? Does this paragraph seem to build towards the final sentence?
4. What method of development does Lynes use in ¶ 10? What effect does the parenthetical remark create?

suggestions for writing

1. Select one of the "dirty words" Lynes discusses and write a paper illustrating your understanding of that word.
2. Write a paper discussing your stand on four-letter words in writing and speech.
3. Almost everyone has a list of words which are offensive to him. Write a paper about a word or group of words which make you cringe.

Up Tight About Hang-ups

[1]   Walter Muir Whitehill, an author and the director of the august Athenaeum library in Boston, couldn't believe what he saw on the annual report from Colonial Williamsburg, Inc., which administers the restored village of Williamsburg, Va. "The title of the report," reports Whitehill, "was 'Williamsburg Tells It Like It Was'."

[2]   *Groovy. Beautiful. Out of sight.* The jargon of the alienated, the oppressed, the discontented is becoming the idiom of Middle—nay, Colonial—America. Television writers babble like acid-heads; newspaper columnists sound like black militants; and advertising copywriters echo the slogans of the teeny-boppers. "Turn on, before you turn in," read one advertisement in The New York Times last week, "with your own fun-at-home steambath." "People used to want to grow up," notes Times columnist Russell Baker, dourly. "Now they just want to sound young."

[3]   The mainstream of language, of course, is always being refreshed by new sources of words and phrases, and only the most doctrinaire purist would argue that lively lingo should be banned from straight usage. "*Hang-up* is good, it replaces psychiatric text-book talk," says Chicago Daily News columnist Mike Royko. Adds writer and press critic Ben Bagdikian: "I think *The Man* expresses very succinctly the idea of the person of authority. It is a private language, a secret sort of handclasp." NBC commentator David Brinkley says he likes the term *up tight* better than earlier, less expressive terms such as tensed up.

[4]   Overkill: But what happens is that the innovators—blacks, young people and, as the sociologists would put it, other "out groups"—find that their cabalistic expressions are taken over by the square world and spoken and written to death. Journalists, too, overkill with jargon and pretentious usages because they come quickly to mind and substitute for thinking. Unfortunately, interment doesn't come fast enough. A chrestomathy of current phrases that a representative group of lovers of English offer up for burial:

[5]   "*Tell it like it is,*" volunteers literary critic Philip Rahv. "It is the supreme cliché of the year. Certainly, the person saying it doesn't know what really 'is'. Who does? What an arrogant statement, a ridiculous request." British writer Katherine Whitehorn can do without *with-it* and *so-called*—"it doesn't mean the object is misnamed, just that the user doesn't like it."

[6]   Bergen Evans, professor of English at Northwestern University and a leading member of the permissive school of language, hopes he will never have to be confronted with the term *confrontation.*

[7]   Robert Manning, editor of The Atlantic, picked up a newspaper

and focused on the phrase *sort of* as an expression he considers "useless, ambiguous and grating." Manning is disturbed also by the proliferation of obscenity. "I wish the problem would go away." says Manning. "The words won't. In some pieces they are essential to convey the point. But in others they are being used more and more for shock purposes only."

[8]   Louis Lyons, former curator of the Nieman Foundation at Harvard, and James Boylan, editor of the Columbia Journalism Review, are exacerbated by *you know*—which both say they hear much too often over radio and TV. "What does it mean," asks Lyons. "What do I know? What is that expression? A nervous tic? A lack of vocabulary?"

[9]   Both Bagdikian and Baker believe that the value of *Establishment* has been debased. "It would be all right to keep the Establishment members," Baker says, "if we got rid of the word."

[10]   Washington newsmen are annoyed most by officialese. "The first expression that I want to go is *viable*," says Art Buchwald. "It dates back to the Kennedy Administration and it just isn't very viable any more." But he also objects to some of the phrases that Mr. Nixon has introduced. "In every speech," says Buchwald, "he throws in a line that goes: 'I want to make this perfectly clear' or 'I want to say this candidly'." Adds Russell Baker: "Republicans go in for Latin stems and roots a lot. We're bound to hear a lot about *definitization* and *implementation*."

[11]   The problem has become an English one as well as an American one. William Davis, the new editor of Punch, says he "would like to dispose of—*crisis, taking into consideration, in the final analysis, within the framework of, at this time, other things being equal* and *alive and well and living in*." Adds Bill Grundy, press critic for the weekly Spectator: "I could do without *participation; charisma* has lost its charisma for me; let's eliminate *teach-ins, sit-ins, live-ins* and any other bloody ins; and I'm sick of *in depth,* which usually means in length."

[12]   NEWSWEEK would like to recommend early retirement for *it's what's happening, where it's at, up against the wall, doing (my, your, his, her) thing, generation gap, name of the game, piece of the action, relevant, commitment, culturally deprived, disadvantaged, value judgment* and *meaningful relationship* (instead of campus sex).

[13]   But Art Buchwald deserves to pronounce the final, meaningful, relevant, viable judgment: "Another thing I'd like to see go," he says, "is stories about words that are in or out."

words and sentences

1. Vocabulary: *dourly* (¶ 2); *doctrinaire* (3); *cabalistic, interment, chrestomathy* (4); *proliferation* (7); *exacerbated* (8); *viable* (10); *charisma* (11).
2. Describe the pattern of the second sentence in ¶ 2; then write a sentence imitating that pattern.
3. Scan as you would a poem the quotation from Philip Rahv in ¶ 5. Then write a sentence imitating the rhythm of Rahv's quotation.
4. Describe the pattern of the sentence in ¶ 13; then write a sentence

imitating that pattern. What effect is the writer working for with the string of adjectives before the word *judgment*?

ideas and implications

1. What arguments are used for favoring some slang words? What against?
2. Are any of the terms mentioned unfamiliar words in the language? Or are they merely new combinations? How is this phenomenon a comment on the flexibility of language?

strategies

1. What kind of research has gone into the writing of the *Newsweek* article? Does the use of sources help the argument?
2. How has the writer organized his material? Describe the opening and closing strategies.

suggestions for writing

1. From your own experience, write about a situation in which you used a private language. Tell why that language was necessary.
2. Though Buchwald might not approve, write a paper examining several "in" words. Try to explain why these words seem to be in favor.
3. Collect a dozen words or phrases which you would like to bury. Write a paper explaining why.
4. Coin a new word; then write a paper arguing for the coinage.

John Lardner

Thoughts on Radio-Televese

[1]　Interviewing Governor Rockefeller recently on Station WMCA, Barry Gray, the discless jockey, felt he needed to ask his guest a certain question. He also felt a clear obligation to put the inquiry in radio-televese, the semi-official language of men who promote conversation on the air. Though it is more or less required, this language is a flexible one, leaving a good deal to the user's imagination. "Governor," Mr. Gray said, after pausing to review the possibilities of the patois, "how do you see your future in a Pennsylvania Avenue sense?" I thought it was a splendid gambit. Another broadcaster might have said "How do you see yourself in the electoral-college picture?" or "How do you project

yourself Chief Executive-wise?" The Gray formula had the special flavor, the colorful two-rings-from-the-bull's-eye quality, that I have associated with the work of this interviewer ever since I began to follow it, several years ago. For the record, Governor Rockefeller replied, "I *could* be happier where I am." He might have meant Albany, he might have meant the WMCA studio. As you see, radio-televese is not only a limber language, it is contagious.

[2]   The salient characteristic of remarks made in radio-televese is that they never coincide exactly with primary meanings or accepted forms. For instance, Mr. Gray, a leader in the postwar development of the lingo, has a way of taking a trenchant thought or a strong locution and placing it somewhere to the right or left of where it would seem to belong. "Is this your first trip to the mainland? How do you feel about statehood?" I have heard him ask a guest from the Philippines on one of his shows (the program runs, at present, from 11:05 P.M. to 1 A.M.). On the topic of Puerto Ricans in New York, he has said, "How can we make these people welcome and not upset the décor of the city?" On a show a few years ago, he described an incident that had taken place in a night club "that might be called a bawd." A drunk at a ringside table, Mr. Gray said, "interrupted the floor show to deliver a soliloquy." "When did the chink begin to pierce the armor?" he once asked, in connection with a decline in the prestige of former Mayor O'Dwyer. "The fault, then," he said on another occasion, "is not with Caesar or with his stars but with certain congressmen." Speaking of the real-life source of a character in a Broadway play, he has observed, "He was the clay pigeon on whom the character was modelled." When Mr. Gray called Brussels "the Paris of Belgium," I was reminded of an editorial I had read in a Long Island newspaper long ago in which Great Neck was called "the Constantinople of the North Shore." There is an eloquence and an easy confidence in Mr. Gray's talk that stimulates even his guests to heights of radio-televese. Artie Shaw, a musician, in describing the art of another performer to Mr. Gray, said, "He has a certain thing known as 'presence'—when he's on-stage, you can see him." Another guest declared that the success of a mutual friend was "owing to a combination of luck and a combination of skill." "You can say that again," Mr. Gray agreed, and I believe that the guest did so, a little later. The same eloquence and the same off-center-ism can be found today in the speech of a wide variety of radio and television regulars. "Parallels are odious," Marty Glickman, a sports announcer, has stated. "The matter has reached a semi-head," a senator—I couldn't be sure which one—said at a recent televised Congressional hearing. "I hear you were shot down over the Netherlands while flying," a video reporter said to Senator Howard Cannon, a war veteran, on a Channel 2 program last winter. "Where in the next year are we going to find the writers to fill the cry and the need?" David Susskind demanded not long ago of a forum of TV directors. "Do you have an emotional umbilical cord with Hollywood?" Mr. Susskind asked a director on the same show.

[3]   Mr. Susskind's second question raises the point that metaphor is indispensable in radio-televese. "Wherein water always finds its own level,

they should start hitting soon," a baseball announcer said about the Yankees the other day. In an earlier year, Red Barber, analyzing a situation in which a dangerous batter had been purposely walked, with the effect of bringing an even more dangerous batter to the plate, remarked that it was a case of "carrying coals to Newcastle, to make use of an old expression." I suspect that Mr. Barber meant that it was a case of the frying pan and the fire, and I also suspect that if he had thought of the right metaphor afterward, would have corrected himself publicly. He is a conscientious man, and therefore by no means a typical user of radio-televese. The true exponent never retraces his steps but moves from bold figure to bold figure without apology. There have been few bolder sequences (or "seg-ways," as they are sometimes called on the air) than the one that Mr. Gray achieved in 1957, during a discussion of the perils faced by Jack Paar in launching a new program. I think I have quoted this passage here once before; it still fills me with admiration. "It's like starting off with a noose around your neck," Mr. Gray said. "You've got twenty-six weeks to make good, or they'll shoot you. That sword of Damocles can be a rough proposition." As most of you know by now, Mr. Paar eventually made good before the sword could explode and throttle him.

[4]   Perhaps the most startling aspect of radio-televese is its power to move freely in time, space, and syntax, transposing past and future, beginnings and endings, subjects and objects. This phase of the language has sometimes been called backward English, and sometimes, with a bow to the game of billiards, reverse English. Dorothy Kilgallen, a television panelist, was wallowing in the freedom of the language on the night she said, "It strikes me as funny, don't you?" So was Dizzy Dean when he said, "Don't fail to miss tomorrow's doubleheader." Tommy Loughran, a boxing announcer, was exploring the area of the displaced ego when he told his audience, "It won't take him [the referee] long before I think he should stop it." Ted Husing was on the threshold of outright mysticism when he reported, about a boxer who was cuffing his adversary smartly around, "There's a lot more authority in Joe's punches than perhaps he would like his opponent to suspect!" It is in the time dimension, however, that radio-televese scores its most remarkable effects. Dizzy Dean's "The Yankees, as I told you later . . ." gives the idea. The insecurity of man is demonstrated regularly on the air by phrases like "Texas, the former birthplace of President Eisenhower" and "Mickey Mantle, a former native of Spavinaw, Oklahoma." I'm indebted to Dan Parker, sportswriter and philologist, for a particularly strong example of time adjustment from the sayings of Vic Marsillo, a boxing manager who occasionally speaks on radio and television: "Now, Jack, whaddya say we reminisce a little about tomorrow's fight?" These quotations show what can be done in the way of outguessing man's greatest enemy, but I think that all of them are excelled by a line of Mr. Gray's, spoken four or five years ago: "What will our future forefathers say?"

[5]   It is occasionally argued in defense of broadcasters (though they need and ask for no defense) that they speak unorthodoxly because they

must speak under pressure, hastily, spontaneously—that their eccentricities are unintentional. Nothing could be farther from the truth. Their language is proud and deliberate. The spirit that has created it is the spirit of ambition. Posterity would have liked it. In times to come, our forebears will be grateful.

words and sentences

1. Vocabulary: *patois* (¶ 1); *salient, trenchant* (2).
2. Scan as you would a poem the last sentence in ¶ 1; then write a sentence imitating that rhythm.
3. Describe the pattern of the second sentence in ¶ 2; then write a sentence imitating that pattern.

ideas and implications

1. What is Lardner's attitude towards radio-televese? Is he writing to criticize only?
2. Compare and contrast Calvin Brown's attitude towards broadcast language with Lardner's.
3. Check the word *spoonerism* in your dictionary. Is there any relationship between spoonerisms and Lardner's radio-televese?

strategies

1. What do the topic sentences of ¶s 2, 3, and 4 promise the reader? How does Lardner develop the ideas in these paragraphs?
2. What strategy does Lardner use to close his essay?

suggestions for writing

1. Write a paper about a radio or television personality you have heard frequently. How does his language characterize him?
2. Watch one of the television talk shows and then write a paper about one of the guests and the moderator.

Stuart Chase

Gobbledygook

[1]   Said Franklin Roosevelt, in one of his early presidential speeches: "I see one-third of a nation ill-housed, ill-clad, ill-nourished." Translated into standard bureaucratic prose his statement would read:

It is evident that a substantial number of persons within the Continental boundaries of the United States have inadequate financial resources with which to purchase the products of agricultural communities and industrial establishments. It would appear that for a considerable segment of the population, possibly as much as 33.333 * of the total, there are inadequate housing facilities, and an equally significant proportion is deprived of the proper types of clothing and nutriment.

* Not carried beyond four places.

[2]   This rousing satire on gobbledygook—or talk among the bureaucrats —is adapted from a report prepared by the Federal Security Agency [1] in an attempt to break out of the verbal squirrel cage. "Gobbledygook" was coined by an exasperated Congressman, Maury Maverick of Texas, and means using two, or three, or ten words in the place of one, or using a five-syllable word where a single syllable would suffice. Maverick was censuring the forbidding prose of executive departments in Washington, but the term has now spread to windy and pretentious language in general.

[3]   "Gobbledygook" itself is a good example of the way a language grows. There was no word for the event before Maverick's invention; one had to say: "You know, that terrible, involved, polysyllabic language those government people use down in Washington." Now one word takes the place of a dozen.

[4]   A British member of Parliament, A. P. Herbert, also exasperated with bureaucratic jargon, translated Nelson's immortal phrase, "England expects every man to do his duty":

England anticipates that, as regards the current emergency, personnel will face up to the issues, and exercise appropriately the functions allocated to their respective occupational groups.

[5]   A New Zealand official made the following report after surveying a plot of ground for an athletic field:

It is obvious from the difference in elevation with relation to the short depth of the property that the contour is such as to preclude any reasonable developmental potential for active recreation.

Seems the plot was too steep.

[6]   An office manager sent this memo to his chief:

Verbal contact with Mr. Blank regarding the attached notification of promotion has elicited the attached representation intimating that he prefers to decline the assignment.

Seems Mr. Blank didn't want the job.

A doctor testified at an English trial that one of the parties was suffering from "circumorbital haematoma."

1 Now the Department of Health, Education, and Welfare.

Seems the party had a black eye.

> In August 1952 the U.S. Department of Agriculture put out a pamphlet entitled: "Cultural and Pathogenic Variability in Single-Condial and Hyphaltip Isolates of Hemlin-Thosporium Turcicum Pass."

Seems it was about corn leaf disease.

[7]   On reaching the top of the Finsteraarhorn in 1845, M. Dollfus-Ausset, when he got his breath, exclaimed:

> The soul communes in the infinite with those icy peaks which seem to have their roots in the bowels of eternity.

Seems he enjoyed the view.

[8]   A government department announced:

> Voucherable expenditures necessary to provide adequate dental treatment required as adjunct to medical treatment being rendered a pay patient in in-patient status may be incurred as required at the expense of the Public Health Service.

Seems you can charge your dentist bill to the Public Health Service. Or can you?

Legal Talk

[9]   Gobbledygook not only flourishes in government bureaus but grows wild and lush in the law, the universities, and sometimes among the literati. Mr. Micawber was a master of gobbledygook, which he hoped would improve his fortunes. It is almost always found in offices too big for face-to-face talk. Gobbledygook can be defined as squandering words, packing a message with excess baggage and so introducing semantic "noise." Or it can be scrambling words in a message so that meaning does not come through. The directions on cans, bottles, and packages for putting the contents to use are often a good illustration. Gobbledygook must not be confused with double talk, however, for the intentions of the sender are usually honest.

[10]   I offer you a round fruit and say, "Have an orange." Not so an expert in legal phraseology, as parodied by editors of *Labor:*

> I hereby give and convey to you, all and singular, my estate and interests, right, title, claim and advantages of and in said orange, together with all rind, juice, pulp and pits, and all rights and advantages therein . . . anything hereinbefore or hereinafter or in any other deed or deeds, instrument or instruments of whatever nature or kind whatsoever, to the contrary, in any wise, notwithstanding.

[11]   The state of Ohio, after five years of work, has redrafted its legal code in modern English, eliminating 4,500 sections and doubtless a blizzard of "whereases" and "hereinafters." Legal terms of necessity must be closely tied to their referents, but the early solons tried to do this the hard way, by adding synonyms. They hoped to trap the physical event in a net of words, but instead they created a mumbo-jumbo beyond the

power of the layman, and even many a lawyer, to translate. Legal talk is studded with tautologies, such as "cease and desist," "give and convey," "irrelevant, incompetent, and immaterial." Furthermore, legal jargon is a dead language; it is not spoken and it is not growing. An official of one of the big insurance companies calls their branch of it "bafflegab." Here is a sample from his collection:

> One-half to his mother, if living, if not to his father, and one-half to his mother-in-law, if living, if not to his mother, if living, if not to his father. Thereafter payment is to be made in a single sum to his brothers. On the one-half payable to his mother, if living, if not to his father, he does not bring in his mother-in-law as the next payee to receive, although on the one-half to his mother-in-law, he does bring in the mother or father.

[12]   You apply for an insurance policy, pass the tests, and instead of a straightforward "here is your policy," you receive something like this:

> This policy is issued in consideration of the application therefor, copy of which application is attached hereto and made part hereof, and of the payment for said insurance on the life of the above-named insured.

Academic Talk

[13]   The pedagogues may be less repetitious than the lawyers, but many use even longer words. It is a symbol of their calling to prefer Greek and Latin derivatives to Anglo-Saxon. Thus instead of saying: "I like short clear words," many a professor would think it more seemly to say: "I prefer an abbreviated phraseology, distinguished for its lucidity." Your professor is sometimes right, the longer word may carry the meaning better—but not because it is long. Allen Upward in his book *The New Word* warmly advocates Anglo-Saxon English as against what he calls "Mediterranean" English, with its polysyllables built up like a skyscraper.

[14]   Professional pedagogy, still alternating betweeen the Middle Ages and modern science, can produce what Henshaw Ward once called the most repellent prose known to man. It takes an iron will to read as much as a page of it. Here is a sample of what is known in some quarters as "pedageese":

> Realization has grown that the curriculum or the experience of learners change and improve only as those who are most directly involved examine their goals, improve their understandings and increase their skill in performing the tasks necessary to reach newly defined goals. This places the focus upon teacher, lay citizen and learner as partners in curricular improvement and as the individuals who must change, if there is to be curriculum change.

[15]   I think there is an idea concealed here somewhere. I think it means: "If we are going to change the curriculum, teacher, parent, and student must all help." The reader is invited to get out his semantic decoder and check on my translation. Observe there is no technical language in this gem of pedageese, beyond possibly the word "curriculum." It is just a simple idea heavily ververbalized.

[16] In another kind of academic talk the author may display his learning to conceal a lack of ideas. A bright instructor, for instance, in need of prestige may select a common sense proposition for the subject of a learned monograph—say, "Modern cities are hard to live in" and adorn it with imposing polysyllables: "Urban existence in the perpendicular declivities of megalopolis . . ." et cetera. He coins some new terms to transfix the reader—"mega-decibel" or "strato-cosmopolis"—and works them vigorously. He is careful to add a page or two of differential equations to show the "scatter." And then he publishes, with 147 footnotes and a bibliography to knock your eye out. If the authorities are dozing, it can be worth an associate professorship.

[17] While we are on the campus, however, we must not forget that the technical language of the natural sciences and some terms in the social sciences, forbidding as they may sound to the layman, are quite necessary. Without them, specialists could not communicate what they find. Trouble arises when experts expect the uninitiated to understand the words; when they tell the jury, for instance, that the defendant is suffering from "circumorbital haematoma."

[18] Here are two authentic quotations. Which was written by a distinguished modern author, and which by a patient in a mental hospital? You will find the answer at the end of the chapter.

> (1) Have just been to supper. Did not knowing what the woodchuck sent me here. How when the blue blue blue on the said anyone can do it that tries. Such is the presidential candidate.
>
> (2) No history of a family to close with those and close. Never shall he be alone to be alone to be alone to be alone to be alone to lend a hand and leave it left and wasted.

Reducing the Gobble

[19] As government and business offices grow larger, the need for doing something about gobbledygook increases. Fortunately the biggest office in the world is working hard to reduce it. The Federal Security Agency in Washington, with nearly 100 million clients on its books, began analyzing its communication lines some years ago, with gratifying results. Surveys find trouble in three main areas: correspondence with clients about their social security problems, office memos, official reports.

[20] Clarity and brevity, as well as common humanity, are urgently needed in this vast establishment which deals with disability, old age, and unemployment. The surveys found instead many cases of long-windedness, foggy meanings, clichés, and singsong phrases, and gross neglect of the reader's point of view. Rather than talking to a real person, the writer was talking to himself. "We often write like a man walking on stilts."

[21] Here is a typical case of long-windedness:

> *Gobbledygook as found:* "We are wondering if sufficient time has passed so that you are in a position to indicate whether favorable action

may now be taken on our recommendation for the reclassification of Mrs. Blank, junior clerk-stenographer, CAF 2, to assistant clerk-stenographer, CAF 3?"

Suggested improvement: "Have you yet been able to act on our recommendation to reclassify Mrs. Blank?"

[22]   Another case:

Although the Central Efficiency Rating Committee recognizes that there are many desirable changes that could be made in the present efficiency rating system in order to make it more realistic and more workable than it now is, this committee is of the opinion that no further change should be made in the present system during the current year. Because of conditions prevailing throughout the country and the resultant turnover in personnel, and difficulty in administering the Federal programs, further mechanical improvement in the present rating system would require staff retraining and other administrative expense which would seem best withheld until the official termination of hostilities, and until restoration of regular operations.

[23]   The F.S.A. invites us to squeeze the gobbledygook out of this statement. Here is my attempt:

The Central Efficiency Rating Committee recognizes that desirable changes could be made in the present system. We believe, however, that no change should be attempted until the war is over.

[24]   This cuts the statement from 111 to 30 words, about one-quarter of the original, but perhaps the reader can do still better. What of importance have I left out?

[25]   Sometimes in a book which I am reading for information—not for literary pleasure—I run a pencil through the surplus words. Often I can cut a section to half its length with an improvement in clarity. Magazines like *The Reader's Digest* have reduced this process to an art. Are long-windedness and obscurity a cultural lag from the days when writing was reserved for priests and cloistered scholars? The more words and the deeper the mystery, the greater their prestige and the firmer the hold on their jobs. And the better the candidate's chance today to have his doctoral thesis accepted.

[26]   The F.S.A. surveys found that a great deal of writing was obscure although not necessarily prolix. Here is a letter sent to more than 100,000 inquirers, a classic example of murky prose. To clarify it, one needs to *add* words, not cut them:

In order to be fully insured, an individual must have earned $50 or more in covered employment for as many quarters of coverage as half the calendar quarters elapsing between 1936 and the quarter in which he reaches age 65 or dies, whichever first occurs.

Probably no one without the technical jargon of the office could translate this: nevertheless, it was sent out to drive clients mad for seven years. One poor fellow wrote back: "I am no longer in covered employment. I have an outside job now."

[27] Many words and phrases in officialese seem to come out automatically, as if from lower centers of the brain. In this standardized prose people never *get jobs*, they "secure employment"; *before* and *after* become "prior to" and "subsequent to"; one does not *do*, one "performs"; nobody *knows* a thing, he is "fully cognizant"; one never *says*, he "indicates." A great favorite at present is "implement."

[28] Some charming boners occur in this talking-in-one's-sleep. For instance:

> The problem of extending coverage to all employees, regardless of size is not as simple as surface appearances indicate.
> Though the proportions of all males and females in ages 16-45 are essentially the same . . .
> Dairy cattle, usually and commonly embraced in dairying . . .

[29] In its manual to employees, the F.S.A. suggests the following:

Instead of	Use
give consideration to	consider
make inquiry regarding	inquire
is of the opinion	believes
comes into conflict with	conflicts
information which is of a confidential nature	confidential information

[30] Professional or office goobledygook often arises from using the passive rather than the active voice. Instead of looking you in the eye, as it were, and writing "This act requires . . ." the office worker looks out of the window and writes: "It is required by this statute that . . ." When the bureau chief says, "We expect Congress to cut your budget," the message is only too clear; but usually he says, "It is expected that the departmental budget estimates will be reduced by Congress."

[31] *Gobbled:* "All letters prepared for the signature of the Administrator will be single spaced."

[32] *Ungobbled:* "Single space all letters for the Administrator." (Thus cutting 13 words to 7.)

Only People Can Read

[33] The F.S.A. surveys pick up the point . . . that human communication involves a listener as well as a speaker. Only people can read, though a lot of writing seems to be addressed to beings in outer space. To whom are you talking? The sender of the officialese message often forgets the chap on the other end of the line.

[34] A woman with two small children wrote the F.S.A. asking what she should do about payments, as her husband had lost his memory. "If he never gets able to work," she said, "and stays in an institution would I be able to draw any benefits? . . . I don't know how I am going to live and raise my children since he is disable to work. Please give me some information. . . ."

[35] To this human appeal, she received a shattering blast of gobbledy-

gook, beginning, "State unemployment compensation laws do not provide any benefits for sick or disabled individuals . . . in order to qualify an individual must have a certain number of quarters of coverage . . ." et cetera, et cetera. Certainly if the writer had been thinking about the poor woman he would not have dragged in unessential material about old-age insurance. If he had pictured a mother without means to care for her children, he would have told her where she might get help—from the local office which handles aid to dependent children, for instance.

[36]   Gobbledygook of this kind would largely evaporate if we thought of our messages as two way—in the above case, if we pictured ourselves talking on the doorstep of a shabby house to a woman with two children tugging at her skirts, who in her distress does not know which way to turn.

Results of the Survey

[37]   The F.S.A. survey showed that office documents could be cut 20 to 50 per cent, with an improvement in clarity and a great saving to taxpayers in paper and payrolls.

[38]   A handbook was prepared and distributed to key officials. They read it, thought about it, and presently began calling section meetings to discuss gobbledygook. More booklets were ordered, and the local output of documents began to improve. A Correspondence Review Section was established as a kind of laboratory to test murky messages. A supervisor could send up samples for analysis and suggestions. The handbook is now used for training new members; and many employees keep it on their desks along with the dictionary. Outside the Bureau some 25,000 copies have been sold (at 20 cents each) to individuals, governments, business firms, all over the world. It is now used officially in the Veterans Administration and in the Department of Agriculture.

[39]   The handbook makes clear the enormous amount of gobbledygook which automatically spreads in any large office, together with ways and means to keep it under control. I would guess that at least half of all the words circulating around the bureaus of the world are "irrelevant, incompetent, and immaterial"—to use a favorite legalism; or are just plain "unnecessary"—to ungobble it.

[40]   My favorite story of removing the gobble from gobbledygook concerns the Bureau of Standards at Washington. I have told it before but perhaps the reader will forgive the repetition. A New York plumber wrote the Bureau that he had found hydrochloric acid fine for cleaning drains, and was it harmless? Washington replied: "The efficacy of hydrochloric acid is indisputable, but the chlorine residue is incompatible with metallic permanence."

[41]   The plumber wrote back that he was mighty glad the Bureau agreed with him. The Bureau replied with a note of alarm: "We cannot assume responsibility for the production of toxic and noxious residues with hydrochloric acid, and suggest that you use an alternate procedure." The plumber was happy to learn that the Bureau still agreed with him.

[42] Whereupon Washington exploded: "Don't use hydrochloric acid; it eats hell out of the pipes!"

Note: The second quotation [in paragraph 18 of this text] comes from Gertrude Stein's *Lucy Church Amiably.*

Time Magazine

Baffle-Gab Thesaurus

As any self-respecting bureaucrat knows, it is bad form indeed to use a single, simple word when six or seven obfuscating ones will do.

But where is the Washington phrasemaker to turn if he is hung up for what Horace called "words a foot and a half long"? Simple. Just glance at the Systematic Buzz Phrase Projector, or S.B.P.P.

The S.B.P.P. has aptly obscure origins but appears to come from a Royal Canadian Air Force listing of fuzzy phrases. It was popularized in Washington by Philip Broughton, a U.S. Public Health Service official, who circulated it among civil servants and businessmen. A sort of mini-thesaurus of baffle-gab, it consists of a three-column list of 30 over-used but appropriately portentous words. Whenever a GS-14 or deputy assistant secretary needs an opaque phrase, he need only think of a three-digit number—any one will do as well as the next—and select the corresponding "buzz words" from the three columns. For example, 257 produces "systematized logistical projection," which has the ring of absolute authority and means absolutely nothing.

Broughton's baffle-gab guide:

	A	B	C
0)	Integrated	Management	Options
1)	Total	Organizational	Flexibility
2)	Systematized	Monitored	Capability
3)	Parallel	Reciprocal	Mobility
4)	Functional	Digital	Programming
5)	Responsive	Logistical	Concept
6)	Optional	Transitional	Time-Phase
7)	Synchronized	Incremental	Projection
8)	Compatible	Third-Generation	Hardware
9)	Balanced	Policy	Contingency

words and sentences

1. Vocabulary: *polysyllabic* (¶ 3); *literati* (9); *tautologies* (11); *pedagogues* (13); *cloistered* (25); *prolix* (26). In "Baffle-Gab Thesaurus" ¶ 1: *obfuscating*.
2. Chase writes of the "verbal squirrel cage" in ¶ 2. What does this comparison suggest?
3. Rewrite the paragraph Chase cites in ¶ 22. Can you improve upon Chase's revision in ¶ 23?
4. Describe the structure of the sentence in ¶ 36; then write a sentence imitating that pattern. What does the "who" clause modify? Can you suggest an improvement on Chase's sentence?
5. Check the word "gobbledygook" in your dictionary. What is the derivation of this word?

ideas and implications

1. How is gobbledygook different from double talk?
2. Where does Chase find most of his examples of gobbledygook? Do these examples comment on the professions from which they are taken? If so, in what ways?
3. What is Chase's attitude towards long words? Why?
4. Examine the language of the widow's letter (¶ 34) and that of the F.S.A.'s response (¶ 35). Are there implications beyond those suggested by Chase?
5. What is the relationship between the size of an organization and the use of gobbledygook? Can you think of any reasons beyond those Chase offers for this relationship?
6. What does Chase say about passive voice verbs? Why?
7. What is Chase's attitude towards the F.S.A.'s attempt to ungobble the gobbledygook?

strategies

1. How many times does Chase define *gobbledygook* in his essay? In what paragraphs does he offer formal definitions for the term?
2. Describe Chase's opening strategy. Can you think of another example which might have worked?
3. What is the function of ¶s 2-8? What is the tone of these paragraphs?
4. In ¶s 33-36, does Chase develop his idea by beginning with a specific statement and then generalizing? Or does he order this part of his essay by generalizing and then presenting specific evidence? Which order seems more effective for this portion of the essay?
5. Chase concludes his essay with an anecdote. Does the pattern of the anecdote resemble the pattern of his essay?

suggestions for writing

1. If you own an insurance policy, trot it out to look at its language. Try to rewrite some paragraphs of the policy in everyday language. Include the paragraphs of the policy with your rewritten version.

2. Nearly everyone has had trouble with directions written on bottles, cans, or instructions for assembling toys. Write a paper about such an experience of your own.

3. Using the "Baffle-Gab Thesaurus," write a paragraph or so of gobbledygook.

4. Compile your own "Baffle-Gab Thesaurus" and write a brief introduction to it.

C. Hugh Holman

Metaphor and Mixed Figures

[1] *Metaphor:* An implied ANALOGY which imaginatively identifies one object with another and ascribes to the first one or more of the qualities of the second or invests the first with emotional or imaginative qualities associated with the second. It is one of the TROPES; that is, one of the principal devices by which poetic "turns" on the meaning of words are achieved. I. A. Richards' distinction between the TENOR and the VEHICLE of a *metaphor* has been widely accepted and is very useful. The TENOR is the idea being expressed or the subject of the comparison; the VEHICLE is the IMAGE by which this idea is conveyed or the subject communicated. When Shakespeare writes

> That time of year thou mayst in me behold
> When yellow leaves, or none, or few, do hang
> Upon those boughs which shake against the cold,
> Bare ruined choirs where late the sweet birds sang.

the TENOR is old age, the VEHICLE is the season of late fall or early winter, conveyed through a group of IMAGES unusually complex in their implications. The TENOR and VEHICLE taken together constitute the FIGURE OF SPEECH, the TROPE, the "turn" in meaning which the *metaphor* conveys. The purposes for using *metaphors* can vary widely. At one extreme, the VEHICLE may merely be a means of decorating the TENOR; at the other extreme, the TENOR may merely be an excuse for having the VEHICLE. ALLEGORY, for example, may be thought of as an elaborate and consistently constructed extended *metaphor* in which the TENOR is never expressed, al-

From C. Hugh Holman, *A Handbook to Literature,* based on the original book by William Flint Thrall and Addison Hibbard, © 1936, 1960 by The Odyssey Press, Inc., © 1972 by The Bobbs-Merrill Company, Inc. Reprinted by permission.

though it is implied. In the simplest kinds of *metaphors* there is an obvious direct resemblance that exists objectively between the TENOR and the VEHICLE, and in some *metaphors,* particularly those which lend themselves to elaborate CONCEITS, the relationship between TENOR and VEHICLE is in the mind of the maker of the *metaphor,* rather than in specific qualities of VEHICLE or TENOR. The first kind tends to be sensuous and the second witty.

[2] Aristotle praised the *metaphor* as "the greatest thing by far" for the poet, and saw it as the product of his insight which permitted him to find the similarities in seemingly dissimilar things. Modern criticism follows Aristotle in placing a similarly high premium on the poet's abilities in the making of *metaphors,* and ANALYTICAL CRITICISM tends to find almost as much rich suggestiveness in the differences between the things compared as it does in the recognition of surprising but unsuspected similarities. Cleanth Brooks uses the term "functional *metaphor*" to describe the way in which the *metaphor* is able to have "referential" and "emotive" characteristics and to go beyond them and become a direct means in itself of representing a truth incommunicable by any other means. Clearly when a *metaphor* performs this function, it is behaving as a SYMBOL.

[3] *Metaphors* may be simple, that is, may occur in the single isolated comparison, or a large *metaphor* may function as the CONTROLLING IMAGE of a whole work, or a series of VEHICLES may all be associated with a single TENOR, as in Hamlet's "To be or not to be" soliloquy. In this last kind of case, however, unless the IMAGES can harmoniously build the TENOR without impressing the reader with a sense of their incongruity, the danger of a MIXED FIGURE is grave.

[4] The whole nature of our language is highly metaphorical. Most of our modern speech, which now seems prosaic enough, was once largely metaphorical. Our ABSTRACT TERMS are borrowed from physical objects. Natural objects and actions have passed over into abstractions because of some inherent metaphorical significance. Thus "transgression"—which today signifies a misdemeanor, an error, or mistake—formerly meant "to cross a line." The metaphorical significance has been lost—is said to be "dead"—and the former figure of speech now stands simply for an abstraction. (It is thus, in fact, that ABSTRACT TERMS possibly first came into language; early man was necessarily content simply to name the objects about him which he could see and feel and smell.)

[5] *Mixed Figures:* The mingling of one FIGURE OF SPEECH with another immediately following with which the first is incongruous. A notable example is the sentence of Castlereagh: "And now, sir, I must embark into the feature on which this question chiefly hinges." Here, obviously, the sentence begins with a nautical figure ("embark") but closes with a mechanical figure ("hinges"). The effect is grotesque. Lloyd George is reported to have said, "I smell a rat. I see it floating in the air. I shall nip it in the bud." Mixed IMAGERY, however, is sometimes deliberately used by writers with great effectiveness, when the differing figures contribute cumulatively to a single referent which is increasingly illuminated

as they pile up. It is important, however, that the cumulative effect of the various IMAGES not be one of incongruity.

words and sentences

1. Vocabulary: *tropes, images, conceits, sensuous* (¶ 1); *referential* (2); *incongruity* (3).
2. How does Holman use the word *turns* in ¶ 1? What special meaning does he attach to it?
3. Describe the pattern of the fourth sentence ("The tenor is the idea") in ¶ 1; then write a sentence imitating that pattern. How useful is this sentence pattern for defining?

ideas and implications

1. Holman refers to "a series of vehicles . . . associated with a single tenor" in Hamlet's "To be, or not to be" speech. Look back to Section 3 and examine that speech for its metaphoric language. How do the metaphors function in this speech? Do the terms *tenor* and *vehicle* help you understand the nature of metaphor?
2. Does Holman suggest that the mixing of metaphors shows a fuzziness of thought? Why or why not?

strategies

1. Holman's aim is to define his two terms. Examine his paragraphs to see *how* he goes about defining. Make a list of the ways he describes his terms. How many items do you have on your list? Are these methods similar to those of a dictionary? How are they different?

suggestions for writing

1. Poets are not the only writers who use metaphors; prose writers also clarify through metaphor. Write a half dozen sentences using metaphor to illuminate or clarify. Then take the most promising sentence and use it as the topic sentence of a paragraph which extends that metaphor.
2. Listen to your classmates as they talk in lunch-rooms or dormitories. How much figurative language do they use? Write a paper about some of the interesting metaphors you hear.
3. Select a poem that you know and write a paper about the way figurative language functions in the poem.

5 The Writer's Words: Social and Human Implications

PEANUTS

Though her husband often went on business trips, she hated to be left alone.

8-6

"I've solved our problem," he said. "I've bought you a St. Bernard. It's name is Great Reluctance."

"Now, when I go away, you shall know that I am leaving you with Great Reluctance!"

She hit him with a waffle iron.

SCHULZ

INTRODUCTION

Sticks and stones
May break my bones,
But words can never harm me!

So goes the chant that defends many a child from playmates' hurtful words. But Author Snoopy knows that words can bring down waffle irons—and worse. Every playground has its Fatty and its Peewee, but unless we have been Fatty or Peewee, we are not likely to know how these names ring upon receiving ears. Words sometimes leave longer scars than waffle irons.

"All that's spoke is marr'd," says Gratiano at the end of Shakespeare's *Othello*. And Iago, whose words have led Othello to murder Desdemona and to kill himself, declares in his final speech, "From this time forth I never will speak word."

The distance between the child's playground and the territory of adults is not so great because words follow us where we will go. As women and men, every day we say words affecting the lives of others, often without being aware of how they fall upon receiving ears. The readings in this section talk about the implications of the words falling from our mouths and pens.

In "The Principles of Newspeak," George Orwell invents a language suitable to the political and human aspirations he foresees in the world of 1984. Filled with *doublethink* to obfuscate meaning, this language makes impossible precision of feelings and ideas. Its purpose is to make men slaves rather than to make them free. Orwell predicts that Newspeak will be the language of English-speaking peoples by 2050. Stefan Kanfer suggests that 2050 may have arrived in "Words from Watergate."

The next four essays deal with censorship, a problem in every society and one that has received new emphasis in the United States by the Supreme Court's recent decision to return jurisdiction on such matters to states and communities. John Milton's classic statement in *Areopagitica* argues that to be free, men must be able to choose what they shall read and write. Opposing both *license* and *licensing* (censorship), Milton says, "I cannot praise a fugitive and cloistered virtue, unexercised and unbreathed, that never sallies out and sees her adversary, but slinks out of the race, where that immortal garland is to be run for not without dust and heat."

George Jean Nathan believes that all men favor some forms of censorship; the problem, he argues, is not censorship, but censors who "disgrace the theory of censorship in its soundest sense." Nathan charges the promiscuous users of the word *vulgar* with betraying their ignorance "that some of the grantedly greatest of art the world has known has been as vulgar as pigs' feet." He cites Shakespeare to prove his point.

Sydney Harris attacks four-letter words, not because they are obscene, but because people use these words instead of inventing original oaths. He wants "more and better swear words."

Malcolm Bradbury comments on the ways our words reveal our moral stance. In "The New Language of Morals," he distinguishes between an Old Style of discourse *describing* "the obligation to choose between right and wrong" and a New Style referring "to *difficulty* of choosing between right and wrong." He defines words like *Youth, Culture,* and *Tradition* in both Styles to point to differences.

"The English Language is My Enemy!" shouts author and playwright Ossie Davis. To prove his point, Davis looks at words associated with *blackness* and *whiteness,* and decides that the language is his enemy because "I cannot conceive of my self as a black man without, at the same time, debasing myself."

Roger D. Abrahams examines some stereotype assumptions about urban Black children and their sense of language. Contrary to the clichés of many white and Black teachers, these children have "a well-developed sense of language and its power to pass on information and to control interpersonal relationships." Middle-class teachers, Black and white, frequently misunderstand these children's cultural heritage and thus fail to recognize their facility with language. Abrahams believes teachers need to be educated out of their prejudices before they can teach these children intelligently.

Claude Brown describes "The Language of Soul" as "simply an honest vocal portrayal of black America." Admiring the vigor and creativity of Spoken Soul, Brown traces its history and shows its cyclical progress. He argues that "the picture looks dark for soul" because conservative and militant Blacks are "trying diligently to relinquish and repudiate whatever vestige they may still possess of soul."

Starting with the stereotype of the "granite-faced grunting redskin," Vine Deloria, Jr., has good sport showing how "Indian Humor" operates. He cites Columbus and Custer jokes and the Indian custom of teasing to make his point. Deloria claims Custer dressed well for the battle of the Little Big Horn; when the Sioux found his body, he was wearing an Arrow shirt.

In "Virgin Power," Art Buchwald tweaks groups formed to protect their sexual freedom by interviewing a fictional character named Sidney Pimpledown, president of the Virgin Anti-Defamation League. While Buchwald is having fun with the language of such movements, he also seems to sympathize with the social injustices suffered by such groups.

The next three readings discuss the ways that language affects the lives of women. Connie C. Eble describes seven ways the language expresses masculine dominance in our culture. Subtly and often unconsciously, our language "undermines a girl's self-respect and bolsters a boy's ego." Eble suggests some reforms to mitigate this discrimination.

Germaine Greer recounts how terms of abuse for women came into being. Citing words that once described both men and women, Greer sees the double standard of conduct as responsible for the increased number of abuse words applied to women, usually by neurotic men. Terms of abuse help women to shape unhealthy images of themselves, says Greer. "As long as women consider themselves sexual objects they will continue to writhe under the voiced contempt of men, and worse, to think of themselves with shame and scorn," she concludes.

In "What Not to Say," Art Buchwald lists thirty remarks that men might make in conversation to enrage women. "I met this woman doctor the other day, at the hospital, and she really seemed to know what she was doing" is one of those remarks.

Finally, Sydney Harris writes, "It is a curious commentary on human nature—and on human speech, which reflects our nature—that we have so few words to designate good things, and so many to designate bad." He is repeating the words that Shakespeare put in Gratiano's mouth more than three hundred years ago: "All that's spoke is marr'd."

Yet men and women continue to speak and write, continue to make worlds of words so that they can share with each other what it is to be human and to be alive. William Faulkner probably characterized this urge as well as any writer; in his Nobel Prize Speech in 1950, he said:

> I decline to accept the end of man. It is easy enough to say that man is immortal simply because he will endure; that when the last ding-dong of doom has clanged and faded from the last worthless rock hanging tideless in the last red and dying evening, that even then there will still be one more sound: that of his puny inexhaustible voice, still talking. I refuse to accept this. I believe that man will not merely endure: he will prevail. He is immortal, not because he alone among creatures has an inexhaustible voice but because he has a soul, a spirit capable of compassion and sacrifice and endurance.[1]

[1] Reprinted from *The Faulkner Reader,* copyright 1954 by William Faulkner (Random House, Inc.).

George Orwell

The Principles of Newspeak

[1] Newspeak was the official language of Oceania and had been devised to meet the ideological needs of Ingsoc, or English Socialism. In the year 1984 there was not as yet anyone who used Newspeak as his sole means of communication, either in speech or writing. The leading articles in the *Times* were written in it, but this was a tour de force which could only be carried out by a specialist. It was expected that Newspeak would have finally superseded Oldspeak (or Standard English, as we should call it) by about the year 2050. Meanwhile it gained ground steadily, all Party members tending to use Newspeak words and grammatical constructions more and more in their everyday speech. The version in use in 1984, and embodied in the Ninth and Tenth Editions of the Newspeak dictionary, was a provisional one, and contained many superfluous words and archaic formations which were due to be suppressed later. It is with the final, perfected version, as embodied in the Eleventh Edition of the dictionary, that we are concerned here.

[2] The purpose of Newspeak was not only to provide a medium of expression for the world-view and mental habits proper to the devotees of Ingsoc, but to make all other modes of thought impossible. It was intended that when Newspeak had been adopted once and for all and Oldspeak forgotten, a heretical thought—that is, a thought diverging from the principles of Ingsoc—should be literally unthinkable, at least so far as thought is dependent on words. Its vocabulary was so constructed as to give exact and often very subtle expression to every meaning that a Party member could properly wish to express, while excluding all other meanings and also the possibility of arriving at them by indirect methods. This was done partly by the invention of new words, but chiefly by eliminating undesirable words and by stripping such words as remained of unorthodox meanings, and so far as possible of all secondary meanings whatever. To give a single example. The word *free* still existed in Newspeak, but it could only be used in such statements as "This dog is free from lice" or "This field is free from weeds." It could not be used in its old sense of "politically free" or "intellectually free," since political and intellectual freedom no longer existed even as concepts, and were therefore of necessity nameless. Quite apart from the suppression of definitely heretical words, reduction of vocabulary was regarded as an end in itself, and no word that could be dispensed with was allowed to survive. Newspeak was designed not to extend but to *diminish* the range of thought, and this purpose was indirectly assisted by cutting the choice of words down to a minimum.

[3] Newspeak was founded on the English language as we now know it, though many Newspeak sentences, even when not containing newly created

words, would be barely intelligible to an English-speaker of our own day. Newspeak words were divided into three distinct classes, known as the A vocabulary, the B vocabulary (also called compound words), and the C vocabulary. It will be simpler to discuss each class separately, but the grammatical peculiarities of the language can be dealt with in the section devoted to the A vocabulary, since the same rules held good for all three categories.

[4]   *The A vocabulary.* The A vocabulary consisted of the words needed for the business of everyday life—for such things as eating, drinking, working, putting on one's clothes, going up and down stairs, riding in vehicles, gardening, cooking, and the like. It was composed almost entirely of words that we already possess—words like *hit, run, dog, tree, sugar, house, field*—but in comparison with the present-day English vocabulary, their number was extremely small, while their meanings were far more rigidly defined. All ambiguities and shades of meaning had been purged out of them. So far as it could be achieved, a Newspeak word of this class was simply a staccato sound expressing *one* clearly understood concept. It would have been quite impossible to use the A vocabulary for literary purposes or for political or philosophical discussion. It was intended only to express simple, purposive thoughts, usually involving concrete objects or physical actions.

[5]   The grammar of Newspeak had two outstanding peculiarities. The first of these was an almost complete interchangeability between different parts of speech. Any word in the language (in principle this applied even to very abstract words such as *if* or *when*) could be used either as verb, noun, adjective, or adverb. Between the verb and the noun form, when they were of the same root, there was never any variation, this rule of itself involving the destruction of many archaic forms. The word *thought,* for example, did not exist in Newspeak. Its place was taken by *think,* which did duty for both noun and verb. No etymological principle was followed here; in some cases it was the original noun that was chosen for retention, in other cases the verb. Even where a noun and verb of kindred meaning were not etymologically connected, one or other of them was frequently suppressed. There was, for example, no such word as *cut,* its meaning being sufficiently covered by the noun-verb *knife.* Adjectives were formed by adding the suffix *-ful* to the noun-verb, and adverbs by adding *-wise.* Thus, for example, *speedful* meant "rapid" and *speedwise* meant "quickly." Certain of our present-day adjectives, such as *good, strong, big, black, soft,* were retained, but their total number was very small. There was little need for them, since almost any adjectival meaning could be arrived at by adding *-ful* to a noun-verb. None of the now-existing adverbs was retained, except for a very few already ending in *-wise;* the *-wise* termination was invariable. The word *well,* for example, was replaced by *goodwise.*

[6]   In addition, any word—this again applied in principle to every word in the language—could be negatived by adding the affix *un-,* or could be strengthened by the affix *plus-,* or, for still greater emphasis, *doubleplus-.*

Thus, for example, *uncold* meant "warm," while *pluscold* and *doubleplus-cold* meant, respectively, "very cold" and "superlatively cold." It was also possible, as in present-day English, to modify the meaning of almost any word by prepositional affixes such as *ante-, post-, up-, down-,* etc. By such methods it was found possible to bring about an enormous diminution of vocabulary. Given, for instance, the word *good,* there was no need for such a word as *bad,* since the required meaning was equally well—indeed, better—expressed by *ungood.* All that was necessary, in any case where two words formed a natural pair of opposites, was to decide which of them to suppress. *Dark,* for example, could be replaced by *unlight,* or *light* by *undark,* according to preference.

[7]   The second distinguishing mark of Newspeak grammar was its regularity. Subject to a few exceptions which are mentioned below, all inflections followed the same rules. Thus, in all verbs the preterite and the past participle were the same and ended in *-ed.* The preterite of *steal* was *stealed,* the preterite of *think* was *thinked,* and so on throughout the langauge, all such forms as *swam, gave, brought, spoke, taken,* etc., being abolished. All plurals were made by adding *-s* or *-es* as the case might be. The plurals of *man, ox, life* were *mans, oxes, lifes.* Comparison of adjectives was invariably made by adding *-er, -est* (*good, gooder, goodest*), irregular forms and the *more, most* formation being suppressed.

[8]   The only classes of words that were still allowed to inflect irregularly were the pronouns, the relatives, the demonstrative adjectives, and the auxiliary verbs. All of these followed their ancient usage, except that *whom* had been scrapped as unnecessary, and the *shall, should* tenses had been dropped, all their uses being covered by *will* and *would.* There were also certain irregularities in word-formation arising out of the need for rapid and easy speech. A word which was difficult to utter, or was liable to be incorrectly heard, was held to be ipso facto a bad word; occasionally therefore, for the sake of euphony, extra letters were inserted into a word or an archaic formation was retained. But this need made itself felt chiefly in connection with the B vocabulary. *Why* so great an importance was attached to ease of pronunciation will be made clear later in this essay.

[9]   *The B vocabulary.* The B vocabulary consisted of words which had been deliberately constructed for political purposes: words, that is to say, which not only had in every case a political implication, but were intended to impose a desirable mental attitude upon the person using them. Without a full understanding of the principles of Ingsoc it was difficult to use these words correctly. In some cases they could be translated into Oldspeak, or even into words taken from the A vocabulary, but this usually demanded a long paraphrase and always involved the loss of certain overtones. The B words were a sort of verbal shorthand, often packing whole ranges of ideas into a few syllables, and at the same time more accurate and forcible than ordinary language.

[10]   The B words were in all cases compound words.* They consisted of

---

* Compound words, such as *speakwrite,* were of course to be found in the A vocabulary, but these were merely convenient abbreviations and had no special ideological color.

two or more words, or portions of words, welded together in an easily pronounceable form. The resulting amalgam was always a noun-verb, and inflected according to the ordinary rules. To take a single example: the word *goodthink,* meaning, very roughly, "orthodoxy," or, if one chose to regard it as a verb, "to think in an orthodox manner." This inflected as follows: noun-verb, *goodthink;* past tense and past participle, *goodthinked;* present participle, *goodthinking;* adjective, *good-thinkful;* adverb, *goodthinkwise;* verbal noun, *goodthinker.*

[11]   The B words were not constructed on any etymological plan. The words of which they were made up could be any parts of speech, and could be placed in any order and mutilated in any way which made them easy to pronounce while indicating their derivation. In the word *crimethink* (thoughtcrime), for instance, the *think* came second, whereas in *thinkpol* (Thought Police) it came first, and in the latter word *police* had lost its second syllable. Because of the greater difficulty in securing euphony, irregular formations were commoner in the B vocabulary than in the A vocabulary. For example, the adjectival forms of *Minitrue, Minipax,* and *Miniluv* were, respectively, *Minitruthful, Minipeaceful,* and *Minilovely,* simply because *-trueful, -paxful,* and *-loveful* were slightly awkward to pronounce. In principle, however, all B words could inflect, and all inflected in exactly the same way.

[12]   Some of the B words had highly subtilized meanings, barely intelligible to anyone who had not mastered the language as a whole. Consider, for example, such a typical sentence from a *Times* leading article as *Oldthinkers unbellyfeel Ingsoc.* The shortest rendering that one could make of this in Oldspeak would be: "Those whose ideas were formed before the Revolution cannot have a full emotional understanding of the principles of English Socialism." But this is not an adequate translation. To begin with, in order to grasp the full meaning of the Newspeak sentence quoted above, one would have to have a clear idea of what is meant by *Ingsoc.* And, in addition, only a person thoroughly grounded in Ingsoc could appreciate the full force of the word *bellyfeel,* which implied a blind, enthusiastic acceptance difficult to imagine today; or of the word *oldthink,* which was inextricably mixed up with the idea of wickedness and decadence. But the special function of certain Newspeak words, of which *oldthink* was one, was not so much to express meanings as to destroy them. These words, necessarily few in number, had had their meanings extended until they contained within themselves whole batteries of words which, as they were sufficiently covered by a single comprehensive term, could now be scrapped and forgotten. The greatest difficulty facing the compilers of the Newspeak dictionary was not to invent new words, but, having invented them, to make sure what they meant: to make sure, that is to say, what ranges of words they canceled by their existence.

[13]   As we have already seen in the case of the word *free,* words which had once borne a heretical meaning were sometimes retained for the sake of convenience, but only with the undesirable meanings purged out of them. Countless other words such as *honor, justice, morality, internationalism, democracy, science,* and *religion* had simply ceased to exist. A few

blanket words covered them, and, in covering them, abolished them. All words grouping themselves round the concepts of liberty and equality, for instance, were contained in the single word *crimethink,* while all words grouping themselves round the concepts of objectivity and rationalism were contained in the single word *oldthink.* Greater precision would have been dangerous. What was required in a Party member was an outlook similar to that of the ancient Hebrew who knew, without knowing much else, that all nations other than his own worshiped "false gods." He did not need to know that these gods were called Baal, Osiris, Moloch, Ashtaroth, and the like; probably the less he knew about them the better for his orthodoxy. He knew Jehovah and the commandments of Jehovah; he knew, therefore, that all gods with other names or other attributes were false gods. In somewhat the same way, the Party member knew what constituted right conduct, and in exceedingly vague, generalized terms he knew what kinds of departure from it were possible. His sexual life, for example, was entirely regulated by the two Newspeak words *sexcrime* (sexual immorality) and *goodsex* (chastity). *Sexcrime* covered all sexual misdeeds whatever. It covered fornication, adultery, homosexuality, and other perversions, and, in addition, normal intercourse practiced for its own sake. There was no need to enumerate them separately, since they were all equally culpable, and, in principle, all punishable by death. In the C vocabulary, which consisted of scientific and technical words, it might be necessary to give specialized names to certain sexual aberrations, but the ordinary citizen had no need of them. He knew what was meant by *goodsex*—that is to say, normal intercourse between man and wife, for the sole purpose of begetting children, and without physical pleasure on the part of the woman; all else was *sexcrime.* In Newspeak it was seldom possible to follow a heretical thought further than the perception that it *was* heretical; beyond that point the necessary words were nonexistent.

[14]   No word in the B vocabulary was ideologically neutral. A great many were euphemisms. Such words, for instance, as *joycamp* (forced-labor camp) or *Minipax* (Ministry of Peace, i.e., Ministry of War) meant almost the exact oposite of what they appeared to mean. Some words, on the other hand, displayed a frank and contemptuous understanding of the real nature of Oceanic society. An example was *prolefeed,* meaning the rubbishy entertainment and spurious news which the Party handed out to the masses. Other words, again, were ambivalent, having the connotation "good" when applied to the Party and "bad" when applied to its enemies. But in addition there were great numbers of words which at first sight appeared to be mere abbreviations and which derived their ideological color not from their meaning but from their structure.

[15]   So far as it could be contrived, everything that had or might have political significance of any kind was fitted into the B vocabulary. The name of every organization, or body of people, or doctrine, or country, or institution, or public building, was invariably cut down into the familiar shape; that is, a single easily pronounced word with the smallest number of syllables that would preserve the original derivation. In the Ministry

of Truth, for example, the Records Department, in which Winston Smith worked, was called *Recdep*, the Fiction Department was called *Ficdep*, the Teleprograms Department was called *Teledep*, and so on. This was not done solely with the object of saving time. Even in the early decades of the twentieth century, telescoped words and phrases had been one of the characteristic features of political language; and it had been noticed that the tendency to use abbreviations of this kind was most marked in totalitarian countries and totalitarian organizations. Examples were such words as *Nazi, Gestapo, Comintern, Inprecorr, Agitprop.* In the beginning the practice had been adopted as it were instinctively, but in Newspeak it was used with a conscious purpose. It was perceived that in thus abbreviating a name one narrowed and subtly altered its meaning, by cutting out most of the associations that would otherwise cling to it. The words *Communist International,* for instance, call up a composite picture of universal human brotherhood, red flags, barricades, Karl Marx, and the Paris Commune. The word Comintern, on the other hand, suggests merely a tightly knit organization and a well-defined body of doctrine. It refers to something almost as easily recognized, and as limited in purpose, as a chair or a table. *Comintern* is a word that can be uttered almost without taking thought, whereas *Communist International* is a phrase over which one is obliged to linger at least momentarily. In the same way, the associations called up by a word like *Minitrue* are fewer and more controllable than those called up by *Ministry of Truth.* This accounted not only for the habit of abbreviating whenever possible, but also for the almost exaggerated care that was taken to make every word easily pronounceable.

[16] In Newspeak, euphony outweighed every consideration other than exactitude of meaning. Regularity of grammar was always sacrificed to it when it seemed necessary. And rightly so, since what was required, above all for political purposes, were short clipped words of unmistakable meaning which could be uttered rapidly and which roused the minimum of echoes in the speaker's mind. The words of the B vocabulary even gained in force from the fact that nearly all of them were very much alike. Almost invariably these words—*goodthink, Minipax, prolefeed, sexcrime, joycamp, Ingsoc, bellyfeel, thinkpol,* and countless others—were words of two or three syllables, with the stress distributed equally between the first syllable and the last. The use of them encouraged a gabbling style of speech, at once staccato and monotonous. And this was exactly what was aimed at. The intention was to make speech, and especially speech on any subject not ideologically neutral, as nearly as possible independent of consciousness. For the purposes of everyday life it was no doubt necessary, or sometimes necessary, to reflect before speaking, but a Party member called upon to make a political or ethical judgment should be able to spray forth the correct opinions as automatically as a machine gun spraying forth bullets. His training fitted him to do this, the language gave him an almost foolproof instrument, and the texture of the words, with their harsh sound and a certain willful ugliness which was in accord with the spirit of Ingsoc, assisted the process still further.

[17]   So did the fact of having very few words to choose from. Relative to our own, the Newspeak vocabulary was tiny, and new ways of reducing it were constantly being devised. Newspeak, indeed, differed from almost all other languages in that its vocabulary grew smaller instead of larger every year. Each reduction was a gain, since the smaller the area of choice, the smaller the temptation to take thought. Ultimately it was hoped to make articulate speech issue from the larynx without involving the higher brain centers at all. This aim was frankly admitted in the Newspeak word *duckspeak,* meaning to "quack like a duck." Like various other words in the B vocabulary, *duckspeak* was ambivalent in meaning. Provided that the opinions which were quacked out were orthodox ones, it implied nothing but praise, and when the *Times* referred to one of the orators of the Party as *doubleplusgood duckspeaker* it was paying a warm and valued compliment.

[18]   *The C Vocabulary.*   The C vocabulary was supplementary to the others and consisted entirely of scientific and technical terms. These resembled the scientific terms in use today, and were constructed from the same roots, but the usual care was taken to define them rigidly and strip them of undesirable meanings. They followed the same grammatical rules as the words in the other two vocabularies. Very few of the C words had any currency either in everyday speech or in political speech. Any scientific worker or technician could find all the words he needed in the list devoted to his own specialty, but he seldom had more than a smattering of the words occurring in the other lists. Only a very few words were common to all lists, and there was no vocabulary expressing the function of Science as a habit of mind, or a method of thought, irrespective of its particular branches. There was, indeed, no word for "Science," any meaning that it could possibly bear being already sufficiently covered by the word *Ingsoc.*

[19]   From the foregoing account it will be seen that in Newspeak the expression of unorthodox opinions, above a very low level, was well-nigh impossible. It was of course possible to utter heresies of a very crude kind, a species of blasphemy. It would have been possible, for example, to say *Big Brother is ungood.* But this statement, which to an orthodox ear merely conveyed a self-evident absurdity, could not have been sustained by reasoned argument, because the necessary words were not available. Ideas inimical to Ingsoc could only be entertained in a vague wordless form, and could only be named in very broad terms which lumped together and condemned whole groups of heresies without defining them in doing so. One could, in fact, only use Newspeak for unorthodox purposes by illegitimately translating some of the words back into Oldspeak. For example, *All mans are equal* was a possible Newspeak sentence, but only in the same sense in which *All men are redhaired* is a possible Oldspeak sentence. It did not contain a grammatical error, but it expressed a palpable untruth, i.e., that all men are of equal size, weight, or strength. The concept of political equality no longer existed,

and this secondary meaning had accordingly been purged out of the word *equal*. In 1984, when Oldspeak was still the normal means of communication, the danger theoretically existed that in using Newspeak words one might remember their original meanings. In practice it was not difficult for any person well grounded in *doublethink* to avoid doing this, but within a couple of generations even the possibility of such a lapse would have vanished. A person growing up with Newspeak as his sole language would no more know that *equal* had once had the secondary meaning of "politically equal," or that *free* had once meant "intellectually free," than, for instance, a person who had never heard of chess would be aware of the secondary meanings attached to *queen* and *rook*. There would be many crimes and errors which it would be beyond his power to commit, simply because they were nameless and therefore unimaginable. And it was to be foreseen that with the passage of time the distinguishing characteristics of Newspeak would become more and more pronounced— its words growing fewer and fewer, their meanings more and more rigid, and the chance of putting them to improper uses always diminishing.

[20] When Oldspeak had been once and for all superseded, the last link with the past would have been severed. History had already been rewritten, but fragments of the literature of the past survived here and there, imperfectly censored, and so long as one retained one's knowledge of Oldspeak it was possible to read them. In the future such fragments, even if they chanced to survive, would be unintelligible and untranslatable. It was impossible to translate any passage of Oldspeak into Newspeak unless it either referred to some technical process or some very simple everyday action, or was already orthodox (*goodthinkful* would be the Newspeak expression) in tendency. In practice this meant that no book written before approximately 1960 could be translated as a whole. Prerevolutionary literature could only be subjected to ideological translation—that is, alteration in sense as well as language. Take for example the well-known passage from the Declaration of Independence:

> *We hold these truths to be self-evident, that all men are created equal, that they are endowed by their Creator with certain inalienable rights, that among these are life, liberty and the pursuit of happiness. That to secure these rights, Governments are instituted among men, deriving their powers from the consent of the governed. That whenever any form of Government becomes destructive of those ends, it is the right of the People to alter or abolish it, and to institute new Government . . .*

[21] It would have been quite impossible to render this into Newspeak while keeping to the sense of the original. The nearest one could come to doing so would be to swallow the whole passage up in the single word *crimethink*. A full translation could only be an ideological translation, whereby Jefferson's words would be changed into a panegyric on absolute government.

[22] A good deal of the literature of the past was, indeed, already being transformed in this way. Considerations of prestige made it desirable to preserve the memory of certain historical figures, while at the same time

bringing their achievements into line with the philosophy of Ingsoc. Various writers, such as Shakespeare, Milton, Swift, Byron, Dickens, and some others were therefore in process of translation; when the task had been completed, their original writings, with all else that survived of the literature of the past, would be destroyed. These translations were a slow and difficult business, and it was not expected that they would be finished before the first or second decade of the twenty-first century. There were also large quantities of merely utilitarian literature—indispensable technical manuals and the like—that had to be treated in the same way. It was chiefly in order to allow time for the preliminary work of translation that the final adoption of Newspeak had been fixed for so late a date as 2050.

words and sentences

1. Vocabulary: *archaic, ambiguities* (¶ 1); *heretical, unorthodox* (2); *etymological* (5); *preterite* (7); *euphony* (8); *amalgam (10); decadence* (12); *euphemisms, spurious, ambivalent* (14); *blasphemy, inimical, palpable* (19); *panegyric* (21); *utilitarian* (22).
2. What does Orwell mean by "Standard English" (¶ 1)? What does this term mean to you?
3. Describe the pattern of the first sentence in ¶ 2; then write a sentence imitating that pattern.
4. Describe the pattern of the first sentence in ¶ 4; then write a sentence imitating that pattern. Do the sentences in ¶s 2 and 4 have qualities in common in their syntax and punctuation?
5. In ¶ 13, Orwell lists words that "had simply ceased to exist." From his examples, make a list of other words that might have disappeared from Ingsoc. Tell why the words on your list might have ceased to exist.
6. Write a sentence or two in Newspeak; then translate those sentences into Oldspeak.
7. Describe the pattern of the last sentence in ¶ 19; then write a sentence imitating that pattern. Does this sentence share any qualities with those cited above in questions 3 and 4?

ideas and implications

1. "The Principles of Newspeak" is an essay appended to Orwell's novel *1984*, published in 1949. Why might Orwell refer to 1984, 1960, and 2050 as important dates in the transformation from Oldspeak to Newspeak?
2. Why was it necessary to invent Newspeak? What were the problems for the dictionary makers of Newspeak? Would dictionaries be more or less important for the citizens of 1984 than for the present-day speakers of English?
3. What is the relationship between thought and language in Newspeak? Why is it necessary to diminish vocabulary?

4. Describe in your own words the grammar of Newspeak. In this language, what has happened to grammar and why?

5. In ¶ 16, Orwell talks of the "willful ugliness" of Newspeak and of the two-syllable words "with stress distributed equally between the first syllable and the last." What are the implications of these observations and others in ¶ 16?

6. Is there any relationship between the translation discussed in ¶ 22 and the updating of the Bible and Shakespeare parodied by Art Buchwald in "First the Bible, then Shakespeare" (Section 3)?

7. In the world of Newspeak, why was it important to sever all links with the past?

8. Why does Orwell divide the language of Newspeak into three vocabularies? Are there equivalents to those three vocabularies in our language today?

strategies

1. In ¶ 3, Orwell describes the strategy for presenting his ideas. What is that strategy?

2. Orwell's essay falls into three sections: ¶s 1-3, 4-18, and 19-22. Describe the purpose of each of the parts of Orwell's essay.

3. Outline ¶s 4-8. What order has Orwell used for presenting his ideas and why?

4. In ¶s 9-17, Orwell discusses the "B vocabulary." Outline this part of the essay to discover the order Orwell uses to convey his ideas. Why is this section of the essay longer than those discussing the "A" and "C" vocabularies?

5. Why does Orwell devote a single paragraph to the discussion of the "C vocabulary"? Does he need to say more on this subject?

6. Orwell develops many of his paragraphs by using examples. Point to two paragraphs using this method of development.

7. In ¶ 13, Orwell compares a "Party member" with "the ancient Hebrew." What is the purpose of this comparison?

suggestions for writing

1. Collect your own examples of *doublethink* (see ¶ 19) and write a paper examining the meanings and purposes of these words and phrases.

2. Find a paragraph of clear and specific prose; then rewrite that paragraph in Newspeak.

3. Write a paragraph in Newspeak; then translate that paragraph into Oldspeak.

4. From your own experience, write a paper about a situation in which you tried to control someone's thinking through careful selection of words and phrases. Did you succeed or fail? Why?

5. Write a paper about an abstract word or subject without using abstract words. Is this assignment possible? Orwell lists several of these words and phrases in his essay.

6. Write a paper describing a situation in which you believe someone used *doublethink* on you. What was your response to this situation and why?

Stefan Kanfer

Words from Watergate

Wilson: How do you know that, Mr. Chairman?
Ervin: Because I can understand the English language. It is my mother tongue.

[1]   Yes, but Lawyer John Wilson's clients, John Ehrlichman and H. R. Haldeman, are also children of that mother tongue. And so are Caulfield and Dean, Odle and Porter, Mitchell and Magruder, and virtually every other Watergate witness. Those witnesses are a peculiar group of siblings, obedient to every authority except that of their parent language.

[2]   Even with the admission of tapes, no one will ever master the entire vocabulary or thought processes of the Nixon Administration. But tantalizing glimpses are possible through the aperture of the Ervin hearings. By now, of course, the Nixonian cadre has turned a few phrases to bromides, notably the sci-fi sounds: "At that point in time," and, "In that time frame." Still, these clichés are excellent indicators of the Administration's unwritten laws of language: 1) never use a word when a sentence will do; 2) obscure, don't clarify; 3) Humpty Dumpty was right when he said to Alice: "When *I* use a word . . . it means just what I choose it to mean."

[3]   Most of the Watergate witnesses prefer not to answer with a simple yes or no. The vagueness shown last week by H. R. Haldeman has been the motto of the month: "I am not sure whether I was or not. I may very well have been." Other witnesses felt that truth was illusory; facts could only be construed "in their context." The quibbling over nuances would do credit to Henry James—as when Erlichman vainly tried to distinguish between "literal" and "actual."

[4]   Perhaps because Haldeman has been characterized as a former adman, he avoided any run-it-up-the-flagpole chatter. Still, he introduced some collector's items: "Zero-defect system," for perfection; "containment" for the withholding of information. Throughout the hearings, where precision would help, a file of worn metaphors and similes appears. Usually the phrases smack of the military or sports—two arenas notable

From *Time Magazine,* August 13, 1973. Reprinted by permission from TIME, The Weekly Newsmagazine; © Time Inc.

for their threadbare lexicons. Porter thought of himself as "a team player," Dean as a soldier who had "earned my stripes." Erlichman considered himself proficient at "downfield blocking." J. Edgar Hoover was "a loyal trooper." Mitchell football-coached, "When the going gets tough, the tough get going"; and everybody worried about the chief "lowering the boom."

[5] Responsibility was obviously diffused; in the New Nixon years, power no longer seems to emanate from persons but from real estate. The President rarely appears in testimony. The word comes from "the Oval Office." When Caulfield carried the fragile promise of Executive clemency, said McCord, he spoke of "the very highest levels of the White House"—perhaps the first time that favors were to be dispensed by architecture.

[6] Euphemisms are to the tongue what novocain is to the gums. In the hearings, criminality is given scores of numbing disguises. For "intelligence-gathering operations" read "breaking and entering," for "plumbers" read "burglars," for "stroking" read "cheap flattery," for "puffing" read "expensive flattery," for "White House horrors" read "Government-sponsored crimes." The roster seems endless: "dirty tricks," "laundered money," "telephone anomalies"—all perform the same function: the separation of words from truth.

[7] Sometimes the resonances are poignant: McCord's use of the familiar "game plan" or young Odle's attempt to "make a couple of things perfectly clear." Occasionally they are mystifying, as in the characterization of CBS Newsman Daniel Schorr as "a real media enemy"—as opposed, perhaps, to an unreal media enemy. Often, however, they are terrifying because they illuminate just how much ignorance the functionaries had—not only of the law but of themselves.

[8] To the Ervin committee, for example, Ehrlichman released a clandestine tape recording of a conversation he had had with Herbert Kalmbach. It contains a dazzling example of self-deception. Kalmbach is asked to testify that he spoke to Erlichman in California, when in fact the conversation took place in Washington. "I wouldn't ask you to lie," says the former presidential aide.

[9] It was this recording that prompted Mary McCarthy to speculate in the London *Observer:* [The tape] shows Ehrlichman demanding that his friend commit perjury. That is the only way it can be read. Perhaps this is illuminating. If Erlichman cannot realize what his taped voice says in plain English, perhaps Nixon cannot either, and so his own battery of tapes may be produced after all."

[10] Whether or not the President can comprehend plain English, it is certain that many on his staff could not or would not. In their obfuscations they were not alone. Long before the Nixon Administration took office, the military had its "pacification" and "fragging." Radical critics led their own assaults on the English language with the substitution of "offing" for killing, the prating of "fascism" every time an obstacle was encountered. At the same time, business gave its own donation at the office, with the computer talk of "inputs," "software" and "print-outs."

[11] Indeed, every sector has its private jargon meant to mystify the outsider, frequently at the cost of undermining the speaker. Yet, all these linguistic abuses have paled beside the rhetorical revelations of Watergate. With that special gift of hindsight so praised by committeemen and witnesses, the spectator can now perceive that the seeds of the affair were planted long ago, in the first days of Nixon's tenure. Once upon a point in time. Administration spokesmen instructed commentators: "Don't judge us by what we say but by what we do." As the world now realizes, verb and act are in the deepest sense inseparable.

[12] In his classic essay, *Politics and the English Language*, George Orwell spoke for all time: "If thought corrupts language, language can also corrupt thought." Yet even with his innate pessimism, Orwell offered a solution—a method more applicable today than it was in the holocaust of the '40s. "One ought to recognize," he wrote, "that the present political chaos is connected with the decay of language, and that one can probably bring about some improvement by starting at the verbal end."

[13] It takes no feminist to see how much the nation owes its mother tongue. If that tongue is to speak again with clarity and force, alterations have to begin, not in the spirit of litigation but in its opposite: the defense of values. The Watergate evasions will have to be swept away with those who mouth them. Honest politics will not miraculously reappear. But in the absence of bromides and shibboleths, Americans may once again be able to put in some good words for their Government. And vice versa.

words and sentences

1. Vocabulary: *siblings* (¶ 1); *aperture, cadre, bromides* (2); *illusory* (3); *lexicons* (4); *diffused, emanate* (5); *clandestine* (8); *obfuscations* (10); *shibboleths* (13).
2. Why does the phrase "the aperture of the Ervin hearings" (¶ 2) seem appropriate? Does the phrase contain a metaphor?
3. What is "run-it-up-the-flagpole chatter" (¶ 4)?
4. Describe the pattern of the first sentence in ¶ 6; then write a sentence imitating this pattern.
5. Examine Kanfer's use of the words *crime* and *criminality*.
6. Nearly everyone has read a James Bond book or seen a James Bond movie. Does the language which Kanfer attributes to the Nixon aides resemble that of a James Bond book or movie? Be specific.
7. What are the connotative associations of the word *functionaries* (¶ 7)?
8. Describe the pattern and punctuation of the last sentence in ¶ 2; then write a sentence imitating that pattern.

ideas and implications

1. Compare the first sentence in ¶ 2 of Kanfer's essay with Orwell's observations about vocabulary in "The Principles of Newspeak." Note that Kanfer quotes Orwell near the end of the essay. Discuss the implications of this comparison.

2. In Kanfer's view, what is the difference between "context" and "quibbling over nuances" (¶ 3)? What are the implications of this distinction?
3. For Kanfer, what is the relationship between words and deeds? Point to specific references to support your answer.
4. For Kanfer, what is the relationship between corruption of language and self-deception?

strategies

1. Describe Kanfer's rhetorical stance.
2. What strategy does Kanfer use for beginning and concluding his essay? Re-examine the first sentence of ¶ 13.
3. What plan of organization has Kanfer used in his essay? Beginning with ¶ 10, where does Kanfer turn his attention?
4. Examine the transitions between paragraphs of the essay to discover how Kanfer carries his reader from one major topic to another.

suggestions for writing

1. Write a paper describing a situation in which you lied and were not discovered. Try to find the reasons for not being discovered.
2. Write a paper describing an occasion when you lied and were discovered. Try to find the reasons for being discovered.
3. If you watched or read about the Watergate hearings, write your observations about the language of a committee member or a witness who caught your interest.
4. President Nixon responded to the Watergate hearings in a speech given on August 15, 1973. Read the speech (reprinted in the New York *Times,* August 16, 1973), and write a paper about the language and meaning of the speech.

John Milton

from **Areopagitica**

[1]   I deny not but that it is of greatest concernment in the Church and Commonwealth to have a vigilant eye how books demean themselves as well as men; and thereafter to confine, imprison, and do sharpest justice on them as malefactors: for books are not absolutely dead things, but do contain a potency of life in them to be as active as that soul was whose progeny they are; nay, they do preserve as in a vial the purest efficacy and extraction of that living intellect that bred them. I know they are as lively, and as vigorously productive, as those fabulous dragons' teeth; and, being sown up and down, may chance to spring up armed men. And yet on the

other hand, unless wariness be used, as good almost kill a man as kill a good book; who kills a man kills a reasonable creature, God's image; but he who destroys a good book kills reason itself, kills the image of God as it were in the eye. Many a man lives a burden to the earth; but a good book is the precious life-blood of a master spirit, embalmed and treasured up on purpose to a life beyond life. 'Tis true, no age can restore a life, whereof perhaps there is no great loss; and revolutions of ages do not oft recover the loss of a rejected truth, for the want of which whole nations fare the worse. We should be wary therefore what persecution we raise against the living labours of public men, how we spill that seasoned life of man preserved and stored up in books; since we see a kind of homicide may be thus committed, sometimes a martyrdom, and, if it extend to the whole impression, a kind of massacre, whereof the execution ends not in the slaying of an elemental life, but strikes at that ethereal and fifth essence, the breath of reason itself, slays an immortality rather than a life. But lest I should be condemned of introducing licence while I oppose licensing, I refuse not the pains to be so much historical as will serve to show what hath been done by ancient and famous Commonwealths against this disorder, till the very time that this project of licensing crept out of the Inquisition, was caught up by our Prelates, and hath caught some of our Presbyters. . . .

[2]   . . . Solomon informs us that much reading is a weariness to the flesh; but neither he nor other inspired author tells us that such or such reading is unlawful: yet certainly had God thought good to limit us herein, it had been much more expedient to have told us what was unlawful than what was wearisome. As for the burning of those Ephesian books by St. Paul's converts, it is replied the books were magic, the Syriac so renders them. It was a private act, a voluntary act, and leaves us to a voluntary imitation; the men in remorse burnt those books which were their own; the magistrate by this example is not appointed; these men practised the books, another might perhaps have read them in some sort usefully. Good and evil we know in the field of this world grow up together almost inseparably; and the knowledge of good is so involved and interwoven with the knowledge of evil, and in so many cunning resemblances hardly to be discerned, that those confused seeds, which were imposed on Psyche as an incessant labour to cull out and sort asunder, were not more intermixed. It was from out the rind of one apple tasted that the knowledge of good and evil as two twins cleaving together leapt forth into the world. And perhaps this is that doom which Adam fell into of knowing good and evil, that is to say, of knowing good by evil. As therefore the state of man now is, what wisdom there be to choose, what continence to forbear, without the knowledge of evil? He that can apprehend and consider vice with all her baits and seeming pleasures, and yet abstain, and yet distinguish, and yet prefer that which is truly better, he is the true warfaring Christian. I cannot praise a fugitive and cloistered virtue, unexercised and unbreathed, that never sallies out and sees her adversary, but slinks out of the race, where that immortal garland is to be run for not without dust and heat. Assuredly we bring not innocence into the world,

we bring impurity much rather: that which purifies us is trial, and trial is by what is contrary. That virtue therefore which is but a youngling in the contemplation of evil, and knows not the utmost that vice promises to her followers, and rejects it, is but a blank virtue, not a pure; her whiteness is but an excremental whiteness; which was the reason why our sage and serious poet Spenser, whom I dare be known to think a better teacher than Scotus or Aquinas, describing true temperance under the person of Guyon, brings him in with his palmer through the cave of Mammon and the bower of earthly bliss, that he might see and know, and yet abstain. Since, therefore, the knowledge and survey of vice is in this world so necessary to the constituting of human virtue, and the scanning of error to the confirmation of truth, how can we more safely and with less danger scout into the regions of sin and falsity, than by reading all manner of tractates, and hearing all manner of reason? And this is the benefit which may be had of books promiscuously read.

words and sentences

1. Vocabulary: *malefactors, progeny, efficacy, ethereal, licensing* (¶ 1).
2. In what ways are the diction, punctuation, syntax, and paragraphing of Milton's *Areopagitica,* published in 1644, different from those of modern prose?
3. In the last sentence of ¶ 1, how is Milton using the words *license* and *licensing?* Check the derivations of this word.
4. What does Milton mean by "excremental whiteness" in ¶ 2?

ideas and implications

1. Does Milton deny the state the power of censorship?
2. What is Milton's argument in ¶ 1 about the relationship between books and men? Why does he make this argument?
3. Though Milton does not use the term "book burning," he speaks of this practice. What is his attitude towards book burning? Is book burning practiced in our time?
4. What are Milton's assumptions about good and evil? How do these assumptions affect his attitudes towards intellectual freedom and freedom of the press?

strategies

1. What method of development does Milton use to argue his point in ¶ 1?
2. What is the purpose of ¶ 2 in Milton's argument? How does he develop this argument? Does he state his purpose at the beginning of ¶ 1 or does he state it elsewhere? Why?

suggestions for writing

1. A recent decision of the United States Supreme Court returned to the states and communities the power to decide what is fit for public

reading and viewing. Write a paper about this decision in light of Milton's observation in *Areopagitica*. Or if you know of a specific occasion on which the state or community exercised this power, you might write a paper about these events and their consequences.

2. The showing of blue movies and skin flicks and the publication of "pornographic" magazines and books are topics of much debate in our society. Write a paper about these movies and publications. Can one justify their existence?

3. Write a paper in which you attack, defend, or qualify Milton's notions about good and evil.

4. From your own experience, write a paper describing your own confrontations with good and evil. Try to focus your paper on an event, character, or specific circumstance.

5. Write a paper about a situation in which a friend or member of your family suppressed the truth from you. What were the consequences of this suppression of truth?

George Jean Nathan

On Censorship

[1]   The plain trouble lies not with censorship, but with censors. There isn't one of us, once his loud talk has died down, but believes in censorship in one degree or another. I should like to inquire of the stoutest foe of all censorship just what his attitude would be were a French peepshow, to which minors were freely admitted, to be opened on either side of his home. I should, further, like to make a similar inquiry of the staunchest opponent of theatrical censorship in the event that, let us say, the curtain to the dramatization of Dreiser's *An American Tragedy* were at one point kept aloft a few moments longer and the seduction episode in which Clyde and Roberta figure pursued with a Zolaesque realism. And I should like to continue the inquiry in the case of the loudest howler against literary censorship in the event that copies of John Cleland's immortal tome were published at a nickel each and sold freely to school-children. The way to beat censorship is not to deny all sense to it and all justification, but to give ground where ground must be given and then, when the enemy oversteps its bounds, to let fly with the full artillery of calm intelligence. The last way in the world in which to win a battle is to try to convince one's self that the enemy has no guns. To contend that the cause of art is in

From *The World of George Jean Nathan*, ed. Charles Angoff. © 1952 by Alfred A. Knopf, Inc. Reprinted by permission of Mrs. George Jean Nathan.

danger because the censors edit or condemn and suppress a lot of dirty postcards, pornographic pamphlets, cheap moving pictures and equally cheap plays, to say nothing of a second-rate novel or so, is to make one's self and one's convictions ridiculous. Now and again, of course, a good piece of work suffers along with the contemptible because of the ignorance of the censors, but art is a poor and pitiable thing if it cannot survive such an occasional calamity. It has stood it in the past, and often enough. A relatively few years pass, the suppressed work duly comes into its own again, and all is as tranquil as before. True art simply can not be suppressed for long; history proves that much. If it can be suppressed and stay suppressed, you may rest assured that it isn't art. In all the centuries, not one genuinely fine piece of work has been suppressed by censorship for more than a little while. Art crushed to earth soon rises again. Only the spurious in art remains lying in the dirt.

[2]   I am against censorship not because it is censorship, but because it is generally ignorant. I am against censors because, all the time, they disgrace the theory of censorship in its soundest sense and make it objectionable even to men who may be willing to grant its periodic integrity. I have before me two documents in illustration. One is a copy of an address, made recently on the floor of the House of Representatives by a Congressman from a Southern State, advocating a general censorship of magazines. After denouncing a certain magazine as immoral and corruptive, this would-be censor quoted at length, in chief and eloquent support of his case, an article which I myself had written, carefully omitting the name of the magazine in which it had appeared. Who among his hearers was to know that the article was published in the very magazine that he was denouncing? What is one to say of such open-and-shut hypocrisy and double-dealing? A second illustration is to be had in a letter lying on my desk as I write this. It comes to me from a gentleman of God and one of the two leading champions of censorship in New York State. This holy gentleman, mistaking my attitude toward censors and censorship, observes that it is his opinion that the stage of New York City is unutterably filthy, that the law should promptly and forcibly be brought down upon it, and then asks me to supply him with the names of any plays that are dirty, confessing that he has not seen any of them himself! In other words, what we engage here is a censor who is certain that censorship is called for but who doesn't know what it is that should be censored. It is men like these— and they are typical of the tong—who bring censorship into vile disrepute and who cause all fair-minded and upright men and women to hold their noses. But let us get on our knees and thank God for them. It is they who are ruining irrevocably the cause of censorship amongst even censorship's more rational proponents.

words and sentences

1. Vocabulary: *peepshow* (¶ 1); *irrevocably* (2).
2. Describe and compare and contrast the patterns of the first sentences in ¶s 1 and 2; then write sentences imitating those patterns.

3. Describe the patterns of sentences three, four, and five in ¶ 1; then write a sequence of sentences imitating these patterns.

ideas and implications

1. Nathan's reference to John Cleland's "immortal tome" is to the novel *Fanny Hill*. When Nathan originally wrote his essay in 1927, this novel was not available to the general public. Is this true today? How do some of Nathan's references and allusions date his essay?
2. Why does Nathan believe that the trouble with censorship lies with the censors?
3. Under what circumstances does Nathan believe censorship to be justified?
4. Why does Nathan believe that true art cannot be suppressed?

strategies

1. How does Nathan open his argument? What strategy is Nathan using in these opening sentences?
2. Does ¶ 2 have a topic sentence? How does Nathan develop his idea in this paragraph?

suggestions for writing

1. Write a paper describing a situation or situations in which you believe censorship to be justified.
2. Write a review of a movie or book that you believe to be in questionable taste. Try to show precisely why you believe the movie or book to be in questionable taste.
3. Write a paper defending the existence of "porno bookstores" and the easy availability of pornography in our society.
4. Pretend that you are a legislator writing a bill to be offered to Congress on the subject of censorship. Your paper will be the bill that you submit.

George Jean Nathan

Vulgarity in Literature

The word vulgar, appearing promiscuously in American criticism, is the emptiest word in the critical vocabulary. Indiscriminately and with a supercilious snoot visited upon the writings of some of our best artists, its users betray simply their own shanty fastidiousness, to say nothing of their

From *The World of George Jean Nathan*, ed. Charles Angoff. © 1952 by Alfred A. Knopf, Inc. Reprinted by permission of Mrs. George Jean Nathan.

ignorance of the platitudinous fact that some of the grantedly greatest art that the world has known has been as vulgar as pigs' feet. What, may one ask, would these critics say today of an artist whose characters expectorated all over the place, talked of whores and intimate biological functions and discoursed on human sex indulgence in terms of animals; who treated of incest, named certain of his women characters after the social diseases and their consequences and descended to the lowest form of gutter speech; whose characters were Christened after the more esoteric portions of the human anatomy and after the act of copulation, drank themselves into a state of stomach sickness, indulged in a prodigious belching, never failed to speak of disgusting odors, and swore like bohunks? That is, conceiving a second coming, of an artist like Shakespeare?

words and sentences

1. Vocabulary: *supercilious, fastidiousness, platitudinous, expectorated, esoteric, prodigious.*
2. Describe the pattern of the third sentence; then write a sentence imitating that pattern.
3. In the first sentence, Nathan uses the word *promiscuously* to describe the way American critics use the word *vulgar?* Why?
4. Check the derivation of the word *vulgar.*
5. Examine the word choices in the second sentence. What does Nathan suggest about the critics who characterize "our best artists" as vulgar?

ideas and implications

1. Why does Nathan believe the word *vulgar* to be empty?
2. Is Nathan's description of the works of William Shakespeare accurate? Be specific.
3. What assumption does Nathan make about vulgarity in literature and life?

strategies

1. Describe Nathan's strategy for presenting his idea. Why does he conclude his paragraph with a question?
2. Why might Nathan choose Shakespeare as an example of the vulgar in literature and art? Nathan knows what his audience's reaction to Shakespeare will be. What is that reaction?

suggestions for writing

1. Write a paper defining the word *vulgar.*
2. The novelist H. G. Wells spoke of the "jolly coarseness of life" as a source of humor and a source for the writer. Write a paper in which you recount from your own experience an event or situation that might reflect this "jolly coarseness of life."
3. Write a paper defining the attitudes of a parent or a friend towards vulgarity.

Sydney J. Harris

Needed: More and Better Swear Words

[1]   Turning in heavy traffic the other afternoon, I heard one motorist lean out of his window and shout at another: "You dirty unprintable blank-blank!"

[2]   These trite and meaningless obscenities reminded me that I had been re-reading *Henry IV* a few evenings ago, and I went back and looked up some of the epithets that Falstaff and his colleagues flung at each other.

[3]   In just riffling through one scene, I came across the following: malt-worm, gor-bellied knave, fat chuff, knot-pated rogue, impudent swine, greasy tallowcatch, dried neat's tongue, elf-skin, stock-fish, vile standing-tuck, stinking mackerel, soused gurnet, cut-purse, and filthy-bung.

[4]   One of the depressing evidences of the decay of the English language since Shakespeare's day is the expulsion of colorful epithets, which have been replaced by nothing except a few boring swear words.

[5]   Anyone who has ever heard a Frenchman, an Italian or, (especially) a Spaniard curse will know what I mean. Terms of sexual deprecation are rarely used, and are not needed; the Latins' vivid and flexible vocabulary of insult is an artistic performance of high skill.

[6]   Such old-fashioned English words as "fop," "jackanapes," and "pop-injay," for instance, have passed out of the language, and our terms of opprobrious description are limited to such limp words as "dope" or "jerk," which have no strength, no precision and no point.

[7]   "Bounder" and "cad" are also *passé* in their serious sense, but how do you designate a man who cheats at cards, kisses and tells, and behaves generally with no regard for fair play?

[8]   "Popinjay," incidentally, is a wonderful word for a certain kind of man who struts pompously and parrots the ideas of his betters. And we have no satisfactory substitute for "coxcomb," to describe a silly and conceited man infatuated with his surface appearance.

[9]   My objection to swear words is not moral, but esthetic. They are unlovely and mean nothing, since they are forced to cover so wide a range of evaluations. And they indicate a verbal poverty on the level of "You're another" and "So's your old man." This is little-boy talk, and not the proper linguistic currency of a mature people with the tradition of a Shakespeare, or even a Dickens, behind them.

words and sentences

    1. Vocabulary: *epithets* (¶ 2); *opprobrious* (6); *esthetic* (9).

    2. Check your dictionary for the words Harris mentions in ¶ 3. Can you find all of these words? Why or why not?

From Sydney J. Harris, *Strictly Personal*. © 1953 by Henry Regnery Co., Chicago. Reprinted by permission of the publisher.

3. Describe the pattern of the sentence in ¶ 6; then write a sentence imitating this pattern. What effect does Harris create with the final clause in his sentence?

ideas and implications

1. What does Harris mean by "little boy talk" (¶ 9)?
2. Why does Harris characterize profanity as "trite and meaningless"? What assumption does he make about language with such a statement?
3. Harris says his objection to swear words "is not moral, but esthetic." Why does he argue in this way?

strategies

1. What strategy does Harris use for beginning and concluding his essay? How are these two paragraphs (¶s 1 and 9) different and how are they alike in content?
2. How much does Harris depend upon comparison and contrast to develop his idea? What comparisons and contrasts does he make?

suggestions for writing

1. Write a paper in which you create some better swear words. Keep in mind Harris's examples from Shakespeare.
2. Write a paper in which you comment on the current state of swearing. You may want to begin with, but do not limit your discussion to, those four-letter words of profanity.
3. Write a paper in which you agree with, disagree with, or modify Harris's observations in ¶ 9. As you write, keep in mind the following questions: Do we have the linguistic resources to swear as our ancestors did? To what extent is swearing related to society's expectations of linguistic conduct?
4. Write a sketch of a person whose distinguishing characteristic is his use of forceful, perhaps even obscene, language.

Malcolm Bradbury

The New Language of Morals

[1] From time to time, the moral vocabulary of a society seems to alter substantially, in response to social changes and the conscious or unconscious election of new leaders of thought and opinion. In these times it is

Reprinted from *Twentieth Century* Vol. 172 (Summer, 1963), pp. 77–84.

easy to tell what side of the fence people are on, not so much by the opinions they express as by the words they use to express them. There grows up an Elect of discourse, using words in a new, a special, a group way, and using a language with its own honorific words and concepts. One interesting example of such a word is *Puritan,* which is used in many quarters to denote a suspicious and repressive attitude towards pleasurable indulgence, but which is esteemed in other quarters as meaning almost the exact opposite. The two groups encountered each other, with perceptible raising of eyebrows, at the *Lady Chatterley's Lover* trial, when Prosecuting Counsel, speaking with the voice of conventional educated culture, confronted Professor Hoggart, speaking with the voice of modern literary culture, and confusion ensued.

[2]   Another similar key-word, conveniently separating Elect from Mass, is *Life.* To most people, Life is what we get up and go to every day, however unwillingly; and it is hard to see how Being on the Side of Life is the property of some persons more than others. But this formulation, taken over apparently from the artists of the Decadence, has now a substantial vogue. The Life Enhancers and the Life Diminishers are seen as two contrary parties in society—seen, of course, by the self-confessed Life Enhancers. The characteristic of moral vocabularies is that they have a way of praising those who use them. There is a modern formulation which divides people into Hips and Squares, but of course it is really only those who are, or think themselves, Hip that use it. The American formulation of Far In and Far Out is a distinction made by the Far Out. It is true that the word *bourgeois* is largely a formulation of the bourgeois, but only because they had sufficient urbanity to see themselves from outside, which meant that they ceased in fact to be bourgeois, in their own view at least. So it is with the Side of Lifers; it is rare to find anyone describing himself, or his friends, as being on the Side of Death.

[3]   There is nothing more dangerous than for a young man in our society to appear in public with the wrong mode of discourse. The honorific words of one group are the condemnatory words of another; hence the difficulty experienced by candidates for certain rather advanced departments in universities when they have the misfortune to be praised by their headmasters as *loyal.* One man's praise is another man's stigma. In a recent *Observer* series on *Patriotism,* a number of eminent people presented themselves before us in poses of acute embarrassment, rather as a bishop might in being found in a brothel in the old days. Here they were, modern men, most of them, being asked to discourse in a traditional vocabulary which was hardly likely to be current among readers who had doubtless sucked in *A Farewell to Arms* with mother's milk:

> I was always embarrassed by the words *sacred, glorious,* and *sacrifice* and the expression *in vain.* We had heard them, sometimes standing in the rain almost out of earshot, so that only the shouted words came through, and had read them, on proclamations that were slapped up by billposters over other proclamations, now for a long time, and I had seen nothing sacred, and things that were glorious had no glory and the sacrifices were like the

stockyards at Chicago if nothing was done with the meat except bury it. There were many words you could not stand to hear and finally only the names of places had dignity. . . . Abstract words such as *glory, honour, courage,* or *hallow* were obscene. . . .

The fact of the matter is that the traditional discourse associated with the public virtues, made up of words like *patriotism, loyalty, courage* and *public spirit,* has tended to lapse, and indeed instead of attributing high motives to people who manifest them many of us are more than ready to be cynical about them. There used once to be a whole pattern of honorific words which described a happy correlation between a man's values and the aims and intentions of his society; but these are as unfashionable as the invocations to *thrift* and *self-help* that were current in Victorian society and have now disappeared in a time when we require people to spend rather than save, consume rather than produce. Most of the words that describe bridging motions between man and society have tended to vanish from the discourse of the moderns, though they remain solidly in the speech of those for whom a degree of social engagement seems impressive and worthy. Similarly many of the words that stigmatized those who made a bad bridge between self and society have lost their force. There used once to be a wealth of words which manifested a general sense of the low repute in which evil and antisocial conduct was held. Nowadays, when we regard evil as a moral preference different from our own, we tend to turn to the neutral discourse of sociology or psychology. We likewise tend to suspect hierarchical words, like *superior, refined* and so on. The preference today seems to be for apparently neutral and seemingly unhierarchical words without a public moral content. In this sense, the power of moral assertion in discourse would appear to be declining. In fact, of course, it is being reformed. New hierarchies and moral inferences emerge.
[4]   Words asserting a public standard of morality, roughly agreed on as a general direction for human aspiration, tend to be replaced by words asserting a relativistic and private conception. Linked with this is the discarding, in the newer vocabulary, of words seeming to imply a preference for fathers over sons. *Paternalism* is a case of a word now demoted and used pejoratively—linguistically the fraternal society is already with us— and *educational* has suffered a similar fate. The word *mature,* on the other hand, has undergone an interesting process of adaptation and reclamation, for it is now regarded as a moral quality almost exclusively the property of the young. This particular corrective process has struck particularly hard at Western religion, which has both a sense of the value of public moral consensus and a strong paternalistic symbolism. In consequence those aspects of religion which tend towards the fatherly, the authoritative or the social have been demoted, while those to do with the youthful and the private have been stressed of late. As more than one vicar has observed, Christianity is really a teenage religion; as others have suggested, it should never have become an institution at all, for this has set an organization intervening between man and his creator; as yet others have indicated, it never intended to become morally assertive, to take up that

most unattractive of properties, a high moral tone. Religion thus tends to be de-moralized, and many of the clergy are at pains to point out that there is little moral consensus in the Church; it is the need to worship they are agreed on, though there are theologians without the clergy's degree of personal interest who hardly see the need for that. Thus in recent months we have heard a great deal about "religionless Christianity," which is, to put the matter crudely, Christianity divested of all the social apparatus which has enabled it to survive and be powerful. The new religionists— who, as a friend of mine once put it, believe in at the most one God and pray To Whom It May Concern—pay little attention to the superb sociology of the Church in the past. How cleverly, by means of great effectiveness and frequent undesirability, it kept alive the power of religion over the community! But for the new religionists it is the individual rather than the social implications of faith that matter; and the whole tone of their discourse reflects this fact, their pronouncements emphasizing contacts between man and creator, their words being personal, unabstract, tentative. As with the new philosophers the point of enquiry is the seeing eye and the thinking mind; and a logical consequence, already being reached in philosophy, is that discourse will in fact totally cease, other people lying beyond the self in a fearsome universe in whose reality one cannot for a moment trust.

[5]   Let me not suggest, however, that the Church is the stronghold of the new moral discourse—this is, on the whole, not so. Generally it is on the side of moral consensus and the moral assertion, offering its positions almost as if they had some external authority. And thus it is the Church's words that are most suspect. In his Reith Lectures Professor Carstairs stigmatized Saint Paul as "an authoritarian character," a man who attempted to insist on a sexual morality remote from that of the Trobriand Islanders, and the tendency towards this sort of insistence is to be found extensively in the history of the Church. In his recent book on *The Family* the sociologist Ronald Fletcher collects together a veritable courtesy-book of old-style moral usages, most of them using the word *moral* itself. Many of the spokesmen he selects were Methodists who espoused a strict and traditional idea of public morality; they are here to be found complaining that the modern family has gone downhill, and in support of their impression they did not quote statistics but spoke rhetorically of the nation's "dire moral peril," of the "seedy dingy moral apathy of our time," "the moral failure of the home" and so on. Mr. Fletcher counters with the new mode of discourse, against moral decline he offers different behaviour. His tone is evidently more permissive but the interesting thing is that it is not without its prophetic note. He expresses "irritation" with the old manner (anger plays a substantial part in the new moral tone) and demands forward-looking thinking, better statistics, other words. So the point is not that the new prophets are without morality but that they have a different and a flatter style of moral speech to distinguish them. (In fact the word *moral* is central to the new discourse; but it means something rather different.)

[6]   What, then, we may perceive in the quiet linguistic changes that are

taking place in our society at the moment is a tendency towards the heightening of private values at the expense of public ones, of the energization of words that tend to express this, and an opprobious weighting to certain traditional words which have been of evident value to public men of the past. The very overtones of the word *establishment* (i.e., that which is established is automatically to be suspected) suggests the fund of resources behind the new-style speakers, while the Conservative Party have long ceased defending the existence of anything on the grounds that it is traditional, though the test of time and the test of existence are as good tests as any. The gradual spreading of the new discourse naturally spreads the implied attitudes behind it (for one of the ways in which we acquire values is through acquiring an organized vocabulary—this is why vocabulary has power). And spreading it is, so that most of us now find that we straddle two linguistic worlds. The new language has extending currency. The ready acceptance of what it is conventional to call "satire" is the acceptance of the tone of voice, quizzical, demanding, informal, vernacular, often faintly offensive and doctrinaire, which is appropriate to the new language, and which many writers have been exploring. The group of new-style speakers is thus spreading, and is leading to some gradual alienation of those who use the older tone of voice. One may examine this process in a number of conscious users of language, such as journalists or broadcasters. The formality of B.B.C. official speech used to be one of our great reassurances; it spoke for order, like guards on trains. Now, in a wave of informality, even the news is changing. The names of contributors to newsreels are frequently mentioned (personal), announcers cough regularly and carefully do not, as they easily can, switch the cough out (informal), the opinions of people in the street are canvassed, though they frequently have none (democratic), and interviewers are aggressive and sometimes even offensive (vernacular). So, personal, informal, democratic and vernacular, comes the new common speech for all things.

[7]   However, the co-existence of the two modes of language can lead to confusion in these intermediate times, and it is not surprising that many people, caught between the two camps, feel now and then that a little assistance is needed. For most of us borrow our speech from all that is available, and these are hard days. One might take again the already mentioned instance of the word *moral*. In the old style of discourse (hereafter designated as OS) the word describes the obligation to choose between right and wrong; in new style (NS) it refers to the *difficulty* of choosing between right and wrong. It should be noted then that many words have diametrically opposite meanings or intonations, and a short glossary here would not come amiss:

> *Youth* = a person not yet fully mature (OS); a person fully mature (NS).
>
> *Mature* = wise, responsible, capable of holding positions of power (OS); wise, conscious of difficulty, incapable of holding positions of power (NS).
>
> *Rebellious* = out of touch with cultural experience (OS); in touch with cultural experience (NS).
>
> *Spontaneous* = ill-considered, hasty (OS); imaginatively perceptive (NS).

Apathy = not being interested in taking on social duties and obligations (OS); being interested in taking on social duties and obligations (NS).

Paternal = taking an intelligent and encouraging interest in the young (OS); imposing upon and destroying the young (NS).

Culture = reading books, pursuing the arts (OS); doing anything (NS).

Commitment = an unfortunate obligation to a cause (OS); a necessary obligation to a cause (NS).

Hypocrisy = pretending to believe in what is self-evident (OS); believing in what pretends to be self-evident (NS).

Sinful = doing what everyone knows to be wrong (OS); knowing what everyone does to be wrong (NS).

Tradition = the proper preoccupation of the living with the dead (OS); the morbid preoccupation of the dead with the living (NS).

The list of course can be extended indefinitely.

[8]   A further problem emerges, however, when we find not the same word for different concepts, but different words for the same concept. Here, once again, a short list might give some guidance:

Guilt (OS) = *shame* (NS).
Puritan (OS) = *censor* (NS).
Libertine (OS) = *puritan* (NS).
Father (OS) = *brother* (NS).
Righteous indignation (OS) = *anger* or *hate* (NS).
Vulgar (OS) = *phoney* (NS).
Us (OS) = *them* (NS).
Them (OS) = *us* (NS).

[9]   There are many deductions that can be made from these slim and summary lists; it is outside my purpose here to make them. Studies are needed of the frequency with which each of these groups uses certain central words, and of particular interest are those words that appear frequently in the discourse of one group and never in the discourse of the other. In some cases they indicate the vanishing of certain concepts (*virginity* might for instance be one among NS-speakers) and the invention of others (*commitment* perhaps, totally irrelevant to OS-speakers). My purpose here is simply to point out, to those who aspire to enter the arena of social discussion, that one's alliances may be determined by the very discourse one has acquired or chooses to espouse. The importance of a common language in establishing the freemasonry of the Elect has been the theme of many modern novels, which frequently show private languages triumphing over public ones, the vernacular defeating the literary, the words of youth defeating the words of the aged. The idea of such an Elect, a central group of moral sophisticates who either triumph over or plunge more deeply into experience, whose private vision is higher than any public one, recurs frequently in fiction; it is present in Hemingway and Salinger, Lawrence and Sillitoe. It is present for that matter in Jane Austen. The logical development of the situation is to be found in the Beat Generation, an out group that distinguishes and selects its members largely by

their language. What this means of course is that common discourse can both include and exclude, and in fact the Beat Generation is a very exclusive club, rather like our image of the traditional aristocracy. This sort of distinction by language has of course always existed, and it suggests that even in a classless society a hierarchy of discourse will survive. The assumption that those who are not *with it* are against it, that *them* is in no way a part of *us,* that the squares and the phoneys and the establishment—or the masses and the hoi polloi and the untutored—are by definition in another camp, means that language retains one of its essential functions. It reassures those who share our words with the warmth of phatic communion; it separates those who do not into their rightful place—beyond the pale.

[10]   In fact, of course, these two different languages represent two different functions of speech. The older language tends to be in character a language of idealism, of hortatory and ennobling concepts. It provides a range of discourse that is extensive and puts its users into touch with a history of language and thought. Its weakness is that it is apt to become detached from realities, to represent nothing but the will to speak. The second language tends, however, in the opposite direction. It is not a language of power, and is poor in abstract concepts. It tends to be anti-cultural. It is a language of uncertainty and scepticism to set off against the discourse of the confident. Its emphasis falls on realism rather than idealism, on descriptive rather than enlarging concepts. Its words for relations outside the self are often thin and indeterminate, and in some auditors it produces an impression akin to disturbed silence. Its best words are those which have to do with immediacy, spontaneity, and the presentation of disguised emotions and indignations. It stresses the value of being in touch and ready with a response. It closes off large areas of traditional thought and speech. Holden Caulfield, with all the resources of the English language behind him, can scarcely get beyond the word *phoney* to describe what he distrusts; we are invited to value him for his immediate touchstones, his vernacular of scepticism, though we tend to note too how narrow a discourse it is. It seems a thin discourse on which to pin a moral life; but the other discourse, with its heavily rhetorical note, its genial gestures toward meaning, can be a language quite as flat. The modern speaker needs to be quite as careful today as in the days when to use the word "notepaper" was enough to damn a man socially for life.

words and sentences

1. Vocabulary: *honorific* (¶ 1); *bourgeois, urbanity* (2); *stigma, brothel, hierarchical* (3); *opprobrious* (6); *phatic* (9); *hortatory* (10).
2. Check the meaning of the word *Elect* in a dictionary. How is Bradbury using this word?
3. What associations does Bradbury make with the following words: *rhetoric, new, discourse*?
4. Describe the structure of the first sentence in ¶ 7; then write a sentence imitating that pattern. Can you improve upon Bradbury's sentence?

ideas and implications

1. Why does Bradbury say (¶ 3), "There is nothing more dangerous than for a young man in our society to appear in public with the wrong mode of discourse"?
2. According to Bradbury, why does the new language of morals suspect abstraction and abstract words?
3. How does Bradbury regard the discourse of sociology and psychology? Why?
4. Describe Bradbury's attitude towards religion.
5. What distinction does Bradbury make between public and private language, morals, and values?
6. What is Bradbury's attitude towards the fiction of Hemingway and J. D. Salinger? Why?
7. Which style—old or new—does Bradbury see as superior? Why?

strategies

1. Describe Bradbury's rhetorical stance. What are his attitudes and his tone of voice?
2. Bradbury uses comparison and contrast as the method for developing his idea and for arguing his thesis. One way to see his argument and the development of that argument is to write the words "Old Style" and "New Style" at the top of two columns on a sheet of paper. Then place under each of these headings those associations which Bradbury makes with each. For example, the words *personal, informal, democratic,* and *vernacular* (¶ 6) are associated with "New Style." On occasion, the parallel quality or characteristic associated with "Old Style" is not stated, but suggested. When this is true, place the suggested quality on your list in brackets. Once you have listed as many comparisons and contrasts as you can, you will begin to see the shape of Bradbury's argument and organization—and should be better able to state your attitudes towards Bradbury's ideas.

suggestions for writing

1. Select one of the abstract words in ¶ 3 and write a paper defining that word.
2. Without using the words "Life Enhancers" and "Life Diminishers," write a paper characterizing a person who in your view fits one of these descriptions. Is your character likely to be one or the other?
3. Write a paper about an occasion when you believe you were a witness to or participant in an evil act.
4. Write a paper attempting to define your attitudes towards religion.

Ossie Davis

The English Language Is My Enemy!

[1]   A superficial examination of Roget's *Thesaurus of the English Language* reveals the following facts: the word WHITENESS has 134 synonyms; 44 of which are favorable and pleasing to contemplate, i.e. purity, cleanness, immaculateness, bright, shining, ivory, fair, blonde, stainless, clean, clear, chaste, unblemished, unsullied, innocent, honorable, upright, just, straight-forward, fair, genuine, trustworthy, (a white man-colloquialism). Only ten synonyms for WHITENESS appear to me have negative implications—and these only in the mildest sense: gloss over, whitewash, gray, wan, pale, ashen, etc.

[2]   The word BLACKNESS has 120 synonyms, 60 of which are distinctly unfavorable, and none of them even mildly positive. Among the offending 60 were such words as: blot, blotch, smut, smudge, sully, begrime, soot, becloud, obscure, dingy, murky, low-toned, threatening, frowning, foreboding, forbidden, sinister, baneful, dismal, thundery, evil, wicked, malignant, deadly, unclean, dirty, unwashed, foul, etc . . . not to mention 20 synonyms directly related to race, such as: Negro, Negress, nigger, darky, blackamoor, etc.

[3]   When you consider the fact that *thinking* itself is sub-vocal speech—in other words, one must use *words* in order to think at all—you will appreciate the enormous heritage of racial prejudgment that lies in wait for any child born into the English Language. Any teacher good or bad, white or black, Jew or Gentile, who uses the English Language as a medium of communication is forced, willy-nilly, to teach the Negro child 60 ways to despise himself, and the white child 60 ways to aid and abet him in the crime.

[4]   Who speaks to me in my Mother Tongue damns me indeed! . . . the English Language—in which I cannot conceive my self as a black man without, at the same time, debasing myself . . . my enemy, with which to survive at all I must continually be at war.

words and sentences

1. Vocabulary: *immaculateness* (¶ 1); *baneful* (2).
2. Describe the pattern of the last sentence in ¶ 3; then write a sentence imitating that pattern. Do the same for ¶ 4.

ideas and implications

1. When Davis says, "my Mother Tongue damns me indeed!" how is he using the word *damns*?
2. Check in a thesaurus or a dictionary of synonyms the words *black* and

Reprinted from the *American Teacher*, April 1967, by permission of the American Federation of Teachers.

white. Make a list of the unfavorable words associated with *white* and the favorable words associated with *black*.

3. Could one argue that the English language is the means by which Davis frees himself for expression of his ideas? Does that argument make less true his perception of the associations his culture and his language make with *black* and *white*?

strategies

1. What method of development does Davis use in ¶s 1 and 2? Why does his opening seem effective?
2. Where does Davis state his thesis idea? What structure has Davis used to convey his ideas?

suggestions for writing

1. Write a paper describing a situation in which you thought the English language was your enemy. Was it the language itself or the user of the language that posed the problems?
2. Check in a dictionary of synonyms or a thesaurus for synonyms of the words *yellow, red, brown, pink*. Then write a paper about the associational meanings with one or more of these words.
3. If you have read Herman Melville's *Moby-Dick*, you might want to reread the chapter on "The Whiteness of the Whale" and write a paper on Melville's perception of *whiteness*. If you have read Joseph Conrad's "Heart of Darkness," you might wish to write on the perception of *darkness* in that story.

Roger D. Abrahams

Language
from *Positively Black*

[1]   One of the statements most often repeated by white elementary teachers about "them"—their Negro charges—is that they have no verbal resources and, because of this, no language ability. This is commonly followed by one of two rationalizing statements: either "these poor children have never been taught to speak correctly" or "they couldn't have developed verbal skills since they come from families with so many children that there isn't any time for communication with their parents." ("Why some of them don't even know who their fathers are!") Both of

these statements are ethnocentric in the extreme, even if they are well-meaning.

[2]   In regard to the supposed substandard language of lower-class Negroes, schooled investigators are just beginning to recognize that Negro speech is not a dialect of English at all but rather part of a language system unto itself which differs from "standard" English in everything but vocabulary. Probably originating from an African Portuguese Creole language, New World Negro dialects developed through a substitution of the vocabularies of the speech of the dominant culture in the places the slaves were deposited (Whinnom). In the United States, rather than viewing the various types of Negro speech as different dialectal corruptions of English, it is more meaningful to view them as one creole language, whole unto itself, which has been progressively gravitating toward the regional English dialects with which it has come into contact (William Stewart). This English creole is not a language *manqué* but a communications system which is as fully developed as any other language. Only by an unfortunate historical accident has it accrued the vocabulary of English, and therefore appeared to many observers as an English dialect. What this means for teachers is that they must learn to deal with the teaching of Standard English as if it were a different language, but one in which most (but not all, by any means) of the vocabulary is the same.

[3]   Furthermore—and this is what I will be documenting in this book—there is not only a different language at work here but a different attitude toward speech and speech acts. We are just beginning to recognize that we don't know very much about information-passing among Negroes; but we can predict with a reasonable degree of accuracy that the subjects and methods of communication of knowledge and feeling will be quite different from white middle-class norms. The implications of such differences are of obvious importance to teachers of Negroes, especially since they have been operating on the assumption that no cultural differences existed in this area.

[4]   One of the basic variations in the passing on of information is in regard to who communicates with whom, and in what recurrent situations; this brings us back to the second ethnocentric judgment commonly made by teachers—that Negro children are not verbal because they don't have a chance to communicate with parents. This attitude makes the assumption that the only communication channel useful for educational development is that which arises between adults and children. This is a natural outgrowth of the image that teachers have of themselves (ratified by the community, of course) that they are surrogate parents. But with children who are not subject to the middle-class family system, this places them immediately at a disadvantage, both in relation to the teacher who has these expectations, and in regard to the educational system in general.

[5]   The fact is that most of the lower-class black children who come into the classroom have a well-developed sense of language and its power to pass on information and to control interpersonal relationships; but

the children derive this language skill not from social interaction with adults (with whom they have been taught to be silent) so much as with other children. This situation is dictated by the custom of care, in which younger children are placed in the care of older ones; it is also assisted by the practice of street play which has older children teaching the younger both verbal and motor play routines. In this milieu, children learn the power of words in the development of their sense of self. They learn the importance of banter, the power of the taunt, the pleasure of playing with words. They develop vocabulary and other skills in active contest situations, for the purpose of winning a verbal game and gaining esteem from this group. If they have little informational exchange with adults, they have a great deal of language-learning play with fellow children, a factor usually ignored in the classroom. Indeed, Negro children find, when they go into school, that the language skills they have learned are in a tongue that is despised as substandard and performed in a manner that is regarded as hostile, obscene, or arrogant. They learn very quickly that the easiest way of getting by in the classroom is to be quiet—and so they are accused of being nonverbal. This derogation of language and language skills, furthermore, does little for the development of self-confidence.

[6]   If this weren't enough, even the best-intentioned language arts teachers commonly carry a further prejudice into the educational encounter with black pupils. It is firmly felt by them that reading is a skill that is the key to learning, that words are *things* that one must learn to recognize on the printed page or blackboard because such recognition will open up the repositories of knowledge, books. The often unconscious assumption made by these teachers is that all children will share the attitude that books are valuable things. But not only do most lower-class Negro children not share this feeling (since like most lower-class people most never encounter much reading material around the house or on the streets) but they don't commonly recognize words as things. Words to them are rather devices to be used in performances. Consequently, the argument that one must learn to read and then write in order to find one's way into the wonderful world of books is totally lost on children from such a background. They have not been concerned with the kinds of information contained in books, the kind that middle-class adults pass on to children, and that teachers expect to feed students.

[7]   But this does not mean that the lower-class black child brings no cultural resources into the classroom—they are just *different* resources. He brings a verbal skill, which, if recognized by the teacher, can be of considerable value in the devlopment of an understanding of language. But to capitalize upon this fund, the child must be allowed to speak, even if this violates the usual sense of decorum the teacher carries into class with her. The teacher must further learn to understand the communication system with which she is dealing, both as it relates to adult-child situations and to those between peers. Once this system is recognized it appears obvious (as it did to Herbert Kohl when he taught Harlem children) that one can teach writing by showing the children how much

more permanent and pleasurable are their verbal performances when written down. Once the value of words as records of speech events has been shown, the reading of other people's performances in book form will come naturally. By attacking the problem this way, the teacher will have served education in two ways. First, the child has been allowed to develop his own resources without having them exhibited as substandard; therefore he has been permitted to retain and develop his self-respect. Second, he has been taught to speak in an appropriate classroom manner (giving him a sense of the appropriateness of different kinds of language), then write, and then read, and he has thus been led to a point where he has been offered a cultural choice. He has learned to recognize alternatives and to make discretions, which I understand are the aims of our educational process. All of this has been achieved through a recognition of cultural variability on the part of the teacher. The only way this can be achieved, however, is through an understanding of the cultural heritage of the black children (and by this heritage, I *don't* mean spirituals or jazz, but those expressions of culture that the children know from their own immediate experience). The only way this cultural relativity can be learned is by breaking through the barriers to understanding erected by stereotyped thinking.

words and sentences

1. Vocabulary: *ethnocentric* (¶ 1); *creole, manqué* (2); *surrogate* (4); *milieu, derogation* (5); *decorum* (7).
2. Describe the structure of the first sentence in ¶ 5; then write a sentence imitating this pattern. Do the same for sentences four and five in ¶ 5.
3. Rewrite the last sentence in ¶ 7.

ideas and implications

1. How does Abrahams regard "standard" English? Why?
2. What prejudices of white elementary teachers is Abrahams dealing with? Why do these prejudices exist?
3. What relationship does Abrahams see between the language of black children and their "sense of self" (¶ 5)?
4. Abrahams believes that these black students speak a different language from white middle-class students. Why? How are black students' attitudes towards speech different?
5. According to Abrahams, what effect does the denigration of his language have upon the black child? Why?
6. How does stereotyping affect the way white teachers sometimes feel and think about black children and their language?

strategies

1. Describe the strategy of Abrahams's opening paragraph. Does the paragraph have a topic sentence?

2. What is the function of ¶ 2? Does Abrahams develop his idea in detail? Why or why not?
3. In ¶s 3-7, Abrahams argues for the differences in language and cultural backgrounds of black students. What are the major points of his argument and in what order does he present these points? Why might he postpone using the word *stereotyping* until the seventh paragraph?
4. What is the purpose of the parenthetical comment in the next-to-the last sentence in ¶ 7?

suggestions for writing

1. Write a paper about an occasion when you felt that your language or your use of language made you want to be silent or to be ashamed of yourself.
2. Write a paper about a situation in which you stereotyped another person or were stereotyped by another person. Try to discover the reasons for this stereotyping.
3. In his opening paragraph, Abrahams refers to "them" and by implication to "us." Write a paper in which you view a problem through the eyes of one group; then rewrite the paper trying to see the same problem from another vantage point.
4. Write a paper about a situation in which you or someone you know used language unconsciously to hurt another person.

Claude Brown

The Language of Soul

[1]   Perhaps the most soulful word in the world is "nigger." Despite its very definite fundamental meaning (the Negro man), and disregarding the deprecatory connotation of the term, "nigger" has a multiplicity of nuances when used by soul people. Dictionaries define the term as being synonymous with Negro, and they generally point out that it is regarded as a vulgar expression. Nevertheless, to those of chitlins-and-neck-bones background the word nigger is neither a synonym for Negro nor an obscene expression.
[2]   "Nigger" has virtually as many shades of meaning in Colored English as the demonstrative pronoun "that," prior to application to a noun. To some Americans of African ancestry (I avoid using the term Negro whenever feasible, for fear of offending the Brothers X, a pres-

sure group to be reckoned with), nigger seems preferable to Negro and has a unique kind of sentiment attached to it. This is exemplified in the frequent—and perhaps even excessive—usage of the term to denote either fondness or hostility.

[3]   It is probable that numerous transitional niggers and even established ex-soul brothers can—with pangs of nostalgia—reflect upon a day in the lollipop epoch of lives when an adorable lady named Mama bemoaned her spouse's fastidiousness with the strictly secular utterance: "Lord, how can one nigger be so hard to please?" Others are likely to recall a time when that drastically lovable colored woman, who was forever wiping our noses and darning our clothing, bellowed in a moment of exasperation: "Nigger, you gonna be the death o' me." And some of the brethren who have had the precarious fortune to be raised up, wised up, thrown up or simply left alone to get up as best they could, on one of the nation's South Streets or Lenox Avenues, might remember having affectionately referred to a best friend as "My nigger."

[4]   The vast majority of "back-door Americans" are apt to agree with Webster—a nigger is simply a Negro or black man. But the really profound contemporary thinkers of this distinguished ethnic group—Dick Gregory, Redd Foxx, Moms Mabley, Slappy White, etc.—are likely to differ with Mr. Webster and define nigger as "something else"—a soulful "something else." The major difference between the nigger and the Negro, who have many traits in common, is that nigger is the more soulful.

[5]   Certain foods, customs and artistic expressions are associated almost solely with the nigger: collard greens, neck bones, hog maws, black-eyed peas, pigs' feet, etc. A nigger has no desire to conceal or disavow any of these favorite dishes or restrain other behavioral practices such as bobbing his head, patting his feet to funky jazz, and shouting and jumping in church. This is not to be construed that all niggers eat chitlins and shout in church, nor that only niggers eat the aforementioned dishes and exhibit this type of behavior. It is to say, however, that the soulful usage of the term nigger implies all of the foregoing and considerably more.

[6]   The Language of Soul—or, as it might also be called, Spoken Soul or Colored English—is simply an honest vocal portrayal of black America. The roots of it are more than three hundred years old.

[7]   Before the Civil War there were numerous restrictions placed on the speech of slaves. The newly arrived Africans had the problem of learning to speak a new language, but also there were inhibitions placed on the topics of the slaves' conversation by slave masters and overseers. The slaves made up songs to inform one another of, say, the underground railroads' activity. When they sang *Steal Away* they were planning to steal away to the North, not to heaven. Slaves who dared to speak of rebellion or even freedom usually were severely punished. Consequently, Negro slaves were compelled to create a semi-clandestine vernacular in the way that the criminal underworld has historically created words to confound law-enforcement agents. It is said that numerous Negro spirituals were inspired by the hardships of slavery, and that what

later became songs were initially moanings and coded cotton-field lyrics.
To hear these songs sung today by a talented soul brother or sister or
by a group is to be reminded of an historical spiritual bond that cannot
be satisfactorialy described by the mere spoken word.

[8]   The American Negro, for virtually all of his history, has constituted a vastly disproportionate number of the country's illiterates.
Illiteracy has a way of showing itself in all attempts at vocal expression
by the uneducated. With the aid of colloquialisms, malapropisms, battered and fractured grammar, and a considerable amount of creativity,
Colored English, the sound of soul, evolved.

[9]   The progress has been cyclical. Often terms that have been dis-
carded from the soul people's vocabulary for one reason or another are
reaccepted years later, but usually with completely different meaning. In
the Thirties and Forties "stuff" was used to mean vagina. In the middle
Fifties it was revived and used to refer to heroin. Why certain expressions
are thus reactivated is practically an indeterminable question. But it is
not difficult to see why certain terms are dropped from the soul language.
Whenever a soul term becomes popular with whites it is common practice
for the soul folks to relinquish it. The reasoning is that "if white people
can use it, it isn't hip enough for me." To many soul brothers there is
just no such creature as a genuinely hip white person. And there is
nothing more detrimental to anything hip than to have it fall into the
square hands of the hopelessly unhip.

[10]   White Americans wrecked the expression "something else." It was
bad enough that they couldn't say "sump'n else," but they weren't even
able to get out "somethin' else." They had to go around saying *something
else* with perfect or nearly perfect enunciation. The white folks invariably
fail to perceive the soul sound in soulful terms. They get hung up in
diction and grammar, and when they vocalize the expression it's no
longer a soulful thing. In fact, it can be asserted that spoken soul is more
of a sound than a language. It generally possesses a pronounced lyrical
quality which is frequently incompatible to any music other than that
ceaseless and relentlessly driving rhythm that flows from poignantly
spent lives. Spoken soul has a way of coming out metered without the
intention of the speaker to invoke it. There are specific phonetic traits.
To the soulless ear the vast majority of these sounds are dismissed as incorrect usage of the English language and, not infrequently, as speech
impediments. To those so blessed as to have had bestowed upon them at
birth the lifetime gift of soul, these are the most communicative and
meaningful sounds ever to fall upon human ears: the familiar "mah" instead of "my," "gonna" for "going to," "yo" for "your." "Ain't" is pronounced "ain' "; "bread" and "bed," "bray-ud" and "bay-ud"; "baby" is
never "bay-bee" but "bay-buh"; Sammy Davis Jr. is not "Sammee" but
a kind of "Sam-eh"; the same goes for "Eddeh" Jefferson. No matter how
many "man's" you put into your talk, it isn't soulful unless the word has
the proper plaintive, nasal "maee-yun."

[11]   Spoken soul is distinguished from slang primarily by the fact that
the former lends itself easily to conventional English, and the latter is

diametrically opposed to adaptations within the realm of conventional English. Police (pronounced pō'lice) is a soul term, whereas "The Man" is merely slang for the same thing. Negroes seldom adopt slang terms from the white world and when they do the terms are usually given a different meaning. Such was the case with the term "bag." White racketeers used it in the Thirties to refer to the graft that was paid to the police. For the past five years soul people have used it when referring to a person's vocation, hobby, fancy, etc. And once the appropriate term is given the treatment (soul vocalization) it becomes soulful.

[12] However, borrowings from spoken soul by white men's slang—particularly teen-age slang—are plentiful. Perhaps because soul is probably the most graphic language of modern times, everybody who is excluded from Soulville wants to usurp it, ignoring the formidable fettering to the soul folks that has brought the language about. Consider "uptight," "strung-out," "cop," "boss," "kill 'em," all now widely used outside Soulville. Soul people never question the origin of a slang term; they either dig it and make it a part of their vocabulary or don't and forget it. The expression "uptight," which meant being in financial straits, appeared on the soul scene in the general vicinity of 1953. Junkies were very fond of the word and used it literally to describe what was a perpetual condition with them. The word was pictorial and pointed; therefore it caught on quickly in Soulville across the country. In the early Sixties when "uptight" was on the move, a younger generation of soul people in the black urban communities along the Eastern Seaboard regenerated it with a new meaning: "everything is cool, under control, going my way." At present the term has the former meaning for the older generation and the latter construction for those under thirty years of age.

[13] It is difficult to ascertain if the term "strung-out" was coined by junkies or just applied to them and accepted without protest. Like the term "uptight" in its initial interpretation, "strung-out" aptly described the constant plight of the junkie. "Strung-out" had a connotation of hopeless finality about it. "Uptight" implied a temporary situation and lacked the overwhelming despair of "strung-out."

[14] The term "cop" (meaning "to get") is an abbreviation of the word "copulation." "Cop," as originally used by soulful teen-agers in the early Fifties, was deciphered to mean sexual coition, nothing more. By 1955 "cop" was being uttered throughout national Soulville as a synonym for the verb "to get," especially in reference to illegal purchases, drugs, pot, hot goods, pistols, etc. ("Man, where can I cop now?") But by 1955 the meaning was all-encompassing. Anything that could be obtained could be "copped."

[15] The word "boss," denoting something extraordinarily good or great, was a redefined term that had been popular in Soulville during the Forties and Fifties as a complimentary remark from one soul brother to another. Later it was replaced by several terms such as "groovy," "tough," "beautiful," and, most recently, "out of sight." This last expression is an outgrowth of the former term "way out," the meaning of which was

equivocal. "Way out" had an ad hoc hickish ring to it which made it intolerably unsoulful and consequently it was soon replaced by "out of sight," which is also likely to experience a relatively brief period of popular usage. "Out of sight" is better than "way out," but it has some of the same negative, childish taint of its predecessor.

[16]   The expression, "kill 'em," has neither a violent nor a malicious interpretation. It means "good luck," "give 'em hell," or "I'm pulling for you," and originated in Harlem from six to nine years ago.

[17]   There are certain classic soul terms which, no matter how often borrowed, remain in the canon and are reactivated every so often, just as standard jazz tunes are continuously experiencing renaissances. Among the classical expressions are: "solid," "cool," "jive" (generally as a noun), "stuff," "thing," "swing" (or "swinging"), "pimp," "dirt," "freak," "heat," "larceny," "busted," "okee doke," "piece," "sheet" (a jail record), "squat," "square," "stash," "lay," "sting," "mire," "gone," "smooth," "joint," 'blow," "play," "shot," and there are many more.

[18]   Soul language can be heard in practically all communities throughout the country, but for pure, undiluted spoken soul one must go to Soul Street. There are several. Soul is located at Seventh and "T" in Washington, D.C.; on One Two Five Street in New York City; on Springfield Avenue in Newark; on South Street in Philadelphia; on Tremont Street in Boston; on Forty-seventh Street in Chicago; on Fillmore in San Francisco, and dozens of similar locations in dozens of other cities.

[19]   As increasingly more Negroes desert Soulville for honorary membership in the Establishment clique, they experience a metamorphosis, the repercussions of which have a marked influence on the young and impressionable citizens of Soulville. The expatriates of Soulville are often greatly admired by the youth of Soulville, who emulate the behavior of such expatriates as Nancy Wilson, Ella Fitzgerald, Eartha Kitt, Lena Horne, Diahann Carroll, Billy Daniels, or Leslie Uggams. The result—more often than not—is a trend away from spoken soul among the young soul folks. This abandonment of the soul language is facilitated by the fact that more Negro youngsters than ever are acquiring college educations (which, incidentally, is not the best treatment for the continued good health and growth of soul); integration and television, too, are contributing significantly to the gradual demise of spoken soul.

[20]   Perhaps colleges in America should commence to teach a course in spoken soul. It could be entitled the Vocal History of Black America, or simply Spoken Soul. Undoubtedly there would be no difficulty finding teachers. There are literally thousands of these experts throughout the country whose talents lie idle while they await the call to duty.

[21]   Meanwhile the picture looks dark for soul. The two extremities in the Negro spectrum—the conservative and the militant—are both trying diligently to relinquish and repudiate whatever vestige they may still possess of soul. The semi-Negro—the soul brother intent on gaining admission to the Establishment even on an honorary basis—is anxiously embracing and assuming conventional English. The other extremity, the Ultra-Blacks, are frantically adopting everything from a Western

version of Islam that would shock the Caliph right out of his snugly fitting shintiyan to anything that vaguely hints of that big, beautiful, bountiful black bitch lying in the arms of the Indian and Atlantic Oceans and crowned by the majestic Mediterranean Sea. Whatever the Ultra-Black is after, it's anything but soulful.

words and sentences

1. Vocabulary: *deprecatory, nuances, chitling* (¶ 1); *fastidiousness, secular, precarious* (3); *clandestine, vernacular* (7); *poignantly, plaintive* (10); *usurp, fettering* (12); *equivocal* (15); *canon* (17); *metamorphosis, expatriates* (19); *repudiate, vestige* (21).
2. Describe the structure of the sentences in ¶ 6; then write a paragraph imitating these patterns. Do the same for the three sentences in ¶ 8. Pay particular attention to the last sentence in ¶ 8. Is the sentence loose or periodic? What effect has Brown gained from structuring his paragraph as he has?

ideas and implications

1. Why does Brown regard the dictionary definition of "nigger" insufficient? Describe the contexts in which Brown re-defines the word.
2. Why is pronunciation so important to the Language of Soul? Does Brown believe that he is reproducing these sounds accurately on the printed page? Why or why not?
3. How important is the Language of Soul in establishing the identity of its speakers? Why?
4. What is the relationship between Spoken Soul and slang? How are they different?
5. When Brown says that the development of Soul has been cyclical (¶ 9), what does he mean?
6. Brown lists the expatriates of Soulville in ¶ 19. Why does he regard them as expatriates? What are the implications of this word as he uses it to describe the people on his list?
7. What is Brown's attitude towards the Language of Soul? How does he see its prospects for the future? Why?

strategies

1. What is the purpose of the first five paragraphs of Brown's essay? What strategies does he use to achieve this purpose?
2. What are the functions of ¶ 6?
3. ¶s 7-17 comprise the center of Brown's essay. How has Brown presented his ideas about the Language of Soul in these paragraphs? In what direction does his presentation move?
4. What method of development does Brown use in ¶ 11?
5. What method of development does Brown use in ¶ 17? Why does this method seem particularly appropriate in the context of the preceding paragraphs?

6. What are the functions of ¶ 18? Does it look back to the preceding paragraphs or ahead to the concluding paragraphs?

7. What is the purpose of ¶s 19-21? How do these paragraphs recall the opening sentence of ¶ 9?

suggestions for writing

1. Write a paper about a person or a group of persons who identify themselves by using language in a special way.

2. Using Brown's treatment of the word "nigger" as a model, select a word you use frequently and write a paper showing how the dictionary definition is inadequate.

3. Brown mentions the word "hip" in ¶ 9. Write your own extended definition of this word.

4. If you know about "the two extremities in the Negro spectrum" (¶ 21), write a paper about one of these groups and the way their use of language reflects their attitudes and beliefs.

Vine Deloria, Jr.

Indian Humor

[1]   One of the best ways to understand a people is to know what makes them laugh. Laughter encompasses the limits of the soul. In humor life is redefined and accepted. Irony and satire provide much keener insights into a group's collective psyche and values than do years of research.

[2]   It has always been a great disappointment to Indian people that the humorous side of Indian life has not been mentioned by professed experts on Indian Affairs. Rather the image of the granite-faced grunting redskin has been perpetuated by American mythology.

[3]   People have little sympathy with stolid groups. Dick Gregory did much more than is believed when he introduced humor into the Civil Rights struggle. He enabled non-blacks to enter into the thought world of the black community and experience the hurt it suffered. When all people shared the humorous but ironic situation of the black, the urgency and morality of Civil Rights was communicated.

[4]   The Indian people are exactly opposite of the popular stereotype. I sometimes wonder how anything is accomplished by Indians because of the apparent overemphasis on humor within the Indian world. Indians have found a humorous side of nearly every problem and the experiences

of life have generally been so well defined through jokes and stories that they have become a thing in themselves.

[5]   For centuries before the white invasion, teasing was a method of control of social situations by Indian people. Rather than embarrass members of the tribe publicly, people used to tease individuals they considered out of step with the consensus of tribal opinion. In this way egos were preserved and disputes within the tribe of a personal nature were held to a minimum.

[6]   Gradually people learned to anticipate teasing and began to tease themselves as a means of showing humility and at the same time advocating a course of action they deeply believed in. Men would depreciate their feats to show they were not trying to run roughshod over tribal desires. This method of behavior served to highlight their true virtues and gain them a place of influence in tribal policy-making circles

[7]   Humor has come to occupy such a prominent place in national Indian affairs that any kind of movement is impossible without it. Tribes are being brought together by sharing humor of the past. Columbus jokes gain great sympathy among all tribes, yet there are no tribes extant who had anything to do with Columbus. But the fact of white invasion from which all tribes have suffered has created a common bond in relation to Columbus jokes that gives a solid feeling of unity and purpose to the tribes.

[8]   The more desperate the problem, the more humor is directed to describe it. Satirical remarks often circumscribe problems so that possible solutions are drawn from the circumstances that would not make sense if presented in other than a humorous form.

[9]   Often people are awakened and brought to a militant edge through funny remarks. I often counseled people to run for the Bureau of Indian Affairs in case of an earthquake because nothing could shake the BIA. And I would watch as younger Indians set their jaws, determined that they, if nobody else, would shake it. We also had a saying that in case of fire call the BIA and they would handle it because they put a wet blanket on everything. This also got a warm reception from people.

[10]   Columbus and Custer jokes are the best for penetration into the heart of the matter, however. Rumor has it that Columbus began his journey with four ships. But one went over the edge so he arrived in the new world with only three. Another version states that Columbus didn't know where he was going, didn't know where he had been, and did it all on someone else's money. And the white man has been following Columbus ever since.

[11]   It is said that when Columbus landed, one Indian turned to another and said, "Well, there goes the neighborhood." Another version has two Indians watching Columbus land and one saying to the other, "Maybe if we leave them alone they will go away." A favorite cartoon in Indian country a few years back showed a flying saucer landing while an Indian watched. The caption was "Oh, no, not again."

[12]   The most popular and enduring subject of Indian humor is, of course, General Custer. There are probably more jokes about Custer and

the Indians than there were participants in the battle. All tribes, even those thousands of miles from Montana, feel a sense of accomplishment when thinking of Custer. Custer binds together implacable foes because he represented the Ugly American of the last century and he got what was coming to him.

[13] Some years ago we put out a bumper sticker which read "Custer Died for Your Sins." It was originally meant as a dig at the National Council of Churches. But as it spread around the nation it took on additional meaning until everyone claimed to understand it and each interpretation was different.

[14] Originally, the Custer bumper sticker referred to the Sioux Treaty of 1868 signed at Fort Laramie in which the United States pledged to give free and undisturbed use of the lands claimed by Red Cloud in return for peace. Under the covenants of the Old Testament, breaking a covenant called for a blood sacrifice for atonement. Custer was the blood sacrifice for the United States breaking the Sioux treaty. That, at least originally, was the meaning of the slogan.

[15] Custer jokes, however, can barely be categorized, let alone sloganized. Indians say that Custer was well-dressed for the occasion. When the Sioux found his body after the battle, he had on an Arrow shirt.

[16] Many stories are derived from the details of the battle itself. Custer is said to have boasted that he could ride through the entire Sioux nation with his Seventh Cavalry and he was half right. He got half-way through.

[17] One story concerns the period immediately after Custer's contingent had been wiped out and the Sioux and Cheyennes were zeroing in on Major Reno and his troops several miles to the south of the Custer battlefield.

[18] The Indians had Reno's troopers surrounded on a bluff. Water was scarce, ammunition was nearly exhausted, and it looked like the next attack would mean certain extinction.

[19] One of the white soldiers quickly analyzed the situation and shed his clothes. He covered himself with mud, painted his face like an Indian, and began to creep toward the Indian lines.

[20] A Cheyenne heard some rustling in the grass and was just about to shoot.

[21] "Hey, chief," the soldier whispered, "don't shoot, I'm coming over to join you. I'm going to be on your side."

[22] The warrior looked puzzled and asked the soldier why he wanted to change sides.

"Well," he replied, "better red than dead."

[24] Custer's Last Words occupy a revered place in Indian humor. One source states that as he was falling mortally wounded he cried, "Take no prisoners!" Other versions, most of them off color, concentrate on where those **** Indians are coming from. My favorite last saying pictures Custer on top of the hill looking at a multitude of warriors charging up the slope at him. He turns resignedly to his aide and says, "Well, it's better than going back to North Dakota."

[25] Since the battle it has been a favorite technique to boost the

numbers on the Indian side and reduce the numbers on the white side so that Custer stands out as a man fighting against insurmountable odds. One question no pseudo-historian has attempted to answer, when changing the odds to make the little boy in blue more heroic, is how what they say were twenty thousand Indians could be fed when gathered into one camp. What a tremendous pony herd must have been gathered there, what a fantastic herd of buffalo must have been nearby to feed that amount of Indians, what an incredible source of drinking water must have been available for fifty thousand animals and some twenty thousand Indians!

[26] Just figuring water-needs to keep that many people and animals alive for a number of days must have been incredible. If you have estimated correctly, you will see that the Little Big Horn was the last great *naval* engagement of the Indian wars.

[27] The Sioux tease other tribes a great deal for not having been at the Little Big Horn. The Crows, traditional enemies of the Sioux, explain their role as Custer's scouts as one of bringing Custer where the Sioux could get at him! Arapahos and Cheyennes, allies of the Sioux in that battle, refer to the time they "bailed the Sioux out" when they got in trouble with the cavalry.

[28] Even today variations of the Custer legend are bywords in Indian country. When an Indian gets too old and becomes inactive, people say he is "too old to muss the Custer anymore."

words and sentences

1. Vocabulary: *stolid* (¶ 3); *depreciate* (6); *extant* (7); *circumscribe* (8); *implacable* (12); *covenants, atonement* (14).
2. Describe the patterns of the sentences of ¶ 5; then write a paragraph imitating these sentence patterns. Then rewrite your own sentences to eliminate needless words.
3. Describe the pattern of the last sentence in ¶ 2; then write a sentence imitating that pattern. Now rewrite the sentence changing the voice of the verb. Which voice verb seems more effective?

ideas and implications

1. What stereotype must Deloria deal with before he can develop his ideas about Indian humor? Why?
2. Why does Deloria say that people have little sympathy with "stolid groups"?
3. According to Deloria, what was the purpose of teasing in Indian cultures?
4. Why does Deloria argue that understanding a people's humor and irony is sometimes more valuable than years of research?

strategies

1. What are the purposes of ¶s 1-10? Why do these paragraphs precede the actual discussion of Indian jokes?

2. Why does Deloria discuss Dick Gregory's contributions to the Civil Rights Movement?
3. Paragraph 10 changes the direction of Deloria's discussion. What strategy does Deloria use to present his ideas in ¶s 10-28?

suggestions for writing

1. Deloria says (¶ 1), "One of the best ways to understand a people is to know what makes them laugh." The same might be said of individuals. Write a paper characterizing a person you know well by describing what makes him laugh. Or write a self-portrait telling what makes you laugh.
2. Write a paper telling a humorous story.
3. Write a paper about a situation in which humor helped you redefine or accept life.
4. Write a paper about stereotypes of American Indians in movies and books.

Art Buchwald

Virgin Power

[1]   There have been so many groups formed lately to protect their sexual freedoms that little attention has been given to a new activist organization called the Virgin Anti-Defamation League.

The organization was started a few years ago by a small group of people who were sick and tired of virgins being the butt of every joke, every salacious comedy and every tired sexual cliché.

Sidney Pimpledown, the president of VADL, told me the response to the organization has been heartwarming. New chapters are springing up all over the country.

Pimpledown said, "We estimate that there are approximately 1,980,543 virgins in the United States at the present, including at least 1,200 women. These people have been led to believe that there is some sort of shame attached to being a virgin. We want virtuous people to be proud of their heritage. We point out that some of our greatest writers, poets and artists have been virgins. Even today, in some primitive cultures, there is a premium placed on virtue."

[5]   "Then one of your goals," I said, "is to bring virginity out in the open and get people to accept it for what it is?"

From Art Buchwald, *Getting High In Government Circles.* © 1968, 1970, 1971 by Art Buchwald. Reprinted by permission o. G. P. Putnam's Sons.

"That's correct. Until recently it was a dark secret one kept to himself. The majority of virgins refused to talk about it even to each other. But now, thanks to VADL, virgins know they are not alone, that there are almost two million people in the same boat with them. They are good people: Priests, college students, university professors, naval officers and even Avon ladies."

"Our job," Pimpledown continued, "is to convince them they are not the monsters society has made them out to be."

"What do you do besides make virgins feel they are not alone?"

"We have been lobbying for equal treatment for virgins. Do you realize a virtuous secretary makes twenty percent less salary than any other kind of secretary? Virgins are discriminated against in bars, at parties and even drive-in theaters."

[10] "We also," continued Pimpledown, "are demanding the employment of more virgins on television commercials. In the past, cast directors for TV commercials refused to hire virgins, as they were afraid the local TV stations would object, but when we proved to them that virgins were as good at performing on TV as anybody else, they changed their policy. It took time, but now all major advertisers include two virgins in their budgets."

"That. is a breakthrough," I said.

"Our main function is education," Pimpledown said. "We go on television and give our side of the story. For years the talk shows refused to book virgins on their programs. But there is a more enlightened view now. We even had a virgin on the Johnny Carson show last week, and they only received a hundred and fifty protest calls. Three years ago, if Carson had interviewed a virgin, the whole board would have lit up."

"You've come a long way," I told Pimpledown.

"We're starting to fight back. The militant arm of our organization is called Virgin Power. We've picketed movies with the word 'virgin' in the title. We've burned pornographic books that show virgins as weak, cringing people. And we've held sit-ins at city halls demanding virgins be permitted to get married."

[15] "Mr. Pimpledown, what do you consider your biggest success so far?"

"Without doubt," he said, "the biggest success we've had so far was getting the Department of Interior to stop referring to Alaska as 'virgin territory.' "

words and sentences

1. Vocabulary: *salacious* (¶ 2).
2. What are the implications of the word "primitive" in the last sentence of ¶ 4?
3. Describe the patterns of the sentences in ¶ 6; then write a paragraph imitating these sentence patterns. Note the sequence Buchwald employs in the last sentence of the paragraph. What is the effect of this

sequence? Does Buchwald use this technique more than once in his essay?

ideas and implications

1. Buchwald has a serious as well as a comic purpose in his essay. Describe these purposes as precisely as you can.
2. What is Buchwald's attitude towards stereotyping? What relationship does he see between language and stereotyping?
3. What seems to be Buchwald's attitude towards sexual freedom? Why?

strategies

1. Could Buchwald have made his point in straightforward expository prose? Why does he choose the strategy of presenting his ideas through an interview with Sidney Pimpledown?
2. What is the purpose of ¶s 1 and 2?
3. What effect do ¶s 15 and 16 have on Buchwald's depiction of VADL and Virgin Power? Why?
4. Could Buchwald be satirizing certain kinds of news and feature reporting as well as the group spokesman being interviewed?

suggestions for writing

1. Write a paper discussing to what extent a specific reform or protest movement is related to the problems of language in a society.
2. Conduct an interview—real or imaginary—with the leader of a campus reform or protest movement. Or any group, for that matter. Write your findings first as an expository paper; then rewrite the paper as a question-and-answer interview. Which strategy seems more effective for your presentation?
3. Select *one* of the following words and write a paper about the stereotypes associated with it: *bachelor, unmarried woman, career woman, widow, widower, lesbian, homosexual.*

Connie C. Eble

Some Broadminded Remarks on Language

[1]   Outside of the context of conversation about women's liberation or the role of women, try this riddle on some of your acquaintances.

Printed with permission of Connie C. Eble, from a speech given in April 1972.

A doctor in New Orleans has a brother who is a lawyer in Atlanta. But this same lawyer in Atlanta does not have a brother who is a doctor in New Orleans. How can that be?

You will be amazed at how few will immediately come up with the simple answer that the doctor in New Orleans is a woman and, therefore, is the sister, not the brother, of the lawyer in Atlanta. I have stumped members of a women's liberation group and even a professional woman whose own sister is a medical doctor with this riddle. Such response shows that the medical profession in America is so dominantly masculine that for most people the vocabulary item *doctor* operates in the language—and perhaps in thinking—exclusively as a masculine noun.

[2]   It is a fact that language reflects culture. It is also a fact that during the course of the development of the English language the male has been the dominant sex. It is not surprising, then, to find this situation of male dominance coded into the language, sometimes quite subtly. In this way the language reinforces the cultural pattern, very often unconsciously, and therefore can operate as an automatic and pervasive tool of sexual dominance. . . .

[3]   Since the English language does not have separate dialects for male and female and since the differentiation of sex in the third person pronouns is a meaningless commentary on sex status, how does English show signs of a long tradition of male dominance? By an accumulation of minor stylistic differences, a few grammatical and lexical features, and naming customs which all give preference to the male. Each of these is minor and inconclusive in itself, but taken together these linguistic features favor the male and, thus, reinforce the cultural bias.

[4]   *Stylistic differences.* That there are at least stylistic differences between the language of men and women seems to be universally admitted. Almost all cultures seem to have notions about how a woman should or does use the language. English speakers, for instance, are brought up with the impression that women speak quicker, more often, and for a longer length of time than men—and wind up saying less. Or that women have a much smaller vocabulary than men. Otto Jespersen's chapter "The Woman," in *Language: Its Nature, Development, and Origin,* is filled with such male-chauvinist-pig misconceptions as follows.[1]

> Those who want to learn a foreign language will, therefore, always do well at the first stage to read many ladies' novels, because they will there continually meet with just those everyday words and combinations which the foreigner is above all in need of, what may be termed the indispensable small-change of language.

[5]   Perhaps the most obvious difference between the language of women and men in our culture is the abundance of euphemisms and absence of swear words and obscenities in the speech of well-mannered women. Men have a language style, characterized by these very features, which is perfectly acceptable around men but which is not for "mixed company."

[1] P. 248.

Jokes and vocabulary which are permissible—even expected—among men are indications of coarseness and indiscretion when used by a woman of comparable social status. A woman who has borne four or five children and has changed thousands of soiled diapers is somehow less qualified to talk about sexual intercourse and defecation than an adolescent male with limited first-hand knowledge of these subjects.

[6]   Psychoanalyst Dr. Theodore Reik observes that the same expression can mean different things depending on the sex of the speaker. For example, the expression "You caught me with my pants down"

> has two meanings when uttered by a man and a woman. In the mouth of a man it denotes only that he was unpleasantly and unpreparedly surprised, was in a state of defenselessness and helplessness. When used by a woman, the same expression brings to mind the image of the lower part of her body.[2]

[7]   Dr. Reik also complains that in analytic sessions women patients speak of sexual matters very indirectly and delicately. There have traditionally been so many "unmentionables" for women in our culture that it is not surprising that women find it difficult to communicate with their analysts about sex or that American mothers have been notoriously bad in instructing their daughters about sex. Perhaps they haven't had the linguistic ability to convey the information readily. It is interesting that one of the most noticeable and often commented on characteristics of the new feminist revolution is the defiant and blatant use of "four-letter words."

[8]   *Use of masculine pronoun when sex of the referent is unknown or of both sexes.* The most noticeable evidence of male favoritism in the English language is the use of the masculine pronoun *he/him/his* in the third person singular when the sex of the referent is either unknown or a group of both males and females.

> (1) The taxpayer is responsible for *his* return.
> (2) Everyone must turn in *his* paper on time.

An alternative is to say:

> (1') The taxpayer is responsible for *his or her* own return.
> (2') Everyone must turn in *his or her* paper on time.

This circumlocution (notice *his* always comes before *her*) is often cumbersome, as in:

> (3) Every motorist must renew *his or her* license on *his or her* birthday.

[9]   In the initial issue of the magazine *MS.*, Kate Miller and Casey Swift propose the adoption of common gender third person singular pronouns to avoid the *his or her* awkwardness: [3]

2 Theodore Reik, "Men and Women Speak Different Languages," *Psychoanalysis* II (1954), 7.
3 Kate Miller and Casey Swift, "De-Sexing the English Language," *MS.* (Spring 1972), p. 7.

NOMINATIVE	tey	*to replace*	he and she
POSSESSIVE	ter(s)	"	his and her(s)
OBJECTIVE	tem	"	him and her

Unfortunately, artificial interventions into the grammatical system of a language rarely work out. However, the solution may be found in extending the plural forms—which do not show sex distinctions—into the singular. This is already well under way in expressions which are plural in notion but singular in form.

(4) Everyone will pay their own way.
(5) Each student wants their grades mailed to them.

It is also not difficult for English speakers to use the plural *they/them/their* in situations in which the referent is anonymous.

(6) In Switzerland *they* have clean streets.

So why not use *they/them/their* instead of the masculine pronoun when the sex of the referent is either unknown or a group of both males and females?

[10] *Generic use of the word 'man'.* Another area in which the male gets the edge is in the generic use of the term *man*. *Man* can mean either 'human being' or 'male member of the human race'. Many languages have separate vocabulary items for these two meanings, and indeed, English did at one time. In Old English *guma*, which has now been lost, meant 'male', and *mann* most often meant 'human being'. The alternatives to using *man* generically are to use *person, people, human being,* etc., all of which are more phonologically complex than *man* and therefore less likely to catch on. Used generically, then, the word *man* can apply to women—which sometimes gives a comic effect. A student newspaper reported about Grace Murray Hopper that "*She* was the first recipient of the 'Computer Sciences *Man* of the Year Award.'" And Humphrey Bogart, in *The Maltese Falcon*, pronounced, "You're a good *man, sister.*"

[11] We use a masculine noun in many common expressions—*man of letters, Renaissance man, man about town, Master of Arts.* But how about *woman of letters* or *Renaissance woman?* And *woman about town* or *Mistress of Arts* would certainly cause a few raised eyebrows.

[12] *Vocabulary.* The English language, like any language, needs lexical items to denote female referents. It is interesting to look at the origin of these terms; most are derivatives from the male counterpart.

[13] *Woman,* from Old English *wif + mann,* is a compound whose parts are no longer apparent—although spelling makes the element *man/men* identifiable. The term *lady* originally meant 'bread kneader,' a formation which identified her in relation to the *lord,* which meant 'bread guardian.' The word *female* has been altered over the years to look and sound like a derivative of *male,* although when originally borrowed from French into Middle English as *femelle,* the root *fem-* meant 'woman' and the suffix *-elle* meant '*little.*'

[14] English also forms feminines from masculines by means of deriva-

tional suffixes, primarily *-ess: author, authoress; baron, baroness; count, countess; host, hostess; prince, princess; proprietor, proprietress; sculptor, sculptress.* Notice the change in connotation from masculine to feminine in the pair *master, mistress.*

[15]   One glaring exception in which the masculine is derived from the feminine is *widow, widower.* It is not surprising, though, in a male-oriented society in which a woman's identity is through her husband that the condition of deprivation of a husband is primary.

[16]   Many words, especially those referring to a profession, have come to be associated with one sex or the other for cultural rather than formal or linguistic reasons. But once we associate one sex with the meaning of the word, it becomes a semantic feature of the word for us and can influence our thinking. The following are masculine for most speakers of English: *baker, bishop, chef, dentist, detective, doctor, judge, lawyer, minister, sailor, shoemaker.* These words have no female counterpart, so we must resort to such circumlocutions as *lady-dentist* or such offensive derived forms as *sailorette.* On the other hand, the words *nurse, dressmaker,* and *milliner* are feminine; the male equivalents are *male-nurse, tailor,* and *hat maker* or *hatter.*

[17]   Pejorative terms for females seem to be in much greater abundance than pejorative terms for males. The terms *hussy* and *whore* are female terms which are the products of pejoration. *Hussy* is from 'house wife'; *whore* is from the same root as *charity* and originally meant 'dear.' Sometimes an equivalent male term exists but is seldom used; *witch* is in common use, whereas *warlock* isn't—as if women have cornered the market on potions and evil spells. The word *nymphomania* is frequently tossed about in casual conversation, yet the male counterpart *satyriasis* is almost unknown. English has a proliferation of synonyms for *prostitute* yet hardly one satisfactory vocabulary item for the male counterpart, except perhaps the borrowed word *gigolo.*

[18]   Very often casual and slang terms for women are taken from the animal world. It is true that men can be called by animal names, such as *dumb ox* or *jackass.* But the number of animal words used to refer exclusively to women, and usually in a derogatory manner, must be significant of a tendency to in some way regard women as animals: *biddie, bird, bitch, chick, chickadee, cow, harpie, shrew, turtle dove.*[4]

[19]   *Names and titles.*   Although we seldom think about it, many of the common surnames we hear every day are patronyms: *Johnson, Wilson, Nelson, Peterson, Richardson; McArthur, McDonald, McNeil, McMillan, McGregor; O'Donnell, O'Neal, O'Reilly, O'Connor.* As for given names, a girl child is frequently named after a male relative, sometimes using a feminizing suffix—*Paul: Paula, Pauline, Paulette.* Sometimes no attempt is made to feminize the name; I have known girls named *Peter* and *Michael.* A boy child, on the other hand, is seldom named for his mother. If he is, it is the mother's family name, like *Carter, Smith,* or *Wilson,*

---

[4] For an extensive treatment of pejorative terms, see "Abuse" in Germaine Greer, *The Female Eunuch* (1971). [Reprinted in the following selection in this volume.]

rather than her given name. We all know from "The Boy Named *Sue*" what misfortunes can befall a boy with a girl's given name. If a name is used for both sexes, there is often a difference in spelling: *Lynne, Lynn; Frances, Francis.*

[20] In our society the woman takes her husband's name and is thus identified according to her role in life as wife to John Smith. There are complicated rules of "etiquette" concerning how a woman who is single, divorced, or widowed should sign her name and be addressed. Amy Van-derbilt's *New Complete Book of Etiquette* (1967) advises that "when a married woman signs her name as an officer of a woman's organization she should use her social form of address, *Mrs. John Jones,* not *Mrs. Mary Jones.*" A divorcee is warned against using *Mrs. Mary Green* instead of the more proper *Mrs. Robertson Green,* the latter not her own name at all, but a combination of her father's name and her former husband's name. Furthermore, a married woman doctor is expected to forgo the title *Dr.* in favor of *Mrs.* socially, even though if her husband is a doctor he should retain his title.[5]

[21] In English we distinguish marital status in the titles of women, but not in the titles of men—showing how important it is for a woman to be chosen by a man and elevated from *Miss* to *Mrs.* Many of my students, unsure of my marital status, call me *Mrs.* because they think it would be less insulting to err in that direction. It's like calling a military officer General when not sure of his rank.

[22] A recent solution proposed to alleviate this discrepancy is the title *Ms.* for all women, regardless of marital status. The suggested pronuncia-tion is *miz,* which will probably not catch on because of its association with the speech of the South. The title, however, is catching on in writ-ing; I have received letters from book publishers, advertising agencies, and even my landlord addressed this way. This title is to be used with the woman's given name: *Ms. Geraldine Snodgrass,* not *Ms. Percival Snod-grass.* If the husband's name is used, the appropriate title is *Mrs.*

[23] Another form of address which favors males is the salutation of business letters. It vexes me to begin a letter to my insurance company or to a department store with *Dear Sir* or *Gentlemen,* when I know very well that a woman secretary (who is probably underpaid) is going to open, read, compose, and type the answer to me—without a *Sir* or a *Gentleman* ever seeing it.

[24] *Word Order.* The order is simple: male first.

> he and she / him and her / his and her(s)
> John and Mary
> Mr. and Mrs.
> man and woman
> male and female
> man and wife
> husband and wife

[5] *Amy Vanderbilt's New Complete Book of Etiquette* (1967), pp. 420, 577, 598.

This consistent procedure of putting male before female reinforces the supremacy of the male. The exception *ladies and gentlemen* is a condescending order in which the male, in a show of courtesy to the "weaker sex," permits ladies to go first.

[25]   *Proverbs.* The number of proverbs about women—especially about their cunning, guile, wastefulness, etc.—far outnumbers those about men in particular, not men generically. Children that grow up hearing such sayings are bound to be affected by it.

> A woman is only a woman, but a good cigar is a smoke.
> —R. Kipling

> Sir, a woman's preaching is like a dog walking on his hinder legs. It is not done well; but you are surprised to find it done at all.
> —Dr. Johnson

> Behind every successful man is a good woman.
> (underlining mine)

[26]   In conclusion, the English language does not show male dominance in any glaring or systematic way. Perhaps it would be better if it did, because then it would be easy to eradicate. But it is the cumulative effect of all these linguistic devices, over a period of years, which from the early stages of language acquistion undermines a girl's self-respect and bolsters a boy's ego.

words and sentences

1. Vocabulary: *pervasive* (¶ 2); *lexical* (3); *chauvinist* (4); *defecation* (5); *blatant* (7); *referent* (8); *circumlocutions* (16); *pejorative* (17); *alleviate* (22); *generically* (25).
2. Describe the pattern of the last sentence in ¶ 5; then write a sentence imitating that pattern. Do the same for the third sentence in ¶ 4. Comment on the function of the dash in that sentence. What effect does Eble gain by using the construction she has chosen?
3. Comment on the effectiveness of the title. How is Eble using the word "broadminded"?

ideas and implications

1. What does Eble mean by "cultural bias" (¶ 3)? How does this cultural bias affect the identities of girls and boys?
2. What is Eble's attitude towards the use of masculine and feminine pronouns? What solution does she recommend? Does she agree with Miller and Swift?
3. Why does Eble insist that male dominance occurs subtly and often unconsciously?
4. Can you list additional stylistic differences in the language of women and men? (See ¶s 4-7.)
5. What is the relationship between pejoratives referring to women and the problem of stereotyping?

6. What are the implications of Eble's observation in the first two sentences of ¶ 16? Can you think of other examples which might support her idea? Can you think of any examples which might disprove her argument?

7. Eble concludes that "the English language does not show male dominance in any glaring or systematic way," but that the cumulative effect of these subtle and unconscious linguistic devices is to undermine "a girl's self-respect" and bolster "a boy's ego." Comment on the implications of this statement.

strategies

1. Eble wrote her essay to be read before an audience. What evidence appears in the first three paragraphs to indicate the awareness of audience? Describe her audience.

2. How effective is Eble's opening strategy employing the riddle?

3. Where does Eble state her thesis? What is the function of the first three paragraphs of her essay?

4. Eble's strategy is to classify and then develop by details and examples the seven ways in which English asserts male dominance. What are those seven ways? How many paragraphs does she devote to each? Which of those seven seem most important to her? Why?

5. Eble uses italicized headings to indicate divisions in her essay. Are there other ways she might have indicated these divisions? If so, what?

6. Describe Eble's rhetorical stance.

suggestions for writing

1. Try Eble's riddle on several of your friends and then write a paper reporting your findings.

2. In ¶ 25, Eble lists ways that proverbs show attitudes towards women. Consult *Bartlett's Familiar Quotations* or a similar collection of sayings for other proverbs describing women. Then write a paper about your findings.

3. Collect several examples of advertising which appeals to female equality or to male dominance. Write a paper about what you find in these advertisements.

4. In ¶ 18, Eble discusses animal words used to characterize women and men. Using her list as a beginning point, write a paper about the use of such words to describe women and men.

5. Make a list of the names of members of your family—parents, sisters, brothers, grandparents, cousins, great-grandparents. You might want to check a dictionary for the meanings of these names. Then write a paper about names in your family.

6. Write a paper describing a situation in which you treated another person as a woman or a man rather than as an individual. Explore the implications of this situation as carefully as you can.

7. Write about a situation in which you were treated as a man or a woman rather than as an individual. Try to recover your feelings as a result of this episode.

Germaine Greer

Abuse
from *The Female Eunuch*

[1] On December 18, 1969, in the case of Regina *versus* Humphreys, Mr. Frisby Q.C. accused the defense of attempting to show that Miss Pamela Morrow, whom the defendant was charged with having raped, was a "flippertigibbit." [1] It seems incredible that twentieth-century lawyers should accuse a girl of being a foul fiend from hell, the same that rode upon poor Tom's back in *King Lear* and bit him so cruelly.[2] The meaning of the word has declined into a pale shadow of its former force, perhaps because of its indiscriminate use in witch-hunts, but its derivation remains a fact. The element of witch-hunt is never far from trials in which not quite virginal girls are required to give evidence against members of Parliament and there may have been more to Mr. Frisby's use of the term than he was aware, but we may follow this pattern of debilitation by indiscriminate use of terms of the greatest reprobation. The word *hag* used also to apply to a direct satanical manifestation of peculiar grisliness; now it simply means a woman who isn't looking her best. *Hag-ridden* meant the condition of a soul who had been tormented by diabolical spirits in his sleep, and not a husband who had been nagged at. The ineffectualness of the victims of such abuse eventually defused the terms of abuse themselves: *termagant* began its history in the *chansons de geste* as a word meaning a Muhammadan deity, now it too means a nagging woman. Indiscriminate application has weakened the force of *broad,* originally derived from *bawd,* and *hoyden, wanton, baggage,* and *fright* (originally a horrifying mask) as well as *tart,* which began as a cant term of affection, became insulting, and is now only mildly offensive.[3]

[2] Unfortunately the enfeeblement of abuse by hysterical overstatement is not the commonest phenomenon in the language of woman-hatred. Many more terms which originally applied to both men and women gained virulence by sexual discrimination. The word *harlot* did not become exclusively feminine until the seventeenth century. There is no male analogue for it in the era of the double standard. The word *bawd* applied to both sexes until after 1700, and the word *hoyden* is no longer applicable to men. Originally a *scold* was a Scots invective poet—now it means, pre-

1 *Evening News,* December 18, 1969.

2 William Shakespeare, *King Lear,* III. iv. 117–22 and IV. i. 62–3 (*op. cit.*), pp. 926, 930.

3 The sources for this section are mainly the *New English Dictionary* (Oxford); Wentworth and Flexner's *Dictionary of American Slang;* E. Partridge, *Smaller Slang Dictionary* (London, 1961); and Farmer and Henley, *Slang and Its Analogues* (London, 1890).

dictably, a nagging woman. *Witches* may be of either sex, but as a term of abuse *witch* is solely directed at women. A *chit* was originally the young of a beast, came to mean a child, and nowadays means a silly girl.

[3]   Class antagonism has had its effect on the vocabulary of female status. Lower-class distrust of airs and graces has resulted in the ironic applications of terms like *madam, lady, dame* and *duchess,* which is fair exchange for the loading of dialect names for women with contemptuous associations, as in *wench, quean, donah, dell, moll, biddy* and *bunter* (once a ragpicker, but now invariably a prostitute). The most recent case in which contempt for menial labor has devised a new term of abuse for women is the usage of *scrubber* for a girl of easy virtue. If such linguistic movements were to be charted comprehensively and in detail, we would have before us a map of the development of the double standard and the degradation of women. As long as the vocabulary of the cottage and the castle are separate, words like *wench* and *madonna* do not clash; when they do, both concepts suffer and woman is the loser. The more body-hatred grows, so that the sexual function is hated and feared by those unable to renounce it, the more abusive terms we find in the language.

[4]   When most lower-class girls were making a living as domestics, struggling to keep clear of the sexual exploitation of the males in the household, the language of reprobation became more and more concerned with lapses in neatness, which were taken to be the equivalent of moral lapses. The concept of sluttishness or slatternliness with its compound implication of dirt and dishonor gave rise to a great family of nasty words, like *drab, slut, slommack, slammerkin, traipse, malkin, trollop, draggletail.* The word *slattern* itself withdrew the male portion of its meaning and became exclusively feminine.

[5]   The most offensive group of words applied to the female population are those which bear the weight of neurotic male disgust for illicit or casual sex. The Restoration, which reaped the harvest of puritan abuse of gay women, invented a completely new word of unknown derivation to describe complaisant ladies, the ubiquitous *punk.* The imagery of venereal disease added a new dimension to the language: diseased women were *fireships, brimstone, laced mutton, blowens, bawdy baskets, bobtails,* although the vestiges of sensual innocence hung around long enough to endow us with obsolete terms like *bed-fagot, pretty horsebreaker,* as well as loving-ironic use of words like *whore* and *trull,* which were not always wholly bitter in their application. More familiar terms in current usage refer to women as receptacles for refuse, reflecting the evaluation that men put upon their own semen, as *tramp, scow, scupper,* or, most contemporary, the hideous transferred epithet *slag.* Even these words fade from vividness: women themselves use a term like *bag* indiscriminately, although they would recoil from the unequivocal original *douche-bag,* or rhyming slang *toe-rag.*

[6]   Perhaps words like *pig, pig-meat* or *dog* are inspired by the sadness which follows unsatisfactory sex: they too lose their efficacy from wide usage as the word *beast* did, and must constantly be replaced. The vocabulary of impersonal sex is peculiarly desolating. Who wants to "tear

off a piece of ass?" "get his greens?" "stretch a bit of leather?" "knock off a bit? of belly? of crumpet?" "have it away?"

[7]   It would be unbearable, but less so, if it were only the vagina that was belittled by terms like *meat, pussy, snatch, slit, crack* and *tail,* but in some hardboiled patois the woman herself is referred to as a *gash,* a *slot.* The poetical figure which indicates the whole by the part is sadly employed when indicating women as *skirts, frills, a bit of fluff* or a *juicy little piece.*

[8]   These terms are all dead, fleshy and inhuman, and as such easy to resent, but the terms of endearment addressed to women are equally soulless and degrading. The basic imagery behind terms like *honey, sugar, dish, sweety-pie, cherry, cookie, chicken* and *pigeon* is the imagery of food. If a woman is food, her sex organ is for consumption also, in the form of *honey-pot, hair-pie* and *cake-* or *jelly-roll.* There are the pretty toy words, like *doll* and *baby* or even *baby-doll.* There are the cute animal terms like *chick, bird, kitten* and *lamb,* only a shade of meaning away from *cow, bitch, hen, shrew, goose, filly, bat, crow, heifer,* and *vixen,* as well as the splendidly ambiguous expression *fox,* which emanates from the Chicago ghetto. The food terms lose their charm when we reflect how close they are to coarse terms like *fish, mutton, skate, crumpet,* a *bit on a fork, cabbage, greens, meat* and *bread,* terms more specifically applied to the female genitalia but often to the female herself. Who likes to be called *drygoods,* a *potato,* a *tomato,* or a *rutabaga?*

[9]   There used to be a fine family of words which described without reprobation or disgust women who lived outside the accepted sexual laws, but they have faded from current usage. Flatly contemptuous words like *kept-woman* and *call-girl* have taken over the field from *adventuress, woman of the world, woman of pleasure, mistress, inamorata, paramour, courtesan, mondaine.* When Frank Zappa launched the mythology of the *groupie* as high priestess of free love and the group grope, he meant the term to remain free from pejorative coloring,[4] but despite the enormous build-up less than six months later most of the women who hung around musicians treated the appellation as an insult. It is the fate of euphemisms to lose their function rapidly by association with the actuality of what they designate, so that they must be regularly replaced with euphemisms for themselves. It is not too farfetched to imagine that fiancée which commonly in the permissive society means *mistress* will itself become a taboo word unless ideology should miraculously catch up with behavior.

[10]   The most scathing vilification of immoral women does not come from men. The feminine establishment which sees its techniques of sexual bargaining jeopardized by the disregard of women who make themselves *cheap* is more vociferous in its condemnation. Too often the errant women abuse themselves with excessive shame and recrimination, degrading themselves more in their own estimation than they do by their behavior. The compulsiveness of this behavior is the direct result of repressiveness in education: women are drawn to sexual license because it seems forbidden

---

4 *Rolling Stone,* No. 27, February 15, 1969.

and exciting, but the price they pay for such delinquency is too heavy. The result is functional nymphomania, described in Nathan Schiff's *Diary of a Nymph*. A woman in this situation refuses to take responsibility for her own behavior and instead attributes her deeds to a paraself which takes over. She cannot choose between one sexual partner and another because her will is in abeyance, so that her course is set for self-destruction. Shiff's heroine Christine describes sex as filthy and low, and yearns to feel free from it to "be clean again." [5] The same self-denigrating syndrome appears in a type of letter which appears regularly in the correspondence columns of women's magazines. "I feel so low and ashamed . . ."; "I was so disgusted with myself I found I couldn't respond to my husband's love. Now it is worse. I have read about V.D. and am terrified I could have been infected . . ." "I have always loved my husband but three years ago I had a sordid affair which he forgave. . . . I have again been strongly tempted by another man . . ."; "I know it is impossible to change my past, but I have learned my lesson and regretted ever since what happened . . ." [6] None of the replying matriarchs inquires why the affair was so sordid, why it must be regretted, what lesson it was that was learnt, why shame is so disproportionate or what the woman is really describing when she speaks of temptation. Instead, all sagely counsel that the woman continue to accept her guilt and find expiation in renewed self-abnegation. In "true romance" stories women mercilessly vilify themselves for quite minor infractions of the sexual code—"It was so horrible I feel I shall never be clean again. Never. I'm too awful to live. I felt utterly ashamed. I hardly knew this man. How could I be so cheap?" [7]

[11]   For educated girls the most telling gibe is that of *promiscuity*, a notion so ill-defined that for practical purposes we must decide that a girl is promiscuous when she thinks herself to be so. Gael Greene's conversations with college girls revealed that while they tolerate sex between people who are "in love," any other kind was promiscuity, an imagined disease so powerful in its effects that according to Dr. Graham B. Blaine it is the commonest reason for their seeking psychiatric help.[8] Girls who pride themselves on their monogamous instincts have no hesitation in using the whole battery of sex-loathing terms for women who are not. They speak of the "campus punchboard" or "an old beat-up pair of shoes," revealing their unconscious fidelity to the notion that for women sex is *despoiling* and *using*.[9] The last word on the pernicious power of the notion of promiscuity was uttered by Jim Moran, battling the double standard in *Why Men Shouldn't Marry*: "Use of this word [promiscuity] has but one re-

---

5 Nathan Shiff, *Diary of a Nymph* (New York, 1961).

6 Letters to "Mary Grant," *Woman's Own*, July 19, 1969, and to "Evelyn Home," *Woman*, March 15, 1969, and to "Mary Marryat," *Woman's Weekly*, July 2, 1969.

7 "Love Needs No Words," *New Romance*, No. 3, November 1969, and "When Someone Needs You," *True Story*, No. 565, December 1969.

8 Gael Greene, *Sex and the College Girl* (London, 1969), p. 111, quoting a Queen's College Conference on Mental Health, reported in the *New York Times*, May 19, 1963.

9 *Ibid.*, pp. 45–6, and 111–3.

deeming feature. It identifies the user as a pro-virginity, problem-ridden, puritanical prunt." [10]

[12] Moran addressed his words chiefly to men: they ought to be more urgently heeded by women. If women are to be better valued by men they must value themselves more highly. They must not allow themselves to be seduced while in a state of self-induced moral paralysis, trusting to the good-will of the seducer so grudgingly served. They must not scurry about from bed to bed in a self-deluding and pitiable search for love, but must do what they do deliberately, without false modesty, shame or emotional blackmail. As long as women consider themselves sexual objects they will continue to writhe under the voiced contempt of men and, worse, to think of themselves with shame and scorn.

words and sentences

1. Vocabulary: *debilitation, reprobation, cant* (¶ 1); *hysterical, virulence* (2); *neurotic, ubiquitous* (5); *efficacy* (6); *patois* (7); *pejorative, appellation* (9); *vilification, vociferous, expiation, self-abnegation* (10); *pernicious* (11).
2. Describe the pattern of the first sentence in ¶ 9; then write a sentence imitating that pattern. Do the same for the first sentence of ¶ 12. Note Greer's use of the colon in this sentence.
3. In ¶ 11, Greer talks of the word *promiscuity*. Check this word in a dictionary and compare that definition with Greer's definition. How is Greer establishing a context for her definition?

ideas and implications

1. According to Greer, what effect has sexual discrimination and woman-hatred had on language since the seventeenth century?
2. How has the double standard of conduct influenced terms of abuse to describe women? What does Greer mean by the double standard?
3. How has class status affected the growth of terms of abuse for women?
4. Why does Greer consider many terms of endearment for women 'equally soulless and degrading"?
5. In what ways have women been responsible for the creation of language vilifying other women? How do some women degrade themselves more in their language than they do in their behavior?
6. What does the presence of so many terms of abuse suggest to Greer?
7. Who are the "replying matriarchs" Greer mentions in ¶ 9? What is her attitude towards them?
8. What relationship does Greer see between the language men and women use to think about themselves and the images they have of one another and themselves?

strategies

1. What is Greer's opening strategy? How effective is it? Does this opening

[10] Jim Moran, *Why Men Shouldn't Marry* (New York, 1970).

strategy help Greer place her observations in a context? Describe that context.

2. One of Greer's strategies is to show how words have changed their meaning. How does such evidence help her argue her point? Cite specific examples.
3. What is the purpose of ¶ 8? How is this paragraph related to ¶s 5-7?
4. What is the purpose of ¶ 9? Why has this "fine family of words" disappeared from the language?

suggestions for writing

1. From your own experience, write a paper describing a situation in which terms of abuse were used to describe a woman or a man. Does the language tell anything about its user?
2. Write a paper in which you show your own attitude or a friend's attitude towards women (or men) by the language used to describe others.
3. Write a paper about a situation in which you played the role of stereotyped "woman" or "man." Try to discover your reasons for playing that role.
4. Terms of abuse extend beyond the relationships between the sexes. Politics, sports, racial prejudice, and almost any part of our lives include terms of abuse. Select a specific situation from your experience where terms of abuse played an important role. Write a paper about this experience.
5. Make a list of terms of endearment familiar to you. Then examine the list of words to discover its implications.
6. Select a love poem you know well. Then look at the language of the poem to discover the implications of its terms of endearment.

Art Buchwald

What Not to Say

[1]   The Women's Liberation people take themselves very seriously, and well they might. It's very hard to say anything to them without getting them very mad. While I have no idea what you *should* say to someone in Women's Lib, here are some of the things you should *not* say:

"Well, now that you've got your college degree, I suppose you're going to find yourself a husband."

From Art Buchwald, *Getting High In Government Circles.* © 1968, 1970, 1971 by Art Buchwald. Reprinted by permission of G. P. Putnam's Sons.

"You ought to meet Hugh Hefner—he's your kind of guy."

"How do you like this picture of the sexy girl in a bathing suit?"

[5] "Have you heard the latest one about the woman driver who—"

"What's the name of your hairdresser?"

"I suppose if you take this job, you'll probably become pregnant."

"You women go in the other room. We'll stay here for cigars and cognac."

"Wouldn't you hate to be married to a man who makes as much money as you do?"

[10] "Here, let me light your cigarette for you."

"For a woman, you play very well."

"My mother always did something stupid like that herself."

"There's a gal in our office who is as good at selling as any man."

"Hey, look, there's a lady taxi driver!"

[15] "We'd be happy to let you in the press box—it's just that we don't have any lavatory facilities."

"Ha-ha-ha . . . A woman President, that's a good one. Ho-ho-ho."

"Would you like to go out to Ladies' Day at the ball park?"

"The thing I like about you the best is your legs."

"I met this woman doctor the other day, at the hospital, and she really seemed to know what she was doing."

[20] "What do you think about when you're having a baby?"

"I beg your pardon, ma'am. Is the head of the house home?"

"Would you like to feel my muscle?"

"Show me a woman who really likes working, and I'll show you a woman who likes other women."

"A penny for your thoughts."

[25] "Hi, how's the better half feeling?"

"Don't feel bad, I even know men who don't understand it."

"No, sit down and join us. We have nothing important to say."

"The newspaper just arrived. Would you like the women's page?"

"Listen, I'm the first one to admit women have gotten a raw deal, but the majority of them wouldn't have it any other way."

[30] "Meet me at the ladies' entrance of the club at five o'clock."

Any of the above statements can cause a Women's Lib backer to get uptight, but if you really want to see her climb the wall start singing:

"You've come a long way, baby,
"To get where you got to today.
"You've got your own cigarette now, baby,
"You've come a long, long way."

words and sentences

1. Comment on the following phrases: "head of the house" (¶ 21) and "better half" (¶ 25).
2. Select two of the items in Buchwald's list and try to rephrase the sen-

tence so that they would not offend Buchwald's idea of the "Women's Liberation people."

ideas and implications

1. Why does Buchwald focus upon what *not* to say rather than *what to say?*
2. Nearly all of the statements Buchwald lists have implicit in them stereo-typed notions about women. From the list, compile some of the qualities associated with these stereotypes.

strategies

1. Buchwald's strategy is simply to list. Is his list a random one or is there some sequence in it? How effective is his listing?
2. Buchwald concludes his remarks with the words from a cigarette commercial. Why is this conclusion particularly effective?

suggestions for writing

1. Compile your own list of what not to say to or about a group other than Women's Liberation. Then write an essay on the subject.
2. Select any one of Buchwald's statements and write a paper exploring the implications and assumptions of that statement.
3. Write a paper about what not to say to parents, to teachers, to girl-friends or boyfriends, etc.
4. Most of us have our lists of things we do not like to have said to us. Compile your list and then write a paper about yourself.

Sydney J. Harris

Soft Words Are Hard to Come by

[1]   It is a curious commentary on human nature—and on human speech, which reflects our nature—that we have so few words to designate good things, and so many to designate bad.

Flying home the other evening, I heard the pilot announce to the passengers, over the intercom: "There's no weather between here and Chicago."

By "no weather" he meant no bad weather. To aviation people, the mere word "weather" signifies a difficult condition; just as on the ground the mere word "traffic" often means a tieup.

From 'Sydney J. Harris, *Last Things First.* © 1961 by Sydney J. Harris. Reprinted by permission of the publisher, Houghton Mifflin Company.

If we think a man is a liar or a drunk or a cheat, we have scores of deprecatory words at our command; the English language (like any language) is rich in scornful epithets. But if we think he is an admirable person, we can only falter and fumble for words . . . and end up calling him "a good guy."

[5]   A nice day is just a nice day; everyone calls it that. But an un-nice day is mean, miserable, drab, ghastly, chilling, bitter, inhuman, depressing, and lots more. We are never at a loss to describe our negative feelings.

This explains, I think, why criticism often seems so much more harsh than it really means to be. When a critic likes a book or a play or a piece of music, he can only murmur a few conventionally grateful phrases. The vocabulary of approval is extremely limited, even among talented writers.

All criticism is therefore distortion, in some sense. Positive feelings, which come from the heart, are difficult and embarrassing to articulate; negative feelings (in which fear or anger or contempt have been aroused) pour forth with hardly any conscious manipulation. Not only do we express ourselves more vividly and vehemently in a negative way; but we obtain a greater enjoyment in hearing such criticism.

None of Wilde's or Shaw's or Dorothy Parker's generous comments have ever won wide currency; it is only their wittily devastating attacks that are repeated with relish. No critic has achieved eminence for kindness of heart.

This may be a pity (it is certainly an injustice) but it seems to be an inevitable part of the human condition. The most we can do is reach a private understanding with ourselves that all negative criticism (including our own) shall be discounted at 50 per cent on the emotional dollar.

words and sentences

1. Vocabulary: *deprecatory, epithets* (¶ 4).
2. Describe the pattern of the sentences in ¶ 1; then write a sentence imitating that pattern.
3. How important is it for Harris to establish the context for his remarks about the word *weather?* Why?

ideas and implications

1. What seems to be Harris's concept of "the human condition"? How does he make this attitude evident?
2. What are Harris's attitudes towards criticism? Why?
3. Would you agree with Harris that the language has more negative words than positive words? Why are positive feelings "embarrassing to articulate"?

strategies

1. Harris announces his thesis in the first paragraph. How does he develop this idea? By examples only?

suggestions for writing

1. Write a paper about a movie or a book that you admire. Try to avoid being mawkish or sentimental.
2. Write a paper about a person you admire. Again, try to avoid the sentimental.
3. Write a paper about a childhood hero or heroine you still admire.
4. Copy a poem or a passage that expresses a positive attitude towards its subject. Then write a paper examining how and why this positive attitude is successfully conveyed by the writer.
5. If you have ever owned a pet, write a paper about that pet and your feelings towards it.

6 Writers Making Words Work

INTRODUCTION

> True wit is nature to advantage dressed,
> What oft was thought, but ne'er so well expressed;
> Something, whose truth convinced at sight we find,
> That gives us back the image of our mind.
> —*Alexander Pope*

Not everyone agrees with Ludwig Wittgenstein that "The limits of my language are the limits of my world." Dreams submerged in our unconscious and images floating in our heads are not always expressed in words, yet these images and dreams may be part of our awareness even though they are unsaid. Philosophers and psychologists debate whether or not we understand these images and dreams until we say them. They do not agree. They do, however, agree that one avenue to our knowing is through words. Most of us have felt the truth of Pope's observations that writers frequently bring to life through words and images the feelings and thoughts we have experienced before, but have been unable to express until a writer does it for us. The readings in this section illustrate in poems, essays, and fiction ways that writers have tried to free their understanding and to share it with others— to give "us back the image of our mind."

The poets of the first group of readings try to give "us back the image of our mind" on a number of subjects. Nikki Giovanni tells about being a child, having dreams, and being Black. Theodore Roethke and Carolyn Kizer write about love—Roethke celebrating "a woman lovely in her bones," and Kizer talking of "love and lust" in "What the Bones Know." Emily Dickinson takes such diverse topics as bees, wild nights, and a walk along the beach with her dog, and turns these experiences into images that project her understanding. Anne Sexton begins her poetic version of "Red Riding Hood" with these lines: "Many are the deceivers." Her imaginings about Little Red Riding Hood are quite different from those of Perrault, Thurber, and Child Guidance Products (see introduction to Section 1). In "His Wonders to Perform," Charles David Wright remarks upon the fall of a sparrow and what that fall means to "doubtless alleycats below."

Michael "Doc" Hunt renders in verse his view of 1900 to 1909, from his unpublished "A Decade to Decade Look at the United States: 1776-1976." He catalogues historic events of the turn-of-the-century, noting ironically that "into each life some rain must fall."

In "Part xxi" from William R. Harmon's long poem *Treasury Holiday*, the speaker turns the phrase "a dirty mind" about in his head to see what it means. He concludes that some of the great men of letters—Chaucer, Shakespeare, Whitman, e e cummings and others—had dirty minds and that the society about which he writes misinterprets the meaning of the phrase.

In "anyone lived in a pretty how town," e e cummings tells the story of "anyone" and "noone," who meet, fall in love, live, and die. And W. H. Auden comments on life in our time by writing an epitaph for "An Unknown Citizen."

These writers send us images of the world from their minds in the compressed language of poetry, hoping to tell us something about themselves and ourselves.

The next group of readings is about people and places. In Chapter Seven from *The Grapes of Wrath*, John Steinbeck visits a used-car lot selling jalopies to Okies looking for a way to their Promised Land—California. Steinbeck gives us sights and sounds of the used-car lot to show the desperation of people uprooted from their land and the exploitation of these folks by the car dealers. Charles Dickens takes us on a tour of nineteenth-century "Gin-Shops," describing these places and their patrons. Dickens contrasts the splendor of the gin-shops with the "dirt and poverty of the surrounding neighborhood" to suggest that one reason "Gin-drinking is the great vice of England" is that drunkenness gives the people a chance to escape momentarily the "wretchedness and dirt" of their lives.

E. B. White finds meaning in the graceful movements of a circus bareback rider at the Ringling Brothers' winter camp at Sarasota, Fla., and following that circle of the circus bareback rider, he discovers resonances of meaning in "The Ring of Time." In "A Piece of Work for Now and Doomsday," Joan Didion tells how the image of Hoover Dam haunted her after her first visit and how she returned for a second visit "to find something about myself." On her second visit to the Dam, she discovers "the image I had always seen" and the reason that this image had dogged her. Annie Dillard sets out to catch the new season during a February walk in the woods, but finds instead an old snakeskin that was "whole and tied in a knot." The snakeskin sets her to thinking about the seasons and their meaning for people; she concludes that "time is a continuous loop" and that "catching the season" is more difficult than she had imagined.

Willie Morris and Samuel L. Clemens write autobiographically—Morris remembering his boyhood in Yazoo, Mississippi, and trying to make sense of where he was and where he is; Clemens recounting his days as a cub pilot on a Mississippi River steamboat and what the Great River came to mean to him.

Susan B. Lindsay's "A Neutral Zone" describes fictionally some difficulties of growing up. She tells a story about Jennifer Rhodes, a lonely child learning to spell and write so that she can compose a letter to her quarrelling parents. Jennifer hides her words in a folder in her treehouse until she can assemble enough of them to make her feelings known.

"*In principio erat Verbum*" begins the sermon of The Right Reverend John Big Bluff Tosamah in the passage from N. Scott Momaday's novel, *House Made of Dawn*. "In the beginning was the Word." This American Indian preacher looks at the white man's subjection to the word and says, "It may well be that he will perish by the Word." But he talks also about the connection between words and things that he believes must be recovered.

Words can imprison men and women to private despairs, but they can also free. The preacher in Momaday's story tells of his grandmother, a Kiowa woman who was a storyteller and who knew her way around words:

> When she told me those old stories, something strange and good and powerful was going on. I was a child, and that old woman was asking me to come directly into the presence of her mind and spirit; she was taking hold of my imagination, giving me to share in the great fortune of her wonder and delight. She was asking me to go with her to the confrontation of something that was sacred and eternal. It was a timeless, *timeless* thing; nothing of her old age or of my childhood came between us.

When words work, they break the isolation and emptiness to which we might otherwise be doomed.

Nikki Giovanni

Dreams

in my younger years
before i learned
black people aren't
suppose to dream
i wanted to be   5
a raelet
and say "dr o wn d in my youn tears"
or "tal kin bout tal king bout"
or margery hendricks and grind
all up against the mic   10
and scream
"baaaaaby nightandday
baaaaaby nightandday"

then as i grew and matured
i became more sensible   15
and decided i would
settle down
and just become
a sweet inspiration

Nikki Giovanni

Nikki-Rosa

childhood rememberances are always a drag
if you're Black
you always remember things like living in Woodlawn
with no inside toilet
and if you become famous or something   5
they never talk about how happy you were to have your mother
all to yourself and
how good the water felt when you got your bath from one of those
big tubs that folk in chicago barbecue in
and somehow when you talk about home   10
it never gets across how much you
understood their feelings
as the whole family attended meetings about Hollydale
and even though you remember
your biographers never understand   15
your father's pain as he sells his stock
and another dream goes
and though you're poor it isn't poverty that
concerns you
and though they fought a lot   20
it isn't your father's drinking that makes any difference
but only that everybody is together and you
and your sister have happy birthdays and very good christmasses
and I really hope no white person ever has cause to write about me
because they never understand Black love is Black wealth
      and they'll   25
probably talk about my hard childhood and never understand that
all the while I was quite happy

Theodore Roethke

I Knew a Woman

I knew a woman, lovely in her bones,
When small birds sighed, she would sigh back at them;
Ah, when she moved, she moved more ways than one:
The shapes a bright container can contain!
Of her choice virtues only gods should speak,   5
Or English poets who grew up on Greek
(I'd have them sing in chorus, cheek to cheek).

How well her wishes went! She stroked my chin,
She taught me Turn, and Counter-turn, and Stand;
She taught me Touch, that undulant white skin;   10
I nibbled meekly from her proffered hand;
She was the sickle; I, poor I, the rake,
Coming behind her for her pretty sake
(But what prodigious mowing we did make).

Love likes a gander, and adores a goose: 15
Her full lips pursed, the errant note to seize;
She played it quick, she played it light and loose;
My eyes, they dazzled at her flowing knees;
Her several parts could keep a pure repose,
Or one hip quiver with a mobile nose   20
(She moved in circles, and those circles moved).

Let seed be grass, and grass turn into hay:
I'm martyr to a motion not my own;
What's freedom for? To know eternity.
I swear she cast a shadow white as stone.   25
But who would count eternity in days?
These old bones live to learn her wanton ways:
(I measure time by how a body sways).

From *Collected Poems of Theodore Roethke.* © 1954 by Theodore Roethke. Reprinted by permission of Doubleday & Company, Inc.

Carolyn Kizer

What the Bones Know

Remembering the past
And gloating at it now,
I know the frozen brow
And shaking sides of lust   5
Will dog me at my death
To catch my ghostly breath.

I think that Yeats was right,
That lust and love are one.   10
The body of this night
May beggar me to death,
But we are not undone
Who love with all our breath.

                                                             15
I know that Proust was wrong,
His wheeze: love, to survive,
Needs jealousy, and death
And lust, to make it strong
Or goose it back alive.
Proust took away my breath.   20

The later Yeats was right
To think of sex and death
And nothing else. Why wait
Till we are turning old?
My thoughts are hot and cold.
I do not waste my breath.

Emily Dickinson

Five Poems

211

Come slowly—Eden!
Lips unused to Thee—
Bashful—sip thy Jessamines—
As the fainting Bee—

Reaching late his flower,
Round her chamber hums—
Counts his nectars—
Enters—and is lost in Balms.

249

Wild Nights—Wild Nights!
Were I with thee
Wild Nights should be
Our luxury!

Futile—the Winds—
To a Heart in port—
Done with the Compass—
Done with the Chart!

Rowing in Eden—
Ah, the Sea!
Might I but moor—Tonight—
In Thee!

341

After great pain, a formal feeling comes—
The Nerves sit ceremonious, like Tombs—
The stiff Heart questions was it He, that bore,
And Yesterday, or Centuries before?

From *The Complete Poems of Emily Dickinson*, ed. Thomas H. Johnson (Little, Brown and Co., 1960).

The Feet, mechanical, go round—
Of Ground, or Air, or Ought—
A Wooden way
Regardless grown,
A Quartz contentment, like a stone—

This is the Hour of Lead—
Remembered, if outlived,
As Freezing persons, recollect the Snow—
First—Chill—then Stupor—then the letting go—

520

I started Early—Took my Dog—
And visited the Sea—
The Mermaids in the Basement
Came out to look at me—

And Frigates—in the Upper Floor
Extended Hempen Hands—
Presuming Me to be a Mouse—
Aground—upon the Sands—

But no Man moved Me—till the Tide
Went past my simple Shoe—
And past my Apron—and my Belt
And past my Bodice—too—

And made as He would eat me up—
As wholly as a Dew
Upon a Dandelion's Sleeve—
And then—I started—too—

And He—He followed—close behind—
I felt His Silver Heel
Upon my Ankle—Then my Shoes
Would overflow with Pearl—

Until We met the Solid Town—
No One He seemed to know—
And bowing—with a Mighty look—
At me—The Sea withdrew—

1732

My life closed twice before its close—
It yet remains to see
If Immortality unveil
A third event to me

So huge, so hopeless to conceive
As these that twice befell.
Parting is all we know of heaven,
And all we need of hell.

Anne Sexton

Red Riding Hood

Many are the deceivers:

The suburban matron,
proper in the supermarket,
list in hand so she won't suddenly fly,
buying her Duz and Chuck Wagon dog food,   5
meanwhile ascending from earth,
letting her stomach fill up with helium,
letting her arms go loose as kite tails,
getting ready to meet her lover
a mile down Apple Crest Road   10
in the Congregational Church parking lot.

Two seemingly respectable women
come up to an old Jenny
and show her an envelope
full of money   15
and promise to share the booty
if she'll give them ten thou
as an act of faith.

Her life savings are under the mattress
covered with rust stains   20
and counting.
They are as wrinkled as prunes
but negotiable.
The two women take the money and disappear.
Where is the moral?   25
Not all knives are for
stabbing the exposed belly.
Rock climbs on rock
and it only makes a seashore.
Old Jenny has lost her belief in mattresses   30
and now she has no wastebasket in which
to keep her youth.

The standup comic
on the "Tonight" show
who imitates the Vice President   35
and cracks up Johnny Carson
and delays sleep for millions
of bedfellows watching between their feet,
slits his wrist the next morning
in the Algonquin's old-fashioned bathroom,   40
the razor in his hand like a toothbrush,
wall as anonymous as a urinal,
the shower curtain his slack rubberman audience,
and then the slash
as simple as opening a letter   45
and the warm blood breaking out like a rose
upon the bathtub with its claw and ball feet.

And I. I too.
Quite collected at cocktail parties,
meanwhile in my head   50
I'm undergoing open-heart surgery.
The heart, poor fellow,
pounding on his little tin drum
with a faint death beat.
The heart, that eyeless beetle,   55
enormous that Kafka beetle,
running panicked through his maze,
never stopping one foot after the other
one hour after the other

until he gags on an apple   60
and it's all over.

And I. I too again.
I built a summer house on Cape Ann.
A simple A-frame and this too was
a deception—nothing haunts a new house.   65
When I moved in with a bathing suit and tea bags
the ocean rumbled like a train backing up
and at each window secrets came in
like gas. My mother, that departed soul,
sat in my Eames chair and reproached me   70
for losing her keys to the old cottage.
Even in the electric kitchen there was
the smell of a journey. The ocean
was seeping through its frontiers
and laying me out on its wet rails.   75
The bed was stale with my childhood
and I could not move to another city
where the worthy make a new life.

Long ago
there was a strange deception: 80
a wolf dressed in frills,
a kind of transvestite.
But I get ahead of my story.
In the beginning
there was just little Red Riding Hood,   85
so called because her grandmother
made her a red cape and she was never without it.
It was her Linus blanket, besides
it was red, as red as the Swiss flag,
yes it was red, as red as chicken blood.   90
But more than she loved her riding hood
she loved her grandmother who lived
far from the city in the big wood.

This one day her mother gave her
a basket of wine and cake   95
to take to her grandmother
because she was ill.
Wine and cake?
Where's the aspirin? The penicillin?
Where's the fruit juice?   100

Peter Rabbit got camomile tea.
But wine and cake it was.

On her way in the big wood
Red Riding Hood met the wolf.
Good day, Mr. Wolf, she said,   105
thinking him no more dangerous
than a streetcar or a panhandler.
He asked where she was going
and she obligingly told him.
There among the roots and trunks   110
with the mushrooms pulsing inside the moss
he planned how to eat them both,
the grandmother an old carrot
and the child a shy budkin
in a red red hood.   115
He bade her to look at the bloodroot,
the small bunchberry and the dogtooth
and pick some for her grandmother.
And this she did.
Meanwhile he scampered off   120
to Grandmother's house and ate her up
as quick as a slap.
Then he put on her nightdress and cap
and snuggled down into the bed.
A deceptive fellow.   125

Red Riding Hood
knocked on the door and entered
with her flowers, her cake, her wine.
Grandmother looked strange,
a dark and hairy disease it seemed.   130
Oh Grandmother, what big ears you have,
ears, eyes, hands and then the teeth.
The better to eat you with, my dear.
So the wolf gobbled Red Riding Hood down
like a gumdrop. Now he was fat.   135
He appeared to be in his ninth month
and Red Riding Hood and her grandmother
rode like two Jonahs up and down with
his every breath. One pigeon. One partridge.

He was fast asleep,   140
dreaming in his cap and gown,
wolfless.

Along came a huntsman who heard
the loud contented snores
and knew that was no grandmother.   145
He opened the door and said,
So it's you, old sinner.
He raised his gun to shoot him
when it occurred to him that maybe
the wolf had eaten up the old lady.   150
So he took a knife and began cutting open
the sleeping wolf, a kind of caesarian section.

It was a carnal knife that let
Red Riding Hood out like a poppy,
quite alive from the kingdom of the belly.   155
And grandmother too
still waiting for cakes and wine.
The wolf, they decided, was too mean
to be simply shot so they filled his belly
with large stones and sewed him up.   160
He was as heavy as a cemetery
and when he woke up and tried to run off
he fell over dead. Killed by his own weight.
Many a deception ends on such a note.

The huntsman and the grandmother and Red Riding Hood 165
sat down by his corpse and had a meal of wine and cake.
Those two remembering
nothing naked and brutal
from that little death,
that little birth,   170
from their going down
and their lifting up.

Charles David Wright

His Wonders to Perform

That God remarks the sparrow's fall
consoles the sparrow none at all.
The stone that fells him from the fence
does not strike him as Providence.
Better no call to feel with awe   5
mysterious ways in fang and claw,
but perch, the one bird in the park
whom Heaven, thank you, does not mark.
Such high design it augurs, though,
to doubtless alleycats below.   10

Michael "Doc" Hunt

from "A Decade to Decade Look at the United States: 1776-1976"

1900–1909

Part I

A new century,
But old miseries,
Poverty,
Greed,
Distrust,   5
Hate.
McKinley dead,
Roosevelt "speaks softly and carries a big stick,"
Carrie Nation carries a bigger one.

A bicycle shop in Dayton turns out to be the nation's
   future airplane factory,   10
And San Francisco rocks with an earthquake.
Roosevelt the Corollary,
The trust buster,
The conservationist,
And into each life some rain must fall.   15
The urban influx,
The immigrant influx,
And into each life some rain must fall.

Part II: *You Can't Fight The Nation*

You can fight city hall,
You can fight the state,   20
You can even fight Mom and Pop's Diner,
But you can't fight the nation (Carrie Nation that is).
What's her game?
She's got an axe,
Don't ask.   25
What's her game?
She's got an axe,
Don't ask.
But if you insist,
She smashes the whiskey rings,   30
Preaches Prohibition and things,
Denounces demon rum,
And gives everyone (a scare).
Don't mess with the Nation,
She's bad,   35
She's mean,
She sees everything,
And may be obscene.
Women's lib!
Women's lip!   40
Carrie Nation is a trip!
Ride on Carrie Nation, ride on!
Turn a pastime into a racketime,
And soon others will get their high.

William R. Harmon

Part xxi
from Treasury Holiday

If you don't like my peaches
why do you shake my tree?
If you don't like my peaches
why do you shake my tree?
Get out of my orchard   5
& let my fruit trees be.

Ah

shit.

Hips, hip-sockets, hip-strength, inward & outward
round, man-balls, man-root   10
not
in the 1st ed. (1855)

Whitman had a dirty mind

In high school we read Leaves of Grass & Venus & Adonis &
Look Homeward Angel & The Catcher in the Rye for their
dirty parts
cummings had a dirty mind   Wolfe had a dirty mind
Shakespeare had a dirty mind   Chaucer had a very dirty
mind   15
I have a very dirty mind indeed for I have breathed the same air
as coroners
I have seen coroners' assistants with their stomachs & photographs
ball-headed men in glasses & plastics & synthetics & technical terms
(Ah   shit   in italics)
with stomachs of steel & bone buttons & stills of corpses   20

I saw one once of a young guy killed in a car crash
He was laid out on his back
Penis & testicles covered up by a little white rectangle

Laurence Sterne & Jonathan Swift & Samuel Richardson had dirty
minds

From *Treasury Holiday*. © 1969, 1970 by William Harmon. Reprinted by permission of Wesleyan University Press.

Charles Darwin had a dirty mind & thought about shit all the
  God-damn time   25

& Benjamin Franklin & J. S. Bach & W. B. Yeats & Franklin
  Delano Roosevelt had dirty minds & were foul of mouth
Woodrow Wilson had one of the dirtiest minds in the world

Bloody Lydia Pinkham had a dirtier mind than the worst Lutheran
  convict lying on his left side in his grey cell thinking
  compulsively obsessively about pussy twenty-four hours a day
  day in and day out seven days a week fifty two weeks a year
  for his entire lifetime plus ninety-nine fiscal years for
  aggravated sodomy & high carnal knowledge
& if it's not pussy you can bet it's something even worse

But in the final analysis I think I would have to say that
  undertakers coroners & policemen have the dirtiest minds   30
& use the foulest language habitually
In high school they told us that the habit-forming use of profane
  obscene vulgar blasphemous language not only stank in the
  nose-drills of Yahweh but also indicated a deficient command
  of the English language
I guess that's right but still have never found a truer clearer or
  more forceful thing to call a son of a bitch than son of a bitch

Sean O'Casey (19 June 1950 Daily Worker): To hell with the
  atom bomb!
But old Allen Ginsberg with his dirty queer dope-fiend commie
  unbusinesslike mind says through his filthy antisocial
  objectionable obnoxious Jewish beard to clean upstanding &
  erect America: Go fuck yourself with your atom bomb.   35
Now how could that be said better?

"How could that be said better?" a nice old Ulster lady once asked
  me (the text in question being "gem of purest ray serene")
& so I honor her   I really & sincerely do
I honor her here by applying her praise to Ginsberg's scatological
  imperative
Go fuck yourself with your atom bomb   40

She was born in 1888 named Jane unmarried & my landlady in
  Londonderry
had been a schoolteacher & I don't doubt that she had given a
  great deal of serious thought to the mechanics & logistics of
  the operation of that place in the Miller's Tale where one guy
  gets back at another guy by shoving a red-hot plow-share
  up his ass

O plow & stars
& that reminds me that once when I was out she went into my
    room & took my copy of O'Casey's six-volume autobiography
    & later told me that O'Casey was dead that day in Turkey
I could not believe that but she explained (calling me Gorman
    because Harmon is somehow impossible in Gaelic she said)
    that Turkey was a place in Devonshire: Torquay   45

Ah   man-balls & root
Imagine all the ladies of the temperance & suffragette persuasions
    sitting & sipping bloody Lydia's vegetable compound which
    was one half booze & other half dope
thinking about the body electric & incleft outswell
Zip Zap snap crackle inward & outward round

my ass   50

e e cummings

"anyone lived in a pretty how town"

anyone lived in a pretty how town
(with up so floating many bells down)
spring summer autumn winter
he sang his didn't he danced his did.

Women and men(both little and small)   5
cared for anyone not at all
they sowed their isn't they reaped their same
sun moon stars rain

children guessed(but only a few
and down they forgot as up they grew   10
autumn winter spring summer)
that noone loved him more by more

when by now and tree by leaf
she laughed his joy she cried his grief

From *Complete Poems 1913–1962* by E. E. Cummings. Copyright 1940 by E. E. Cummings; renewed 1968 by Marion Morehouse Cummings. Reprinted by permission of Harcourt Brace Jovanovich, Inc.

bird by snow and stir by still   15
anyone's any was all to her

someones married their everyones
laughed their cryings and did their dance
(sleep wake hope and then)they
said their nevers they slept their dream   20

stars rain sun moon
(and only the snow can begin to explain
how children are apt to forget to remember
with up so floating many bells down)

one day anyone died i guess   25
(and noone stooped to kiss his face)
busy folk buried them side by side
little by little and was by was

all by all and deep by deep
and more by more they dream their sleep   30
noone and anyone earth by april
wish by spirit and if by yes.

Women and men(both dong and ding)
summer autumn winter spring
reaped their sowing and went their came   35
sun moon stars rain

W. H. Auden

The Unknown Citizen

(To JS/07/M/378
This Marble Monument
Is Erected by the State)

He was found by the Bureau of Statistics to be
One against whom there was no official complaint,
And all the reports on his conduct agree

From *Collected Shorter Poems 1927–1957*, by W. H. Auden. Copyright 1940 and renewed 1968 by W. H. Auden. Reprinted by permission of Random House, Inc. and
Faber and Faber Limited.

That, in the modern sense of an old-fashioned word, he
   was a saint,
For in everything he did he served the Greater Community.   5
Except for the War till the day he retired
He worked in a factory and never got fired,
But satisfied his employers, Fudge Motors Inc.
Yet he wasn't a scab or odd in his views,
For his Union reports that he paid his dues,   10
(Our report on his Union shows it was sound)
And our Social Psychology workers found
That he was popular with his mates and liked a drink.
The Press are convinced that he bought a paper every day
And that his reactions to advertisements were normal in
   every way.   15
Policies taken out in his name prove that he was fully insured,
And his Health-card shows he was once in hospital but left
   it cured.
Both Producers Research and High-Grade Living declare
He was fully sensible to the advantages of the Instalment Plan
And had everything necessary to the Modern Man,   20
A phonograph, a radio, a car and a frigidaire.
Our researchers into Public Opinion are content
That he held the proper opinions for the time of year;
When there was peace, he was for peace; when there was war,
   he went.
He was married and added five children to the population,   25
Which our Eugenist says was the right number for a parent of
   his generation,
And our teachers report that he never interfered with
   their education.
Was he free? Was he happy? The question is absurd:
Had anything been wrong, we should certainly have heard.

John Steinbeck

from The Grapes of Wrath

[1] In the towns, on the edges of the towns, in fields, in vacant lots, the used-car yards, the wreckers' yards, the garages with blazoned signs—Used Cars, Good Used Cars. Cheap transportation, three trailers. '27 Ford, clean. Checked cars, guaranteed cars. Free radio. Car with 100 gallons of gas free. Come in and look. Used Cars. No overhead.

A lot and a house large enough for a desk and chair and a blue book. Sheaf of contracts, dog-eared, held with paper clips, and a neat pile of unused contracts. Pen—keep it full, keep it working. A sale's been lost 'cause a pen didn't work.

Those sons-of-bitches over there ain't buying. Every yard gets 'em. They're lookers. Spend all their time looking. Don't want to buy no cars; take up your time. Don't give a damn for your time. Over there, them two people—no, with the kids. Get 'em in a car. Start 'em at two hundred and work down. They look good for one and a quarter. Get 'em rolling. Get 'em out in a jalopy. Sock it to 'em! They took our time.

Owners with rolled-up sleeves. Salesmen, neat, deadly, small intent eyes watching for weaknesses.

[5] Watch the woman's face. If the woman likes it we can screw the old man. Start' em on that Cad'. Then you can work 'em down to that '26 Buick. 'F you start on the Buick, they'll go for a Ford. Roll up your sleeves an' get to work. This ain't gonna last forever. Show 'em that Nash while I get the slow leak pumped up on that '25 Dodge. I'll give you a Hymie when I'm ready.

What you want is transportation, ain't it? No baloney for you. Sure the upholstery is shot. Seat cushions ain't turning no wheels over.

Cars lined up, noses forward, rusty noses, flat tires. Parked close together.

Like to get in to see that one? Sure, no trouble. I'll pull her out of the line.

Get 'em under obligation. Make 'em take up your time. Don't let 'em forget they're takin' your time. People are nice, mostly. They hate to put you out. Make 'em put you out, an' then sock it to 'em.

[10] Cars lined up, Model T's, high and snotty, creaking wheel, worn bands. Buicks, Nashes, De Sotos.

Yes, sir. '22 Dodge. Best goddamn car Dodge ever made. Never wear out. Low compression. High compression got lots a sap for a while, but the metal ain't made that'll hold it for long. Plymouths, Rocknes, Stars.

Jesus, where'd that Apperson come from, the Ark? And a Chalmers and a Chandler—ain't made 'em for years. We ain't sellin' cars—rolling junk. Goddamn it, I got to get jalopies. I don't want nothing for more'n twenty-five, thirty bucks. Sell 'em for fifty, seventy-five. That's a good profit. Christ, what cut do you make on a new car? Get jalopies. I can sell 'em fast as I get 'em. Nothing over two hundred fifty. Jim, corral that old bastard on the sidewalk. Don't know his ass from a hole in the ground. Try him on that Apperson. Say, where is that Apperson? Sold? If we don't get some jalopies we got nothing to sell.

Flags, red and white, white and blue—all along the curb. Used Cars. Good Used Cars.

Today's bargain—up on the platform. Never sell it. Makes folks come in, though. If we sold that bargain at that price we'd hardly make a dime. Tell 'em it's jus' sold. Take out that yard battery before you make delivery. Put in that dumb cell. Christ, what they want for six bits? Roll up your sleeves—pitch in. This ain't gonna last. If I had enough jalopies I'd retire in six months.

[15]   Listen, Jim, I heard that Chevvy's rear end. Sounds like bustin' bottles. Squirt in a couple quarts of sawdust. Put some in the gears, too. We got to move that lemon for thirty-five dollars. Bastard cheated me on that one. I offer ten an' he jerks me to fifteen, an' then the son-of-a-bitch took the tools out. God Almighty! I wisht I had five hundred jalopies. This ain't gonna last. He don't like the tires? Tell 'im they got ten thousand in 'em, knock off a buck an' a half.

Piles of rusty ruins against the fence, rows of wrecks in back, fenders, grease-black wrecks, blocks lying on the ground and a pig weed growing up through the cylinders. Brake rods, exhausts, piled like snakes. Grease, gasoline.

See if you can't find a spark plug that ain't cracked. Christ, if I had fifty trailers at under a hundred I'd clean up. What the hell is he kickin' about? We sell 'em, but we don't push 'em home for him. That's good! Don't push 'em home. Get that one in the Monthly, I bet. You don't think he's a prospect? Well, kick 'im out. We got too much to do to bother with a guy that can't make up his mind. Take the right front tire off the Graham. Turn that mended side down. The rest looks swell. Got tread an' everything.

Sure! There's fifty thousan' in that ol' heap yet. Keep plenty oil in. So long. Good luck.

Lookin' for a car? What did you have in mind? See anything attracts you? I'm dry. How about a little snort a good stuff? Come on, while your wife's lookin' at that La Salle. You don't want no La Salle. Bearings shot. Uses too much oil. Got a Lincoln '24. There's a car. Run forever. Make her into a truck.

[20]   Hot sun on rusted metal. Oil on the ground. People are wandering in, bewildered, needing a car.

Wipe your feet. Don't lean on that car, it's dirty. How do you buy a car? What does it cost? Watch the children, now. I wonder how much for this one? We'll ask. It don't cost money to ask. We can ask, can't we? Can't pay a nickel over seventy-five, or there won't be enough to get to California.

God, if I could only get a hundred jalopies. I don't care if they run or not.

Tires, used, bruised tires, stacked in tall cylinders; tubes, red, gray, hanging like sausages.

Tire patch? Radiator cleaner? Spark intensifier? Drop this little pill in your gas tank and get ten extra miles to the gallon. Just paint it on— you got a new surface for fifty cents. Wipers, fan belts, gaskets? Maybe it's the valve. Get a new valve stem. What can you lose for a nickel?

[25] All right Joe. You soften 'em up an' shoot 'em in here. I'll close 'em, I'll deal 'em or I'll kill 'em. Don't send in no bums. I want deals.

Yes, sir, step in. You got a buy there. Yes, sir! At eighty bucks you got a buy.

I can't go no higher than fifty. The fella outside says fifty.

Fifty. Fifty? He's nuts. Paid seventy-eight fifty for that little number. Joe, you crazy fool, you tryin' to bust us? Have to can that guy. I might take sixty. Now look here, mister, I ain't got all day. I'm a business man but I ain't out to stick nobody. Got anything to trade?

Got a pair of mules I'll trade.

[30] *Mules!* Hey, Joe, hear this? This guy wants to trade mules. Didn't nobody tell you this is the machine age? They don't use mules for nothing but glue no more.

Fine big mules—five and seven years old. Maybe we better look around.

Look around! You come in when we're busy, an' take up our time an' then walk out! Joe, did you know you was talkin' to pikers?

I ain't a piker. I got to get a car. We're goin' to California. I got to get a car.

Well, I'm a sucker. Joe says I'm a sucker. Says if I don't quit givin' my shirt away I'll starve to death. Tell you what I'll do—I can get five bucks apiece for them mules for dog feed.

[35] I wouldn't want them to go for dog feed.

Well, maybe I can get ten or seven maybe. Tell you what we'll do. We'll take your mules for twenty. Wagon goes with 'em, don't it? An' you put up fifty, an' you can sign a contract to send the rest at ten dollars a month.

But you said eighty.

Didn't you never hear about carrying charges and insurance? That just boosts her a little. You'll get her all paid up in four-five months. Sign your name right here. We'll take care of ever'thing.

Well, I don't know—

[40] Now, look here. I'm givin' you my shirt, an' you took all this time. I might a made three sales while I been talkin' to you. I'm disgusted. Yeah, sign right there. All right, sir. Joe, fill up the tank for this gentleman. We'll give him gas.

Jesus, Joe, that was a hot one! What'd we give for that jalopy?

Thirty bucks—thirty-five wasn't it? I got that team, an' if I can't get seventy-five for that team, I ain't a business man. An' I got fifty cash an' a contract for forty more. Oh, I know they're not all honest, but it'll surprise you how many kick through with the rest. One guy come through with a hundred two years after I wrote him off. I bet you this guy sends the money. Christ, if I could only get five hundred jalopies! Roll up your sleeves, Joe. Go out an' soften 'em, an' send 'em in to me. You get twenty on that last deal. You ain't doing bad.

Limp flags in the afternoon sun. Today's Bargain. '29 Ford pickup, runs good.

What do you want for fifty bucks—a Zephyr?

Horsehair curling out of seat cushions, fenders battered and hammered back. Bumpers torn loose and hanging. Fancy Ford roadster with little colored lights at fender guide, at radiator cap, and three behind. Mud aprons, and a big die on the gear-shift lever. Pretty girl on tire cover, painted in color and named Cora. Afternoon sun on the dusty windshields.

[45]   Christ, I ain't had time to go out an' eat! Joe, send a kid for a hamburger.

Spattering roar of ancient engines.

There's a dumb-bunny lookin' at that Chrysler. Find out if he got any jack in his jeans. Some a these farm boys is sneaky. Soften 'em up an' roll 'em in to me, Joe. You're doin' good.

Sure, we sold it. Guarantee? We guaranteed it to be an automobile. We didn't guarantee to wet-nurse it. Now listen here, you—you bought a car, an' now you're squawkin'. I don't give a damn if you don't make payments. We ain't got your paper. We turn that over to the finance company. They'll get after you, not us. We don't hold no paper. Yeah? Well you jus' get tough an' I'll call a cop. No, we did not switch the tires. Run 'im outa here, Joe. He bought a car, an' now he ain't satisfied. How'd you think if I bought a steak an' et half an' try to bring it back? We're runnin' a business, not a charity ward. Can ya imagine that guy, Joe? Say—looka there! Got a Elk's tooth! Run over there. Let 'em glance over that '36 Pontiac. Yeah.

Square noses, round noses, rusty noses, shovel noses, and the long curves of streamlines, and the flat surfaces before streamlining. Bargains Today. Old monsters with deep upholstery—you can cut her into a truck easy. Two-wheel trailers, axles rusty in the hard afternoon sun. Used Cars. Good Used Cars. Clean, runs good. Don't pump oil.

[50]   Christ, look at 'er! Somebody took nice care of 'er.

Cadillacs, La Salles, Buicks, Plymouths, Packards, Chevvies, Fords, Pontiacs. Row on row, headlights glinting in the afternoon sun. Good Used Cars.

Soften 'em up, Joe. Jesus, I wisht I had a thousand jalopies! Get 'em ready to deal, an' I'll close 'em.

Goin' to California? Here's jus' what you need. Looks shot, but they's thousan's of miles in her.

Lined up side by side. Good Used Cars. Bargains. Clean, runs good.

Charles Dickens

Gin-Shops
from *Sketches by Boz*

[1] It is a remarkable circumstance, that different trades appear to partake of the disease to which elephants and dogs are especially liable, and to run stark, staring, raving mad, periodically. The great distinction between the animals and the trades, is, that the former run mad with a certain degree of propriety—they are very regular in their irregularities. We know the period at which the emergency will arise, and provide against it accordingly. If an elephant run mad, we are all ready for him— kill or cure—pills or bullets, calomel in conserve of roses, or lead in a musket-barrel. If a dog happen to look unpleasantly warm in the summer months, and to trot about the shady side of the streets with a quarter of a yard of tongue hanging out of his mouth, a thick leather muzzle, which has been previously prepared in compliance with the thoughtful injunctions of the Legislature, is instantly clapped over his head, by way of making him cooler, and he either looks remarkably unhappy for the next six weeks, or becomes legally insane, and goes mad, as it were, by Act of Parliament. But these trades are as eccentric as comets; nay, worse, for no one can calculate on the recurrence of the strange appearances which betoken the disease. Moreover, the contagion is general, and the quickness with which it diffuses itself, almost incredible.

[2] We will cite two or three cases in illustration of our meaning. Six or eight years ago, the epidemic began to display itself among the linen-drapers and haberdashers. The primary symptoms were an inordinate love of plate-glass, and a passion for gas-lights and gilding. The disease gradually progressed, and at last attained a fearful height. Quiet, dusty old shops in different parts of town, were pulled down; spacious premises with stuccoed fronts and gold letters, were erected instead; floors were covered with Turkey carpets; roofs supported by massive pillars; doors knocked into windows; a dozen squares of glass into one; one shopman into a dozen; and there is no knowing what would have been done, if it had not been fortunately discovered, just in time, that the Commissioners of Bankruptcy were as competent to decide such cases as the Commissioners of Lunacy, and that a little confinement and gentle examination did wonders. The disease abated. It died away. A year or two of comparative tranquillity ensued. Suddenly it burst out again amongst the chemists; the symptoms were the same, with the addition of a strong desire to stick the royal arms over the shop-door, and a great rage for mahogany, varnish, and expensive floor-cloth. Then, the hosiers were infected, and began to pull down their shop-fronts with frantic recklessness. The mania again died away, and the public began to congratulate themselves on its entire disappearance, when it burst forth with tenfold violence among the publicans, and keepers of "wine vaults." From that moment it has spread

among them with unprecedented rapidity, exhibiting a concatenation of all the previous symptoms; onward it has rushed to every part of town, knocking down all the old public-houses, and depositing splendid mansions, stone balustrades, rosewood fittings, immense lamps, and illuminated clocks, at the corner of every street.

[3]   The extensive scale on which these places are established, and the ostentatious manner in which the business of even the smallest among them is divided into branches, is amusing. A handsome plate of ground glass in one door directs you "To the Counting-house"; another to the "Bottle Department"; a third to the "Wholesale Department"; a fourth, to "The Wine Promenade"; and so forth, until we are in daily expectation of meeting with a "Brandy Bell," or a "Whiskey Entrance." Then, ingenuity is exhausted in devising attractive titles for the different descriptions of gin; and the dram-drinking portion of the community as they gaze upon the gigantic black and white announcements, which are only to be equalled in size by the figures beneath them, are left in a state of pleasing hesitation between "The Cream of the Valley," "The Out and Out," "The No Mistake," "The Good for Mixing," "The real Knock-me-down," "The celebrated Butter Gin," "The regular Flare-up," and a dozen other, equally inviting and wholesome *liqueurs*. Although places of this description are to be met with in every second street, they are invariably numerous and splendid in precise proportion to the dirt and poverty of the surrounding neighbourhood. The gin-shops in and near Drury-lane, Holborn, St. Giles's, Covent-garden, and Clare-market, are the handsomest in London. There is more of filth and squalid misery near those great thoroughfares than in any part of this mighty city.

[4]   We will endeavour to sketch the bar of a large gin-shop, and its ordinary customers, for the edification of such of our readers as may not have had opportunities of observing such scenes; and on the chance of finding one well suited to our purpose, we will make for Drury-lane, through the narrow streets and dirty courts which divide it from Oxford-street, and that classical spot adjoining the brewery at the bottom of Tottenham-court-road, best known to the initiated as the "Rookery."

[5]   The filthy and miserable appearance of this part of London can hardly be imagined by those (and there are many such) who have not witnessed it. Wretched houses with broken windows patched with rags and paper: every room let out to a different family, and in many instances to two or even three—fruit and "sweet-stuff" manufacturers in the cellars, barbers and red-herring vendors in the front parlours, cobblers in the back; a bird-fancier in the first floor, three families on the second, starvation in the attics, Irishmen in the passage, a "musician" in the front kitchen, and a charwoman and five hungry children in the back one—filth everywhere—a gutter before the houses and a drain behind —clothes drying and slops emptying, from the windows; girls of fourteen or fifteen, with matted hair, walking about barefoot, and in white great-coats, almost their only covering; boys of all ages, in coats of all sizes and no coats at all; men and women, in every variety of scanty and

dirty apparel, lounging, scolding, drinking, smoking, squabbling, fighting, and swearing.

[6]   You turn the corner. What a change! All is light and brilliancy. The hum of many voices issues from that splendid gin-shop which forms the commencement of the two streets opposite; and the gay building with the fantastically ornamented parapet, the illuminated clock, the plate-glass windows surrounded by stucco rosettes, and its profusion of gas-lights in richly-gilt burners, is perfectly dazzling when contrasted with the darkness and dirt we have just left. The interior is even gayer than the exterior. A bar of French-polished mahogany, elegantly carved, extends the whole width of the place; and there are two side-aisles of great casks, painted green and gold, enclosed within a light brass rail, and bearing such inscriptions, as "Old Tom, 549;" "Young Tom, 360;" "Samson, 1421"—the figures agreeing, we presume, with "gallons," understood. Beyond the bar is a lofty and spacious saloon, full of the same enticing vessels, with a gallery running round it, equally well furnished. On the counter, in addition to the usual spirit apparatus, are two or three little baskets of cakes and biscuits, which are carefully secured at top with wicker-work, to prevent their contents being unlawfully abstracted. Behind it, are two showily-dressed damsels with large necklaces, dispensing the spirits and "compounds." They are assisted by the ostensible proprietor of the concern, a stout, coarse fellow in a fur cap, put on very much on one side to give him a knowing air, and to display his sandy whiskers to the best advantage.

[7]   The two old washerwomen, who are seated on the little bench to the left of the bar, are rather overcome by the headdresses and haughty demeanour of the young ladies who officiate. They receive their half-quartern of gin and peppermint, with considerable deference, prefacing a request for "one of them soft biscuits," with a "Jist be good enough, ma'am." They are quite astonished at the impudent air of the young fellow in a brown coat and bright buttons, who, ushering in his two companions, and walking up to the bar in as careless a manner as if he had been used to green and gold ornaments all his life, winks at one of the young ladies with singular coolness, and calls for a "kervorten and a three-out-glass," just as if the place were his own. "Gin for you, sir?" says the young lady when she has drawn it: carefully looking every way but the right one, to show that the wink had no effect upon her. "For me, Mary, my dear," replies the gentleman in brown. "My name an't Mary as it happens," says the young girl, rather relaxing as she delivers the change. "Well, if it an't, it ought to be," responds the irresistible one; "all the Marys as ever *I* see, was handsome gals." Here the young lady, not precisely remembering how blushes are managed in such cases, abruptly ends the flirtation by addressing the female in the faded feathers who has just entered, and who, after stating explicitly, to prevent any subsequent misunderstanding, that "this gentleman pays," calls for "a glass of port wine and a bit of sugar."

[8]   Those two old men who came in "just to have a drain," finished

their third quartern a few seconds ago; they have made themselves crying drunk; and the fat comfortable-looking elderly women, who had
"a glass of rum-srub" each, having chimed in with their complaints on
the hardness of the times, one of the women has agreed to stand a glass
round, jocularly observing that "grief never mended no broken bones,
and as good people's wery scarce, what I says is, make the most on 'em,
and that's all about it!" a sentiment which appears to afford unlimited
satisfaction to those who have nothing to pay.

[8]   It is growing late, and the throng of men, women, and children,
who have been constantly going in and out, dwindles down to two or
three occasional stragglers—cold, wretched-looking creatures, in the last
stage of emaciation and disease. The knot of Irish labourers at the lower
end of the place, who have been alternately shaking hands with, and
threatening the life of each other, for the last hour, become furious in
their disputes, and finding it impossible to silence one man, who is particularly anxious to adjust the difference, they resort to the expedient
of knocking him down and jumping on him afterwards. The man in the
fur cap, and the potboy rush out; a scene of riot and confusion ensues;
half the Irishmen get shut out, and the other half get shut in; the potboy
is knocked among the tubs in no time; the landlord hits everybody, and
everybody hits the landlord; the barmaids scream; the police come in;
the rest is a confused mixture of arms, legs, staves, torn coats, shouting,
and struggling. Some of the party are borne off to the station-house, and
the remainder slink home to beat their wives for complaining, and kick
the children for daring to be hungry.

[10]   We have sketched this subject very slightly, not only because our
limits compel us to do so, but because, if it were pursued farther, it
would be painful and repulsive. Well-disposed gentlemen, and charitable
ladies, would alike turn with coldness and disgust from a description
of the drunken besotted men, and wretched broken-down miserable
women, who form no inconsiderable portion of the frequenters of these
haunts; forgetting, in the pleasant consciousness of their own rectitude,
the poverty of the one, and the temptation of the other. Gin-drinking
is a great vice in England, but wretchedness and dirt are a greater; and
until you improve the homes of the poor, or persuade a half-famished
wretch not to seek relief in the temporary oblivion of his own misery,
with the pittance which, divided among his family, would furnish a
morsel of bread for each, gin-shops will increase in number and splen-
dour. If Temperance Societies would suggest an antidote against hunger,
filth, and foul air, or could establish dispensaries for the gratuitous
distribution of bottles of Lethe-water, gin-palaces would be numbered
among the things that were.

E. B. White

A Letter from the South

Fiddler Bayou, March 22, 1956

[1]   After the lions had returned to their cages, creeping angrily through the chutes, a little bunch of us drifted away and into an open doorway nearby, where we stood for a while in semidarkness, watching a big brown circus horse go harumphing around the practice ring. His trainer was a woman of about forty, and the two of them, horse and woman, seemed caught up in one of those desultory treadmills of afternoon from which there is no apparent escape. The day was hot, and we kibitzers were grateful to be briefly out of the sun's glare. The long rein, or tape, by which the woman guided her charge counterclockwise in his dull career formed the radius of their private circle, of which she was the revolving center; and she, too, stepped a tiny circumference of her own, in order to accommodate the horse and allow him his maximum scope. She had on a short-skirted costume and a conical straw hat. Her legs were bare and she wore high heels, which probed deep into the loose tanbark and kept her ankles in a state of constant turmoil. The great size and meekness of the horse, the repetitive exercise, the heat of the afternoon, all exerted a hypnotic charm that invited boredom; we spectators were experiencing a languor— we neither expected relief nor felt entitled to any. We had paid a dollar to get into the grounds, to be sure, but we had got our dollar's worth a few minutes before, when the lion trainer's whiplash had got caught around a toe of one of the lions. What more did we want for a dollar?

[2]   Behind me I heard someone say, "Excuse me, please," in a low voice. She was halfway into the building when I turned and saw her—a girl of sixteen or seventeen, politely threading her way through us onlookers who blocked the entrance. As she emerged in front of us, I saw that she was barefoot, her dirty little feet fighting the uneven ground. In most respects she was like any of two or three dozen showgirls you encounter if you wander about the winter quarters of Mr. John Ringling North's circus, in Sarasota—cleverly proportioned, deeply browned by the sun, dusty, eager, and almost naked. But her grave face and the naturalness of her manner gave her a sort of quick distinction and brought a new note into the gloomy octagonal building where we had all cast our lot for a few moments. As soon as she had squeezed through the crowd, she spoke a word or two to the older woman, whom I took to be her mother, stepped to the ring, and waited while the horse coasted to a stop in front of her. She gave the animal a couple of affectionate swipes on his enormous neck and then swung herself aboard. The horse immediately resumed his

From "The Ring of Time" in *The Points of My Compass* by E. B. White. © 1956, 1962 by E. B. White. Originally appeared in *The New Yorker*. Reprinted by permission of Harper & Row, Publishers, Inc.

rocking canter, the woman goading him on, chanting something that sounded like "Hop! Hop!"

[3]   In attempting to recapture this mild spectacle, I am merely acting as recording secretary for one of the oldest of societies—the society of those who, at one time or another, have surrendered, without even a show of resistance, to the bedazzlement of a circus rider. As a writing man, or secretary, I have always felt charged with the safekeeping of all unexpected items of worldly or unworldly enchantment, as though I might be held personally responsible if even a small one were to be lost. But it is not easy to communicate anything of this nature. The circus comes as close to being the world in microcosm as anything I know; in a way, it puts all the rest of show business in the shade. Its magic is universal and complex. Out of its wild disorder comes order; from its rank smell rises the good aroma of courage and daring; out of its preliminary shabbiness comes the final splendor. And buried in the familiar boasts of its advance agents lies the modesty of most of its people. For me the circus is at its best before it has been put together. It is at its best at certain moments when it comes to a point, as through a burning glass, in the activity and destiny of a single performer out of so many. One ring is always bigger than three. One rider, one aerialist, is always greater than six. In short, a man has to catch the circus unawares to experience its full impact and share its gaudy dream.

[4]   The ten-minute ride the girl took achieved—as far as I was concerned, who wasn't looking for it, and quite unbeknownst to her, who wasn't even striving for it—the thing that is sought by performers everywhere, on whatever stage, whether struggling in the tidal currents of Shakespeare or bucking the difficult motion of a horse. I somehow got the idea she was just cadging a ride, improving a shining ten minutes in the diligent way all serious artists seize free moments to hone the blade of their talent and keep themselves in trim. Her brief tour included only elementary postures and tricks, perhaps because they were all she was capable of, perhaps because her warmup at this hour was unscheduled and the ring was not rigged for a real practice session. She swung herself off and on the horse several times, gripping his mane. She did a few knee-stands—or whatever they are called—dropping to her knees and quickly bouncing back up on her feet again. Most of the time she simply rode in a standing position, well aft on the beast, her hands hanging easily at her sides, her head erect, her straw-colored ponytail lightly brushing her shoulders, the blood of exertion showing faintly through the tan of her skin. Twice she managed a one-foot stance—a sort of ballet pose, with arms outstretched. At one point the neck strap of her bathing suit broke and she went twice around the ring in the classic attitude of a woman making minor repairs to a garment. The fact that she was standing on the back of a moving horse while doing this invested the matter with a clownish significance that perfectly fitted the spirit of the circus—jocund, yet charming. She just rolled the strap into a neat ball and stowed it inside her bodice while the horse rocked and rolled beneath her in dutiful innocence. The bath-

ing suit proved as self-reliant as its owner and stood up well enough without benefit of strap.

[5]   The richness of the scene was in its plainness, its natural condition—of horse, of ring, of girl, even to the girl's bare feet that gripped the bare back of her proud and ridiculous mount. The enchantment grew not out of anything that happened or was performed but out of something that seemed to go round and around and around with the girl, attending her, a steady gleam in the shape of a circle—a ring of ambition, of happiness, of youth. (And the positive pleasures of equilibrium under difficulties.) In a week or two, all would be changed, all (or almost all) lost: the girl would wear makeup, the horse would wear gold, the ring would be painted, the bark would be clean for the feet of the horse, the girl's feet would be clean for the slippers that she'd wear. All, all would be lost.

[6]   As I watched with the others, our jaws adroop, our eyes alight, I became painfully conscious of the element of time. Everything in the hideous old building seemed to take the shape of a circle, conforming to the course of the horse. The rider's gaze, as she peered straight ahead, seemed to be circular, as though bent by force of circumstance; then time itself began running in circles, and so the beginning was where the end was, and the two were the same, and one thing ran into the next and time went round and around and got nowhere. The girl wasn't so young that she did not know the delicious satisfaction of having a perfectly behaved body and the fun of using it to do a trick most people can't do, but she was too young to know that time does not really move in a circle at all. I thought: "She will never be as beautiful as this again"—a thought that made me acutely unhappy—and in a flash my mind (which is too much of a busybody to suit me) had projected her twenty-five years ahead, and she was now in the center of the ring, on foot, wearing a conical hat and high-heeled shoes, the image of the older woman, holding the long rein, caught in the treadmill of an afternoon long in the future. "She is at that enviable moment in life [I thought] when she believes she can go once around the ring, make one complete circuit, and at the end be exactly the same age as at the start." Everything in her movements, her expression, told you that for her the ring of time was perfectly formed, changeless, predictable, without beginning or end, like the ring in which she was traveling at this moment with the horse that wallowed under her. And then I slipped back into my trance, and time was circular again—time, pausing quietly with the rest of us, so as not to disturb the balance of a performer.

[7]   Her ride ended as casually as it had begun. The older woman stopped the horse, and the girl slid to the ground. As she walked toward us to leave, there was a quick, small burst of applause. She smiled broadly, in surprise and pleasure; then her face suddenly regained its gravity and she disappeared through the door.

[8]   It has been ambitious and plucky of me to attempt to describe what is indescribable, and I have failed, as I knew I would. But I have discharged my duty to my society; and besides, a writer, like an acrobat, must occasionally try a stunt that is too much for him. At any rate, it is worth reporting that long before the circus comes to town, its most notable per-

formances have already been given. Under the bright lights of the finished show, a performer need only reflect the electric candle power that is directed upon him; but in the dark and dirty old training rings and in the makeshift cages, whatever light is generated, whatever excitement, whatever beauty, must come from original sources—from internal fires of professional hunger and delight, from the exuberance and gravity of youth. It is the difference between planetary light and the combustion of stars.
[9]   The South is the land of the sustained sibilant. Everywhere, for the appreciative visitor, the letter "s" insinuates itself in the scene: in the sound of sea and sand, in the singing shell, in the heat of sun and sky, in the sultriness of the gentle hours, in the siesta, in the stir of birds and insects. In contrast to the softness of its music, the South is also cruel and hard and prickly. A little striped lizard, flattened along the sharp green bayonet of yucca, wears in its tiny face and watchful eye the pure look of death and violence. And all over the place, hidden at the bottom of their small sandy craters, the ant lions lie in wait for the ant that will stumble into their trap. (There are three kinds of lions in this region: the lions of the circus, the ant lions, and the Lions of the Tampa Lions Club, who roared their approval of segregation at a meeting the other day—all except one, a Lion named Monty Gurwit, who declined to roar and thereby got his picture in the paper.)
[10]   The day starts on a note of despair: the sorrowing dove, alone on its telephone wire, mourns the loss of night, weeps at the bright perils of the unfolding day. But soon the mockingbird wakes and begins an early rehearsal, setting the dove down by force of character, running through a few slick imitations, and trying a couple of original numbers into the bargain. The redbird takes it from there. Despair gives way to good humor. The Southern dawn is a pale affair, usually, quite different from our northern daybreak. It is a triumph of gradualism; night turns to day imperceptibly, softly, with no theatrics. It is subtle and undisturbing. As the first light seeps in through the blinds I lie in bed half awake, despairing with the dove, sounding the A for the brothers Alsop. All seems lost, all seems sorrowful. Then a mullet jumps in the bayou outside the bedroom window. It falls back into the water with a smart smack. I have asked several people why the mullet incessantly jump and I have received a variety of answers. Some say the mullet jump to shake off a parasite that annoys them. Some say they jump for the love of jumping—as the girl on the horse seemed to ride for the love of riding (although she, too, like all artists, may have been shaking off some parasite that fastens itself to the creative spirit and can be got rid of only by fifty turns around a ring while standing on a horse).
[11]   In Florida at this time of year, the sun does not take command of the day until a couple of hours after it has appeared in the east. It seems to carry no authority at first. The sun and the lizard keep the same schedule; they bide their time until the morning has advanced a good long way before they come fully forth and strike. The cold lizard waits astride his warming leaf for the perfect moment; the cold sun waits in his nest of clouds for the crucial time.

[12] On many days, the dampness of the air pervades all life, all living. Matches refuse to strike. The towel, hung to dry, grows wetter by the hour. The newspaper, with its headlines about integration, wilts in your hand and falls limply into the coffee and the egg. Envelopes seal themselves. Postage stamps mate with one another as shamelessly as grasshoppers. But most of the time the days are models of beauty and wonder and comfort, with the kind sea stroking the back of the warm sand. At evening there are great flights of birds over the sea, where the light lingers; the gulls, the pelicans, the terns, the herons stay aloft for half an hour after land birds have gone to roost. They hold their ancient formations, wheel and fish over the Pass, enjoying the last of day like children playing outdoors after suppertime.

[13] To a beachcomber from the North, which is my present status, the race problem has no pertinence, no immediacy. Here in Florida I am a guest in two houses—the house of the sun, the house of the State of Florida. As a guest, I mind my manners and do not criticize the customs of my hosts. It gives me a queer feeling, though, to be at the center of the greatest social crisis of my time and see hardly a sign of it. Yet the very absence of signs seems to increase one's awareness. Colored people do not come to the public beach to bathe, because they would not be made welcome there; and they don't fritter away their time visiting the circus, because they have other things to do. A few of them turn up at the ballpark, where they occupy a separate but equal section of the left-field bleachers and watch Negro players on the visiting Braves team using the same bases as the white players, instead of separate (but equal) bases. I have had only two small encounters with "color." A colored woman named Viola, who had been a friend of my wife's sister years ago, showed up one day with some laundry of ours that she had consented to do for us, and with the bundle she brought a bunch of nasturtiums, as a sort of natural accompaniment to the delivery of clean clothes. The flowers seemed a very acceptable thing and I was touched by them. We asked Viola about her daughter, and she said she was at Kentucky State College, studying voice.

[14] The other encounter was when I was explaining to our cook, who is from Finland, the mysteries of bus travel in the American Southland. I showed her the bus stop, armed her with a timetable, and then, as a matter of duty, mentioned the customs of the Romans. "When you get on the bus," I said, 'I think you'd better sit in one of the front seats— the seats in back are for colored people." A look of great weariness came into her face, as it does when we use too many dishes, and she replied, "Oh, I know—isn't it silly!"

[15] Her remark, coming as it did all the way from Finland and landing on this sandbar with a plunk, impressed me. The Supreme Court said nothing about silliness, but I suspect it may play more of a role than one might suppose. People are, if anything, more touchy about being thought silly than they are about being thought unjust. I note that one of the arguments in the recent manifesto of Southern Congressmen in support of the doctrine of "separate but equal" was that it had been founded on

"common sense." The sense that is common to one generation is uncommon to the next. Probably the first slave ship, with Negroes lying in chains on its decks, seemed commonsensical to the owners who operated it and to the planters who patronized it. But such a vessel would not be in the realm of common sense today. The only sense that is common, in the long run, is the sense of change—and we all instinctively avoid it, and object to the passage of time, and would rather have none of it.

[16]   The Supreme Court decision is like the Southern sun, laggard in its early stages, biding its time. It has been the law in Florida for two years now, and the years have been like the hours of the morning before the sun has gathered its strength. I think the decision is as incontrovertible and warming as the sun, and, like the sun, will eventually take charge.

[17]   But there is certainly a great temptation in Florida to duck the passage of time. Lying in warm comfort by the sea, you receive gratefully the gift of the sun, the gift of the South. This is true seduction. The day is a circle—morning, afternoon, and night. After a few days I was clearly enjoying the same delusion as the girl on the horse—that I could ride clear around the ring of day, guarded by wind and sun and sea and sand, and be not a moment older.

[18]   P.S. (April 1962).   When I first laid eyes on Fiddler Bayou, it was wild land, populated chiefly by the little crabs that gave it its name, visited by wading birds and by an occasional fisherman. Today, houses ring the bayou, and part of the mangrove shore has been bulkheaded with a concrete wall. Green lawns stretch from patio to water's edge, and sprinklers make rainbows in the light. But despite man's encroachment, Nature manages to hold her own and assert her authority: high tides and high winds in the Gulf sometimes send the sea crashing across the sand barrier, depositing its wrack on lawns and ringing everyone's front door bell. The birds and the crabs accommodate themselves quite readily to the changes that have taken place; every day brings herons to hunt around among the roots of mangroves, and I have discovered that I can approach to within about eight feet of a Little Blue Heron simply by entering the water and swimming slowly toward him. Apparently he has decided that when I'm in the water, I am without guile—possibly even desirable, like a fish.

[19]   The Ringling circus has quit Sarasota and gone elsewhere for its hibernation. A few circus families still own homes in the town, and every spring the students at the high school put on a circus, to let off steam, work off physical requirements, and provide a promotional spectacle for Sarasota. At the drugstore you can buy a postcard showing the bed John Ringling slept in. Time has not stood still for anybody but the dead, and even the dead must be able to hear the acceleration of little sports cars and know that things have changed.

[20]   From the all-wise New York Times, which has the animal kingdom ever in mind, I have learned that one of the creatures most acutely aware of the passing of time is the fiddler crab himself. Tiny spots on his body enlarge during daytime hours, giving him the same color as the mudbank

he explores and thus protecting him from his enemies. At night the spots shrink, his color fades, and he is almost invisible in the light of the moon. These changes are synchronized with the tides, so that each day they occur at a different hour. A scientist who experimented with the crabs to learn more about the phenomenon discovered that even when they are removed from their natural environment and held in confinement, the rhythm of their bodily change continues uninterrupted, and they mark the passage of time in their laboratory prison, faithful to the tides in their fashion.

Joan Didion

A Piece of Work for Now and Doomsday

[1]   I had better tell you first about the pull it has on me, that place, that thing, that idea, whatever it is you would call Hoover Dam. I first saw Hoover Dam on a burning afternoon in 1967, a day when I was in Las Vegas and wanted to be somewhere else and so, in the dull trance induced by having an air-conditioned car when the temperature is 110°, drove on out through the desert to the nearest large feature on the map, Lake Mead, the Colorado River, the Nevada-Arizona line. I would see the dam. I would watch the Bureau of Reclamation movie. I would forget Las Vegas for an hour or so and then I would drive back and forget whatever it was I had seen. But since that afternoon in 1967 the image of Hoover Dam has never been entirely absent from my inner eye. I will be talking to someone in Los Angeles, say, or New York, and suddenly the dam will materialize, its pristine concave face gleaming white against the harsh rusts and taupes and mauves of that rock canyon hundreds or thousands of miles from where I am. I will be driving down Sunset Boulevard, or about to enter a freeway, and abruptly those power transmission towers will appear before me, canted vertiginously over the tailrace. Sometimes I am confronted by the intakes and sometimes by the shadow of the heavy cable that spans the canyon and sometimes by the ominous outlets to unused spillways, black in the lunar clarity of the desert light. Quite often I hear the turbines. Frequently I wonder (even now I wonder) what is happening at the dam this instant, at this precise intersection of time and space, how much water is being released to fill downstream orders and what lights are flashing and which generators are in full use and which just spinning free.

[2]   A few weeks ago I went to Hoover Dam a second time, I suppose to

find out something about myself. I wanted to know what it was about the dam that made me think of it at times and in places where I once thought of the Mindanao Trench, or of the stars wheeling in their courses, or of the words *As it was in the beginning, is now, and ever shall be, world without end. Amen.* Dams, after all, are commonplace: we have all seen one. This particular dam had existed as an idea in the world's mind for almost 40 years before I saw it. Hoover Dam, showpiece of the Boulder Canyon project, the seven million tons of concrete that made the Southwest plausible, the *fait accompli* that was to convey, in the innocent time of its construction, the notion that mankind's brightest promise lay in American engineering.

[3]   Of course the dam derives some of its emotional effect from precisely that aspect, that sense of being a monument to a faith since misplaced. "They died to make the desert bloom," reads a plaque dedicated to the 96 men who died building this first of the great high dams, and *in situ* the worn phrase touches, suggests all of that trust in harnessing resources, in the meliorative power of the dynamo, so central to the early 1930s. Boulder City, built in 1931 as the construction town for the dam, retains the ambience of a model city, a new town, a toy triangular grid of green lawns and trim bungalows, all fanning out from the Reclamation building. The bronze sculptures at the dam itself evoke muscular citizens of a tomorrow that never came, sheaves of wheat clutched heavenward, thunderbolts defied. Winged Victories guard the flagpole. The flag whips in the canyon wind. An empty Pepsi-Cola can clatters across the terrazzo. The place is perfectly frozen in time.

[4]   But history does not explain it all, does not suggest what makes that damn so affecting. Nor, even, does energy, the massive involvement with power and pressure and the transparent sexual overtones to that involvement. On that day when I revisited the dam I walked through it with a man from the Bureau of Reclamation. For a while we trailed behind a guided tour, and then we went on, went into parts of the dam where visitors do not generally go. Once in a while he would explain something in that recondite language having to do with "peaking power," with "outages" and "dewatering," but on the whole we spent the afternoon in a world so alien, so complete and so beautiful unto itself that it was scarcely necessary to speak at all. We saw almost no one. Cranes moved above us as if under their own volition. Generators roared. Transformers hummed. The gratings on which we stood vibrated. We watched a 100-ton steel shaft plunging down to the place where the water was. And finally we got down to that place where the water was, where the water sucked out of Lake Mead roared through 30-foot penstock pipes and then into 13-foot penstocks and finally into the turbines themselves. "Touch it," the Reclamation man said, and I did, and for a long time I just stood there with my hands on the turbine. It was a peculiar moment, but so explicit as to suggest nothing beyond itself.

[5]   There was something beyond all that, beyond history, beyond energy, something I could not fix in my mind. When I came up from the dam the wind was blowing harder, through the canyon and all across the

Mojave. Later, toward Henderson and Las Vegas, there would be dust blowing, blowing past the Country-Western Casino FRI & SAT NITES and blowing past the Shrine of Our Lady of Safe Journey STOP & PRAY, but out here there was no dust, only the rock and the dam and a little grease-wood and a few garbage cans, their tops chained, banging against a fence. I walked across the marble star map that traces a sidereal revolution of the equinox and fixes forever, the Reclamation man had told me, for all time and for all people who can read the stars, the date the dam was dedicated. The star map was, he had said, for when we are all gone and the dam is not. I had not thought much of it when he said it, but I thought of it now, with the wind whining and the sun dropping behind a mesa with the finality of a sunset in space. Of course that was the image I had seen always, seen it without quite realizing what I saw, a dynamo finally free of man, splendid at last in its absolute isolation, releasing water and transmitting power to a world where no one is.

Annie Dillard

Catching the Season

[1]   Yesterday I set out to catch the new season, and instead I found an old snakeskin. I was in the sunny February woods by the quarry; the snakeskin was lying in a heap of leaves right next to an aquarium someone had thrown away. I don't know why that someone hauled the aquarium deep into the woods to get rid of it; it had only one broken glass side. The snake found it handy, I imagine; snakes like to rub against something rigid to help them out of their skins, and the broken aquarium looked like the nearest likely object. Together the snakeskin and the aquarium made an interesting scene on the forest floor. It looked like an exhibit at a trial—circumstantial evidence—of a wild scene, as though a snake had burst through the broken side of the aquarium, burst through his ugly old skin, and disappeared, perhaps straight up in the air, in a rush of freedom and beauty.

[2]   The snakeskin had unkeeled scales, so it belonged to a non-poisonous snake. It was roughly five feet long by the yardstick, but I'm not sure because it was very wrinkled and dry, and every time I tried to stretch it flat it broke. I ended up with seven or eight pieces of it all over the kitchen table in a fine film of forest dust.

[3]   The point I want to make about the snakeskin is that when I found

it, it was whole and tied in a knot. Now there have been stories told, even by reputable scientists, of snakes that have deliberately tied themselves in a knot to prevent larger snakes from trying to swallow them— but I couldn't imagine any way that throwing itself into a half hitch would help a snake trying to escape its skin. Still, ever cautious, I figured that one of the neighborhood boys could possibly have tied it in a knot in the fall, for some whimsical boyish reason, and left it there, where it dried and gathered dust. So I carried the skin along thoughtlessly as I walked, snagging it sure enough on a low branch and ripping it in two for the first of many times. I saw that thick ice still lay on the quarry pond and that the skunk cabbage was already out in the clearings, and then I came home and looked at the skin and its knot.

[4]   The knot had no beginning. I turned it around in my hand, searching for a place to untie; I came to with a start when I realized I must have turned the thing around fully ten times. Carefully then, I traced the knot's lump around with a finger: it was continuous. I couldn't untie it any more than I could untie a doughnut; it was a loop without beginning or end. These snakes *are* magic, I thought for a second, and then of course I figured out what had happened. The skin had been pulled inside-out like a peeled sock for several inches; then an inch or so of the inside-out part—a piece whose length was coincidentally equal to the diameter of the skin—had somehow been turned right-side out again, making a thick lump whose edges were lost in wrinkles, looking exactly like a knot.

[5]   So. I have been thinking about the change of seasons. I don't want to miss spring this year. I want to distinguish the last winter frost from the out-of-season one, the frost of spring. I want to be there on the spot the moment the grass turns green. I always miss this radical revolution; I see it the next day from a window, the yard so suddenly green and lush I could envy Nebuchadnezzar down on all fours eating grass. This year I want to stick a net into time and say "now," as men plant flags on the ice and snow and say, "here." But it occurred to me that I could no more catch spring by the tip of the tail than I could untie the apparent knot in the snakeskin; there are no edges to grasp. Both are continuous loops.

[6]   I wonder how long it would take you to notice the regular recurrence of the seasons if you were the first man on earth. What would it be like to live in open-ended time broken only by days and nights? You could say, "it's cold again; it was cold before," but you couldn't make the key connection and say, "it was cold this time last year," because the notion of "year" is precisely the one you lack. Assuming that you hadn't yet noticed any orderly progression of heavenly bodies, how long would you have to live on earth before you could feel with any assurance that any one particular long period of cold would, in fact, end? "While the earth remaineth, seedtime and harvest, and cold and heat, and summer and winter, and day and night shall not cease." God makes this guarantee very early in Genesis to a people whose fears on this point had been perhaps not completely allayed.

[7]   It must have been fantastically important, at the real beginnings of human culture, to conserve and relay this vital seasonal information, so that the people could anticipate dry or cold seasons, and not huddle on some November rock hoping pathetically that spring was just around the corner. We still very much stress the simple fact of four seasons to schoolchildren; even the most modern of modern new teachers, who don't seem to care if their charges can read or write or name two products of Peru, will still muster some seasonal chitchat and set the kids to making paper pumpkins, or tulips, for the walls. "The people," wrote Van Gogh in a letter, "are very sensitive to the changing seasons." That we are "very sensitive to the changing seasons" is, incidentally, one of the few good reasons to shun travel. If I stay at home I preserve the illusion that what is happening on Tinker Creek is the very newest thing, that I'm at the very vanguard and cutting edge of each new season. I don't want the same season twice in a row; I don't want to know I'm getting last week's weather, used weather, weather broadcast up and down the coast, old-hat weather.

[8]   But there's always unseasonable weather. What we think of the weather and behavior of life on the planet at any given season is really all a matter of statistical probabilities; at any given point, anything might happen. There is a bit of every season in each season. Green plants—deciduous green leaves—grow everywhere, all winter long, and small shoots come up pale and new in every season. Leaves die on the tree in May, turn brown, and fall into the creek. The calendar, the weather, and the behavior of wild creatures have the slimmest of connections. Everything overlaps smoothly for only a few weeks each season, and then it all gets mixed up again. The temperature, of course, lags far behind the calendar seasons, since the earth absorbs and releases heat slowly, like a leviathan breathing. Migrating birds head south in what appears to be dire panic, leaving mild weather and fields full of insects and seeds; they reappear as if in all eagerness in January, and poke about in the snow. Several years ago our October woods would have made a dismal colored photograph for a sadist's calendar: a killing frost came before the leaves had even begun to brown; they drooped from every tree like crepe, blackened and limp. It's all a chancy, jumbled affair at best, as things seem to be below the stars.

[9]   Time is the continuous loop, the snakeskin with scales endlessly overlapping without beginning or end, or time is an ascending spiral if you will, like a child's toy Slinky. Of course we have no idea which arc on the loop is our time, let alone where the loop itself is, so to speak, or down whose lofty flight of stairs the Slinky so uncannily walks.

[10]   The power we seek, too, seems to be a continuous loop. I have always been sympathetic with the early notion of a divine power that exists in a particular place, or that travels about over the face of the earth as a man might wander—and when he is "there" he is surely not here. You can shake the hand of a man you meet in the woods; but the spirit seems to roll along like the mythical hoop snake with its tail in its mouth. There are no hands to shake or edges to untie. It rolls along

the mountain ridges like a fireball, shooting off a spray of sparks at random, and will not be trapped, slowed, grasped, fetched, peeled or aimed. "As for the wheels, it was cried unto them in my hearing, O wheel." This is the hoop of flame that shoots the rapids in the creek or spins across the dizzy meadows; this is the arsonist of the sunny woods: catch it if you can.

Willie Morris

Mississippi
from *North Toward Home*

[1]   Half an hour north of Jackson on U.S. 49, not far beyond the Big Black River, the casual rolling land gives way to a succession of tall, lush hills, one after another for twelve or fifteen miles. In spring and summer the trees and underbrush are of an almost tropical density, and the whole terrain is grown over with a prolific green creeping vine, right up to the highway, and sometimes onto the concrete itself when the highway workers have let up a day too long. On a quiet day after a spring rain this stretch of earth seems prehistoric—damp, cool, inaccessible, the moss hanging from the giant old trees—and if you ignore the occasional diesel, churning up one of these hills on its way to Greenwood or Clarksdale or Memphis, you may feel you are in one of those sudden magic places of America, known mainly to the local people and merely taken for granted, never written about, not even on any of the tourist maps. To my knowledge this area of abrupt hills and deep descents does not have a name, but if you drive up and down them once on a fine day and never see them again, you will find them hard to forget.
[2]   Beyond these hills, if you follow the highway as it forks north and slightly west, the hills suddenly come to an end and there is one long, final descent. Out in the distance, as far as the eye can see, the land is flat, dark, and unbroken, sweeping away in a faint misty haze to the limits of the horizon. This is the great delta. Once it was the very floor under the sea; later knee-deep in waters and covered with primordial forests—a dank shadowy swampland, fetid and rich. There will not be a hill or a rise now until just below Memphis, 180 miles away. In a fast car a man can almost make it to Tennessee on automatic pilot, driving the straight, level road in a kind of euphoria, past the cotton fields and

the tenant shacks, the big plantation houses and the primitive little Negro churches, over the muddy creeks and rivers, through the counties with the forgotten Indian names—Leflore, Coahoma, Tallahatchie, Tunica.

[3]   The town where I grew up sits there on the edge of the delta, straddling that memorable divide where the hills end and the flat land begins. The town itself was half hills and half delta, only forty miles from the Mississippi as the crow flies. One afternoon when I was ten years old, lounging in front of the Phillips station on the street which came hell-bent out of the hills as the highway, I watched a man and his wife emerge from a Buick with Illinois plates. The woman smoothed out the wrinkles in her dress with her palm, paused for a second to look at the drab vistas of the downtown, and whispered, "My God!"

[4]   Its name was Yazoo City, from the river that flows by it from farther up in the delta—a muddy winding stream that takes in the Talla-hatchie, the Sunflower, and God knows how many less ambitious creeks and rivers in its southward course before it empties itself into the greater River a few miles north of Vicksburg. "Yazoo," far from being the ludi-crous name that others would take it, always meant for me something dark, a little blood-crazy and violent. It is, in fact, an old Indian name that means "Death," or "waters of the dead"; the Indians who once inhabited the region as fighters and hunters had died by the scores of some horrible disease. Stephen Foster at first meant his song to be "Way Down upon the Yazoo River," but it was rumored he found out about the meaning of the word, and felt he had been tricked. Hence the town was "death city" to its detractors, and to my contemporaries when I left the place later for college, I was called "Yazoo," such was the spell the very name exerted on you long after you had left it. When the Grey-hound out of Jackson stops at some dilapidated grocery store covered with patent medicine posters to pick up a few Negroes, or a solitary traveler waving a white handkerchief in the middle of nowhere, the driver will ask "Where to?" and the passenger will say "Yazoo," with the accent on the last syllable, rich and bass like a quick rumble of thunder.

[5]   In the nineteenth century the cotton growers, adventurous younger sons and brothers, came here from the older South where the land had played out, seeking the rich alluvial earth. Later the merchants came to exploit the commerce of the Yazoo River, where the old river boats were stacked ten and fifteen deep in cotton bales, and steamboats with names like the *Hard Cash,* the *City of Greenwood,* and the *Katie Robbins* plied their trade from the upper delta to Vicksburg. Keel- and flatboats laden with flour and apples started out on the Yazoo River, then entered the Mississippi and went all the way south to New Orleans. These early settlers had names like Beatty, Adams, Bull, Clark, Gray, Howard, Little, Robertson, Sparks, Taylor, Thompson, Walton, Whitehead, Young. The slaves had the names of the masters, and for years the tax lists of the place suggested the old Anglo-Saxon blood-source. Later others came to this lower delta—Italians, Irish, Jews, Syrians, even Chinese—to pro-

duce a curious melting pot, black, yellow, and white, and all the grada-
tions known to man.

[6]   For a white boy growing up in the 1940s it was a pleasant old
town; many of its streets were unpaved, although most of them in the
white neighborhoods would be sooner or later. Broadway, the street
that came swooping out of the hills, was the most unusual of all. Its
angle was so steep, and its descent from the top so long, that ever so
often the driver of some doomed car or truck would discover that his
brakes were not nearly sufficient to deal with this reckless terrain. His
path to death would be an agonizing one, as he whipped 80 or 90 miles
an hour out of those hills, usually crashing into another car or truck
where the ground leveled off at the intersection with Main Street. Once,
as we were told it later as children, a truckful of Negro cottonpickers
got out of control coming down that street and crashed into a big pecan
tree at 70 miles an hour; the dead and dying were thrown for yards
around, even into the broad limbs of the pecan tree.

[7]   The main street, stretching its several blocks from the Dixie
Theater at Broadway down to the cabin that housed Western Union
at the bend of the river, was always narrow and dingy, so that the gaudy
colored postcard of the "business district" on display in the drugstore
seemed more like another place altogether; and out along the highways
where the town began there was that raw, desperate, unsettled look,
much like towns I later would know in West Texas and the red-clay parts
of Louisiana. But down in the settled places, along the quiet, shady streets
with their pecan and elm and magnolia and locust trees were the stately
old houses, slightly dark and decaying before the descendants became
prosperous enough to have them "restored," which usually meant one
coat of white enamel. Even the names of the streets suggested they
might have been there for a while: Washington, Jefferson, Madison,
Monroe, Jackson, Calhoun, and, of course, College, which ran by the
high school.

[8]   All this was before the advent of a certain middle-class prosperity,
before the big supermarkets and the neighborhood "shopping centers,"
back when the game laws were the only device protecting Republicans,
both New ones and Old. Then it was a lazy town, stretched out on its
hills and its flat streets in a summer sun, a lethargic dreamy place, green
and lush all year except for those four stark months at the end and the
beginning, heavy with leafy smells, at night full of rumblings and lost
ghosts—the Yankees in the sunken gunboat down in the river, the witch
in the cemetery who burned down the whole town in 1904, Casey Jones
crashing headlong into that unfortunate Illinois Central freight. So isolated was the place that when a big passenger plane mistook the few
lights of the dirt airport for Jackson, circled around town and finally
came to a skidding halt in the mud, everyone who heard the motors
drove out to the airport before the lost plane landed, and a representative of the chamber of commerce put up a stepladder and said to each
passenger climbing down, "Welcome to Yazoo." All over the town,
everywhere, the Negro sections surrounded the white, and in that curious

fractured pattern which Northerners have never quite comprehended, many Negro and white houses sat side by side. But in the larger, unbroken Negro sections—on Brickyard Hill, in the river bottom with its shacks on stilts, around the town dump and the Cotton Club honkytonk where all the killings were said to take place Saturday nights—even in these a white boy would wander about any time he felt like it, feeling that damp adventure and pulsing of blood of walking through niggertown alone. I have a vivid image of myself as a child, on the first day the "city bus line" opened, riding all one afternoon in the only bus they owned, paying a nickel every time the rickety old vehicle turned around at the end of the line. We rode in great excitement and pride, having never had a bus line before, down Grand Avenue and Canal to Main, then turned around at the old Western Union station, headed up Main and Canal again and along the rim of Brickyard Hill over the same route: these were the limits of my world.

[9]   Somewhere I once saw a roster of the prominent people the place had produced. General Pershing's aide-de-camp. Senator John Sharp Williams, a friend and advisor of Woodrow Wilson. Hershel Brickell, a literary critic in New York, who died the day I finished my last examinations in high school. Who remembers them now, who knows much about them or cares? And who knows, for no one has any records, what Negroes came from this common place, moved to Chicago or Harlem, and remembered in pleasure or anguish what they had left behind? As a boy Richard Wright lived on a tenant farm not far from the town. Once, many years later, when I was full grown and twenty-two, I found myself in Paris; I got Wright's phone number and called him, saying I was a white Yazoo boy. "You're from Yazoo?" he asked. "Well, come on over." We went out to an Arab bar and got a little drunk together, and talked about the place we both had known. I asked him, "Will you ever come back to America?" "No," he said. "I want my children to grow up as human beings." After a time a silence fell between us, like an immense pain—or maybe it was my imagining.

Samuel L. Clemens

Continued Perplexities
from Life on the Mississippi

[1]   There was no use in arguing with a person like this. I promptly put such a strain on my memory that by and by even the shoal water and the countless crossing-marks began to stay with me. But the result was just the same. I never could more than get one knotty thing learned

before another presented itself. Now I had often seen pilots gazing at
the water and pretending to read it as if it were a book; but it was a
book that told me nothing. A time came at last, however, when Mr.
Bixby seemed to think me far enough advanced to bear a lesson on water-
reading. So he began:

"Do you see that long, slanting line on the face of the water?
Now, that's a reef. Moreover, it's a bluff reef. There is a solid sand-bar
under it that is nearly as straight up and down as the side of a house.
There is plenty of water close up to it, but mighty little on top of it.
If you were to hit it you would knock the boat's brains out. Do you see
where the line fringes out at the upper end and begins to fade away?"

"Yes, sir."

"Well, that is a low place; that is the head of the reef. You can
climb over there, and not hurt anything. Cross over, now, and follow
along close under the reef—easy water there—not much current."

[5]   I followed the reef along till I approached the fringed end. Then
Mr. Bixby said:

"Now get ready. Wait till I give the word. She won't want to
mount the reef; a boat hates shoal water. Stand by—wait—*wait*—keep
her well in hand. *Now* cramp her down! Snatch her! snatch her!"

He seized the other side of the wheel and helped to spin it around
until it was hard down, and then we held it so. The boat resisted, and
refused to answer for a while, and next she came surging to starboard,
mounted the reef, and sent a long, angry ridge of water foaming away
from her bows.

"Now watch her; watch her like a cat, or she'll get away from you.
When she fights strong and the tiller slips a little, in a jerky, greasy sort
of way, let up on her a trifle; it is the way she tells you at night that the
water is too shoal; but keep edging her up, little by little, toward the
point. You are well up on the bar now; there is a bar under every point,
because the water that comes down around it forms an eddy and allows
the sediment to sink. Do you see those fine lines on the face of the water
that branch out like the ribs of a fan? Well, those are little reefs; you
want to just miss the ends of them, but run them pretty close. Now look
out—look out! Don't you crowd that slick, greasy-looking place; there
ain't nine feet there; she won't stand it. She begins to smell it; look
sharp, I tell you! Oh, blazes, there you go! Stop the starboard wheel!
Quick! Ship up to back! Set her back!"

The engine bells jingled and the engines answered promptly,
shooting white columns of steam far aloft out of the 'scape-pipes, but it
was too late. The boat had "smelt" the bar in good earnest; the foamy
ridges that radiated from her bows suddenly disappeared, a great dead
swell came rolling forward, and swept ahead of her, she careened far
over to larboard, and went tearing away toward the shore as if she were
about scared to death. We were a good mile from where we ought to
have been when we finally got the upper hand of her again.

[10]   During the afternoon watch the next day, Mr. Bixby asked me if
I knew how to run the next few miles. I said:

"Go inside the first snag above the point, outside the next one, start out from the lower end of Higgins's woodyard, make a square crossing, and—"

"That's all right. I'll be back before you close up on the next point."

But he wasn't. He was still below when I rounded it and entered upon a piece of the river which I had some misgivings about. I did not know that he was hiding behind a chimney to see how I would perform. I went gaily along, getting prouder and prouder, for he had never left the boat in my sole charge such a length of time before. I even got to "setting" her and letting the wheel go entirely, while I vaingloriously turned by back and inspected the stern marks and hummed a tune, a sort of easy indifference which I had prodigiously admired in Bixby and other great pilots. Once I inspected rather long, and when I faced to the front again my heart flew into my mouth so suddenly that if I hadn't clapped my teeth together I should have lost it. One of those frightful bluff reefs was stretching its deadly length right across our bows! My head was gone in a moment; I did not know which end I stood on; I gasped and could not get my breath; I spun the wheel down with such rapidity that it wove itself together like a spider's web; the boat answered and turned square away from the reef, but the reef followed her! I fled, but still it followed, still it kept—right across my bows! I never looked to see where I was going, I only fled. The awful crash was imminent. Why didn't that villain come? If I committed the crime of ringing a bell I might get thrown overboard. But better that than kill the boat. So in blind desperation, I started such a rattling "shivaree" down below as never had astounded an engineer in this world before, I fancy. Amidst the frenzy of the bells the engines began to back and fill in a curious way, and my reason forsook its throne—we were about to crash into the woods on the other side of the river. Just then Mr. Bixby stepped calmly into view on the hurricane-deck. My soul went out to him in gratitude. My distress vanished; I would have felt safe on the brink of Niagara with Mr. Bixby on the hurricane-deck. He blandly and sweetly took his toothpick out of his mouth between his fingers, as if it were a cigar— we were just in the act of climbing an overhanging big tree, and the passengers were scudding astern like rats—and lifted up these commands to me ever so gently:

"Stop the starboard! Stop the larboard! Set her back on both!"

[15]   The boat hesitated, halted, pressed her nose among the boughs a critical instant, then reluctantly began to back away.

"Stop the larboard! Come ahead on it! Stop the starboard! Come ahead on it! Point her for the bar!"

I sailed away as serenely as a summer's morning. Mr. Bixby came in and said, with mock simplicity:

"When you have a hail, my boy, you ought to tap the big bell three times before you land, so that the engineers can get ready."

I blushed under the sarcasm, and said I hadn't had any hail.

[20]   "Ah! Then it was for wood, I suppose. The officer of the watch will tell you when he wants to wood up."

I went on consuming, and said I wasn't after wood.

"Indeed? Why, what could you want over here in the bend, then? Did you ever know of a boat following a bend up-stream at this stage of the river?"

"No, sir—and *I* wasn't trying to follow it. I was getting away from a bluff reef."

"No, it wasn't a bluff reef; there isn't one within three miles of where you were."

[25] "But I saw it. It was as bluff as that one yonder."

"Just about. Run over it!"

"Do you give it as an order?"

"Yes. Run over it!"

"If I don't, I wish I may die."

[30] "All right; I am taking the responsibility."

I was just as anxious to kill the boat, now, as I had been to save it before. I impressed my orders upon my memory, to be used at the inquest, and made a straight break for the reef. As it disappeared under our bows I held my breath; but we slid over it like oil.

"Now, don't you see the difference? It wasn't anything but a *wind* reef. The wind does that."

"So I see. But it is exactly like a bluff reef. How am I ever going to tell them apart?"

"I can't tell you. It is an instinct. By and by you will just naturally *know* one from the other, but you never will be able to explain why or how you know them apart."

[35] It turned out to be true. The face of the water, in time, became a wonderful book—a book that was a dead language to the uneducated passenger, but which told its mind to me without reserve, delivering its most cherished secrets as clearly as if it uttered them with a voice. And it was not a book to be read once and thrown aside, for it had a new story to tell every day. Throughout the long twelve hundred miles there was never a page that was void of interest, never one that you could leave unread without loss, never one that you would want to skip, thinking you could find higher enjoyment in some other thing. There never was so wonderful a book written by man; never one whose interest was so absorbing, so unflagging, so sparklingly renewed with every reperusal. The passenger who could not read it was charmed with a peculiar sort of faint dimple on its surface (on the rare occasions when he did not overlook it altogether); but to the pilot that was an *italicized* passage; indeed, it was more than that, it was a legend of the largest capitals, with a string of shouting exclamation-points at the end of it, for it meant that a wreck or a rock was buried there that could tear the life out of the strongest vessel that ever floated. It is the faintest and simplest expression the water ever makes, and the most hideous to a pilot's eye. In truth, the passenger who could not read this book saw nothing but all manner of pretty pictures in it, painted by the sun and shaded by the clouds, whereas to the trained eye these were not pictures at all, but the grimmest and most dead-earnest of reading-matter.

Now when I had mastered the language of this water, and had come to know every trifling feature that bordered the great river as familiarly as I knew the letters of the alphabet, I had made a valuable acquisition. But I had lost something, too. I had lost something which could never be restored to me while I lived. All the grace, the beauty, the poetry, had gone out of the majestic river! I still kept in mind a certain wonderful sunset which I witnessed when steamboating was new to me. A broad expanse of the river was turned to blood; in the middle distance the red hue brightened into gold, through which a solitary log came floating, black and conspicuous; in one place a long, slanting mark lay sparkling upon the water; in another the surface was broken by boiling, tumbling rings, that were as many-tinted as an opal; where the ruddy flush was faintest, was a smooth spot that was covered with graceful circles and radiating lines, ever so delicately traced; the shore on our left was densely wooded, and the somber shadow that fell from this forest was broken in one place by a long, ruffled trail that shone like silver; and high above the forest wall a clean-stemmed dead tree waved a single leafy bough that glowed like a flame in the unobstructed splendor that was flowing from the sun. There were graceful curves, reflected images, woody heights, soft distances; and over the whole scene, far and near, the dissolving lights drifted steadily, enriching it every passing moment with new marvels of coloring.

I stood like one bewitched. I drank it in, in a speechless rapture. The world was new to me, and I had never seen anything like this at home. But as I have said, a day came when I began to cease from noting the glories and the charms which the moon and the sun and the twilight wrought upon the river's face; another day came when I ceased altogether to note them. Then, if that sunset scene had been repeated, I should have looked upon it without rapture, and should have commented upon it, inwardly, after this fashion: "This sun means that we are going to have wind to-morrow; that floating log means that the river is rising, small thanks to it; that slanting mark on the water refers to a bluff reef which is going to kill somebody's steamboat one of these nights, if it keeps on stretching out like that; those tumbling 'boils' show a dissolving bar and a changing channel there; the lines and circles in the slick water over yonder are a warning that that troublesome place is shoaling up dangerously; that silver streak in the shadow of the forest is the 'break' from a new snag, and he has located himself in the very best place he could have found to fish for steamboats; that tall dead tree, with a single living branch, is not going to last long, and then how is a body ever going to get through this blind place at night without the friendly old landmark?"

No, the romance and beauty were all gone from the river. All the value any feature of it had for me now was the amount of usefulness it could furnish toward compassing the safe piloting of a steamboat. Since those days, I have pitied doctors from my heart. What does the lovely flush in a beauty's cheek mean to a doctor but a "break" that ripples above some deadly disease? Are not all her visible charms sown thick with what are to him the signs and symbols of hidden decay? Does he ever see her beauty at all, or doesn't he simply view her professionally, and comment upon her unwholesome condition all to himself? And doesn't he sometimes wonder whether he has gained most or lost most by learning his trade?

Susan B. Lindsay

A Neutral Zone

Dennis Gregg swung Jennifer's orange folder back and forth so that the pages flashed white in the schoolyard playground.

"Give it, Dennis."

"Well why do you bring it out here to recess all the time anyway?"

"Give me back my folder." Jennifer glanced over her shoulder. The last of the class was entering the squat rectangular school building.

"Dumb girls, what does anybody want a stupid folder with 'em for just to play kickball?"

"You listen here, Dennis Gregg," Jennifer stepped towards him, "give me back that folder—RIGHT NOW!"

He let it slide through his fingers. Weakly, the folder slapped the asphalt. "Or you're going to do what, Jennifer? Tell on me?"

She lunged, but Dennis reached it first and shoved her backwards.

"Jennifer is a crybaby. Crybaby. Crybaby." He tipped his chin to look at her through one half-closed eye. "What you got in here anyway, Jennifer?"

"None of your business," she said, stiffening.

"So special you won't let anybody see, huh?"

"Dennis," Jennifer curled her fingers into her palms and squeezed. "Give it here." She stopped, considered, thought she'd better not, but then said it anyway. "Besides, you couldn't even read it if you tried! Now give it!"

"Oh yea, I almost forgot, Jennifer." He backed away. "You're so smart you don't have to be in any spelling bees . . ."

No. Jennifer ground her tightly balled fist on her hips, till she could feel the bone almost poking through.

"You know so many words . . ."

He ought to stumble when he backs off the pavement. Maybe.

"So many big words, Jennifer. And you don't want to make us feel dumb, so . . ."

Shut up, Dennis Gregg, shut shut shut SHUT UP! Then quietly, "Give it Dennis," counting his steps. Eight more maybe.

". . . and Miss Mendel gives you stars on your spelling words without even looking . . ."

Two more steps.

". . . wanna see me read it? Huh Jennifer?"

He jerked backwards, caught himself with one hand, and then ran—holding the folder open in front of him. "Parent, me," he yelled.

Jennifer ran, too.

"home, don't, . . ."

Stop it. It's mine.

"fight . . ." Dennis dodged the water fountain, pausing for breath. "Dear Mom and Da-"

Driving her shoulder into his knee, she felt the ground hit them both through his shudder. Anything soft she pounded with her fists.

When Miss Mendel arrived, Jennifer had already smoothed the wrinkled pages; she stood with her back to Dennis, arms folded across the dirt-streaked notebook like a shield she was trying to hide.

"All right. What's going on out here? Jennifer. Dennis?"

"Nothing," Jennifer said, staring at the building. She cradled a raw elbow with one hand so Miss Mendel wouldn't see.

"Get up off the ground, Dennis. Now, what happened? Something must have hap-."

"Nothing happened." Jennifer walked stiffly towards the front entrance. She'd put it under her arithmetic book, at the bottom of her desk. For today at least. By the time Miss Mendel and Dennis got back it would be safe.

"All right, class. All right—Dennis, you sit down, recess is over—." Miss Mendel smiled a cheerleader smile. The box of stars and red marking pens she held up should have been pom-poms. "I want everybody to take out your spelling notebooks and I'll come around to check this week's lesson."

"Just for a stupid folder," Dennis hissed on the way to his seat.

Jennifer looked down her shins at the brown and white saddle oxfords in the middle of the aisle.

This is Mission Control. Do you read me, Toes?

Toes to Mission Control, we read you loud and clear.

Toes, we're going to check out that pair of shoes out there, are you ready?

Toes ready, Mission Control.

Here we go then. Left big toe—up.

Roger, left big toe up.

"No Dennis, and starts with an A, not an E. If the word starts with an E then it spells end. E-N-D spells end. A-N-D spells and." Miss Mendel gave him a check.

Dennis always got a check.

Right big toe—up.

Right big toe beginning to go up. Mission Control, what does it look like up there? We can't go any farther.

She'd have to leave the folder at home now.

Calling all toes.

Couldn't leave it in her room though, probably in the treehouse.

Calling all toes. Toes, this is Mission Control. The shoes are definitely ours.

We see two white bumps from up here.

Good job men.

"Jennifer, I keep telling you that if you insist on sitting sideways with your feet in the aisle like that someone is going to trip. Then you'd feel awfully bad, wouldn't you?" Miss Mendel tilted her head sideways so that her hair stuck inside her collar. "There, now that you've seated yourself properly, like a lady, let's see if you've done your usual excellent job."

Jennifer raised the desk top. Set on top of her books was another orange folder. SPELLING printed at the top in Miss Mendel's magic marker and JENNIFER RHODES under that. Before she took it out she touched under her arithmetic book.

"Mmm." Miss Mendel bent over Jennifer's shoulder, frowning at the neat column of words.

Left toe up—and keep it quiet.

Left toe up, Mission Control.

We can't go any farther. What's going on up there?

Don't worry about it, we'll take care of it from up here.

Down now. Thanks, we found out what we wanted to know.

"Mm-hmm," Miss Mendel turned the page and frowned her way down the exercise where they had to make sentences with all the words they'd had during the week. The box of stars seemed to hang over Jennifer's head.

"Well, that just about does it." Miss Mendel pressed a star onto the corner of the page. "You've still got a perfect record, Jennifer." She nodded, leaning closer as if she was going to tell Jennifer a secret. "You know, I bet you're the best speller in the class. It's too bad nobody else—"

Jennifer shut the spelling folder and put it away. Dennis was probably looking at her. She'd definitely keep her folder in the treehouse.

"You really ought to try the spelling bees again. Why, Jennifer, you won the first few we had." Miss Mendel kneeled down, steadying herself with a hand on the back of Jennifer's seat. "—And I just don't understand why you won't take part . . ."

Dennis was staring at her for sure, now.

"No," Jennifer said, looking at the desk top.

"And you're such a good speller! It's lots of fun . . ."

Jennifer looked down into Miss Mendel's face. "No," she said, forcing the big word through a tiny opening in her lips. Miss Mendel's eyes got very round. She moved to the next desk.

Halfway down the dark stairs, Jennifer squatted on the landing to look through the bannister poles. Her heels made two round cold spots on her haunches.

The den always looked so warm after dinner was all out of the way, like somebody had painted a picture inside the door frame. She wrapped her arms around her legs and squeezed her spelling book between thighs and chest. A neutral zone between warm skin and warm skin.

The couch was almost hidden by the door. She could just see the back of her mother's head and beyond that, Bobby sprawled on his stomach watching TV and drawing circles in the air with one foot. Her dad usually worked down the basement after dinner.

Jennifer eased over the squeaky stair and tip-toed up behind her mother.

"Boo!"

"Jennifer!" Mrs. Rhodes snapped her chin to her shoulder, then smiled. "Jennifer, you startled me. Time for your spelling words, right?"

Jennifer grinned and nodded. "Yup—" she didn't have to ask. "I mean, yes m'am."

"OK, run up and get your book, silly child. It never ceases to amaze me that you can forget your spelling words from one night to the next."

Jennifer waited. Now her mother would shake her head and sigh, and Jennifer would look at the floor and shrug her shoulders.

She shrugged.

Mission Control to Jennifer.

Mission Control to Jennifer.

Check, roger, over and out.

"Now go get your book."

Jennifer sashayed around the sofa's end, her upper lip stretching across the gap where one front tooth was missing. *My Spelling Words— Book Two* rested on a platform she made with her hands.

"I declare, I don't know what I'm going to do with you, child. You're just getting to be so smart. Come on up here."

Settling herself on the couch, Jennifer smiled to the room over the crook in her mother's elbow. Bobby glanced back and rolled his eyes. She stuck her tongue out at him.

"Ready?" her mother said.

They spelled. Jennifer's mother calling the words softly. Jennifer feeling her own warm breath bounce from her mother's arm back over her face with each letter. Bobby leaned forward once to turn up the TV.

"OK, Jennifer, that's it. Up to bed."

"Let's do it once more mom." Please. "Just to make sure I know 'em?"

"Oh all right. Once more smartypants, but after that you've got to run up to bed. Agreed?"

Jennifer relaxed, smiling.

"Him."

"H-I-M."

"Food."

"F-O-O-D."

The basement door squeaked. Her dad must be finished working.

"House."

"H-O-U-S-E."

Jennifer's mother half-rose and twisted around so that she had to scramble sideways to avoid getting bumped. "Carl," she said. No answer. Mrs. Rhodes settled back on the couch. "Please," she said, still facing the door.

"P-L-E-A-S-E," Jennifer whispered.

"What?" her mother turned to the spelling book.

"P-L-E-A-S-E—mama?"

"OK Jennifer, up to bed."

"Come up with me, mom."

"I'll be up in a little while to check on you."

"Ple—"

Bobby sat up so he could see the television better. He spoke to the two football teams preparing for kick-off: "What's wrong, can't the baby put herself to bed?"

Jennifer glared, drew herself up and walked out of the room. In the kitchen her mother and father were starting again. They'd talk in angry whispers for a while because they thought she was asleep, and then they'd forget and she'd hear them yelling until Bobby turned up the TV even louder.

P-L-E-A-S-E, P-L-E-A-S-E, P-L-E-A-S-E, she spelled softly. One letter for each stair. P-L-E-A-S-E, P-L-E-A-S-E, she whispered, sliding between cold sheets, curling inward like a pill bug. Please, she whispered to her knees.

"Jennifer!" Bobby called from the back porch.

Jennifer wrinkled her nose so the knots in the pine boards looked like big beetles creeping towards the orange folder open in her lap. The treehouse wasn't much bigger than she was. When she lay on her stomach and spread her arms she could dangle both hands underneath, and she liked to think about hugging it to her.

"What do you want?" She yelled through the screen of leaves toward the house. Leaning on her good elbow, Jennifer frowned at the smudged fingerprints on the paper. "Mom said to come inside!"

When she put one fist on one cheek and one on the other, and pushed, the list of words blurred into a single grey column.

"Jennifer! Mom said to come inside, dinner's ready, Jennifer! . . . Mom! Jennifer won't come!"

She let the words refocus, examined her pencil point, took a deep breath, and began to write. P—her eyebrows tried to touch and then gave up . . . L—it was almost as if . . . E—she could squeeze . . . A—herself . . . S—out . . . E—of the pencil point and onto the page.

Whew! Jennifer rested against the tree trunk. It was going to be so neat when her parents got the letter. Some things you just didn't say to people right out. Like when she talked about the space between Karen Bright's teeth at dinner one night. "You don't want to make her feel bad about it, besides, she probably already knows," her mother had said. "Anyway, it might make you feel bad, too, after you said it." She couldn't tell Jennifer why.

One more thing to take care of. Jennifer bit her pencil behind her two front teeth and flipped past all the pages starting with "Dear Mom and Dad." If she started with "Dear Mom and Dad," they'd know who sent it. At the top of a clean page she copied "Mr. and Mrs. Carl R. Rhodes" from the envelope she'd already addressed. That might do. She riffled the pages next to her ear for the whirring sound, and climbed down to go to dinner.

Hot dogs! Good. Applesauce. Bleah. Without pulling the chair away from the table, Jennifer slipped into her seat across from Bobby. Her father must have come home late. He still wore his tie close up around his neck.

"Jennifer, you're late," he said. "Are your hands clean?"

"Nope . . ." Jennifer glanced sideways at her mother, "No sir, be back in a minute."

"Jennifer?" Mrs. Rhodes lowered her eyebrows.

"Oh, sorry. Excuse me please."

When she came back her mother was pushing her corn around with her fork like she couldn't find a piece worth eating. Jennifer questioned her own small pile of yellow kernels. It looked OK. Must be all right the way dad was eating his; in fact, he'd probably be ready for seconds soon. Anyway, the hot dog first.

"Pardon me, Carl. I didn't mean to bring up something that was going to become another 'issue.' "

Jennifer stopped the hot dog half-way to her mouth. It hung there, stupidly, in mid-air.

"No wait, Marilyn. Just because I said I was going to stay home with my family for my two weeks of vacation, my only two weeks, instead of going to a convention, you say I should go away—and take a rest."

"All I said was—"

Jennifer ignored Bobby's pointed stare at the napkin beside her plate and bit a chunk off her hot dog, chomping deliberately. He shook his head and looked back to his own plate.

"Dammit, Marilyn. I know what you said, but I also know what you meant."

Jennifer dropped her spoon into the mound of applesauce in the center of her plate so that it made smacking noises when it landed and sucking noises when she pulled it out.

"What do you think you're doing?" Bobby said, stretching to see over the ketchup bottle, mustard jar, lemon juice, and salt and pepper shakers.

"None of your beeswax," she said, and raised her spoon.

"That's enough, Carl. Let's just don't discuss it."

Bobby stabbed his fork at her. "You're going to get in trouble."

"Certainly, Marilyn, we're going to drop the whole thing, just like it never happened."

"Who says?" Jennifer pointed her spoon at him.

"You just are. Wait and see."

"Bet-cha," Jennifer said, "Watch!" But Bobby drained his milk glass, garbled "May I be excused?" through a mouthful of cookie crumbs, and was out the door before her spoon slapped wetly on the plate. She heard him kick the trash can on his way around the corner of the garage.

"Carl—all I meant was that I thought it might be good if you—"

"That's all right, Marilyn, we won't discuss it."

Jennifer hooked her ankles over the chair rung. Maybe she ought to copy over one of the words from fighting to hurting. The watery puddle of applesauce stared limpidly at her like a big wet eye. Words. She couldn't find all the words. Her throat closed around the chunk of hot dog and squeezed.

Her father scraped his fork across his plate for the last of the corn; her mother didn't say anything. She always got funny wrinkles at the corner of her mouth when she tried not to cry.

Jennifer strained against the chair rung till the indentations in the wood started to carve red-purple notches in her skin. They just didn't realize what they were doing. Her mother said that a lot. Like when she'd ask why Bobby was so mean to her. "He's just teasing," she'd say. "If he knew it hurt that much he wouldn't do it. For the time being you just pretend it doesn't bother you. Can you do that for me?" Jennifer smiled.

Her father's fist struck the table, jarring silverware. "I wish someone would let me know what is so amusing."

Jennifer froze. He had seen her smile? She looked at the corner of her place mat. Then his tie. Finally his eyes.

He was looking at her mother.

Jennifer left the table.

Jennifer sat sideways in her seat, copying the words Miss Mendel wrote on the board. The long stick of chalk looked like an extension of her index finger. T-O-G-E-T-H-E-R. The words were getting longer.

"Wow Jennifer," Dennis said sarcastically. "You gonna get a star this week, too?"

"You shut up Dennis." Jennifer turned in her seat and copied the last word. He sat behind her now.

"Hey Jennifer." She could feel him breathing on her shoulder. Sticky. "Where's your orange folder?" The muscles in her neck drew up like wet twine.

"Dennis and Jennifer." Miss Mendel called from the front. "If I have to tell either of you to be quiet once more, you'll both be punished."

Jennifer leaned forward and set her chin in the pencil holder. That way she didn't have to feel him breathing on her at least. He better shut up about that folder.

"Is everybody finished?" The spelling bee was set for after recess.

Jennifer sighed; Miss Mendel had finally given up trying to make her take part. Usually she sat sideways and stared at the chalkboard, or her desk, trying to figure out if any of the new words would fit in her letter. It was almost finished now. All she needed was an ending, but she didn't have a word for that yet.

"All right, class, since everybody's finished the spelling words you can go out for recess now." Miss Mendel waved towards the back playground. "Jennifer, can you stay a minute? I'd like to talk to you."

Jennifer slid her shoe tips down the metal legs of the next desk. They hit the floor with a muffled smack. After the others had left, Miss Mendel came and sat in front of her.

"Jennifer, I know you don't like the spelling bees—and that's all right—" Jennifer turned sideways again. "Really, Jennifer, that's all right, you don't have to be in them if you don't want to."

Jennifer pressed her thumb into her thigh. The round patch of skin went white, then pink.

"Anyway, Jennifer, I just wondered if maybe you wanted to tell me why they bother you so much?"

This time it went white, pink, then red.

"I mean, you don't have to tell me, don't feel you have to tell me. It's just that you're such a good speller and I guess I don't understand. Are you afraid . . . maybe?"

"No," Jennifer barely opened her mouth.

"I didn't really think so since you did so well at the beginning." She coughed. "Is it . . . maybe something at home is bothering you?"

"No." Jennifer said sharply, covering the small red welt with her hand. No.

"The only reason I asked was because you've seemed so preoccupied—not paying attention lately—Jennifer?" Miss Mendel sighed. "I'm glad nothing's wrong."

Jennifer concentrated instead on her saddle oxfords.

Toes, this is Mission Control, do you read me?

Do you read me Toes?

"I guess that's all then, Jennifer. I won't force you to be in the spelling bees if you just don't want to be. That's all it is, isn't it?"

"Yes m'am," Jennifer said. Nothing's wrong.

Toes, do you read me?

It seemed like Dennis Gregg was tearing the pages out of her folder, dropping them over the edge of her treehouse, one by one.

"I thought about calling your mother a number of times, but I'm glad I waited to ask you first, Jennifer? . . . if you ever want to be in a spelling bee would you let me know?"

Jennifer pulled her chin up twice in reply.

"I guess you can go play now."

Jennifer didn't stop walking when she got to the playground; she didn't even slow down till the lady in front of the Winn-Dixie stopped

her and asked her what school she went to. "So you'd rather be an anonymous truant, is that it?" The lady had said when Jennifer just shook
her head.

"What's that mean?" Jennifer asked. "Anonymous or truant."

"A truant is somebody who isn't in school when they're supposed
to be. Anonymous is when nobody knows who you are."

"I'm the second one," Jennifer said before she ran.

She'd just show them. She sneaked through the back yard but the
car wasn't in the driveway anyway. Clamping her pencil between her
teeth, she grabbed the first rung of the ladder.

All she had to do now was stick the letter in the mailbox.

Anonymous. She thumbed through the folder till the envelope
slipped out and then spread the letter. "Mr. and Mrs. Carl R. Rhodes,"
she skimmed it, moving her lips. Some of those words, like family and
children, had taken a long time to collect.

Down at the bottom where it said "love," she wrote AN. Onimus
was going to be harder. She sounded it to herself the way Miss Mendel
made them read words they didn't know, one syllable at a time: "On-im-
us," she said softly. O-N. Im, like in *him,* I-M. Us, that was an easy one,
U-S. "An onimus, an onimus, an onimus."

The words blurred into each other.

N. Scott Momaday

The Priest of the Sun

Sunday 8:30 P.M.
"The Way to Rainy Mountain"
Be kind to a white man today

[1]   The basement was cold and dreary, dimly illuminated by two 40-
watt bulbs which were screwed into the side walls above the dais. This
platform was made out of rough planks of various woods and dimensions,
thrown together without so much as a hammer and nails; it stood seven
or eight inches above the floor, and it supported the tin firebox and the
crescent altar. Off to one side was a kind of lectern, decorated with red
and yellow symbols of the sun and moon. In back of the dais there was
a screen of purple drapery, threadbare and badly faded. On either side
of the aisle which led to the altar there were chairs and crates, fashioned

into pews. The walls were bare and gray and streaked with water. The only windows were small, rectangular openings near the ceiling, at ground level; the panes were covered over with a thick film of coal oil and dust, and spider webs clung to the frames or floated out like smoke across the room. The air was heavy and stale; odors of old smoke and incense lingered all around. The people had filed into the pews and were waiting silently.

[2] Cruz, a squat, oily man with blue-black hair that stood out like spines from his head, stepped forward on the platform and raised his hands as if to ask for the quiet that already was. Everyone watched him for a moment; in the dull light his skin shone yellow with sweat. Turning slightly and extending his arm behind him, he said, "The Right Reverend John Big Bluff Tosamah."

[3] There was a ripple in the dark screen; the drapes parted and the Priest of the Sun appeared, moving shadow-like to the lectern. He was shaggy and awful-looking in the thin, naked light: big, lithe as a cat, narrow-eyed, suggesting in the whole of his look and manner both arrogance and agony. He wore black like a cleric; he had the voice of a great dog:

[4] " '*In principio erat Verbum.*' Think of Genesis. Think of how it was before the world was made. There was nothing, the Bible says. 'And the earth was without form, and void; and darkness was upon the face of the deep.' It was dark, and there was nothing. There were no mountains, no trees, no rocks, no rivers. There was nothing. But there was darkness all around, and in the darkness something happened. *Something happened!* There was a single sound. Far away in the darkness there was a single sound. Nothing made it, but it was there; and there was no one to hear it, but it was there. It was there, and there was nothing else. It rose up in the darkness, little and still, almost nothing in itself—like a single soft breath, like the wind arising; yes, like the whisper of the wind rising slowly and going out into the early morning. But there was no wind. There was only the sound, little and soft. It was almost nothing in itself, the smallest seed of sound—but it took hold of the darkness and there was light; it took hold of the stillness and there was motion forever; it took hold of the silence and there was sound. It was almost nothing in itself, a single sound, a word—a word broken off at the darkest center of the night and let go in the awful void, forever and forever. And it was almost nothing in itself. It scarcely was; but it was, and everything began."

[5] Just then a remarkable thing happened. The Priest of the Sun seemed stricken; he let go of his audience and withdrew into himself, into some strange potential of himself. His voice, which had been low and resonant, suddenly became harsh and flat; his shoulders sagged and his stomach protruded, as if he had held his breath to the limit of endurance; for a moment there was a look of amazement, then utter carelessness in his face. Conviction, caricature, callousness: the remainder of his sermon was a going back and forth among these.

[6] "Thank you so much, Brother Cruz. Good evening, blood brothers

and sisters, and welcome, welcome. Gracious me, I see lots of new faces
out there tonight. *Gracious me!* May the Great Spirit—can we knock off
that talking in the back there?—be with you always.

[7]   " 'In the begining was the Word.' I have taken as my text this
evening the almighty Word itself. Now get this: 'There was a man sent
from God, whose name was John. The same came for a witness, to bear
witness of the Light, that all men through him might believe.' Amen,
brothers and sisters, *Amen.* And the riddle of the Word, 'In the beginning
was the Word. . . .' Now what do you suppose old John *meant* by that?
That cat was a preacher, and, well, you know how it is with preachers; he
had something big on his mind. Oh my, it was big; it was the *Truth,* and
it was heavy, and old John hurried to set it down. And in his hurry he
said too much. 'In the begining was the Word, and the Word was with
God, and the Word was God.' It was the Truth, all right, but it was
more than the Truth. The Truth was overgrown with fat, and the fat
was God. The fat was *John's* God, and God stood between John and the
Truth. Old John, see, he got up one morning and caught sight of the
Truth. It must have been like a bolt of lightning, and the sight of it
made him blind. And for a moment the vision burned on in back of his
eyes, and he *knew* what it was. In that instant he saw something he had
never seen before and would never see again. That was the instant of
revelation, inspiration, Truth. And old John, he must have fallen down
on his knees. Man, he must have been shaking and laughing and crying
and yelling and praying—all at the same time—and he must have been
drunk and delirious with the Truth. You see, he had lived all his life
waiting for that one moment, and it came, and it took him by surprise,
and it was gone. And he said, 'In the beginning was the Word. . . .'
And, man, right then and there he should have stopped. There was
nothing more to say, but he went on. He had said all there was to say,
everything, but he went on. 'In the beginning was the Word. . . .'
Brothers and sisters, *that* was the Truth, the whole of it, the essential
and eternal Truth, the bone and blood and muscle of the Truth. But he
went on, old John, because he was a preacher. The perfect vision faded
from his mind, and he went on. The instant passed, and then he had
nothing but a memory. He was desperate and confused, and in his confusion he stumbled and went on. 'In the beginning was the Word, and
the Word was with God, and the Word was God.' He went on to talk
about Jews and Jerusalem, Levites and Pharisees, Moses and Philip and
Andrew and Peter. Don't you see? Old John *had* to go on. That cat had
a whole lot at stake. He couldn't let the Truth alone. He couldn't see
that he had come to the end of the Truth, and he went on. He tried to
make it bigger and better than it was, but instead he only demeaned
and encumbered it. He made it soft and big with fat. He was a preacher,
and he made a complex sentence of the Truth, two sentences, three, a
paragraph. He made a sermon and theology of the Truth. He imposed
his idea of God upon the everlasting Truth. 'In the beginning was the
Word. . . .' And that is all there was, and it was enough.

[8]   "Now, brothers and sisters, old John was a white man, and the

white man has his ways. Oh gracious me, he has his ways. He talks about the Word. He talks through it and around it. He builds upon it with syllables, with prefixes and suffixes and hyphens and accents. He adds and divides and multiplies the Word. And in all of this he subtracts the Truth. And, brothers and sisters, you have come here to live in the white man's world. Now the white man deals in words, and he deals easily, with grace and sleight of hand. And in his presence, here on his own ground, you are as children, mere babes in the woods. You must not mind, for in this you have a certain advantage. A child can listen and learn. The Word is sacred to a child.

[9]   "My grandmother was a storyteller; she knew her way around words. She never learned to read and write, but somehow she knew the good of reading and writing; she had learned how to listen and delight. She had learned that in words and in language, and there only, she could have whole and consummate being. She told me stories, and she taught me how to listen. I was a child and I listened. She could neither read nor write, you see, but she taught me how to live among her words, how to listen and delight. 'Storytelling; to utter and to hear . . .' And the simple act of listening is crucial to the concept of language, more crucial even than reading and writing, and language in turn is crucial to human society. There is proof of that, I think, in all the histories and prehistories of human experience. When that old Kiowa woman told me stories, I listened with only one ear. I was a child, and I took the words for granted. I did not know what all of them meant, but somehow I held on to them; I remembered them, and I remember them now. The stories were old and dear; they meant a great deal to my grandmother. It was not until she died that I knew how *much* they meant to her. I began to think about it, and then I knew. When she told me those old stories, something strange and good and powerful was going on. I was a child, and that old woman was asking me to come directly into the presence of her mind and spirit; she was taking hold of my imagination, giving me to share in the great fortune of her wonder and delight. She was asking me to go with her to the confrontation of something that was sacred and eternal. It was a timeless, *timeless* thing; nothing of her old age or of my childhood came between us.

[10]   "Children have a greater sense of the power and beauty of words than have the rest of us in general. And if that is so, it is because there occurs—or reoccurs—in the mind of every child something like a reflection of all human experience. I have heard that the human fetus corresponds in its development, stage by stage, to the scale of evolution. Surely it is no less reasonable to suppose that the waking mind of a child corresponds in the same way to the whole evolution of human thought and perception.

[11]   "In the white man's world, language, too—and the way in which the white man thinks of it—has undergone a process of change. The white man takes such things as words and literatures for granted, as indeed he must, for nothing in his world is so commonplace. On every side of him there are words by the millions, an unending succession of

pamphlets and papers, letters and books, bills and bulletins, commentaries and conversations. He has diluted and multiplied the Word, and words have begun to close in upon him. He is sated and insensitive; his regard for language—for the Word itself—as an instrument of creation has diminished nearly to the point of no return. It may be that he will perish by the Word.

[12] "But it was not always so with him, and it is not so with you. Consider for a moment that old Kiowa woman, my grandmother, whose use of language was confined to speech. And be assured that her regard for words was always keen in proportion as she depended upon them. You see, for her words were medicine; they were magic and invisible. They came from nothing into sound and meaning. They were beyond price; they could neither be bought nor sold. And she never threw words away.

[13] "My grandmother used to tell me the story of Tai-me, of how Tai-me came to the Kiowas. The Kiowas were a sun dance culture, and Tai-me was their sun dance doll, their most sacred fetish; no medicine was ever more powerful. There is a story about the coming of Tai-me. This is what my grandmother told me:

[14]   Long ago there were bad times. The Kiowas were hungry and there was no food. There was a man who heard his children cry from hunger, and he began to search for food. He walked four days and became very weak. On the fourth day he came to a great canyon. Suddenly there was thunder and lightning. A Voice spoke to him and said, "Why are you following me? What do you want?" The man was afraid. The thing standing before him had the feet of a deer, and its body was covered with feathers. The man answered that the Kiowas were hungry. "Take me with you," the Voice said, "and I will give you whatever you want." From that day Tai-me has belonged to the Kiowas.

[15] "Do you see? There, far off in the darkness, something happened. Do you see? Far, far away in the nothingness something happened. There was a voice, a sound, a word—and everything began. The story of the coming of Tai-me has existed for hundreds of years by word of mouth. It represents the oldest and best idea that man has of himself. It represents a very rich literature, which, because it was never written down, was always but one generation from extinction. But for the same reason it was cherished and revered. I could see that reverence in my grandmother's eyes, and I could hear it in her voice. It was that, I think, that old Saint John had in mind when he said, 'In the beginning was the Word. . . .' But he went on. He went on to lay a scheme about the Word. He could find no satisfaction in the simple fact that the Word *was*; he had to account for it, not in terms of that sudden and profound insight, which must have devastated him at once, but in terms of the moment afterward, which was irrelevant and remote; not in terms of his imagination, but only in terms of his prejudice.

[16] "Say this: 'In the beginning was the Word. . . .' There was nothing. There was *nothing!* Darkness. There was darkness, and there was no end

to it. You look up sometimes in the night and there are stars; you can see all the way to the stars. And you begin to know the universe, how awful and great it is. The stars lie out against the sky and do not fill it. A single star, flickering out in the universe, is enough to fill the mind, but it is nothing in the night sky. The darkness looms around it. The darkness flows among the stars, and beyond them forever. In the beginning that is how it was, but there were no stars. There was only the dark infinity in which nothing was. And something happened. At the distance of a star something happened, and everything began. The Word did not come into being, but *it was*. It did not break upon the silence, but *it was older than the silence and the silence was made of it.*

[17]   "Old John caught sight of something terrible. The thing standing before him said, 'Why are you following me? What do you want?' And from that day the Word has belonged to us, who have heard it for what it is, who have lived in fear and awe of it. In the Word was the beginning; *'In the beginning was the Word. . . .'*"

[18]   The Priest of the Sun appeared to have spent himself. He stepped back from the lectern and hung his head, smiling. In his mind the earth was spinning and the stars rattled around in the heavens. The sun shone, and the moon. Smiling in a kind of transport, the Priest of the Sun stood silent for a time while the congregation waited to be dismissed.

[19]   "Good night," he said, at last, "and get yours."

RHETORICAL STRATEGIES

Classifying prose and poetry by rhetorical modes or strategies is difficult because most writing mixes methods. This alternate table of contents lists the readings by the principal rhetorical strategy used to present the writer's ideas and feelings. Several readings appear under more than one heading because they emphasize more than a single rhetorical strategy.

Analogy

Analysis and Cause and Effect

Analysis and Cause and Effect (cont'd)

Argument and Persuasion

Classification

Description

Details, Examples, or Incidents

Keeping a Journal

Process

INDEX

In addition to authors and titles, this index includes important rhetorical terms and problems addressed in the study questions—problems such as sentence structure, methods of development, and diction. Since the study questions refer to specific examples in the text, students can find in this index (1) references to questions identifying special problems, and (2) illustrations of writers' solutions to these problems in the readings.